Fourth Edition

The Policy-Based Profession

An Introduction to Social Welfare Policy Analysis for Social Workers

Philip R. Popple
University of Texas at Arlington

Leslie Leighninger
Arizona State University

PEARSON

Boston   New York   San Francisco
Mexico City   Montreal   Toronto   London   Madrid   Munich   Paris
Hong Kong   Singapore   Tokyo   Cape Town   Sydney

Senior Series Editor: Patricia Quinlin
Editorial Assistant: Nakeesha Warner
Marketing Manager: Laura Lee Manley
Editorial Production Service: Omegatype Typography, Inc.
Composition Buyer: Linda Cox
Manufacturing Buyer: JoAnne Sweeney
Electronic Composition: Omegatype Typography, Inc.
Photo Researcher: Omegatype Typography, Inc.
Cover Administrator: Kristina Mose-Libon

For related titles and support materials, visit our online catalog at www.ablongman.com.

Between the time website information is gathered and then published, it is not unusual for some sites to have closed. Also, the transcription of URLs can result in typographical errors. The publisher would appreciate notification where these errors occur so that they may be corrected in subsequent editions.

ISBN-13: 978-0-205-48592-5   ISBN-10: 0-205-48592-8

Library of Congress Cataloging-in-Publication Data

Popple, Philip R.
  The policy-based profession: an introduction to social welfare policy analysis for social
  workers / Philip R. Popple, Leslie Leighninger.—4th ed.
    p. cm.
  Includes bibliographical references and index.
  ISBN 0-205-48592-8 (alk. paper)
    1. Social workers—United States. 2. Public welfare—United States. 3. Social
  service—United States. 4. United States—Social policy. I. Leighninger, Leslie.
  II. Title.

HV91.P677 2008
361.3'2—dc22   2006043012

Printed in the United States of America

10 9 8 7 6 5 4   10 09

To my kids, Rich and Nancy,
David and Jennifer, Jeff and Heather
—PRP

In memory of my mother,
Paulette Kahn Hartrich,
social worker and fighter for social causes
1916–2002
—LL

Contents

Preface

Social welfare policy is currently not high on the national agenda. Since the attack on the World Trade Center and the subsequent invasions of Afghanistan and Iraq, issues of national security and international relations (e.g., the price of oil) have dominated the policy landscape to the near exclusion of domestic issues other than immigration reform (which is presented as a national security issue). Domestic social welfare issues, however, have not gone away and in fact continue to fester and grow below the radar screen. Prominent issues exist that will need attention in the near future:

- Supports for retirement are deteriorating at an alarming rate. The private pension system appears to have been abandoned by corporate America, and the government Pension Benefits Guaranty Corporation is already overwhelmed by the amount of need. Also, the Social Security system, although not in as bad shape as critics often paint it, will need some careful analysis and adjustment for it to remain a critical component of citizens' retirement planning.
- The health care system is currently so inefficient and poorly managed that major reform is needed to prevent its collapsing under its own weight. Medicare and Medicaid, which are often pointed to by critics as the major cause of health care financing problems are, in reality, only two components of a whole system in crisis.
- The Personal Responsibility and Work Opportunity Reconciliation Act was scheduled for reauthorization in 2001, but has been operating on continuing resolutions for the past five years because Congress and the administration have been unable to agree on a plan.
- As clearly demonstrated by Hurricane Katrina, not only is our disaster response system inadequate for major events, but our social service system is woefully inadequate to provide people with the emergency supports they need.

Social work as a profession has always operated within the context of social policy—whether this policy stems from agency rules and guidelines, the decisions of boards of directors, organizational accreditation or licensing regulations, state and national legislation, court rulings, or administrative and implementation procedures. Social work practice takes place in accordance with policies large and small, such as federal public welfare legislation, state guidelines for Medicaid reimbursements, court orders removing abused children from their homes, the waiting list practices of a United Way family counseling center, or a religious denomination's policy regarding the recognition of gay and lesbian relationships. In fact, we argue in this book that social work's intimate connection to social policy makes it unique among the professions, many of which are only now becoming enmeshed in the expectations of external bodies such as the corporation, the state legislature, and the federal bureaucracy.

Despite the relationship between social welfare policy and social work practice, few students have a good grasp of how to analyze and evaluate the policies that will affect their work, the lives of their clients, and the larger community. The purpose of this book is to help students acquire these policy analysis skills. We are not interested in policy analysis as a mere academic exercise. We are convinced that the understanding of policies—how they have developed, whom they affect, and how they affect those people—enables social workers to effectively use, implement, and, when necessary, change policies and programs for the good of their clients. One of our students referred to this text as "not overwhelming, as one might expect, . . . but more of a journey." Our intention is to make this journey as interesting and useful as possible.

There are particular reasons for social workers to have an informed view of today's social welfare policy world. The policy environment of social work is changing at an extraordinary rate. Economic, demographic, and political developments have opened the way for major welfare reform, reevaluation of immigration policies, a rethinking of the purpose and structure of Social Security, and a revolution in health care emanating from the private sector. Social work practitioners need tools to understand and respond to these changes; the profession as a whole needs to revitalize itself as an actor, rather than reactor, in the policy arena. We hope that this book will help achieve these goals.

This book, which is written for students at both the baccalaureate and master's levels of social work education, begins by outlining a policy-based model of the social work profession that explicitly recognizes the social welfare policy system as a major factor in social work practice. The second section delineates four major facets of the policy context: historical, economic, social, and political. Because both authors were trained as social welfare historians, there is an emphasis on history as an overarching approach to the study of policy. All four facets are then combined in a policy analysis framework that can provide the basis of a practitioner policy analysis.

The final section of the book applies the framework to representative policies in the fields of public welfare, aging, mental health, substance abuse, and child welfare. Rather than attempt a comprehensive (and soon outdated) overview of current policies, our intent has been to choose a current example of a major social welfare initiative within each policy area. Most important, we have sought to acquaint students with a process for understanding policies that they can continue to apply in their professional practice. This book ends with a brief discussion of policy practice skills. Our purpose is not to provide in-depth materials on these skills, for that is the job of a policy practice text. We are simply trying to sensitize students to the existence and importance of these skills and, we hope, inspire them to study further. We hope that by teaching students to use a policy analysis technique, which we have termed *practitioner policy analysis*, we will equip them with a skill that will be useful throughout their careers and from which they can develop additional policy practice skills.

Acknowledgments

We are grateful to the following people for assistance in researching and writing this text: Laura Dase, Barry Daste, Joseph Delatte, Wendy Franklin, Kenneth Millar, Matt Leighninger, Robert D. Leighninger, Jr., Judith Kolb Morris, Shannon Robshaw, Todd Atkins, J. Dennis Tyler, Catherine Lemieux, Anita Evans, Tanya Blom, Kim Chapman, Natisha Nason, David Austin, Ronald B. Dear, Nelson Reid, Paul H. Stuart, James L. Wolk, the members of the first Ph.D. class of the School of Social Work at Louisiana State University, and the students in the spring 1999 section of Social Work 3202, Social Welfare Policy, in the Social Work Department at the University of North Carolina at Charlotte. Many thanks to the reviewers of this edition: Sarah Cearley, University of Arkansas, Little Rock; Patricia Cianciolo, Northern Michigan University; and Patrick Dattalo, Virginia Commonwealth University.

1

Social Welfare Policy and the Social Work Profession

The Policy-Based Profession

For me the realization of the importance of policy to social work practice came in a blinding flash, or an epiphany, as my theologically inclined friends would say. As a social work master's student, I had had little interest in policy, preferring to spend my time learning psychopathology, therapeutic techniques, group process, and all of the other sexy stuff taught in a typical social work graduate program. When I graduated, I became a training specialist for a large state department of social services; my primary assignment was to train the child welfare staff. In my new position, I developed and provided training programs on behavior modification techniques, risk assessment, and transactional analysis. I even included a session on an early version of the Diagnostic and Statistical Manual. The only time I ever thought about policy was during the session for new employees in which I would discuss office hours, dress code, sick leave, vacation, and retirement.

I'm not sure whether it was because state office staff thought I was especially good or because they thought I was especially obnoxious, but I became the person of choice to supply mandated training in regions lacking training specialists. So it was that I was sent to the largest office in the state—which had a staff so hostile that they had run out three training specialists in less than a year—to provide a series of three-day training sessions on how to fill out a new form.

This was a guaranteed loser for me. The staff hated state office, hated training, and, most of all, hated forms. I asked the director of training why she didn't just issue the staff guns and then dress me in a shirt with a target on it. The director told me not to worry, this was going to be great. This was not merely a simple bureaucratic form we were asking the staff to use but really a system to train them in principles and techniques of task-oriented social services (which the state office had begun to call TOSS). The staff would fill out a simple form for each of their cases, a form that would require them to select and prioritize, from a standard list of codes, one or more goals for each case and then to list objectives required to reach each goal. The form would be updated each month with progress monitored by a computerized information system. The director showed me all the professionally developed curriculum material I would be supplied with to teach the staff this new problem-solving approach to social work practice.

When I began my first training session, it was as big a nightmare as I had imagined. The staff argued every step of the way. They said that task-oriented social services and the problem-solving method were fine, but they were already using this approach without the use of any long and complicated form. They argued that the reporting system would just get in the way of their work. They presented case after case that none of the preselected goals would fit. One guy, wearing the uniform of the professional radical of the era (beard, semilong hair, denim workshirt, American flag tie), selected a chair at the back of the room, leaned it against the wall, and promptly fell asleep. I figured that as long as he didn't start snoring I would consider the day a success. He did and I didn't.

The training was held on the campus of a college with a school of social work. By the end of the first day, I was thoroughly depressed and wandered over to the school in hopes of finding someone who could help me salvage this disaster. I ran into an acquaintance who was a professor of social policy. As she liked to keep tabs on activities of the Department of Social Services, she was happy to talk to me. She patiently listened to a lengthy tirade about my day, looked at the training material, and said, "Of course this is going badly. This form has nothing to do with social work practice and the staff knows it. This form has to do with social policy, but your state office staff doesn't think the field staff can understand and appreciate policy. They think the staff will only respond to issues if they are presented in terms of direct practice." Over take-out Chinese food, she spent much of the evening explaining social service funding to me, pointing out that the state could receive reimbursement from the federal government for 90 percent of the cost of services related to family planning, 75 percent for social services to welfare-eligible children, but less than 50 percent for services to children not eligible for welfare. She said, "Obviously, the state wants to report services in the categories where they will receive the highest match. The higher the rate of reimbursement, the greater the amount of services the state will be able to provide. Staff can understand and appreciate this; why don't you just tell them?"

Following the professor's advice, and with an armload of books and photocopied journal articles she lent me, I returned to my hotel and stayed up most of the night revising my curriculum. The next morning I faced my now more-hostile-than-ever class and explained that we were going to approach the TOSS form from a slightly different angle. I spent about an hour discussing social service funding streams and how the state could maximize services by accurately reporting services to the federal government. I then deconstructed the form to show how, although it might have some slight relation to task-oriented social services, its actual purpose was to get the best reimbursement rate we could for services provided. To my surprise, the staff had become quiet and attentive and were even showing some glimmer of interest. At the end of my presentation, the guy at the back of the room, who had resumed leaning against the wall but had not fallen asleep, leaned forward so the front legs of his chair hit the floor with a crash, and almost yelled, "Oh, I get it. This form's to screw the feds. I can do that!" I responded that I preferred to view it as a system to maximize the federal reimbursement the state could legitimately claim under existing laws, but if he wished to view it as screwing the feds, that was all right with me.

Once I made the purpose of the form clear, teaching the staff how to use it was relatively simple. In fact, we finished the training session a whole day early. I surveyed the class to see how they would like to spend the time left. They decided that they would like to discuss new techniques of social work practice, as long as the techniques did not involve any state office forms.

—Philip Popple

The state office administrators in the previous example assumed that the social workers to be trained would not be receptive to a social policy explanation because of what Bruce Jansson refers to as the mythology of autonomous practice. By this he means that social workers tend to approach practice assuming that they and their clients are relatively insulated from external policies. This mythology has led the profession to develop practice theories that focus heavily on the individual dimension of problems, causing a general disinterest in their *policy* context. Jansson states, "This notion of autonomous practice has had a curious and persistent strength in the social work profession."[1] This perception of social policy also appears internationally, as illustrated by a study of the social policy curriculum in Australia. The author, Philip Mendes, states that "in practice social policy seems to be peripheral to most social work courses in Australia" and that "social work students [have] the impression that social policy is simply about theoretical knowledge, without any need for practical application."[2] In this chapter we argue that the mythology of autonomous practice has been directly related to social work's efforts to achieve professional status. These efforts have been based on a flawed theory of what professionalization means, a theory that equated autonomy with private practice and that assigned primary importance to the development of practice techniques. We will argue that looking at social work within a more up-to-date and accurate theory of professions leads to the conclusion that policy is not only relevant to the day-to-day activities of social workers but is also central to the definition and mission of the profession. Before we can get to this topic, however, we must first look at the function of social work in society and how policy became relegated to secondary status in the profession, a victim of social work's professional aspirations.

The Target of Social Work—The Individual and Society

Stuart observes that "social work's unique and distinctive contribution to American life, often expressed as a dual focus on the person and his or her environment, resulted from a specific frame of reference that linked clients and social policy."[3] By this he means that we do not limit our concern to a person's intrapsychic functioning; we also seek to understand and manipulate factors in the environment that contribute to his or her problems. Some of these environmental factors are close to the person—for example, family, job, and neighborhood. However, people are also affected by factors in the larger environment—affirmative action laws, public welfare programs, United Way fund-raising campaigns, church positions on social issues, and the like. The social work profession is distinctive for its interest in all these factors and issues.

The Social Function of Social Work

Social work's concern with person-in-environment stems from the profession's social function. Social work is the core technology in the social welfare institution, the institution in society that deals with the problem of dependency. Dependency occurs when an individual is not adequately fulfilling a role (for example, providing physical care for his children) and social institutions are not providing adequate supports to enable the individual to fulfill a role (for example, good quality, affordable child care is not available) and this causes problems for the community that requires a response. By this we mean that every person in society occupies a number of social positions or statuses (mother, teacher, consumer, citizen, etc.), and attached to each of these positions are a number of social roles (nurturing children, communicating information, shopping, voting, etc.). These statuses and roles are located within social institutions that support people in their efforts to meet role expectations successfully. For example, the role of employee occurs within the economic institution, which must be functioning well enough to provide jobs for most people. When an individual is doing everything necessary to fulfill a role and the appropriate social institutions are functioning well enough to support the person's role performance, we have a situation we refer to as interdependence.[4]

When most people and institutions are functioning interdependently, society operates smoothly. However, when people fail to perform roles adequately or social institutions fail to sufficiently support people in their role performance, social stability is threatened. Common examples of individual role failure are:

- A woman is unemployed because she has difficulty controlling her temper.
- A single father leaves his two-year-old son at home alone for an extended time while he goes fishing.
- A fifteen-year-old does not attend school because he prefers to sleep late and watch MTV.

Examples of failure of social institutions to support individual role performance are:

- A woman is unemployed because, due to plant closings, there are jobs in her town for only seven of ten people who need to work.
- A single father leaves his two-year-old son at home alone while he works because there is no affordable day care available.
- A fifteen-year-old with a learning disability does not attend school because the school does not offer a program that meets his special needs.

The Dual Targets of Social Work

Because of the dual focus of the social welfare institution, the social work profession also has two targets. One target is helping individuals having difficulty meeting individual role expectations. This is the type of social work generally referred to as social work practice with individuals, families, and small groups, also referred to as *micropractice* or clinical social work. The other goal of social work concerns those aspects of social institutions that fail to support individuals in fulfilling role expectations.[5] This type of social work, sometimes referred to as *macropractice* or social work administration, policy, and planning, is what we are concerned with in the study of social welfare policy.

The Dominance of Micropractice

Social workers have long recognized that micro- and macropractice are complementary, but they have generally emphasized the micro, individual treatment aspect of the profession. The early social work leader and theoretician Mary Richmond referred to the dual nature of social work as *retail* and *wholesale*, saying, "The healthy and well-rounded reform movement usually begins in the retail method and returns to it again, forming in the two curves of its upward push and downward pull a complete circle."[6] By this she meant, according to Richmond scholar Peggy Pittman-Munke,

> To utilize the rich material gathered through painstaking casework in a way which causes the problem to wear flesh and bones and breathe, to aggregate the data to present statistics which will convince policy makers of the need for reform, to organize and mount a successful campaign to see the legislation become a reality, and then to use case work as a way to evaluate the outcome of the legislation.[7]

Another early leader, Porter R. Lee, referred to these aspects of social work as *cause* (working to effect social change) and *function* (treatment of individual role difficulties). He felt that function was the proper professional concern of social work. Lee argued that a cause, once successful, naturally tended to "transfer its interest and its responsibility to an administrative unit" that justified its existence by the test of efficiency, not zeal—by its "demonstrated possibilities of achievement" rather than by the "faith and purpose of its adherents." The emphasis of the function was on "organization, technique, standards, and efficiency." Fervor inspired the cause, whereas intelligence directed the function. Lee felt that once the cause had been won it was necessary that it be institutionalized as a function to make the gains permanent. He saw this as the primary task of professional social work.[8]

The opinions of Richmond and Lee have continued to represent the position of the vast majority of social work professionals. Practice with individuals, families, and small groups to treat problems of individual role performance continues to be the focus of most social work. Even though social workers will admit that problems with social institutions are at the root of most client problems, we have tended to persist in dealing primarily with the individual client. There are three main reasons for this: (1) the individual is the most immediate target for change, (2) U.S. society is generally conservative, and (3) social work has chosen to follow a particular model of professionalism throughout most of the twentieth century.

The Individual Is the Most Immediate Target for Change

An individual with a problem cannot wait for a social policy change to come along and solve the problem. For example, the main reason a welfare mother runs out of money before the end of the month is, no doubt, the extremely small amount of money she receives, an *institutional* problem. If the size of the mother's grant were to increase, her problem might well disappear. However, this is not going to happen in the near future, so the social worker must concentrate on aspects of the mother's behavior that can be changed to stretch out her small budget and to help her develop skills in manipulating the system to ensure that she receives the maximum benefits to which she is entitled.

The Conservative Nature of U.S. Society

Another reason for the social work profession's strong emphasis on individual role performance is that U.S. society is rather conservative and firmly believes in the notion of individualism. We strongly believe that people deserve the majority of credit for any success they experience and, conversely, deserve most of the blame for any failures. We resent, and often make fun of, explanations of people's personal situations that attribute anything to factors external to the individual.[9] Explanations that attribute poverty, for example, to factors such as the job market, neighborhood disintegration, racism, and so forth will often be dismissed as "bleeding-heart liberal" explanations. In a society characterized by such attitudes, a model of social work that concentrates on problems of individual role performance is obviously much more readily accepted and supported than one that seeks environmental change.

Professionalization

The final explanation of social work's emphasis on treating individual causes of dependency and deemphasizing institutional causes is little recognized but of key importance. This is the model of professionalism that social work subscribed to early in the twentieth century, and social work's subsequent efforts to achieve professional status have been based on this model. It is to this model that we now turn.

Social Work's Pursuit of Professional Status

Social work as a paid occupation has existed for only a little over 100 years. From the very beginning, those engaged in the provision of social services have been concerned, some would say preoccupied, with the status of their activities in the world of work, specifically with gaining recognition as a profession rather than simply as an occupation.

When social workers began to actively organize to improve their status, there was a conflict between those who thought the new profession should concentrate on institutional causes of dependency (social welfare policy) and those who were more interested in developing techniques and knowledge useful for helping individuals experiencing role failure (social work practice). Social work leaders such as Samuel McCune Lindsey at the New York School of Social Work, Edith Abbott at the Chicago School of Civics and Philanthropy, and George Mangold at the Missouri School of Social Economy argued for a profession based on social and economic theory and with a social reform orientation. Mangold stated:

> The leaders of social work . . . can subordinate technique to an understanding of the social problems that are involved. . . . Fundamental principles, both in economics and in sociology are necessary for the development of their plans of community welfare. . . . Courses in problems of poverty and in the method and technique of charity organizations are fundamental to our work. But the study of economics of labor is quite as important, and lies at the basis of our living and social condition. . . . The gain is but slight if our philanthropy means nothing more than relieving distress here and helping a family there; the permanent gain comes only as we are able to work out policies that mean the permanent improvement of social conditions.[10]

On the other hand, there were a number of social work leaders who believed that the new profession should concentrate on the development of practical knowledge related to addressing problems of individual role performance. The Charity Organization Society leader Mary Richmond advocated using case records and the experiences of senior social workers to train new workers in practical techniques of work with individuals. Frank Bruno argued that social work should be concerned with "processes . . . with all technical methods from the activities of boards of directors to the means used by a probation officer to rectify the conduct of a delinquent child."[11]

The debate regarding the focus of the new social work profession came to a head at the 1915 meeting of the National Conference of Charities and Correction. Abraham Flexner, famed critic of the medical profession, had been asked to prepare a paper for the conference analyzing social work as a profession. Flexner began his analysis with the first clear statement of traits that differentiate professions from "lesser occupations." He asserted that

> Professions involve essentially intellectual operations with large individual responsibility; they derive their raw material from science and learning; this material they work up to a practical and definite end; they possess an educationally communicable technique; they tend to self-organization; they are becoming increasingly altruistic in motivations.[12]

Following his definition of profession as a concept, Flexner measured social work against this definition. He found that social work strongly exhibited some professional traits—it was intellectual, derived its knowledge from science and learning, possessed a "professional self-consciousness," and was altruistic. However, in several important criteria, mainly those of educationally communicable technique and individual responsibility, Flexner found social work lacking.

Regarding social work's lack of an educationally communicable technique, Flexner felt the source of the deficiency was the broadness of its boundaries. He believed that professions should have definite and specific ends. However, "the high degree of specialized competency required for action and conditioned on limitation of area cannot possibly go with the width and scope characteristic of social work." Flexner believed that this lack of specificity seriously affected the possibility of professional training. "The occupations of social workers are so numerous and diverse that no compact, purposefully organized educational discipline is possible."[13]

In the area of individual responsibility, Flexner felt that social workers were mediators rather than responsible parties.

> The social worker takes hold of a case, that of a disintegrating family, a wrecked individual, or an unsocialized industry. Having localized his problem, having decided on its particular nature, is he not usually driven to invoke the specialized agency, professional or other, best equipped to handle it? . . . To the extent that the social worker mediates the intervention of the particular agent or agency best fitted to deal with the specific emergency which he has encountered, is the social worker himself a professional or is he the intelligence that brings this or that profession or other activity into action?[14]

Social workers took Flexner's message to heart such that "Is Social Work a Profession?" is probably the most frequently cited paper in the social work literature. David Austin asserts that Flexner's "model of an established profession became the most important organizing concept in the conceptual development of social work and, in particular, social work education."[15] Following the presentation of the paper, social workers consciously set out to remedy the deficiencies identified by

Flexner, mainly the development of an educationally communicable technique and the assumption of "large individual responsibility."

In the area of technique, the profession chose to emphasize practice with individuals, families, and small groups, or *social casework* as it was then called. The committee charged with responding to Flexner's paper stated, "This committee . . . respectfully suggests that the chief problem facing social work is the development of training methods which will give it [a] technical basis."[16] The committee felt that the social work profession had the beginning of an educationally communicable technique in the area of social casework; the profession should narrow its focus to emphasize this. This view was institutionalized in 1919 when the American Association of Professional Schools of Social Work was founded, dominated by educators who subscribed to the Flexner model for the profession. At an early meeting, it was voted that students receive training in casework, statistics, and community service. F. Stuart Chapin, director of the Smith College Training School for Social Work, proposed that social legislation be included as a fundamental curriculum area. This was voted down, based on the argument that social legislation lacked clarity and technique and was not suitable for fieldwork. Likewise, settlement house work was considered to be unsuitable for professional education. Settlements emphasized "mere neighborliness" and were opposed to the idea that their residents were more expert than their neighbors.[17] Thus, within a relatively few years following Flexner's paper, social work had all but eliminated knowledge and skills related to social policy from the profession's domain, substituting a nearly exclusive focus on techniques demonstrated as useful in helping individuals solve problems of role functioning.

The second area in which Flexner considered social work deficient in meeting the criteria of professionalization is that of "assuming large individual responsibility." By this, Flexner was referring to what is now generally termed *professional authority* or *autonomy*. According to Greenwood, "In a professional relationship . . . the professional dictates what is good or evil for the client, who has no choice but to accede to professional judgement."[18] Professional autonomy is closely related to professional expertise because it is on expertise that authority or autonomy is based.

Although neither Flexner nor any other theorist said it directly, social workers have come to equate professional autonomy with a private practice model of service delivery. Two reasons for this interpretation come to mind. The first is that Flexner's model of a profession was based on medicine, which he viewed as the prototypical "true" profession. Because the predominant model of medicine during most of the twentieth century was private practice, social workers naturally assumed that private practice was the key to autonomy. The second reason is that it is obvious on the face of it that a person with no boss—as is the case in private practice—is autonomous. But whatever the reason, the result of this interpretation has been to push social work further away from policy toward an individual treatment model of practice. As Austin has observed,

> The emphasis on distinctive method also reinforced a focus on the casework counseling interview as the core professional technique in social work. This was a technique that could most readily be adapted to a private-practice model—a model that has been viewed by many practitioners as a close approximation to the medical model of professionalism that Flexner had in mind.[19]

In summary, for better or for worse, the adoption of a model of professionalization based on the Flexner's criteria caused, or perhaps simply accelerated, the trend in social work to define the profession as being focused on role difficulties of individuals (casework) and to deemphasize concern with the institutional causes of role failure (social welfare policy). Social workers were concerned with identifying and demonstrating an educationally communicable technique. Casework with individuals and families appeared to be more promising than a concern with social welfare policy, which was—and still is—amorphous and hard to conceptualize. Social workers were also concerned with being able to practice autonomously, which they came to associate with private practice. The types of professional roles associated with social policy almost always occur in large organizations, which have traditionally been viewed as threats to autonomy. The definition of professional autonomy as ideally occurring in private practice has furthered the perception of social welfare policy as tangential to the social work profession.

Thus, social workers' concern with professionalization has been an important reason for the relatively low interest in social welfare policy in the profession. It appears, however, that this model of professionalism contains some major errors. Flexner's model of professionalism was based on medicine; it assumed that medicine was a prototypical profession and that as other occupations began to achieve professional status they would more closely resemble medicine. It is now apparent that medicine, rather than being a prototypical profession, was in fact an anomaly.[20] For various social and political reasons, medicine was able to escape both the corporation and the bureaucracy and thus was able to completely control its domain and determine most of its own working conditions.[21] However, rather than developing and becoming more like medicine as everyone assumed it would, social work has moved in quite the opposite direction. Medicine is now coming under the control of the corporation and the bureaucracy and, in terms of occupational organization, is coming more and more to resemble social work. These developments indicate errors in the Flexner model of professions and call for a reexamination of the concept. This reexamination should develop the concept in such a way that professionalism can be understood without assuming that professionals should be private practitioners and high-level technicians. In the following section, we attempt such a reexamination.

The Policy-Based Profession

The model developed by Flexner might well be termed the *market-based profession*. This model, based on the medical profession in the early part of the twentieth century, assumes that the professional is essentially a small business person. The product the professional is selling is his or her expertise. The basic relationship, illustrated in Figure 1.1, is dyadic. The consumer comes to the professional stating a problem, the professional diagnoses the problem and prescribes a solution, the consumer requests the solution that the professional provides, and the consumer pays the bill. The demonstration of specific techniques is key in the market-based model because these represent the "products" the professional is selling. Autonomy is assumed in this model to result from the fact that the professional is his or her own boss.

Two general developments accelerated over the course of the twentieth century and indicate that the market-based model of professions no longer accurately reflects reality, if it ever did. The first is that the trend in all professions has been for professionals to become employees in organizations rather than private practitioners. Even medicine, long viewed as the ideal independent profession, shows signs of an eroding independent practice base. Paul Starr observes:

> The AMA [American Medical Association] is no longer as devoted to solo practice either. "We are not opposed to the corporate practice of medicine," says Dr. Sammons of the AMA. "There is no way that we could be," he adds, pointing out that a high proportion of the AMA's members are now involved in corporate practice. According to AMA data, some 26 percent of physicians have contractual relationships with hospitals; three out of five of these doctors are on salary. . . . Many physicians in private practice receive part of their income through independent practice associations, HMO's, and for-profit hospitals and other health care companies. The growth of corporate medicine has simply gone too far for the AMA to oppose it outright.[22]

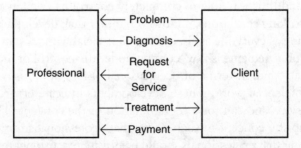

Figure 1.1   The Market-Based Profession

Although the number of social workers in private practice has steadily increased in recent years—and, as social workers succeed in their efforts to be eligible for third-party reimbursement (insurance), this number may increase even more—it is certain that a high proportion of social workers will continue to earn their living within organizational settings. Thus, a common work setting for professional persons in many fields has become a public or private bureaucracy rather than a private practice.

The second development that indicates the market-based model of professions is outdated is that professional practice, even in private settings, is increasingly subject to the dictates of external bodies. The psychiatry profession developed the *Diagnostic and Statistical Manual* in response to pressure from insurance companies to classify various treatments for insurance reimbursement. This manual is now the bible guiding the practice of mental health professionals, regardless of what they may feel about the evil of labeling. The practice of lawyers is subject to the dictates of banks, title companies, and state and federal justice departments, as well as the entire court system. Before a physician can hospitalize a patient, an insurance company generally has to approve the proposed treatment for payment; once the patient is in the hospital, the length of stay is usually determined not by the patient's physician but by the insurance company, managed care organization, or governmental agency that will eventually pay most of the bill. Social workers in "private practice" receive most their income through membership in managed care panels, where they are paid by large insurance companies or HMOs. The list of examples could go on and on to illustrate our point that even professionals who are in so-called independent practice are now subject to all sorts of influences and controls by external organizations.

The model of professionalism reflecting occupational reality in the early twenty-first century is called the *policy-based profession*. This model, illustrated in Figure 1.2, is based on a triadic relationship. The triad is composed of three systems—the professional system, the client system, and the policy system. The policy-based model recognizes that although a professional provides services on behalf of a client, it is often not the client who requests the services, defines the problem, or pays the professional.

Recognizing that professions are now predominantly policy based rather than market based leads to two major revisions of the traditional way of looking at professions, each contributing to the argument that social welfare policy must be a central concern of the social work profession. The first regards the matter of expert technique and the second regards practice within an organizational setting.

Expert Technique

According to Flexner and all the social theorists following him who subscribe to the market-based model, an occupation becomes recognized as a profession by developing techniques in the same way a business develops a product, marketing the

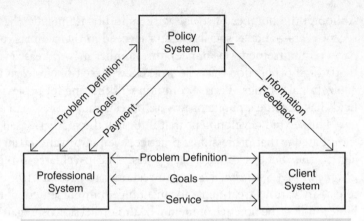

Figure 1.2   The Policy-Based Profession

technique and, if successful, to use Robert Dingwall's term, "accomplishing profession."[23] This process, however, does not follow from what we know of the history of professions. All professions were recognized as professions *before* they had any particularly effective techniques. This includes medicine, which was not particularly effective until the twentieth century. Many professions—the clergy, for example—do not now and probably never will have such techniques. By pursuing this trait (developing marketable techniques), social workers have defined a number of areas as outside the scope of the profession, generally areas related to social welfare policy, because they were not seen as amenable to the development of specific, educationally communicable techniques.

Rather than the possession of expert technique, *social assignment* appears to be crucial for an occupation to be recognized as a profession. Professions exist for the purpose of managing problems critical to society; the successful profession is recognized by society as being primarily responsible for a given social problem area. Medicine is charged with dealing with physical health, law with management of deviance and civil relations, engineering with the practical applications of technology, education with the communication of socially critical knowledge and skills, and, finally, social work with the management of dependency. All professions have wide and complex bodies of knowledge, and all have a theory base. However, the degree to which this knowledge and theory is translated into educationally communicable techniques varies widely. Medicine and engineering have rather precise educationally communicable techniques; law and the clergy have techniques that are somewhat less precise. Rather than specific techniques, these professions base their authority on mastery of complex cultural traditions. The important point is that it is not the possession of technique that is crucial for the development of a profession. Rather, what is crucial is the identification of one occupation over others as being given primary responsibility for the management of a social problem.[24]

Professional Practice within an Organizational Context

Traditional theory, based on Flexner's work, equates professional autonomy with the autonomy of the independent practitioner who is his or her own boss. Over the course of the twentieth century, more and more professionals came to work in traditional bureaucratic organizations, and the question arose whether this development erodes the very basis of professional autonomy. The theoretical position that argues this most forcefully is called *proletarianization*. This thesis emphasizes the loss of control that professionals supposedly experience when they work in large organizations. According to Eliot Freidson,

> This thesis stems from Marx's theory of history, in which he asserts that over time the intrinsic characteristics of capitalism will reduce virtually all workers to the status of the proletariat, i.e., dependent on selling their labor in order to survive and stripped of all control over the substance and process of their work.[25]

Supposedly, in organizations the authority of the office is substituted for the authority of professional expertise. In other words, a person working in a bureaucracy is required to take direction from any person who occupies a superior position in the organization, regardless of whether the person has equal or greater expertise in the professional task being performed. Thus, when employed in an organization, a professional does not have autonomy.

Sociologists who have studied professionals working in organizations have found that the fears of losing professional autonomy in such settings have been greatly exaggerated. Instead, the organizations in which professionals typically work—hospitals, schools, law firms, social agencies, and so forth—have developed as hybrid forms that deviate from the ideal type of bureaucracy in order to accommodate professionals. Freidson states that

> studies [of professionals in organizations], as well as more recent developments in organizational theory, call into question the validity of the assumption that large organizations employing professionals are sufficiently bureaucratic to allow one to assume that professional work within them is ordered and controlled by strictly bureaucratic means.[26]

A number of developments have enabled professionals to work in organizations while maintaining sufficient autonomy to perform their professional roles. First, professionals have come to be recognized as a special group under U.S. labor law because they are expected to exercise judgment and discretion on a routine, daily basis in the course of performing their work. In other words, discretion is a recognized and legitimate part of their work role. Second, professionals are subject to a different type of supervision than are ordinary rank and file workers. Ordinary workers are generally supervised by someone who has been trained as a manager, not as a worker in the area being supervised. Professionals, however, generally are entitled to expect supervision only from a member of their own profession. In social agencies, supervisors, managers, and often even executive positions are reserved for persons trained and licensed as social workers.[27]

Summary and Practice Implications

Recognizing that social work is a policy-based rather than a market-based profession clarifies and legitimizes the place of social welfare policy as a central concern. First, the policy-based model, while recognizing that the development of technique is important for any profession, also recognizes that functions do not need to be excluded from a profession's concern simply because they are not amenable to the development of narrow, specific procedures. This recognition legitimizes the inclusion of policy content such as policy analysis, administration, negotiation, planning, and so forth. Such inclusion has often been questioned because it was viewed as not being amenable to the development of "educationally communicable techniques." Second, the policy-based model recognizes that the social work profession will probably always exist in an organizational context and that social work's long experience in providing services within this context should be viewed as a strength rather than a weakness of the profession. Finally, the policy-based model explicitly recognizes the policy system as a major factor in social work practice and emphasizes that understanding this system is every bit as important for social work practitioners as understanding basic concepts of human behavior.

A number of roles within social work are described as policy practice roles, including roles mentioned previously—planner, administrator, policy analyst, program evaluator, and so on. In the years following the Flexner report, there was a good deal of debate whether these were really social work practice roles or something else, perhaps public administration. Tortured rationales were often developed that defined these roles as casework techniques applied to different settings and populations. The 1959 Council on Social Work Education curriculum study, for example, concluded, "As the administration project progressed, it became more and more clear that what we were discussing in the preparation of social work students for executive level positions was social work [practice] in an administrative setting and not administration in a social work setting."[28] Over the years, however, these roles have come to be defined as legitimate areas of social work practice without resorting to defining them as social casework applied to a different setting. Many graduate schools of social work now offer a concentration in administration, policy, and planning, often called macro social work practice.

This book, however, is not aimed only at social workers preparing for specialized policy practice roles. Rather, it is aimed at people interested in more traditional direct practice roles with individuals, families, and small groups. In this chapter, we have argued that the study of policy is relevant, in fact a *necessity*, for this group because policy is built into the very fabric of social work practice just as much as the study of human behavior. Social work's concern with policy is a logical extension of our person-in-environment perspective. Up to this point, this discussion has been rather abstract and theoretical. The reader is justified at this point in looking for specific examples of the ways policy affects direct practice. The following, although not a complete classification of ways that policy directly relates to practice, offers a few of many possible examples.

Policy Determines the Major Goals of Service

A basic component of social work practice is the setting of case goals. As illustrated by the vignette at the beginning of the chapter, the range of possible goals is not entirely up to the judgment of the individual social work practitioner but rather is greatly restricted, and sometimes actually prescribed, by agency policy. A good example of this is shown in child protective services. For a number of years, protective service policy was based on goals that have come to be referred to as "child rescue." The idea was that when the level of child care in a home had sunk to the level of neglect or abuse, the family was probably irredeemable and the appropriate strategy was to get the child out of the home and placed in a better setting. Based to a certain degree on case experience and research results, but probably more on the outcomes of a number of lawsuits, policy is now shifting to the goal of family preservation. This means that before a child is removed from the home, the social worker must demonstrate that a reasonable effort has been made to help the family while the child is still in the home. The point is that family preservation now figures prominently among the goals of child protection social workers, not because thousands of social workers have individually come to the conclusion that this is the most appropriate goal, but because policy now specifies that this be the goal of choice.

Policy Determines Characteristics of Clientele

Policy analyst Alvin Schorr has pointed out how agency policy, often in subtle ways, determines the type of clients that social agency staff will deal with. If the agency wishes to serve a middle-class clientele, they can attract this type of client and discourage poorer clients by means of several policy decisions. First, by locating in the suburbs, the agency services become more accessible to the middle class and less so to poorer segments of the population. Second, what Schorr terms *agency culture* can be designed to appeal to the middle class—whether the waiting room is plush or bare and functional; whether appointments are insisted on or drop-in visits are permitted; whether the agency gives priority to clients who can pay for services; whether the agency has evening and weekend hours or is open only during the day, and so forth.[29]

Policy Determines Who Will Get Services

Ira Colby relates a situation in which an anonymous caller contacted a state department of social services to report that a fourteen-year-old girl had been at home alone for several days with nothing to eat, and the caller wanted the department to "do something." The supervisor who was working intake that day

> was torn about what action to take. On the one hand, [she] wanted to send a worker out to verify the referral and provide any and all available services; yet, the department's policy clearly classified this case as a priority three—a letter would be sent to the caretakers outlining parental responsibilities. . . . In [this state], each child protective services' referral is classified as a priority one, two, or three. A priority one requires that a worker begin work within twenty-four hours after the agency receives a referral; a priority two mandates that contact be made within ten days; a priority three requires no more action than a letter or phone call. Cases are prioritized based on a number of variables, including the alleged victim's age and the type and extent of the alleged abuse.[30]

Most social workers are employed in agencies with policies specifying who can and who cannot receive services and some method of prioritizing services.

Policy Specifies, or Restricts, Certain Options for Clients

Policy often requires that a social worker either offer or not offer certain options. For example, social workers who are employed by Catholic Social Services are generally forbidden to discuss abortion as an option for an unplanned pregnancy. Social workers at a Planned Parenthood center are required to explore this option. When one of the authors began work for a state welfare department, during the first six months of his employment he was explicitly prohibited by agency policy from discussing birth control with welfare recipients. During the last six months of his employment there, policy was changed to explicitly *require* him to discuss birth control with all welfare recipients.

Policy Determines the Theoretical Focus of Services

Although less common than the other examples, in certain instances agencies will have policies that require social workers to adopt a certain theoretical orientation

toward their practice. For a number of years there was a schism in social work between the diagnostic school (followers of Sigmund Freud) and the functional
school (followers of Otto Rank). Social agencies sometimes defined themselves as
belonging to one school or the other and would not employ social workers who
practiced according to the other perspective. Currently, there are agencies that define themselves as behavioral, ecosystems, feminist (or whatever) and frown on
other approaches being applied by their staff. One of the authors once prepared a
training curriculum for child protective services workers on behavioral principles;
it was rejected by the state office training division because "this is not the way we
wish our staff to practice."

Conclusion

Although few social workers enter the profession because of an interest in social
welfare policy, every social work practitioner is in fact involved in policy on a daily
basis. Social work agencies are created by policies, their goals are specified by policies, social workers are hired to carry out policy-specific tasks, and the whole environment in which social workers and clients exist is policy determined. We often
think of policy in terms of social legislation, but it is much broader than that. As
Schorr has noted,

> Power in terms of policy is not applied on a grand scale only; the term "practi-
> tioner" implies consideration of policy in terms of clinical relationships and rela-
> tively small groups. These may be as consequential or more consequential for the
> quality of everyday life than the large-scale government and private hierarchical
> actions that are more commonly regarded as policy. As practitioners practice
> policy, they may choose any of a variety of instruments. They may simply decide
> differently about matters that lie within their own control, they may attempt to
> influence their agencies or they may take on more deep-seated and, chances are,
> conflict-ridden change. These are also choices that practitioners make.[31]

The problem with which we began this chapter shows why social work
students who desire to be direct practitioners need to study social welfare policy.
The answer should be clear by now. Because social work is a policy-based profession, practitioners need to be sensitive to, and knowledgeable about, the dynamics of three systems—the client system, the practitioner system, and the policy
system. Human behavior in the social environment curriculum concentrates on
the dynamics of the client system; the social work practice curriculum concentrates
on the practitioner system; and the social welfare policy and services curriculum
focuses on the policy system. All three are equally important to the preparation of
a direct practice social worker.

Notes

1. Bruce Jansson, *Social Welfare Policy: From Theory to Practice* (Belmont, CA: Wadsworth, 1990), p. 2.

2. Philip Mendes, "Teaching Social Policy to Social Work Students: A Critical Reflection," *Australian Social Work* 56 (September 2003), p. 220.

3. Paul H. Stuart, "Linking Clients and Policy: Social Work's Distinctive Contributions," *Social Work* 44 (July 1999), p. 335.

4. For a detailed discussion of the social welfare institution and the social work profession's place within it, see Philip R. Popple and Leslie Leighninger, *Social Work, Social Welfare, and American Society*, 5th ed. (Boston: Allyn and Bacon, 2002), pp. 23–52.

5. Charles Atherton, "The Social Assignment of Social Work," *Social Service Review* 43 (May 1969), pp. 421–429.

6. Joanna C. Colcord and Ruth Mann, Eds., *Mary E. Richmond, The Long View: Papers and Addresses* (New York: Russell Sage Foundation, 1930), pp. 111–112.

7. Peggy Pittman-Munke, "Bridging the Divide: The Casework Policy Link," *Journal of Sociology and Social Welfare* 26 (June 1999), p. 210.

8. Porter R. Lee, *Social Work as Cause and Function, and Other Papers* (New York: New York School of Social Work, 1937), pp. 4–9.

9. For a classic discussion of individualism in U.S. society as it relates to social work and social welfare, see Harold Wilensky and Charles Lebeaux, *Industrial Society and Social Welfare*, 2nd ed. (New York: Russell Sage Foundation, 1965).

10. George B. Mangold, "The New Profession of Social Service," in J. E. McCullock, Ed., *Battling for Social Betterment* (Nashville, TN: Southern Sociological Congress, 1914), pp. 86–90.

11. Frank J. Bruno, "The Project of Training for Social Work," *Adult Education Bulletin* 3 (June 1928), p. 4.

12. Abraham Flexner, "Is Social Work a Profession?" *Proceedings of the National Conference of Charities and Correction, 1915* (Chicago: Hildmann Printing Co., 1915), p. 581.

13. Flexner, "Is Social Work a Profession?" pp. 285–288.

14. Flexner, "Is Social Work a Profession?" p. 585.

15. David M. Austin, "The Flexner Myth and the History of Social Work," *Social Service Review* 57 (September 1983), p. 367.

16. Porter R. Lee, "Committee Report: The Professional Basis of Social Work," *Proceedings of the National Conference of Charities and Correction, 1915* (Chicago: Hildmann Printing Co., 1915), pp. 576–590.

17. Roy Lubove, *The Professional Altruist: The Emergence of Social Work as a Career, 1880–1930* (Cambridge, MA: Harvard University Press, 1965), p. 147.

18. Ernest Greenwood, "Attributes of a Profession," *Social Work* 2 (July 1957), p. 46.

19. Austin, "The Flexner Myth," p. 369.

20. George Ritzer, "Professionalization, Bureaucratization, and Rationalization: The Views of Max Weber," *Social Forces* 53 (June 1975), p. 628.

21. See Paul Starr, *The Social Transformation of American Medicine* (New York: Basic Books, 1982).

22. Starr, *The Social Transformation of American Medicine*, p. 446.

23. Robert Dingwall, "Accomplishing Profession," *Sociological Review* 24 (June 1976), pp. 331–349.

24. Philip R. Popple, "The Social Work Profession: A Reconceptualization," *Social Service Review* (December 1985), pp. 560–577.

25. Eliot Freidson, "The Changing Nature of Professional Control," *Annual Review of Sociology* 10 (1984), p. 3.

26. Freidson, "The Changing Nature of Professional Control," pp. 10–11.

27. Freidson, "The Changing Nature of Professional Control," pp. 10–12.

28. Sue Spencer, *The Administration Method in Social Work Education*, Vol. III, Social Work Curriculum Study (New York: Council on Social Work Education, 1959), p. 9.

29. Alvin L. Schorr, "Professional Practice as Policy," *Social Service Review* 59 (June 1985), pp. 185–186.

30. Ira C. Colby, *Social Welfare Policy: Perspectives, Patterns, Insights* (Chicago: The Dorsey Press, 1989), p. v.

31. Schorr, "Professional Practice as Policy," pp. 193–194.

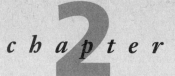

Defining Social
Welfare Policy

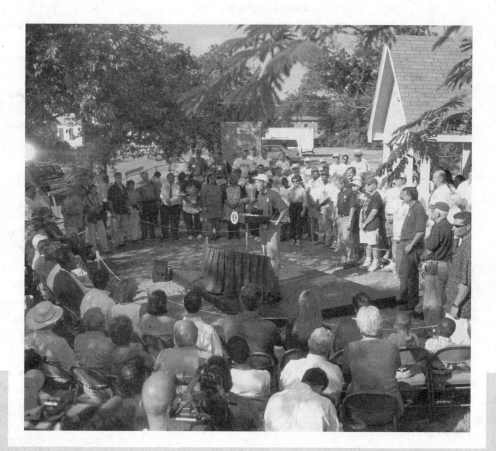

The last time Bud hit her, something deep inside of Sarah snapped. She yelled, screamed, hit him with a sixteen-ounce can of pork and beans, and finally, after regaining some control, called the police. By the time the officers arrived, Bud had agreed to move to his brother's, at least for a while. After four years of physical and emotional abuse, Sarah just wanted to take her four-year-old daughter, Megan, and get out of the situation and begin putting her life back together. However, it seemed that at every step there was some policy or other to contend with.

First, there was the problem of getting untangled from the criminal justice system. Sarah really did not want Bud to go to jail; she just wanted him out of the house. She explained this to the police officers when they arrived and requested that the complaint be dropped. They said they would like to do that, but department policy stated that an arrest had to be made any time there was a domestic violence complaint. After Bud spent the night in jail, Sarah explained the same thing to the judge. The judge said that it was his policy in domestic violence cases to send the perpetrator to prison unless the couple agreed to attend marital counseling. Sarah and Bud agreed to do this, even though Sarah was not optimistic about it.

The next problem was in complying with the judge's order. Sarah first called their medical insurance company, who explained that their benefits policy paid for marital counseling only if alcohol or drug abuse was the cause of the problem. Simple relationship difficulties were not covered. Sarah then called the mental health unit at the Methodist hospital; they told her that their policy excluded clients who were seeking counseling due to a court order. The hospital board felt that involuntary clients were not motivated and therefore would not benefit from treatment. Finally, Sarah was able to get an appointment with a social worker at the local YWCA women's center.

Bud lasted in counseling exactly one session. He said that the social worker, Julie Draughn, was a "feminazi" and he wasn't about to listen to her. Sarah was not surprised at Bud's reaction, but she thought what Julie had to say was kind of nice and was certainly food for thought. Julie believed that social policy in our country was evolving from a traditionally patriarchal, hierarchical system that forced women into dependent roles, into a more egalitarian system that freed women from subservience, at the same time placing greater demands on them for independent contributions. She tried to explain to Bud that this policy evolution would also eventually free men from burdens that had often crushed them in the past, but he wasn't having any of it. His last words to Sarah were that if she was so damn liberated she had better not count on him for any support at all, financial support included.

After Bud made good on his threat and refused to contribute anything to Sarah and Megan's expenses, Julie Draughn referred Sarah to the state Department of Human Resources (DHR) office to apply for assistance. The eligibility worker at DHR told Sarah that state policy required that a child support order be obtained before she would be eligible for any help. When she did obtain an order, the amount, $400 per month, when combined with the small income she received from a part-time job, exceeded the maximum that eligibility policy allowed for receipt of financial assistance. Eligibility policy for the food stamp program is somewhat less stringent (income less than 125 percent of the poverty level), so Sarah and Megan at least got some food assistance. In a similar fashion, Sarah found she was eligible for rental assistance under a policy referred to simply as Section VIII, so she was able to get a decent apartment for a very affordable rent. After a few payments, Bud disappeared, never to be seen again, so Sarah and Megan were able to qualify for public assistance.

Two years after her separation and subsequent divorce, Sarah has become somewhat of an expert on social welfare policy. After her living situation became stabilized, Sarah researched educational assistance policy and was able to develop a strategy to obtain assistance with tuition, books, and day care while she attended a local university to obtain a degree and a teaching certificate. However, halfway through the program, public assistance policy changed; it no longer permitted recipients to attend a four-year program. Sarah was forced to drop out of the teacher education curriculum and reevaluate her options, finally deciding to enroll in the local two-year technical college in a dental assistant training program. She is still working part time but carefully monitors her income to be sure that it does not exceed the maximum allowable for the various benefits she receives. She occasionally feels guilty about not contributing as much as she possibly can to her own support, but she realizes that the purpose of all these policies is to encourage her to become a self-supporting, tax-paying citizen, and that is exactly her own goal.

Sarah's story illustrates the vast impact of policy on social welfare clients, but more important for our purposes in this chapter, it illustrates the multiple meanings of the term *social welfare policy* and hence some of the difficulties in discussing and studying the subject. The term *social welfare policy* sometimes refers to broad social philosophy, sometimes to the narrowest administrative rule. When people use the term *policy*, they are usually referring to the actions of government, but social welfare policy often involves activities of the voluntary sector of the economy, of religious groups, and (more and more) of profit-making businesses. The purpose of this chapter is to look at the many meanings of the term *social welfare policy* and to clarify the way it is used in this book.

Social Welfare Policy—Basic Definition

To define the concept of social welfare policy, we must break the concept into its two constituent parts—*social welfare* and *policy*. We dealt briefly with the term *social welfare* in Chapter 1, where it was defined as the institution in society that deals with the problem of dependency. Recall that by *dependency* we mean situations in which individuals are not fulfilling critical social roles (a parent is not adequately caring for a child, a person is unable to support himself or herself financially, a child consistently breaks the law, etc.) or in which social institutions are not functioning well enough to support people in their role performance (the unemployment level is so high that a person cannot get a job despite being qualified, for example). The social welfare institution deals with these situations in order to help maintain social equilibrium.

Policy is a rather loose and imprecise term for which there is no generally accepted definition in the academic literature.[1] Some frequently cited definitions from political scientists are:

- A purposive course of action followed by an actor or set of actors in dealing with a problem or matter of concern.
- A course of action or inaction chosen by public authorities to address a given problem or interrelated set of problems.
- A "standing decision" characterized by behavioral consistency and repetiveness on the part of both those who make it and those who abide by it.
- In its most general sense, the pattern of action that resolves conflicting claims or provides incentives for cooperation.[2]

As the term is generally used, *policy* means principles, guidelines, or procedures that serve the purpose of maximizing uniformity in decision making.

Thus, the very simple beginning definition we will use for the term *social welfare policy* is: principles, guidelines, or procedures that serve the purpose of maximizing uniformity in decision making regarding the problem of dependency in our society. This seems simple enough but, as you will see in the remainder of this chapter, *social welfare policy* is a slippery and elusive term.

Factors Complicating the Definition of Social Welfare Policy

Complicating any attempt to reach a clear and simple definition of *social welfare policy* is the fact that the term is used in many different ways by many different people and to refer to many different things by any one individual. The following are some aspects of the term that often lead to a lack of clarity and precision in its use.

Social Welfare Policy and Social Policy

As you become familiar with the literature of social work and social welfare, you will find that the terms *social welfare policy* and *social policy* are often used interchangeably. This practice can be misleading because the terms do not have exactly the same meaning. Social welfare policy is a subcategory of social policy, which has a broader and more general meaning. David Gil, for example, uses the term *social welfare policy* to refer to societal responses to specific needs or problems such as poverty, child maltreatment, substandard housing, and so forth, and uses *social policy* to refer to efforts to "shape the overall quality of life in a society, the living conditions of its members, and their relations to one another and to society as a whole." In a similar fashion, Ronald Dear defines social policy as

> those principles, procedures, and courses of action established in statute, admin-istrative code, and agency regulation that affect people's social well-being. Thus, tax, transportation, public health, environmental, and social security statutes, as well as the implementation of codes and regulations that directly influence indi-vidual well-being, may be thought of as social policies. . . . Social welfare policy, in turn, is a subset or one portion of social policy. Social welfare policies may be thought of as those policies that affect the distribution of resources.

Martin Rein says that social policy is "not the social services alone, but the social purposes and consequences of agricultural, economic, manpower, fiscal, physical development, and social welfare policies that form the subject matter of social policy."[3]

The term *social policy* is frequently used in a philosophic sense. As Gil observes, when used in this sense the term refers to the collective struggle to seek enduring social solutions to social problems and conveys a meaning almost the opposite of the term *rugged individualism*. When used in this sense, social policy is equated with the struggle for equality in social and economic life. The term *social policy* as used by many theorists "goes far beyond conventional social welfare policies and programs. . . . Core functions of social policies [are viewed as] the reduction of so-cial inequalities through redistribution of claims, and access to, resources, rights, and social opportunities."[4] Much of British writing on social policy, notably that of Richard Titmuss and T. H. Marshall, reflects the social policy as social philos-ophy approach. These writers view social policy as synonymous with increasing government involvement in social life and the pursuit of greater equality, equity, and social justice.[5]

Thus, *social policy* is a term that includes some elements that we exclude from our definition of *social welfare policy*. Items such as libraries, parks and recreation, and various aspects of the tax codes and of family law are included in the domain of social policy because they deal with the integrative system and the overall qual-ity of life. The continuing struggle of humanity for equality is also a central fea-ture of social policy discussions. Although these things are clearly related to *social welfare policy*, they are not central to the way we use the term in this book. We do not include these in our definition of the domain of social welfare policy because they are not related to the problem of dependency or to specific categorical programs.

Social Welfare Policy as an Academic Discipline and a Social Work Curriculum Area

There is an additional complication for the social worker seeking to understand the term *social welfare policy:* The term has somewhat different meanings when used to refer to an area of academic inquiry as opposed to an area of the social work curriculum. As an area of academic inquiry, social welfare policy is a subfield of sociology, political science, history, economics, and—of course—social work. In addition, over the past decade or so a number of academic schools and departments have emerged specifically for the study of policy; social welfare policy is a basic area of study in these schools. As the term *social welfare policy* is used in these disciplines, it refers nearly exclusively to the activities of government. In addition to the definitions cited earlier, scholars in these disciplines generally add something to the effect of:

- Public policies are those policies developed by governmental bodies and officials.
- Public policy is the combination of basic decisions, commitments, and actions made by those who hold or affect government positions of authority.
- Public policy is what governments do, why they do it, and what difference it makes.
- Social welfare policy is anything government chooses to do, or not to do, that affects the quality of life of its people.[6]

Although many social workers in the area of social welfare policy share the traditional academic definition, the term is often used by social workers in a broader fashion. As will be discussed in the next section, many social welfare services are provided by private nonprofit, many times religious, agencies. These agencies have policies that affect social workers and their clients and must be understood if social workers are to comprehend their working environments fully. Also, an increasing number of services are being provided by the profit-making sector. Day care for children, disabled adults, and the elderly; residential and foster care for children; home health services; behavioral health care; retirement and nursing homes; and low-income housing are only a few examples of rapidly growing social welfare services provided by the profit-making sector.[7] Scholars in traditional policy areas would be quick to point out that services provided by private nonprofit agencies and by private businesses often receive a portion of their funding from government programs and so should probably come under the heading of actions of government. This is true, but it is also true that the social workers employed by these organizations are not government employees, and the programs come under a wide range of policies that are entirely nongovernmental in nature.

The term *social welfare policy* also refers to a specific area of the professional social work curriculum. The accrediting body of social work programs is the Council on Social Work Education (CSWE). The Educational Policy and Accreditation Standards of CSWE under the heading of Social Welfare Policy and Services reads:

> Programs provide content about the history of social work, the history and current structures of social welfare services, and the role of policy in service delivery, social work practice, and attainment of individual and social well being. Course content provides students with knowledge and skills to understand major policies that form the foundation of social welfare; analyze organizational, local, state, national, and international issues in social welfare policy and social service delivery; analyze and apply the results of policy research relevant to social service delivery; understand and demonstrate policy practice skills in regard to economic, political, and organizational systems, and use them to influence, formulate, and advocate for policy consistent with social work values; and identify financial, organizational, administrative, and planning processes required to deliver social services.[8]

This definition encompasses the term *social welfare policy* as used in traditional academic disciplines but also contains tangential areas. Thus, in social work programs, it is not uncommon to find courses with titles such as The Social Work Profession or Social Welfare History included as part of the social welfare policy curriculum.

Also, in the social work curriculum, *social welfare policy* often refers to a practice method. Policy analysis as taught in the traditional academic disciplines is central to the method, but additional, generally *interpersonal*, skills are also included that are usually not central to these other fields. Jansson identifies four basic policy practice skills needed by social workers:

> They need analytic skills to evaluate social problems and develop policy proposals, analyze the severity of specific problems, identify barriers to policy implementation, and develop strategies for assessing programs. They need political skills to gain and use power and to develop and implement political strategy. They need interactional skills to participate in task groups, such as committees and coalitions, and persuade other people to support specific policies. They need value-clarifying skills to identify and rank relevant principles when engaging in policy practice.[9]

Social Workers Are Interested in Social Welfare Policy in All Sectors of the Economy

Although social welfare is generally thought of as the responsibility of government, keep in mind that the social welfare system in the United States grew out of activities of the private sector; the government assumed responsibility very reluctantly. It would not be an overstatement to say that the social work profession itself is a result of policies of private, voluntary, social welfare agencies. In the nineteenth century, private agencies joined to form Charity Organization Societies specifically for the purpose of developing policies and procedures that would rationalize dealing with the growing problem of dependency in large cities. Shortly thereafter, the agencies realized that a major barrier to the rationalization of philanthropy was the lack of qualified staff. The agencies then began to formulate policies for training and hiring personnel; this eventually resulted in the emergence of social work as a profession.

During the course of the last century, the government assumed a larger and larger role in the provision of social welfare services. However, the private sector still provides a significant proportion of services. In 1995, public social welfare expenditures amounted to more than 1,504 billion dollars; private social welfare expenditures were almost 925 billion dollars.[10] Thus, the private sector of the economy still provides approximately 38 percent of all social welfare services and benefits, a very significant proportion.

Private social service agencies have policies that affect their employees and clients in much the same manner as governmental policies. For example, every area United Way organization has policies on criteria and procedures for an agency to become affiliated with the United Way, on the setting of priorities for funding, on financial accounting and reporting, on personnel, and on other concerns that, to use our earlier definition of *policy*, set down principles, guidelines, and procedures that maximize uniformity in decision making for member agencies.

It is apparent that the private, for-profit sector is becoming increasingly important in the social welfare enterprise. Ryan observes,

> The real revolution is that the social service market is now accepting providers that have a decided for-profit bent. In marked contrast with earlier years, when for-profits were excluded from the social services—frowned upon as unfit partners for government—the public sector now sees business not as a pariah but as a role model. This radical transformation in public-sector attitudes has spurred— even dared—for-profits to move into the social services delivery system.[11]

For-profit nursing homes, adult and child day care, home health services, alcohol and drug treatment centers, managed care mental health systems, phobic and eating disorder clinics—all have appeared on the scene in recent years. Like public and voluntary agencies, these for-profit organizations all have policies that affect clients and staff. As we will discuss in the chapters on physical and mental health, policies of profit-making agencies present a special concern to the social work profession because of the high potential for conflict between providing services that are in the best interest of the client and services that are most profitable for the organization.

There is a tendency to define policy as only public policy. To fully understand the context in which they practice, social workers need to understand the policies of all three sectors of the social welfare system and the interaction among them.

The Multiple Levels of Social Welfare Policy

An additional point that needs to be dealt with before we can fully define social welfare policy is that policy exists on several levels. These levels are referred to as macro-, mezzo-, and microlevel policy.

Macrolevel Policy

Macrolevel social welfare policy involves the broad laws, regulations, or guidelines that provide the basic framework for the provision of services and benefits. Most macrolevel policy is generated by the public and the private nonprofit sectors. The macrolevel policy arena we most commonly think of is the public sector, in which macrolevel policies take the form of laws and regulations. Examples are Title XX of the Social Security Act, the Americans with Disabilities Act, and the Older Americans Act. After passage, all of these acts were translated into detailed federal regulations that specify issues of implementation, evaluation, and so forth. The private nonprofit sector also generates macrolevel policy to guide its efforts to deal with problems of dependency. For example, the 200th General Assembly of the Presbyterian Church (U.S.A.) developed an eighty-three-page policy statement on health care that dealt with health care benefits for church employees and with the church's stand on the general problems of the health care system.[12] The private for-profit sector responds to, and attempts to influence, macrolevel policy more than it generates such policy on its own.

Mezzolevel Policy

Mezzolevel (midlevel) policy is administrative policy that organizations generate to direct and regularize their operations. Every social worker who has ever worked for a state social services department is familiar with the ritual followed with new employees: A supervisor sets three or four giant manuals before the new employee with instructions to spend the day reviewing them. There will generally be a personnel policy manual, which sets out all the rules and regulations regarding pay, benefits, insurance, office hours, holidays, evaluations, grievances, retirement, and the like. Then there will be a financial policy manual, which outlines procedures and forms for budgeting, purchasing, travel, supplies, financial reporting, and so on. Finally, there will be one or more manuals outlining the policies governing the particular program area in which the social worker is employed. For example, the food stamp program will have manuals describing intake, eligibility, record keeping, what is and is not appropriate to discuss with an applicant, referrals, and so forth.

Much of mezzolevel policy is, of course, in direct response to macrolevel policy. For example, the food stamp program, as set out in federal regulations, requires that state welfare departments respond to an application within thirty days, except in cases in which the family is expected to have an income for the month of less than $150, in which case the department must respond within five days. The macrolevel federal regulations containing this policy are sent to the state agencies, which must translate it into mezzolevel policy by setting out specific procedures so the department can comply with the policy of the federal Food and Nutrition Service.

Microlevel Policy

Microlevel policy is what happens when individuals such as social workers translate macro- and mezzolevel policy into actual service to clients. As we discussed in Chapter 1, social work is a profession with a good deal of autonomy; this means individual social workers have great latitude for interpreting and implementing a given policy. The political scientist Michael Lipsky refers to social workers as "street-level bureaucrats" who, he says, "make policy in two related respects. They exercise wide discretion in decisions about citizens with whom they interact. Then, when taken in concert, their individual actions add up to agency behavior."[13] Recognizing the importance of microlevel policy making rests on the question: If Congress passes a law stating that individuals are entitled to a certain benefit (macrolevel policy) and state and local agencies develop regulations and procedures for delivering the benefit (mezzolevel policy) but the social workers charged with delivering the benefit do not support the policy and obstruct the process to an extent that few people actually receive the benefit, what actually is the policy? The policy is that people do not get the benefit.

The following example will illustrate the importance of microlevel policy far better than any theoretical discussion. One of the authors was at one time the training director for a large region of a state social services department. He would periodically get requests from the state office to conduct training for the food stamp program staff on eligibility policy. The request would be the result of complaints from college students who had applied for food stamps and whose applications had dragged on and on over one technicality after another. The problem, however, had nothing to do with the staff not *understanding* eligibility policy. Rather, the eligibility determination workers tended to be women who, due to one life situation or another (marriage, pregnancy, husband becoming unemployed, etc.), had dropped out of college after two years (the amount of college required for a food stamp eligibility worker position) and taken a job with the welfare department in order to support their families. The attitude of the workers in this particular office was "When I needed money, I dropped out of school and got a job; I didn't expect the government to support me." They collectively felt that the policy of making college students eligible for food stamps was wrong. As a result, they had developed techniques to discourage applications from this group, and if a student persisted in applying, the workers would do everything possible to slow the process further. The result? The actual policy in this particular office was that college students were not eligible for food stamps.

Many people would say that the existence of microlevel policy significantly different from macro- and mezzolevel policy is an indication of bad management. Effective management should be able to bring individual practice into line with organization policy. Due to the nature of their work, however, this is not possible with social workers. As Lipsky observes, because problems resulting from microlevel policy

> would theoretically disappear if workers' discretion were eliminated, one may wonder why discretion remains characteristic of their jobs. The answer is that certain characteristics of the jobs of street-level bureaucrats make it difficult, if not impossible, to severely reduce discretion. They involve complex tasks for which elaboration of rules, guidelines, or instructions cannot circumscribe the alternatives.

This situation is the result of two factors: "First, street-level bureaucrats often work in situations too complicated to reduce to programmatic formats . . . [and] second, street-level bureaucrats work in situations that often require responses to the human dimensions of situations" which are too varied and complex to reduce to routinized procedures.[14]

Recognition of the existence of microlevel policy provides one of the strongest arguments for the promotion of policy-driven professions such as social work. If the performance of workers cannot be controlled by standardized work rules, as is the natural practice in bureaucracies, then controls must be internal to the workers. The most effective means of developing these internal controls is through professional training and socialization in certain values and a code of ethics. The food stamp eligibility workers described here, incidentally, were not professional social workers. At one time they would have been, but in the late 1960s, in what was known as separation of services, eligibility functions in welfare departments were redesignated from professional social work positions to high-level clerical jobs.

One of the rationales for this change was that social workers exercised too much individual discretion and that clerical-level staff would be more amenable to organizational control. The result appears to have been the creation of a workforce that is effectively under the control of neither organizational rules nor professional ethics and standards of behavior.

Social Welfare Policy—A Working Definition

By now it should be apparent that there is no one correct (or incorrect for that matter) definition of *social welfare policy*. The term is broad and general, and its definition is similar to the story of the blind people describing an elephant—how you define it depends on which part you are in contact with. The upshot of this is that it is crucial for people addressing the subject of social welfare policy to be clear on how they are using the term. For our purposes in this book, we will use the following definition:

> Social welfare policy concerns those interrelated, but not necessarily logically consistent, principles, guidelines, and procedures designed to deal with the problem of dependency in our society. Policies may be laws, public or private regulations, formal procedures, or simply normatively sanctioned patterns of behavior. Social welfare policy is a subset of social policy. Social welfare policy as an academic discipline is less concerned with specific policies than it is with the process by which those policies came into being, the societal base and effects of those policies, and the relationship between policies. Those studying social welfare policy as an area of the professional social work curriculum share the concerns of the traditional academic disciplines but have as primary concerns the relationship of policy to social work practice and the ways that social workers both as individuals and as members of an organized profession can influence the policy process.

Conclusion

This book is aimed mainly at people training to be direct service social work practitioners. Therefore, our major goal is to help develop skills of policy analysis that will enable practitioners to understand and, when possible, affect the policy context of their practice. We will pay a great deal of attention to macrolevel policy in the public sector because this is the area having the greatest effect on social work practice. However, recognizing their great impact on social work practice, we will also devote significant attention to mezzo- and microlevel policy and the influence of voluntary sector and for-profit sector policy.

Notes

1. Leslie Pal, *Public Policy Analysis: An Introduction* (Toronto: Methuen, 1987), p. 2.

2. James E. Anderson, *Public Policy-Making*, 3rd ed. (New York: Holt, Rinehart and Winston, 1984), p. 3; Leslie Pal, *Beyond Policy Analysis: Public Issue Management in Turbulent Times*, 3rd ed. (Toronto: Thompson/Nelson, 2006), p. 2; Heinz Eulau and Kenneth Prewitt, *Labyrinths of Democracy* (Indianapolis: Bobbs-Merrill, 1973), p. 465; Fred M. Frohock, *Public Policy: Scope and Logic* (Englewood Cliffs, NJ: Prentice-Hall, 1979), p. 11.

3. Ronald B. Dear, "Social Welfare Policy," in Richard L. Edwards, Ed., *Encyclopedia of Social Work*, 19th ed. (Washington, DC: NASW Press, 1995), p. 2227; David Gil, *Unravelling Social Policy*, 5th ed. (Rochester, VT: Schenkman Books, 1992), p. 9; Martin Rein, *Social Policy: Issues of Choice and Change* (New York: Random House, 1970), p. 4.

4. Gil, *Unravelling Social Policy*, p. 3.

5. Ken Blakemore, *Social Policy—An Introduction* (Philadelphia: Open University Press, 1998), pp. 8–11.

6. Anderson, *Public Policy-Making*, p. 3; Thomas R. Dye, *Understanding Public Policy*, 6th ed. (Upper Saddle River, NJ: Prentice-Hall, 2006), p. 2; Richard Simeon, "Studying Public Policy," *Canadian Journal of Political Science* 9 (December 1976), p. 548; Ira Sharkansky, "The Political Scientist and Policy Analysis," in Ira Sharkansky, Ed., *Policy Analysis in Political Science* (Chicago: Markham, 1970), p. 1; Diana M. DiNitto, *Social Welfare: Politics and Public Policy*, 5th ed. (Boston: Allyn and Bacon, 2003), p. 2; Larry N. Gerston, *Public Policy Making, Process and Principles*, 2nd ed. (Armonk, NY: M. E. Sharpe, 2004), p. 6.

7. William P. Ryan, "The New Landscape for Nonprofits," *Harvard Business Review* 7(1) (January–February 1999), pp. 127–136.

8. Commission on Accreditation, *Educational Policy and Accreditation Standards* (Alexandria, VA: Council on Social Work Education, 2002), pp. 7–8.

9. Bruce S. Jansson, *Social Welfare Policy: From Theory to Practice*, 2nd ed. (Belmont, CA: Wadsworth, 1994), p. 25.

10. "Social Welfare and the Economy," *Social Security Bulletin* (December 31, 1999), p. 136.

11. Ryan, "The New Landscape for Nonprofits," pp. 129–130.

12. Office of the General Assembly of the Presbyterian Church (U.S.A.), *Life Abundant: Values, Choices, and Health Care: The Responsibility and Role of the Presbyterian Church (U.S.A.)* (Louisville, KY: Author, 1988).

13. Michael Lipsky, *Street-Level Bureaucracy: Dilemmas of the Individual in Public Services* (New York: Russell Sage Foundation, 1980), p. 13.

14. Lipsky, *Street-Level Bureaucracy*, p. 15.

Social Welfare Policy Analysis

In Part I, we sought to identify policy as central to the social work profession and to define the term. It logically follows that if policy is as important as we assert, then it is important to develop systematic means of studying and understanding policy in all its dimensions. This is the goal of Part II. We begin this section by discussing what policy analysis is (a very slippery subject in its own right), and we then move on to discuss the analysis of various dimensions of social welfare policy. We will basically follow the outline presented below. Before you become overwhelmed with the level of detail presented, note that we are presenting this as a way of discussing the immensely complex subject of policy analysis, not as a model to be actually applied in all its detail by a social work practitioner. This outline can be applied at any level of detail, from one very specific policy (i.e., the Older Americans Act) to a general policy area (i.e., social welfare policies enacted to deal with the problems of elderly citizens). It is not always necessary to apply the whole framework in every policy analysis; policy analysts in the real world selectively apply various parts of the outline, guided by the specific policy they are concerned with and the purpose of the analysis. In Part III of this book, we will demonstrate how practitioner policy analyses are done using examples from fighting poverty, aging, mental health, substance abuse, and child welfare.

Policy Analysis Outline

I. Delineation and Overview of the Policy under Analysis
    A. What is the specific policy or general policy area to be analyzed?
    B. What is the nature of the problem being targeted by the policy?
       1. How is the problem defined?
       2. For whom is it a problem?

    C. What is the context of the policy being analyzed (i.e., how does this specific policy fit with other policies seeking to manage a social problem)?

    D. Choice analysis (i.e., what is the design of programs created by a policy and what are alternatives to this design?)

        1. What are the bases of social allocation?

        2. What are the types of social provisions?

        3. What are the strategies for delivery of benefits?

        4. What are the methods of financing these provisions?

II. Historical Analysis

    A. What policies and programs were previously developed to deal with the problem? In other words, how has this problem been dealt with in the past?

    B. How has the specific policy/program under analysis developed over time?

        1. What people, or groups of people, initiated and/or promoted the policy?

        2. What people, or groups of people, opposed the policy?

    C. What does history tell us about effective/ineffective approaches to the problem being addressed?

    D. To what extent does the current policy/program incorporate the lessons of history?

III. Social Analysis

    A. Problem description

        1. How complete is our knowledge of the problem?

        2. Are our efforts to deal with the problem in accord with research findings?

        3. What population is affected by the problem?

            a. Size

            b. Defining characteristics

            c. Distribution

    B. What theory or theories of human behavior are explicit or, more likely, implicit in the policy?

    C. What are major social values related to the problem and what value conflicts exist?

    D. What are the goals of the policy under analysis?

        1. Manifest (stated) goals

        2. Latent (unstated) goals

        3. Degree of consensus regarding goals

E. What are the hypotheses implicit or explicit in the statement of the problem and goals?

IV. Economic Analysis
  A. What are the effects and/or potential effects of the policy on the functioning of the economy as a whole—output, income, inflation, unemployment, and so forth? (macroeconomic analysis)
  B. What are the effects and/or potential effects of the policy on the behavior of individuals, firms, and markets—motivation to work, cost of rent, supply of commodities, etc.? (microeconomic analysis)
  C. Opportunity cost; cost/benefit analysis

V. Political Analysis
  A. Who are the major stakeholders regarding this particular policy/program?
    1. What is the power base of the policy/program's supporters?
    2. What is the power base of the policy/program's opponents?
    3. How well are the policy/program's intended beneficiaries represented in the ongoing development and implementation of the policy/ program?
  B. How has the policy/program been legitimized? Is this basis for legitimation still current?
  C. To what extent is the policy/program an example of rational decision making, incremental change, or of change brought about by conflict?
  D. What are the political aspects of the implementation of the policy/program?

VI. Policy/Program Evaluation
  A. What are the outcomes of the policy/program in relation to the stated goals?
  B. What are the unintended consequences of the policy/program?
  C. Is the policy/program cost effective?

VII. Current Proposals for Policy Reform

chapter **3**

Social Welfare Policy Analysis: Basic Concepts

Every once in a while, a policy study appears that is so interesting and well written that people read it for relaxation and enjoyment. Jason DeParle's book *American Dreams: Three Women, Ten Kids, and a Nation's Drive to End Welfare* is one example.[1] This, unfortunately, is a rare occurrence. Generally, people read policy literature for practical reasons, namely to gain an understanding of the dynamics of our collective response to various social problems. Policy analyses are read to answer questions such as: How do we deal with poverty? What do we do about health care for people who are sick but have no insurance and no money? What is being done to help children who are being mistreated? Is our response to drug abuse the best one and, if not, what other options are available?

When you seek the answers to questions such as these, you will first consult the policy analysis literature. Two aspects of this literature will, at least initially, puzzle you. First, you will notice that the policy analysis literature is spread all over the library. Some is shelved, as you would expect, with the social work literature. You probably won't be too surprised to find some policy material with sociology, political science, history, and economics. A small amount, less predictably, will be with business, and a rather substantial amount will be with religion and philosophy.

Second, once you have ferreted out sources on a policy issue (for example, on antipoverty policy), you will find that, though different sources deal with the same topic, the approaches look very different. Some policy analyses look like literature, being composed mostly of stories. Some look like mathematics texts, with lengthy and complex formulas, tables, graphs, and so forth. Some look like stories in a newspaper or magazine (in fact, may *be* stories in newspapers and magazines). To help prevent the confusion you may experience in simply identifying and locating sources of policy analysis, we begin with a discussion of the policy analysis field.

The Many Meanings of Policy Analysis

Like most terms and concepts in the study of social welfare policy, the term *policy analysis* tends to be used in vague and inconsistent ways. David Bobrow and John Dryzek refer to the policy analysis field as "home to a babel of tongues."[2] The late Aaron Wildavsky, a leading figure in the policy analysis field, argued that it is unwise to even try to define the term, saying, "At the Graduate School of Public Policy in Berkeley, I discouraged discussions on the meaning of policy analysis. Hundreds of conversations on this slippery subject had proven futile, even exasperating, possibly dangerous." He referred to policy analysis as that which "could be learned but not explained, that all of us could sometimes do but that none of us could ever define."[3] Although we sympathize with Wildavsky's frustration, we believe that, at least for social workers whose primary interest is not policy, it is necessary to deal with the term before any progress can be made in learning policy analysis skills. The definition we like is based on the one offered by the Canadian political scientist Leslie Pal: Policy analysis is the disciplined application of intellect to the study of collective responses to public (in our case social welfare) problems. This definition is sufficiently broad to include the wide range of policy analysis approaches we describe but is still precise enough to exclude many other types of social work knowledge-building activities.[4]

A key to defining and dealing with the term *policy analysis* is the recognition that it is broad and general. In many ways, it is analogous to the term *research*, which we all realize means many different things depending on how it is used by different people in different contexts. We all recognize the difference between a husband saying to his wife, "We need to do some research on state parks before we plan our summer vacation," and a social worker saying, "I have received a $250,000 grant to do research on the relationship between drug usage and marital instability." In a similar fashion, the term *policy analysis* is used to refer to everything from the processes citizens use to familiarize themselves with issues prior to voting, to a multiyear, multimillion dollar project to set up and evaluate programs using different approaches to financial assistance.

Table 3.1 presents a typology for categorizing different approaches to policy analysis. The table identifies four major dimensions on which policy analysis approaches vary. The first is the sophistication required of the person conducting the analysis. From the top of the table downward, the sophistication required diminishes. For the top two types, academic social science research and applied policy research, the analyst is generally educated at the doctoral level in policy analysis or in a related social science or applied social profession such as public administration or social work. These analysts generally spend a large proportion of their time conducting policy studies that are read and critiqued by other policy researchers and/or by actual policymakers. Because their purpose is to create new knowledge, the results are generally published in fairly accessible sources. These may range from books and articles available in a good library, to proceedings of professional conferences that may be widely circulated, to monographs and reports available in microform and on the Internet, to photocopied in-house reports, which are less widely distributed. Because of the rigorous nature of the methodology and the wide availability of results of these types of analyses, they often form the database for other approaches to policy analysis.

The next two approaches, social planning and agency planning/policy management, are generally conducted by professionals educated at the master's or doctoral level in applied social professions, often social work. They generally have specialized in policy/planning/administration in graduate school. Policy analysis usually constitutes only a small proportion of their jobs, with most of their time being devoted to running an agency, coordinating a community social service program, monitoring program compliance, or any of a number of other macropractice roles. The results

Table 3.1   Approaches to Policy Analysis

Policy Analysis Approach	Purpose	Consumer	Method
Academic social science research	Constructing theories for understanding society	Academic community	Rigorous empirical methodology, often quantitative
Applied policy research	Predicting or evaluating impacts of changes in variables that can be altered by public and/or private programs	Decision makers in the policy area	Formal research methodology applied to policy-relevant questions
Social planning	Defining and specifying ways to ameliorate social problems and to achieve a desirable future state	The "public interest" as professionally defined	Survey research, public forums, expert and/or citizen panels
Agency planning/ policy management	Defining and clarifying agency goals; explicating alternatives for achieving those goals; evaluating outcomes of attempts to achieve those goals	Boards of directors, funding agencies, interested citizens	Databases, management techniques (PERT, flow charting, decision analysis), survey research, public forums, expert and/or citizen panels
Journalistic	Focusing public attention on social welfare problems	General public	Existing documents, expert sources (professionals, scholars, people affected by the problem)
Practitioner policy analysis	Understanding the policy context within which an individual social worker functions	The social worker doing the analysis	Existing literature, government and other documents available on the Internet, expert sources
Citizen policy analysis	Clarifying issues for participation as an involved citizen in a democracy	The citizen involved in the analysis of elected officials that citizen wishes to influence	Existing literature, elected and appointed officials

Source: Adapted from D. L. Weiner and A. R. Vining, *Policy Analysis: Concepts and Practice,* 4th ed. (Upper Saddle River, NJ: Pearson/Prentice Hall, 2004), p. 26.

of these analyses are generally published in-house and are distributed to members of the organization employing the analyst as well as interested community persons.

The next two types are journalistic and practitioner policy analysis. The people who do these analyses generally are not educated specifically in policy analysis, and policy research is only tangential to their primary professional role. However, they need to develop a fairly sophisticated understanding of complex policy issues. The journalist needs to communicate with the general public and the social work practitioner needs to understand and effectively function on a daily basis. Journalistic policy analysis is generally presented in either written or electronic form in the public media and is generally based entirely on the work of academic social science researchers or applied policy researchers, usually supplemented by original reporting on the effects (both intended and unintended) of policies on beneficiaries. It is important to note that although journalistic policy analysis is not based on original research, this in no way detracts from its importance. The inspiration for the massive social programs of the Kennedy and Johnson administrations in the 1960s is generally credited to an essay review of several policy studies, notably Michael Harrington's *The Other America*, written by journalist Dwight McDonald and published in *New Yorker Magazine*. Randy Shilts's *And the Band Played On: Politics, People, and the AIDS Epidemic* has had a significant impact on AIDS policy.[5] Practitioner policy analysis is the focus of the remainder of this book, so it won't be described further here.

The lowest level of sophistication is that of the citizen analyst. The purpose of this type of analysis is for a person to obtain the information required to carry out the responsibilities of an informed citizen. Although we classify this as the least sophisticated approach to policy analysis, we should note that many citizens become quite skilled in studying policy. This type of analysis is the major focus of voluntary citizen groups such as the League of Women Voters.

The next three dimensions of the approaches to policy analysis (purpose, consumer, and method) are sufficiently explained in the table. The main point is that when you read policy analysis literature you need to identify which approach to analysis the author is using. Most of the literature concerns the top two levels of sophistication and is generally read by people who identify themselves as policy analysis professionals. This literature can be frustrating for the social work practitioner who has neither the time nor the inclination to become skilled in the application of highly sophisticated, often mathematical, techniques such as difference equations, queuing models, simulations, Markov chains, and the like. Fortunately, in recent years a literature has been developing that addresses the needs of practitioners.[6]

Methods of Policy Analysis

In addition to different approaches to policy analysis, different methods may be employed within any of the approaches. A number of different schemes have been developed for differentiating among methods of policy analysis. Our discussion categorizes policy analysis as descriptive analysis, process analysis, or evaluation.[7]

Descriptive Analysis

Descriptive policy analysis can be further subdivided into four types. These are content, choice, comparative, and historical analysis.

Content Analysis

Content analysis* is the most straightforward type of policy analysis. It is simply an empirical description of an existing policy in terms of its intentions, problem definition, goals, and means employed for achieving the goals. Content analysis is most often employed by agencies charged with administering a policy and is generally published in manuals, brochures, and annual reports of the agency. Occasionally, special interest groups such as the National Association of Retired Persons will publish content analyses of policies under which members may receive benefits.

Content analysis is generally not widely circulated to the general public and rarely is published in standard academic outlets. One of the most accessible, and certainly the most useful, sources of content analysis is the *Green Book*[8] published every two years by the U.S. Government Printing Office and also available on the House of Representatives Committee on Ways and Means web site. The most recent edition was published in 2000 and provides 1,500 pages of largely descriptive information about federal assistance programs, such as Social Security, Medicare, Supplemental Security Income, Unemployment Compensation, Railroad Retirement, Trade Adjustment Assistance, Temporary Assistance to Needy Families, child support enforcement, child care, child protection, foster care and adoption assistance, tax provisions, and the Pension Benefit Guaranty Corporation.

Choice Analysis

Largely developed by social workers Neil Gilbert, Paul Terrell, and the late Harry Specht, choice analysis is a systematic process of looking at the options available to planners for dealing with a social welfare problem. Gilbert and Terrell, describe this type of analysis as dealing with choices that "may be framed in program proposals, laws and statutes, or standing plans which eventually are transformed into programs. The analytic focus of such studies is upon issues of choice: What is the form and substance of the choices that compose the policy design? What options did these choices foreclose?"[9] The four primary dimensions of choice are described in some detail below.

Bases of Allocations.   The first dimension of choice involves the following question: *What are the bases of social allocations?* Gilbert and Terrell use this phrase to describe decisions about who will benefit from a policy. They draw two major distinctions in allocation: universal and selective provision. In the first case, "benefits [are] made available to an entire population as a social right." Universalism assumes that all citizens are "at risk," at some point, for common problems.[10] The classic example of universal benefits is Social Security for the elderly and those with disability. Unemployment Insurance is another example of a benefit

---

*This is not to be confused with the research methodology of content analysis, in which qualitative data, such as words or themes in a text, are subject to quantitative analysis.

made available to an entire group of people—those who have worked a specified length of time and are now unemployed. Since the 1930s, provision for these groups of people has been considered a basic right and therefore a responsibility of the government. Eligibility depends solely on characteristics such as age and prior attachment to the workforce. Factors such as present income or geographic location are irrelevant.

The alternative to universal allocation is selectivity. In the language of social welfare policy, *selectivity* has a specialized meaning: the allocation of benefits based on individual economic need. This is generally determined through an income test; those below a certain income level are eligible to receive benefits. Students often get confused about this concept because "selectivity" suggests a variety of ways to distinguish who will be provided for (such as all mothers of young children, all nearsighted people, or all intelligent high school students seeking college scholarships). The best way to understand selectivity in social welfare is to remember its tie to income level and the fact that there is no national consensus that the benefits are a fundamental right of the recipient.

Social welfare policymakers also speak of "universal versus categorical" distinctions. In this context, the word *categorical* refers to particular categories of poor people, for example, low-income women and children, elderly individuals, or those with handicaps. Public welfare benefits and Supplemental Security Income (SSI) are examples of categorical public assistance programs. Because these programs are based on need, they are also considered a selective approach to allocating benefits.

There are many arguments for and against each type of approach. The universal basis of allocation carries relatively little stigma and fits with democratic notions of equal treatment for all. Recipients can be seen as citizens or consumers. Proponents of selectivity herald its cost effectiveness; instead of resources being spread over a vast population, money or services can be used where they are most needed. This can help fill in the gaps between needy and nonneedy groups. Debates over the future shape of Social Security in our society involve these issues, with some observers suggesting that we should stop paying Social Security to those who don't need it and instead target more money to the less-well-off elderly.

Critics of selectivity argue, however, that it may be more cost effective to provide social welfare benefits across the board rather than to spend time and money sorting out those who are "truly disadvantaged." These critics add that selectivity leads to a two-track system; benefits for low-income groups don't seem as important to society as benefits for the majority and are thus allowed to be of lesser quality. This is a common argument today in discussions of health care; the system people can afford to pay for (on their own or through insurance) is often superior to publicly financed health care for the indigent.

The broad universal–selective distinction is perhaps most helpful in discussing government income maintenance programs such as Social Security and Temporary

Assistance to Needy Families. Within the wide variety of social welfare programs, however, there are additional ways of allocating benefits. Benefits can, for example, be provided to groups of people with specific common needs that are not met in the economic market. Such groups might include high school dropouts or the residents of a deteriorated urban neighborhood. Another principle of allocation is compensation; this is based on membership in a group, such as war veterans, that has made a specific contribution to society. Veterans' benefits are generally made available to individuals without regard to economic need. Finally, people may qualify for assistance through technical diagnosis of a condition such as a physical handicap or mental illness. Table 3.2, developed by Gilbert and Terrell, gives a good example of various bases for allocations of benefits.

Types of Benefits.   The second dimension of choice is concerned with the following question: *What are the types of social benefits to be provided?* A traditional way of categorizing types of provision is to distinguish between "in-cash" or "in-kind" benefits. Monthly unemployment checks are a good example of the former. Indirect forms of cash benefits, although not often viewed as such, include tax credits and exemptions such as the homeowner's deduction for mortgage interest.[11] Benefits-in-kind are actual goods or services. They include such things as used clothing from the Salvation Army, free inoculations for schoolchildren, and subsidized housing. Social services (for example, counseling, job training, or referrals) are a special type of in-kind benefit.

As in the case of universal and selective bases of allocation, policymakers debate the merits of cash versus in-kind benefits. Cash benefits are credited with allowing

Table 3.2   Alternative Bases for Allocation of Day Care Services

Conditions of Eligibility	Examples of Alternative Bases for Allocations
Attributed need	All families
	Single-parent families
	Families with working parents
	Families with student parents
Compensation	Minority families
	Families of servicemen and servicewomen
	Families of workers in specified occupational groups
Diagnostic differentiation	Families with physically or emotionally handicapped children
	Families in short-term crises
Means-tested need	Families whose earnings and resources fall beneath a designated standard of economic need

Source: Neil Gilbert and Paul Terrell, *Dimensions of Social Welfare Policy,* 6th ed. by Allyn and Bacon. Reprinted/Adapted by permission.

the recipient to maintain some sense of choice and control, a feature held to be important both in a democracy and a market economy. In-kind benefits, especially concrete goods, can be seen as undermining an individual's dignity and sense of responsibility. A familiar example is the Christmas basket for the poor, which may be perceived by recipients as a demeaning and patronizing type of assistance.

An advantage attributed to benefits-in-kind is the ability to ensure that the provisions will be used exactly as intended. Parents won't be tempted to "drink the welfare money"; a box of surplus foodstuffs will feed the family, whereas a food allowance might be absorbed into the general household income. These arguments imply that recipients, for whatever reasons, make unwise choices. A different, less judgmental, justification for in-kind benefits stresses efficiency and economy of scale, as in the publicly funded school lunch program.

Vouchers constitute a compromise between the two types of benefits. These are used like cash but are targeted for particular purchases. Housing vouchers, for example, guarantee that the government will pay the landlord a part of a family's rent. Vouchers are touted both for providing freedom of choice in a particular commodity or service area and for ensuring that the benefit is used as intended. However, the notion of freedom of choice may be illusory, as when housing discrimination prevents minority families from using their vouchers in certain neighborhoods. Some voucher systems, such as food stamps, are more successful, although even here individuals can encounter stigma as they proceed through the grocery checkout line.

Experiments in vouchers for private schools have attracted a good deal of attention lately. President George W. Bush has championed the use of vouchers, although Congress did not support his 2002 proposal to provide federal vouchers for poor students in "failing" schools. Some states and cities have established their own voucher programs. Polls indicate that many Americans like the idea of vouchers, although support weakens if funding for them would decrease money for public schools. So far, research on the use of vouchers for children attending substandard public schools has failed to yield "conclusive evidence that these programs consistently improve student achievement."[12]

Critics of publicly funded vouchers include not only those worried about funding of public schools but also African American parents who are skeptical about the acceptance of their children in white suburban schools. The fact that vouchers are often used for attendance at religious schools is another concern. In 2002, a close decision of the U.S. Supreme Court upheld the state of Ohio's publicly financed voucher program, even though nearly all the vouchers were used for religious schools. Decisive as the ruling seemed, policy analysts noted at the time that it might not translate into widespread use of vouchers, because opposition to them in other states would continue and because private and parochial schools lacked the space to accommodate all applicants. In fact, in 2006 the Florida Supreme Court struck down a voucher program for students attending failing schools. The court based its ruling on the fact that the state constitution barred Florida from using taxpayer money to finance a private alternative to the public system. The lawyer speaking against the voucher system represented the NAACP, the ACLU, and the Florida Education System, the state's largest teachers union. He argued that the state was paying for the "religious indoctrination of young children." The ruling ordered the end of a program that Governor Jeb Bush had considered one of his chief accomplishments. As in housing vouchers, discrimination against minorities and the poor will probably persist. In Ohio, for example, suburban schools had to agree to accept voucher students, yet none of them did.[13]

One further distinction in benefits occurs most frequently in, but is not limited to, the area of services. Receipt of services such as counseling or medical care can be voluntary or mandatory. Court-ordered therapy for people who abuse children may have a different success rate than that chosen more or less freely by a client (we say "more or less" because the decision to seek counseling may well be influenced by family, peers, or others). Social workers struggle these days with decisions over voluntary versus mandatory services in a number of areas. For example, should we force "street people" to enter shelters or insist that emotionally withdrawn nursing home residents join in the daily crafts class?

Delivery Structure.   The third dimension of choice is concerned with *the structure of the delivery system.* This set of policy choices relates to the details of how services or benefits will be delivered. There are a variety of administrative or organizational structures for doing this. A key distinction is the degree of centralization and/or coordination within the system. Will benefits be provided by a variety of agencies with little coordination, or will they be brought together, either under one roof or through an interorganizational network? Children's services are an example of a decentralized system in many states: Foster care and protective services are handled through a public child welfare department; adoptions programs are carried out through both public and private agencies; and children's health care is provided in public health departments, school clinics, and private doctors' offices. These separate organizations may have little interaction with one another. Even within a single agency, the various programs and departments may operate relatively autonomously.[14]

One way to centralize services is to link them together within one organization. For example, a shelter for homeless families might provide job counseling, health care, day care for children, recreation programs, and a public welfare office branch all within one facility, stressing careful coordination between units. Another approach linking the programs of various agencies is utilized in the field of gerontology. Publicly funded local Area Agencies on Aging are responsible for area-wide planning of social services for the elderly, for monitoring local programs affecting the elderly, and for coordination of specific federal programs.

Centralized or coordinated systems are often more convenient for clients to use, can allow for comprehensive planning of benefits, and tend to lessen duplication of services. On the other hand, centralization (in particular) usually involves a more complex bureaucracy, increasing the distance between clients and administrators.[15] Decentralized or less coordinated systems generally increase autonomy and diversity in mission and approach and may lead to a competition among programs that may increase quality. In implementing policy, planners have to decide which type of structure is best in meeting policy goals.

There are many other features of delivery system structure that policymakers must consider. These include the degree of citizen participation in program decisions, the types of employees used to provide benefits (professionals, nonprofessionals, or consumers), and ways of relating to racial and ethnic needs.[16] A particularly important distinction among the organizations providing benefits is that between public and private agencies. We turn to that distinction in the following discussion of modes of finance.

Financing Benefits.   The final dimension of choice analysis relates to decisions on *how benefits are financed.* This can be done in a variety of ways: through taxation, voluntary contributions, or fees. Federal, state, and local taxation is, of course, a public levy on citizens; it supports public social welfare programs such as public assistance, Social Security (through a special payroll tax), public health programs, and services to veterans. Voluntary contributions are charitable donations, particular private agencies or programs, and the like. Local giving is often coordinated by United Way or Community Fund organizations. Fees for services are charged by both private nonprofit and for-profit agencies and occasionally by public agencies.

Social welfare benefits are provided by public governmental organizations on federal, state, and local levels; by private nonprofit or voluntary agencies; and by private for-profit groups. The last two decades have seen rapid growth in entrepreneurial social welfare services run on a corporate model. Important examples of these human services corporations include for-profit psychiatric and medical hospitals, home health care systems for the elderly, child care programs, and job training and job placement programs for welfare recipients.[17]

The social policy picture would be much simpler if each category of organization depended on a single type of funding, but one of the most important characteristics of the U.S. social welfare system today is its complicated mixture of funding sources for all three types of agencies. This mixture has a long tradition in the United States, though it has become more complex in recent years. Before discussing the overlapping nature of funding, however, we will look at the goals, advantages, and disadvantages of each type of agency in its purest form.

A system of public social welfare programs can be described as representing the general public will. It is financed by all of us and thus publicly sanctioned to do certain things. Theoretically, at least, public agencies will be openly account-able for their actions. Public social services are presumed to be available on an equitable and nondiscriminatory basis. Public financing means command of greater resources than are generally available in the private sector. Finally, the public services can reap the advantages of economies of scale as they provide their benefits.

Private agencies have certain general characteristics, although the nonprofit and for-profit versions each have their own particular attributes. Private social service agencies are often thought to be more innovative in services and more likely to experiment with alternative organizational models. Many of the crisis phone lines of the 1970s and 1980s, for example, were developed by small private organizations. Proponents of private agencies also describe them as more respon-sive to the needs of specific groups in the community (as in the case of religious social service agencies) and better able than large government organizations to per-sonalize services. Voluntary agencies, which receive a great deal of support from the public, have been characterized as performing social welfare tasks that neither the government nor the for-profit sector is willing to carry out. Because they are generally directed by community boards, it is assumed that they respond to community needs and goals. The for-profit sector is touted particularly for its cost-effectiveness and ability to produce better services through competition. Because consumers pay for services, it is argued, the for-profit agency will be responsive to their choices.[18]

The truth lies somewhere among all of these claims. Although the possibility for accountability is probably greater in the public sector, the public may have only limited influence on government agency policy. By the same token, volun-tary agencies do not always represent their total communities; boards may consist of businesspeople and professionals who do not necessarily respond to the needs or desires of disadvantaged groups. Consumers of services in for-profit agencies may not have sufficient information to make informed choices about which service is best, as in the cases of mental and physical health care. In addition, the goal of maximizing profits may take precedence over a commitment to meeting clients' needs. The idea of establishing patients' rights in managed care is seen as one solution to this problem.[19]

In addition, cost-effectiveness may or may not occur in any of the three types of agencies; for example, in the health arena, it can be argued that duplication of expensive equipment by private hospitals has contributed to the rise in health care costs. Although for-profit and voluntary agencies can indeed experiment in new kinds of service delivery, some public agencies have been able to do this as well. Sometimes private agencies avoid what they consider to be unpopular innovations for fear of discouraging contributors. Often an important variable is the size of the organization; large bureaucracies in both public and private agencies may hamper innovation and lead to impersonal treatment (the big private hospital may be just as daunting to patients as the large public welfare office is to its clients). In sum, though certain broad distinctions can be made about the differences in mission and operation among the three agency types, it is clear that these distinctions are sometimes blurred.

Rather than relying on any one approach to social welfare, the United States has opted for a mixed public/voluntary/for-profit system. What is known as "contracting out" for services—a process in which a state public welfare department, for example, pays a private organization to provide child welfare services—has been with us in some form for a long time. By the mid-1830s, for example, many states subsidized private institutions, such as orphanages run by religious groups, for the care of dependent children. Since the 1960s, government subsidies have increased dramatically. Until recently, the bulk of government social welfare contracts have gone to voluntary agencies; now, however, an increasing number involve for-profit groups. Four states, for example, contract out case management, skills training, and job placement assistance for public welfare clients to a division of the huge defense company Lockheed Martin.[20] Similar patterns are occurring in the public schools (see Box 3.1).

The U.S. government has also been taking a new look at federal funding for social services provided by religious groups, including churches. Such funding has occurred on a small scale for some time, and in 1996 Congress passed legislation allowing religious groups to compete for contracts from the U.S. Department of Health and Human Services. Building on a campaign promise, President George W. Bush began work on his "faith-based initiative" shortly after taking office. Arguing that faith can accomplish what secular programs cannot, Bush proposed that religious groups have the right to contract with other federal agencies and to use federal dollars for a wide variety of services for people in need. Whereas earlier recipients of federal money were generally large agencies such as Catholic Charities, Bush was particularly interested in bringing federal money to religious congregations. It appeared that this focus might be especially appealing to African American congregations, which have had a long tradition of providing charitable aid in their communities.[21]

Not surprisingly, Bush's proposals unleashed a vigorous debate, both in Congress and among the public at large, over the boundaries between church and state. According to one survey, most Americans were ambivalent about the president's plan. Although they supported giving federal grants to religious social service providers, they believed the proposal placed too little emphasis on holding religious groups accountable. The plan raised fears that religious agencies and congregations would attempt to proselytize, forcing their beliefs on recipients of aid. Opponents also pointed out that some religious agencies do not hire people of different religious backgrounds and discriminate against gays and lesbians.

box
3.1

Will Privatization Approaches Work in the Public Schools?

The 2002 No Child Left Behind Act made it possible for private companies to offer tutoring to students in "failing public schools." These tutoring programs can now be financed by federal money formerly spent on the schools themselves. As a result, "the federally financed tutoring industry has doubled in size in each of the past two years, with the potential to become a $2 billion-a-year enterprise."[1] How well has this experiment in privatization worked? In Chicago's Wentworth Elementary School, tutors from a private company offering after-school classes failed to control the rambunctious students of Room 2007. The school's principal noted that the tutors weren't prepared "to deal with challenging inner city children. . . . I think they expected to find children who'd just sit down and wait for them to expound." In fact, private tutoring companies have ended up trying to deal with the same discipline, attendance, and other problems "that have kept failing schools from raising proficiency levels on their own."[2]

According to a Harvard University Study of eleven school districts in three states, the need to oversee private tutoring programs put heavy administrative burdens on those districts. In addition, "the requirement to withhold 20 percent of Title I money" for these programs ended up diverting resources "from the neediest schools."[3] Issues of poor learning in public schools have to do with many problems, including poverty, poor health care, low expectations, discrimination, and lack of adequate child care for low-income working parents. Private services, such as tutoring, have so far not been the panacea for resolving such problems.

Sources: (1) Susan Saulny, "A Lucrative Brand of Tutoring Grows Unchecked," *New York Times* (4 April 2005), p. 1; (2) Sam Dillon, "For Children Being Left Behind, Private Tutors Face Rocky Start," *New York Times* (16 April 2004), p. 16; (3) Dillon, "For Children Being Left Behind," p. 26.

Religious groups themselves were divided, some welcoming the prospect of government resources, others worrying about red tape and federal regulations.[22]

Failing to get legislation passed to sanction expansion of federal funding for religious social services, Bush has recently turned to a series of executive orders. One such order makes it easier for religious groups to be funded by allowing those receiving federal contracts to maintain the practice of taking religious affiliation into account when hiring staff. Such changes in federal regulations have served to relax laws that previously made some groups ineligible to receive government funds. In the meantime, the debate over federal support for religious social services continues.[23]

The growth in government contracts for social welfare services, whether secular or religious, is one factor in the increasingly close relationship between the public and private sectors. The private sector also depends to a great extent on government funding sources such as Medicaid and Medicare. The striking rise in the number of for-profit hospitals and home health care facilities, for example, is due in large part to an increase in government expenditures on health care. To make things even more complex, the line between for-profit and nonprofit social welfare activities has blurred. As voluntary agencies have witnessed a decline in contributions as a portion of their resources, they have turned more and more to what has been called the "commercialization" of their financial base, charging more fees for services and even selling products. In addition, for-profit companies have begun to compete successfully with nonprofit groups for government funding, leading some charitable organizations to seek to work collaboratively with the for-profits. For example, when Lockheed Martin received a contract for welfare-to-work services in Dade County, Florida, it subcontracted with a number of nonprofit agencies to deliver those services.[24]

By now, you may be thoroughly confused and wondering what all of this has to do with social work. The bottom line is effective and equitable service to clients. Social workers must continue to gauge what these developments mean to people who need assistance and whether they ameliorate such problems as poverty and poor health. Evaluation research is needed to determine the advantages and disadvantages of specific public and private approaches, and social work practitioners must observe and evaluate the results of different programs for their individual clients.

Comparative Analysis

This type of policy analysis involves systematically comparing policies across two or more settings. The most common form is cross-national analysis: The policy in one nation (in these examples, the United States) is compared with policies of other nations regarding the same problem. More limited comparisons, between states or communities or between public and private service provisions, for example, are also possible and useful. This is a rich approach because it provides policy analysts with "natural experiments" of alternative approaches to social welfare problems.

The recognized masters of this type of analysis in social work are Sheila Kamerman and Alfred Kahn, who have produced a number of comparative studies of social welfare policies. An example of a cross-national analysis is their study of child care, family benefits, and working parents in which they compared policies in the United States with those of five European countries. They introduce this study as follows:

> This report . . . deals with one of the major family policy questions facing industrial urban societies, or perhaps the major question: . . . what are the optimum response alternatives . . . to a situation in which parents are in the paid labor force,

want to have children, and want to rear them successfully? Modern societies have a stake in both childbearing and successful child rearing, but the consequences of different policy responses have not been given detailed, systematic examination. After surveying fourteen country patterns, we selected six countries which have adopted different approaches. The options represent a continuum, with those in the middle involving different mixes. . . . We have placed all this in societal context, given an overview of where children under three actually are during the day, and assessed the debate and interest group positions in each country. There is a secondary review of research on costs, effects, prices, and who pays.[25]

An example of comparative analysis of policies within the United States is Kamerman and Kahn's study of child care policy. In this study, they compare local child care initiatives, state child care actions, private approaches, public school systems as child care providers, employers and child care, and family day care.[26] Comparative analysis may use any or all of the methods of policy analysis discussed in this chapter.

Historical Analysis

It is difficult, if not impossible, to analyze any current policy without at least a brief review of preceding events. Historical analysis, as a policy analysis type, goes well beyond this and is based on the assumption that current policies can be fully understood only if we have a thorough understanding of their evolution. Content analysis defines *policy* as what currently exists, but the historical orientation views policy as patterns of behavior by the state and private groups extending over a long period of time. If a policy is the continuation of a long trend, as in the case of the recent welfare reform legislation, historical analysis seeks to explicate that trend and to understand why it has continued. On the other hand, if a policy is significantly different from earlier policies in the same area, such as the old-age insurance portion of the Social Security Act of 1935, for example, the purpose of historical analysis is to explain the reasons for the departure from standard practice. Historical policy analysis methods will be discussed in greater detail in Chapter 4.

Process Analysis

Process analysis is less concerned with policy content than with how a policy comes into being. The focus of this analytic approach is on the interactions of the many political actors, which include public officials, bureaucrats, media, professional associations, and special interest groups representing those likely to be affected either positively or negatively by a policy. An understanding of the process is necessary to fully understand the content of a policy.

One of the better examples of a process analysis is Steiner's study of family policy in the United States. As part of this study, Steiner looks at foster care policy, specifically at the process that eventually resulted in the Adoption Assistance and Child Welfare Act of 1980.[27] Steiner found a number of dynamics to be important in shaping the bill that was eventually passed. These included:

- The Catholic church, which in the 1930s opposed inclusion in the Social Security Act of federally funded foster care for urban areas. This was to protect already existing agreements between the church and several large cities for the funding of Catholic children's homes.
- Academicians, who failed to develop a useful theory on which to base public policy for children in foster homes.
- Child welfare social workers, who often did not actively seek to involve biological parents in case planning because "deemphasizing the biological parent is the safest approach for the child welfare worker, who carries in his or her head two injunctions: do the child no harm and do not embarrass the agency."
- Foster parents, who were too diverse a group to be able to get together to support a specific program.
- The Department of Health, Education, and Welfare (now Health and Human Services), which had no new data or new plans to bring to Congress in support of any expansion of services.
- The Child Welfare League of America, whose main concern was opposing any attempt to put a cap on spending for foster care and related services.

The result of all these forces was a piece of legislation that did not break significant new ground in dealing with the problem of children who need substitute care.

Evaluation

If there is a theme that describes social welfare policy in recent years it is increasing skepticism. Voters, elected representatives, bureaucrats, and academics have all ceased to assume that social welfare programs are good simply because they have good intentions. One result is a demand for evaluation of all aspects of social welfare policy. Rather than simply describing or explaining social welfare policy, evaluation is intended to judge it. The evaluation process may judge a policy's logical consistency, empirically evaluate its effectiveness and efficiency, or analyze its ethical character.

Logical Evaluation

Logical evaluation is similar to content analysis in looking at the content of a social welfare policy in detail. It goes beyond content analysis, however, by assessing a policy's internal rigor and consistency. Logical evaluation generally evaluates a policy in terms of three possible dimensions—singly or in combination—as the following discussion indicates. Because social welfare policies generally have more than one goal, the first dimension of logical evaluation entails assessing the internal consistency of a policy's multiple goals. Financial assistance policy, for example, has a goal of getting people to go to work and also has a goal of enabling mothers to take good care of their children. Because taking good care of children may well involve staying home with them rather than working, these goals are often in conflict.

The second dimension of logical evaluation involves assessing the consistency between a policy's goals and the means for achieving these goals. For example, the report of the Ford Foundation Project on Social Welfare and the American Future is very critical of the internal logic of our social welfare policies because they do not have the means to achieve the desired ends. The report argues that

> The current social welfare system appears oriented to picking up pieces rather than preventing the original breakage. Our policies typically do not help families with children until there is a crisis and the children are hurt. We spend large amounts to save the life of each low-birthweight baby, but skimp on the prenatal care that helps avoid future suffering. We stand aside as large numbers of children are damaged intellectually and socially in their first few years of life, and then rush in with remedial school programs and anti-crime measures when the inevitable consequences of such neglect occur. We also ask the poor to go on welfare before health care is made accessible to them. We expect most jobless and very poorly paid workers to exhaust their unemployment benefits and their own resources before they can receive any help with retraining or other means of securing mobility in the labor market. . . . As taxpayers and as victims of a violent society we end up paying for the social wreckage that results from a lack of earlier investments in other people and their children. We cannot build enough prisons or buy enough home security systems to protect our private worlds from the social decay that spreads when true opportunity is denied to large numbers of people.[28]

The third dimension of logical evaluation involves assessing the difference between intended and unintended consequences. As Pal has observed, "Even when goals are consistent and there is a clear logical relationship between ends and means, public policies may have unintended consequences that can be worse than the original problem."[29] A well-known example of this type of evaluation is the 1984 critique of the welfare system conducted by conservative analyst Charles Murray. Murray argues that although the goals of social welfare policy between 1950 and 1980 were to help people become self-sufficient, the effect was exactly the opposite. The reason he gives for this is that, in his opinion, the system became so generous in its attempts to help people that it became more attractive to go on welfare, and once on to stay on welfare, than to "tough it out" by getting a job, getting married, and working to rise through the system.[30]

Quantitative Evaluation

Social welfare policies are created to solve pressing social problems, and in so doing they expend large sums of money. Thus it is natural to demand a rigorous, data-based evaluation of whether policies achieve their intended goals and at what cost. There are generally two parts to quantitative evaluations: effectiveness (sometimes called *outcome*) evaluations and efficiency (sometimes called *cost-effectiveness*) evaluations. These evaluations encompass a wide range of research methodology, and a huge literature has developed related to both the methods and the politics of evaluation.[31]

The most common type of evaluations are ex post facto evaluations of programs that are set up and operating at the time researchers are brought in to assess their effectiveness and efficiency. One of the best-known examples of this is the evaluation of the Head Start Program conducted by Westinghouse Learning Corporation and Ohio University in 1968. The Head Start Program was begun in 1964 as one of the main efforts of the Office of Economic Opportunity. The premise of the program (heavily influenced by culture of poverty theory) was that poor children performed at a lower level in school than nonpoor children because they came from homes in which adequate cognitive preparation for school was absent. The program originally provided eight weeks of intensive educational preparation, and in many areas this was soon increased to one year. The intent was that poor children would be brought up to the same level of educational readiness as nonpoor children and hence would be able to compete successfully in school. The evaluators randomly selected 104 Head Start programs from across the country; about two-thirds were eight-week and one-third were full-year programs. Children who had completed the program and were, at the time of the study, in first, second, or third grade were matched in socioeconomic background with children who had not gone through the program. The children were all given batteries of tests of educational achievement and cognitive development. In addition, parents were interviewed and teachers of both groups were asked to rate the children on achievement and motivation. The results of the evaluation were disappointing because the researchers found little evidence of effectiveness, although the parents of the children in the program voiced great satisfaction with it.[32] In spite of the evidence of low effectiveness, Head Start remained, and still remains, a very popular program. This fact relates to the political nature of policy in general, as discussed in Chapter 6, and of evaluation in particular, which will be discussed later in this chapter.

A less common type of evaluation is the policy experiment. In this type of evaluation, research questions and hypotheses are developed and a program to test them is designed following generally accepted social science criteria. A recent example of a well-done policy experiment concerns the disappointing results of early Head Start evaluations. Reviewing the weak Head Start results, policy makers theorized that perhaps Head Start intervention needed to begin before age three. The Secretary of the Department of Health and Human Services appointed an Advisory Committee on Services for Families with Infants and Toddlers, and this committee recommended a "comprehensive, two-generation program [that] includes intensive services that begin before the child is born and concentrates on enhancing the child's development and supporting the family during the critical first three years of the child's life"[33] The program, called Early Head Start, began in 1995/96 with programs funded at 143 sites. Mathematica Policy Research was hired to conduct an experimental evaluation of the results of this program. The evaluation was conducted by selecting seventeen sites and then randomly assigning program applicants to the Early Head Start Program or to a comparison group not assigned to the program. The children and families in both groups were then monitored and measured on a number of variables, including cognitive development, language development, social–emotional development, parenting outcomes, parent's progress toward self-sufficiency, subsequent births to parents, and father–child interaction. The results of this study, completed in 2005, were summarized as "a consistent pattern of statistically significant, modest, favorable impacts across a range of outcomes when children were two and three years old, with larger impacts in several subgroups. Although little is known about how important this pattern of impacts sustained through toddlerhood will be in the long run, reductions in risk factors and improvements in protective factors may support improved later outcomes."[34]

Ethical Evaluation

All types of policy analysis discussed thus far are, at least theoretically, value-free. To demonstrate this, Pal uses the following example of an analyst asked to evaluate the Nazi regime's policy of concentration camps:

> It would be possible to provide a description of the "final solution," an analysis of the processes that caused it, and a logical and empirical evaluation. Auschwitz could be described, its background and establishment detailed, determining political forces as well as its organizational processes outlined, logical consistency of policy probed and even an analysis of efficiency conducted. The analyst's ethical judgement could be withheld while these technical analyses were undertaken. But the concentration camps were and are an affront to civilized ethics, and it is entirely appropriate to judge them in these terms.[35]

One of the major points we make throughout this book is that social welfare policy is heavily value laden. The issues that social welfare policy deals with are, at their core, issues of good and bad, right and wrong, should and shouldn't. Therefore ethical evaluation is a common and important type of social welfare policy analysis. Because there are sharp differences between value systems, ethical policy evaluations are often controversial. One of the best examples is the pastoral letter of the American Catholic bishops, "Economic Justice for All: Catholic Social Teaching and the U.S. Economy."[36] The bishops begin the letter by clearly stating six moral principles that provide an overview for the vision they wish to share:

1. Every economic decision and institution must be judged in light of whether it protects or undermines the dignity of the human person.
2. Human dignity can be realized and protected only in community.
3. All people have a right to participate in the economic life of society.
4. All members of society have a special obligation to the poor and vulnerable.
5. Human rights are the minimum conditions for life in community.
6. Society as a whole, acting through public and private institutions, has the moral responsibility to enhance human dignity and protect human rights.

Based on these moral principles, the bishops then analyzed a number of policy issues. They found the U.S. social welfare system deficient in a number of areas and recommended changes such as providing financial assistance recipients with an adequate level of support (they deplored the finding that "only 4 percent of poor families with children receive enough cash welfare benefits to lift them out of poverty"), establishing national eligibility standards and a national minimum welfare benefit level, and making two-parent families eligible for welfare assistance in all states. It is interesting to note that, although the bishops were almost certainly aware of the discouraging final report of the Seattle and Denver Income Maintenance Experiments (SIME/DIME—see Chapter 7), which found more generous approaches to income maintenance such as a negative income tax actually reduced work participation by recipients, one of their concluding recommendations was that the negative income tax "is another major policy proposal that deserves continued discussion." Apparently, based on the moral principles the bishops were using as the framework for their analysis, the fact that a quantitative evaluation had indicated that the negative income tax resulted in lowered labor force participation did not detract from the attractiveness of this approach.

Policy Analysis Methods as Ideal Types

While reading the preceding discussion of policy analysis methods, you may have asked yourself questions such as: How can you do a historical analysis without its also being descriptive? Aren't empirical evaluations based on some ethical principles (for example, SIME/DIME obviously embraces the work ethic)? Don't ethical evaluations use data as the basis for some of their arguments? These questions point out that none of the methods we have described actually exists in pure form in the real world. Rather, they are what sociologists refer to as *ideal types*. That is, we have artificially separated them and described what they would look like in pure form if such a form existed. In reality, there is much overlap among the methods, and most policy analyses contain elements from several of them. Good policy analysis almost always begins with solid description and historical analysis, always is based on the best empirical data available, and then proceeds to focus on logic, efficiency, effectiveness, or ethics. In addition, good policy analysis is often comparative.

Policy Analysis as Science, Art, and Politics

As a rule, policy analysts consider themselves to be social scientists and what they do to be science. Policy analysts generally employ conventional methods of social science, beginning with formulating the problem and proceeding to stating the hypotheses, developing data collection procedures, collecting and analyzing data, drawing conclusions, and generalizing from the results. When attempting to read a policy analysis textbook, the lay reader can easily be overwhelmed by the complexity of the technical methods employed.

Although there is no doubt that policy analysis seeks to be a science, and there is little doubt as to the appropriateness of this quest, it is important to understand that there are limits to the degree that conclusive knowledge can be obtained regarding policy questions. Charles Lindblom gives four reasons why analysis cannot provide conclusive answers to policy questions:

1. Policy problems are simply beyond the analytic capacities of human beings. Lindblom explains that "the basic difficulty stems from a discrepancy between the limited cognitive capacities of the human animal and the complexities of policy problems. Even when extended by a range of devices from written language to electronic computers, the mind at its best simply cannot grasp the complexity of reality."

2. Policy issues are based on values and interests that are often in conflict. A policy that may be optimal based on the values and interests of one group may be in conflict with those of another group. For example, what is the correct abortion policy? For one group, the right of a woman to choose is the paramount value, and for another, the right of a fetus to live is most important. It is impossible to quantify these values and reach an absolute conclusion.

3. The more a policy analysis approaches complete understanding of an issue, the more time and money will be required to conduct it. Most policy decisions cannot wait until "all the data are in" and therefore are made based on less than complete information. For example, the SIME/DIME studies referred to previously took nine years and many millions of dollars to conduct yet provided

only partial answers to a few rather limited questions regarding the optimal approach to income maintenance.

4. A purely analytic formulation of the question a policy addresses is impossible. What is the problem for antipoverty policy? Is it lack of motivation among the poor? Lack of equal opportunity? Inadequate economic growth? These questions contain moral components and, as such, must be settled by politics rather than analysis.[37]

If policy analysis cannot be purely scientific in the sense that single, definitive answers are rarely found, what does this mean? First, it means that we must recognize that policy analysis is as much an art as it is a science. Wildavsky asserts that policy analysis is synonymous with creativity. "Analysis is imagination. Making believe the future has happened in the past, analysts try to imagine events as if those actions already had occurred."[38] One of the means for doing this is what is known as the "thought experiment." This means simply taking a program, either real or imaginary, and—as systematically as possible, based only on logical thought—analyzing the likely effects. The conservative analyst Charles Murray does this to great effect in *Losing Ground*. He describes a young couple, Harold and Phyllis, who are not married but are seriously involved; they have learned that Phyllis is pregnant. Murray proceeds to imagine what their behavior would have been in 1960, when there were few social programs to assist them, and in 1970, when there were generous AFDC benefits (he places them in Pennsylvania, a state with benefits among the highest in the nation), public housing, Medicaid, food stamps, as well as other programs. His conclusion from the thought experiment is that in 1960 they would have chosen to get married and to take jobs, even unattractive ones, because there were no other options available. This choice, he argues, would have put them on the first rung of the ladder of success, or at least to participation in mainstream U.S. society. In 1970, Murray imagines, they again would have taken the rational course of action—which now would be to *not* get married so Phyllis could avail herself of all the "generous" social program benefits. This would result in Harold's eventually drifting off because his role had become extraneous to the lives of Phyllis and the baby, who would be doomed (his view) to a life as a single-parent welfare family. From this, Murray concludes that present social welfare policies result in more harm than good and probably should be discontinued.[39] As this example illustrates, thought experiments, perhaps even more than other forms of policy analysis, are heavily influenced by the political perspective of the analyst.

Whatever the technique employed, the impact of those policy analyses is due more to their art than to their science. Analyses such as Murray's conservative *Losing Ground,* or Harrington's liberal *The Other America*, or even television documentaries such as Public Broadcasting's *Eyes on the Prize* or Edward R. Murrow's famous *Harvest of Shame* have been well written and well organized and because of this have had great impact.

This leads us to introduce an important point that will be noted again in Chapter 6: Policy analysis—whether conducted using rigorous, scientific methodology or more as an art—is, in the final analysis, political. Lindblom argues that analysis, regardless of its form, becomes part of the play of power, a tool of persuasion. He uses the term *partisan policy analysis.* By this he means that effective policy analysts realize that their analysis will be used in the play of power. They therefore target it to people or groups of people they wish to influence. This is done by taking the values of the group or person to be influenced and analyzing the policy to show how those values can be furthered.[40] For example, imagine that an advocate for increased economic assistance to the poor was attempting to get support for increased welfare benefits from a member of Congress known for supporting defense spending. The advocate for the poor would attempt to demonstrate that increased welfare benefits would in some way serve the interests of national defense, perhaps by improving the health, education, or social adjustment of the young people who make up the pool of potential soldiers. Although this example may be a little farfetched, the point is not. Policy analysis, be it art or science, is used as one of a number of tools of persuasion in the political process.

Conclusion

In this chapter, we have knowingly strayed a bit from the major focus of this book; we have addressed policy analysis more from the perspective of professional academic policy analysts and less from the viewpoint of practicing social workers who need to understand the context of their practice. There is a reason for this: When you begin to conduct your own practitioner policy analysis using the methods described in the following chapters, you will be relying heavily on the work of professional academic analysts. Their work can be confusing unless you understand a few simple points, described in this chapter. Now, with this basic understanding of the policy analysis field, we proceed to address methods you can use in your own practice.

Notes

1. Jason DeParle, *American Dream: Three Women, Ten Kids, and a Nation's Drive to End Welfare* (New York: Viking, 2004).

2. Davis B. Bobrow and John S. Dryzek, *Policy Analysis by Design* (Pittsburgh: University of Pittsburgh Press, 1987), p. 5.

3. Aaron Wildavsky, *Speaking Truth to Power: The Art and Craft of Policy Analysis* (Boston: Little, Brown, 1979), p. 2.

4. Leslie A. Pal, *Beyond Policy Analysis: Public Issue Management in Turbulent Times,* 3rd ed. (Toronto: Thomson/Nelson, 2006), p. 14.

5. Michael Harrington, *The Other America: Poverty in the United States* (New York: Penguin Books, 1962); Dwight McDonald, "Our Invisible Poor," *New Yorker Magazine* 38 (19 January 1963), pp. 82–132; Randy Shilts, *And the Band Played On: Politics, People, and the AIDS Epidemic* (New York: St. Martin's Press, 1987).

6. See, for example, Donald Chambers and Kenneth Wedel, *Social Policy and Social Programs: A Method for the Practical Policy Analyst*, 4th ed. (Boston: Allyn and Bacon, 2005); Lewis G. Irwin, *The Policy Analysts Handbook: Rational Problem Solving in a Political World* (Armonk, New York: M. E. Sharp, 2003).

7. See, for example, Leslie A. Pal, *Public Policy Analysis: An Introduction*, (Toronto: Methuen, 1987), pp. 27–38; Neil Gilbert and Paul Terrell, *Dimensions of Social Welfare Policy*, 6th ed. (Boston: Allyn and Bacon, 2005), pp. 11–15.

8. *Green Book, 2004: Background Material and Data on Programs within the Jurisdiction of the Committee on Ways and Means* (Washington, DC: U.S. Government Printing Office, 2004).

9. Gilbert and Terrell, *Dimensions of Social Welfare Policy*, pp. 42–43.

10. Gilbert and Terrell, *Dimensions of Social Welfare Policy*, p. 71.

11. Elizabeth Huttman, *Introduction to Social Policy* (New York: McGraw-Hill, 1981), p. 123.

12. Kate Zernike, "Vouchers: A Shift, but Just How Big?" *New York Times* (30 June 2002), p. 3; "Court Begins Hearing School Vouchers Case," *Arizona Republic* (22 February 2002), p. 4; "Reality of Vouchers Gets Mixed Reactions, Poll Says," *Arizona Republic* (7 August 2002), p. 3; Diana Jean Schemo, "Voucher Study Indicates No Steady Gains in Learning," *New York Times* (9 December 2001), p. 33.

13. Robert E. Pierre, "Skeptical about Vouchers," *Washington Post National Weekly Edition* (5–11 August 2002), p. 29; Sam Dillon, "Florida Supreme Court Blocks School Vouchers," *New York Times* (6 January 2002), p. 14; Joe Follick, "Florida Supreme Court Takes Up Vouchers," *New York Times* (8 June 2005), p. 13; Jacques Steinberg, "Cleveland Case Poses New Test for Vouchers," *New York Times* (10 February 2002), p. 1.

14. Chambers and Wedel, *Social Policy and Social Programs*, pp. 108–115.

15. Chambers and Wedel, *Social Policy and Social Programs*, pp. 115–116.

16. For a detailed discussion of social service delivery system options, see Gilbert and Terrell, *Dimensions of Social Welfare Policy*, pp. 125–158.

17. Howard Karger and David Stoesz, *American Social Welfare Policy: A Pluralist Approach*, 2nd ed. (New York: Longman, 1994), pp. 222–231; Mary Ann Jimenez, "Historical Evolution and Future Challenges of the Human Services Professions," *Social Service Review* 67 (March 1993), pp. 3–12.

18. Michael Hill and Glen Bramley, *Analyzing Social Policy* (New York: Basil Blackwell, 1986), pp. 101–106; *Giving and Volunteering in the United States* (Washington, DC: Independent Sector, 1988), p. 5.

19. Michael Sosin, *Private Benefits: Material Assistance in the Private Sector* (Orlando, FL: Academic Press, 1986), p. 166; Hill and Bramley, *Analyzing Social Policy*, pp. 109–110.

20. Walter I. Trattner, *From Poor Law to Welfare State: A History of Social Welfare in America*, 6th ed. (New York: Free Press, 1999), pp. 113–115; Matthew A. Crenson, *Building the Invisible Orphanage: A Prehistory of the American Welfare System* (Cambridge, MA: Harvard University Press, 1998), pp. 3, 46–48; Christopher G. Petr and Ivy C. Johnson, "Privatizing of Foster Care in Kansas: A Cautionary Tale," *Social Work* 44 (May 1999), pp. 263–267.

21. Frank Bruni and Laurie Goodstein, "Bush to Focus on a Favorite Project: Helping Religious Groups to Help the Needy," *New York Times* (26 January 2001), p. 17; Mark Silk, "New Rules for an Old Alliance," *Washington Post Weekly Edition* (26 February–4 March 2001), p. 22.

22. "A Conversation with Amy Sherman: Faith-Based Organizations and Welfare Reform," *Policy and Practice* 59 (September 2001), p. 16; Kenneth Woodward, "Of God and Mammon," *Newsweek* (12 February 2001), pp. 24–25; Kelly Ettenborough and Maureen West, "Valley Organizations View Plan as Godsend or Intrusion," *Arizona Republic* (30 January 2001), pp. 1, 4; Jerry Keister, "Faith Based Initiative, Red Flags Right, Left, and Center," *Social Work Today I* (20 August 2001), pp. 10–14.

23. "Faith-Based by Fiat," *Washington Post Weekly Edition* (23 December 2002–5 February 2003), p. 25; Laura Meckler, "Faith-Based Treatment for Addicts Draws Fire," *Arizona Republic* (29 January 2003), p. 13.

24. William P. Ryan, "The New Landscape for Nonprofits," *Harvard Business Review* (January–February 1999), pp. 127–136.

25. Sheila B. Kamerman and Alfred J. Kahn, *Child Care, Family Benefits, and Working Parents: A Study in Comparative Policy* (New York: Columbia University Press, 1981), p. xi.

26. Alfred J. Kahn and Sheila B. Kamerman, *Child Care: Facing the Hard Choices* (Dover, MA: Auburn House, 1987).

27. Gilbert Y. Steiner, *The Futility of Family Policy* (Washington, DC: The Brookings Institution, 1981), pp. 130–155.

28. Ford Foundation Project on Social Welfare and the American Future, *The Common Good: Social Welfare and the American Future* (New York: Ford Foundation, 1989), pp. 5–6.

29. Pal, *Public Policy Analysis: An Introduction*, p. 33.

30. Charles Murray, *Losing Ground: American Social Policy 1950–1980*, 2nd ed. (New York: Basic Books, 1994).

31. See, for example, David Weisburd, Anthony Petrosino, and Cynthia M. Lum, Eds., *Assessing Systematic Evidence in Crime and Justice: Methodological Concerns and Empirical Outcomes* (Thousand Oaks, CA: Sage, 2003); Jane E. Davidson, *Evaluation Methodology Basics: The Nuts and Bolts of Sound Evaluation* (Thousand Oaks, CA: Sage, 2005); Robert L. Schalock, *Outcome-Based Evaluation* (New York: Plenum, 2001); Huey-tsyh Chen, *Practical Program Evaluation: Assessing and Improving Planning, Implementation, and Effectiveness* (Thousand Oaks, CA: Sage, 2005); Yvonne Unrau, Peter Gabor, and Richard Grinnell, Jr., "Program Evaluation," in Richard M. Grinnell, Jr., and Yvonne A. Unrau, Eds., *Social Work Research and Evaluation: Quantitative and Qualitative Approaches*, 7th ed. (New York: Oxford University Press, 2005), pp. 453–468; older but still of value is Carol H. Weiss, *Evaluation Research: Methods for Assessing Program Effectiveness* (Englewood Cliffs, NJ: Prentice-Hall, 1972).

32. Westinghouse Learning Corporation and Ohio University, *The Impact of Head Start: An Evaluation of the Effects of Head Start on Children's Cognitive and Affective Development* (Washington, DC: Office of Economic Opportunity, 1969).

33. Mathmatica Policy Research, Inc., *Overview of the Early Head Start Research and Evaluation Project* (Princeton, NJ: Author, 2005), online at www.mathmatica-mpr.com/earlycare/ehsover.asp, p. 4.

34. John Love, Ellen Kisker, Christine Ross, and Peter Schochet, *Making a Difference in the Lives of Infants and Toddlers and Their Families: The Impacts of Early Head Start* (Washington, DC: Department of Health and Human Services, 2005), online at www.acf.dhhs.gov/programs/core/ongoing_research/ehs/ehs_intro. html, p. 6.

35. Pal, *Public Policy Analysis: An Introduction*, p. 36.

36. Catholic Church, National Conference of Catholic Bishops, *Economic Justice for All: Pastoral Letter on Catholic Social Teaching and the U.S. Economy* (Washington, DC: Office of Publishing and Promotion Service, United States Catholic Conference, 1986), p. 3.

37. Charles E. Lindblom, *The Policy-Making Process*, 2nd ed. (Englewood Cliffs, NJ: Prentice-Hall, 1980), pp. 19–25.

38. Wildavsky, *Speaking Truth to Power*, pp. 3, 16.

39. Murray, *Losing Ground*, pp. 154–166.

40. Lindblom, *The Policy-Making Process*, 2nd ed., pp. 33–34.

Policy Analysis from a Historical Perspective

In Chapters 3, 5, and 6, we describe a number of things that are useful to know about particular social welfare policies, including their political implications, their economic contexts, and their social consequences. Historical analysis of policies includes all these elements and more, as they existed in the past. Such analysis helps us understand how and why a particular policy or social welfare program developed. Policy history addresses such questions as: Why did the federal government (or the state government, or the Greenacres Children's Treatment Center) pick that particular problem to address, and why did it proceed to deal with it the way it did?

This chapter discusses the historical analysis of policies. We describe the role and usefulness of a historical approach in understanding and dealing with the policies you will encounter on the job. We give examples of policy history, briefly discuss how such histories are developed, and talk about common errors that can lead to misinterpretation of historical evidence. Such errors are particularly troublesome in policy histories because these studies are often used to support or to criticize existing programs and approaches. When done well, however, historical studies are an indispensable tool for policy analysis.

Historical Context of Social Welfare Policies

The junior staff of a small outpatient mental health center were concerned about a center policy regarding information gathered from clients. When an individual came to the center seeking help voluntarily or under the direction of a court or other agency, he or she went through a lengthy intake process. As part of this process, the social worker interviewing the client prepared an intake form that included personal items such as name, age, marital status, and employment; a short description of the client's perception of his or her current difficulties; a psychiatric diagnosis; and details on any past psychiatric hospitalization. Because the center received the bulk of its funding through the state, a copy of the form was sent to the state Department of Mental Health. The state department used these records in research on such factors as the numbers of persons with a particular diagnosis served in a given year.

The staff members' concern stemmed from the fact that although clients were not identified by name, their Social Security numbers were to be provided at the top of the form. Fresh out of graduate training that stressed client rights and the importance of maintaining confidentiality, several social workers worried that client names and details of their emotional difficulties could be linked through use of their Social Security numbers. What was to prevent this information from being shared with other departments in the state bureaucracy? The fact that the State Department of Motor Vehicles had a policy of denying drivers' licenses to people who had been hospitalized for psychiatric problems was especially worrisome. What if, the staff members speculated, the Department of Motor Vehicles could gain access to the mental health department records and use them when clients applied for drivers' license renewals? One social worker who had served in the U.S. Army likened this to the past use of military discharge codes to discriminate against job applicants.

These new employees had been taught that evaluating the effects of agency policies on clients was a legitimate part of their job and that changing policies was sometimes necessary. They reasoned that in order to try to change the intake form policy, they would have to discover its origin. At first they assumed that the state Department of Mental Health mandated the use of Social Security numbers. This, in fact, is what they were told by several mental health aides and one of the clinic's secretaries. ("Oh, that's a state policy" is a common response when one is looking into an unpopular or cumbersome regulation.) Yet when they examined the state mental health handbook, they could not find the policy. They consulted a reference librarian at the local university; he was unable to find any such rule in the published regulations related to state legislation on mental health. The social work supervisor at the mental health center, who had worked there for four years, couldn't supply an answer.

Finally, they approached the senior psychologist, who had been with the clinic since its founding twelve years earlier. "Oh, that rule," he said, "actually, as far as the state's concerned, the information on Social Security numbers is optional. But you know how our director is—Dr. Molson is really a very traditional psychiatrist who believes in detailed record keeping and crossing all the t's. I don't think it would occur to him to worry about protecting clients from possible information leaks within the bureaucracy. He's pretty strong-minded, you know—you don't want to suggest changes to him unless it's really serious."

Having discovered the source of the policy, the new staff worked hard to convince the senior psychologist that the practice was unnecessary and potentially harmful to clients. They elicited his help in initiating a discussion of the use of Social Security numbers at the next staff meeting. With the legitimacy that the psychologist lent to their issue, they were able to convince the clinic director that client identities were not really necessary for mental health research and that leaks of information could jeopardize the trust that the clinic attempted to develop with its clients. As a result of this intervention, the space for Social Security numbers was deleted from the intake form.

This incident illustrates the use of historical analysis in understanding and changing a policy. In this case, the staff discovered where the policy came from, who initially promoted it, and why. They used this information in their successful effort to eliminate the policy. Without such information, the staff might have wasted time advocating for change with the wrong people and might have lost credibility by showing ignorance of the policy's origin.

The Role of History in Understanding Policy

All too often, history is treated as a "frill," or as an obligatory but not particularly enlightening preface to the "real analysis" of a social policy, problem, or program. Social work students, for example, may be given a short description of the goals and activities of reformer Dorothea Dix and a review of the community mental health movement of the 1960s before being exposed to a more thorough analysis of current policies and approaches in the field of mental health. This brief introduction often does little to demonstrate the evolution of policies over time, the similarities and differences between policies of different periods, the criticisms levied against particular approaches, the strategies used by policymakers in the past, their underlying assumptions about causes of social problems, and the impact of social, political, and economic factors on the policies they promoted and the programs they designed. Yet knowledge of all these factors is relevant to understanding, evaluating, and even changing current policies.

In the case of today's mental health programs, for example, it is important to understand that the debate over institutionalization versus community treatment of those with mental illness is a long-standing one. Historical analysis increases awareness of the pros and cons of each treatment approach as it has been tried out in the past. In addition, study of Dorothea Dix's techniques in promoting change can inform current attempts to "sell" new approaches. Dix published dramatic accounts of the conditions in which many insane people lived and spoke personally with as many state legislators as she could. More generally, knowledge of the role of underlying assumptions and the impact of societal factors on past social welfare developments, such as those in mental health, increases our awareness of these factors in current policy making.[1]

In addition, an understanding of the outcome of previous policies helps us evaluate present proposals and claims for success. For example, many people regard the changes in public welfare instituted in the mid-1990s as an abrupt shift in the way we deal with families with dependent children, not realizing that the new program follows a long history of welfare-to-work initiatives, which have met with only limited success. Marketing the program as the way "to end welfare as we know it" may raise false expectations.

These points apply to policies at all levels, from federal laws to organizational decisions. Not understanding the history of an agency policy could lead a worker to make serious mistakes. A new staff member at a family counseling agency, for instance, might unwittingly walk into an ongoing debate about methods of treatment, a debate that has degenerated from professional disagreements into personal feuds. If he questions the policy developed to deal with that debate—assignment of clients to particular counselors by the director rather than by group decision—he may be surprised by the strong negative reaction of other staff. His actions will probably be seen as the naive response of "someone who doesn't know the agency very well."

History, then, helps us understand and deal with current policies. It gives us some sense of how and why particular programs and approaches developed and how well they achieved what they set out to do. Of course, what they "set out to do" is a matter of interpretation. As we will see in Chapter 5, the *manifest* (openly acknowledged) goals of a program are often different from the *latent* (indirect) functions of that same program. For example, the manifest function of a particular drop-in day activities center for those with mental illness was to provide socialization in a therapeutic setting. However, the latent function of such a center was to keep "crazy" people from wandering in the downtown shopping mall. Because historical analysis includes the examination of a policy or program's goals and effects, such analysis is an important tool in recognizing and evaluating both latent and manifest functions.

Despite these arguments in support of the contribution history makes to policy analysis, some researchers criticize the historical approach as lacking the "scientific precision" of other methods.[2] These critics are often quantitative methodologists who stress careful construction of hypotheses and the use of statistical data. What they fail to recognize is that much historical research relies on elements familiar to social scientists: the development of hypotheses or guiding questions, systematic gathering and analysis of evidence to understand the relationships between factors being studied, and the discovery of patterns or the creation of principles to explain these relationships.[3] Although historical study can make use of statistical data, it draws also on a rich variety of other sources: interviews, memoirs, government documents, minutes of meetings in which policies are debated, and so forth. Overall, as Michael Reisch has persuasively argued, the study of history helps one develop "essential skills of analysis and critical judgement"— elements central to any research endeavor.[4]

Examples of Policy History

What does policy history actually look like? The following examples include both national and regional social welfare policies and policies developed within social work agencies. Each example includes discussion of the questions asked by the researcher, the sources used, and the conclusions drawn.

Colonial Poor Relief

The problem of dealing with the continued existence of poverty in the United States dominates much current social policy debate. What is the best way to help individuals off the welfare rolls, what is the most effective way to provide for those who remain on welfare, and how can we structure our economy to provide employment opportunities for all are questions that policy analysts struggle with almost every day. Geoffrey Guest's study of colonial poor relief documents suggests that these same questions have been asked for several hundred years. As Guest notes, boarding paupers in private homes was the principle method of poor relief in colonial America. Local governments paid families to house dependent individuals such as widows and the destitute aged. Despite the prevalence of this approach, Guest could find no detailed historical accounts of how the system worked in practice.[5] Most of the surviving county, town, and parish records gave only the names of the householders who kept the poor and the amounts paid to them. Guest argues that lack of detailed evidence to the contrary has allowed historians to assume that people's willingness to take dependent individuals into their own homes was a sign of widespread generosity to the poor during the colonial period. Historians have posited that a decline in this humanitarian spirit helped lead to a shift in policy during the mid-1800s, in which the boarding system was phased out "in favor of committing the destitute to poorhouses."[6]

The discovery of a remarkable collection of court records from Somerset County, Maryland, for the period 1725–1759 enabled Guest to examine the boarding-out program more carefully and to come to conclusions that conflict with earlier interpretations of the motives behind colonial poor relief. The new data consisted of the "actual petitions for poor relief by householders who were keeping the poor and by individuals seeking relief for themselves or their dependents."[7] Using these petitions, Guest could ask: How did the boarding-out policy actually work? Why did private householders agree to care for the poor? Did the demise of this system and the development of institutions for the poor signify a decline in the charitable impulse?

Guest found that most householders (usually wealthy planters) who took in paupers did so reluctantly. Many of the boarders were incapacitated and needed constant care. Once individuals had kept a pauper, they almost never volunteered to take in another. Officials rarely considered the wishes of the poor in making placements. To maintain the cooperation of householders, the court paid much more to those who boarded paupers than it did to those recipients of relief who were allowed to remain in their own homes. In other words, care of the dependent poor in Somerset County during the colonial period was not the sympathetic and generous response envisioned by most historians. The large payments made to householders keeping paupers were more indicative of the influence of the householders than of attention to the needs and wants of the poor. Guest concludes that colonial communities used the boarding-out approach primarily because the number of dependent individuals was small and because it was more cost effective to board them than to institutionalize them. The later use of poorhouses did not signify a change in attitude so much as a reaction to the higher costs of boarding an increasing number of poor people.

What Guest has presented is a careful study of the reasons behind the choice of a boarding system that kept poor people in a family setting as opposed to the use of institutions such as poorhouses. Much of social welfare history documents the shift back and forth between community-based and institutional responses to dependency. Case histories such as this one examine the implementation and effects of these responses in the past. They also give us important insights into the motives behind such policy choices. Guest's conclusion that economic considerations played a larger role than humanitarian impulses in the maintenance of a boarding system for the poor is food for thought when we analyze current social welfare programs.

The Use of Orphan Asylums

Guest examined a policy related to a public welfare measure operating in the community. Other researchers have explored the history of various institutional responses to social problems. Eve Smith, for example, analyzed the use of orphan asylums from the later part of the nineteenth century through the 1930s.[8] She was drawn to this topic in part because problems in the present foster care system have caused some social workers, and even some politicians, to suggest a return to institutions for the care of dependent and neglected children. In what ways, Smith asked, did institutions such as orphanages function in the past? How well did they work? Are they appropriate models for today's needs?

To answer these questions, Smith used annual reports of orphanages from the time along with magazine articles, government reports, and social welfare conference speeches describing the treatment of children in institutions. In addition, like Guest, she turned to a less-used source of data: the actual case records of children from two different orphan asylums. These records included not only the comments of orphanage workers about children and their families but also letters back and forth between parents, children, and staff. Such sources provide an intriguing insight into daily life in the orphan asylum and the purposes that these asylums served.

You may have noted with surprise the references to parents and families in the preceding paragraph. Smith found, as have other researchers, that orphanages dealt more often with children who had parents than with actual orphans. "From the beginning," she explains, "most institutionalized children were 'half-orphaned' children of single or deserted parents and most would eventually return to their families."[9] Smith's contribution to our understanding of the functions of orphanages is her stress on the way single parents were served by such institutions and on the way they themselves used the orphanages to cope with the problems of single parenthood. As the case records show, many parents, usually single mothers, voluntarily placed their children in institutions when they could no longer afford to care for them on their own. Often they contributed a small sum of money

box
4.1
Cooperation between Parents and "Orphanages"

Beginning in the mid-1920s . . . the [New York] Society for the Relief of Destitute Children of Seamen offered supplementary pensions to a number of parents in order to keep families together. While some parents accepted the assistance and the social work supervision that went with the money, others did not.

An example of a deserted mother who refused the agency's offer, saying she "preferred work to charity," was Mrs. E. When her husband left, she asked for care for her three children, went to work as a domestic (caring for her employer's child), and paid the Society approximately half of her wages. Thereupon began an eight-year partnership—agency and parent—in raising the children.

Mrs. E. bought the children's clothes, and visited regularly. She took them to the doctor and dentist when she could get time away from her job, and had much to say about the course of their lives. The society supervised the children and their schooling (they were "A" students), eventually placing them in foster homes found by Mrs. E.; arranged for medical and dental services; and supplemented Mrs. E.'s financial contribution. They discontinued assistance in 1933, when Mrs. E.'s salary had increased and the Society was pressed for funds.

Source: Eve Smith, "The Care of Children of Single Parents: The Use of 'Orphan Asylums' through the 1930's," presented at the Annual Program Meeting of the Council on Social Work Education, March 1990.

toward the children's support. Generally, they maintained contact with their children and orphanage staff and were involved in decisions about their children's upbringing. If family finances improved, sometimes due to the return of a deserting father, the children left the institution to rejoin the family. (See Box 4.1.) The orphanage thus served as an important resource for poor single parents and as a way for society to deal with children in poverty.

Smith's study suggests several important conclusions. First, she argues there is little evidence that past children's institutions would be appropriate programs for today's foster children. The orphanages served a population of dependent children with parents who generally remained involved in their care and who, by paying part of the bill and advocating for their children, were able to retain some power over their youngsters' lives. Most children in orphanages were "normal"; their institutionalization was due largely to poverty. Today's foster children, Smith maintains, "are much less likely to have a parent or parents who can or will ever assume their care."[10] In addition, they appear to have higher levels of emotional and physical problems. The two groups of children thus have different needs that will not be served by the same types of programs.

Smith's study also reminds us that the people served by social welfare programs should not be viewed simply as passive recipients of care. Her documentation of parents' use of the orphanage system as a way to provide for their children when their own resources had failed is evidence of the way in which clients can influence the shape of social policies and programs.

Smith's emphasis on clients—their problems and strengths—represents a relatively new kind of history, sometimes called "history from the bottom up." In chronicling social welfare developments, this approach focuses not on presidents, lawmakers, and heads of national organizations, but rather on more anonymous policymakers and on the "recipients" of social welfare programs. It looks at "ordinary people," working class and poor; immigrants, minorities, and women; members of self-help groups; and laypeople involved in creating policies. It uses sources such as social work agency case histories, the records of mutual aid associations, and the minutes of local chapters of national reform organizations. This type of history is particularly fruitful for social workers due to its emphasis on the stresses and strengths of ordinary individuals and on how social movements and institutions affect them and are affected by them. Some further examples of the approach are Anne Firor Scott's study of women's associations and their gradual shift from self-help to social reform activities, and Susan L. Smith's *Sick and Tired of Being Sick and Tired*, a record of the health activism of African American midwives, nurses, and women's club members.[11]

Policies for Those with Handicaps

Smith and Guest are both social workers with research competence in social welfare policy history. Historians have also become interested in the examination of social policy, and in fact policy history or "public history" is a newly emerging area of the discipline. Its practitioners seek "to sort out the relationships among policymakers' intentions, the evolution of governmental policy, and the short-range and long-term impact of specific measures."[12] Edward D. Berkowitz presents a good example of public history in his work on the development of state and national policies to deal with disability.[13] Berkowitz, like other public historians, uses his historical analysis to understand current policy problems and to make recommendations for reform.

In his exploration of disability policy in the United States, Berkowitz asks two major questions: (1) How does U.S. public policy respond to the situation of physical disability, and (2) How have these responses developed? The study is based on the hypothesis that the United States has no single disability policy, but rather a set of disparate programs working at cross-purposes.[14] In order to understand the nature of these programs, Berkowitz relied primarily on the records of the U.S. Social Security Administration and of state offices for the handicapped as well as on interviews with past and present policymakers.

Berkowitz studied five major disability programs in the United States, including workers' compensation, national disability insurance, and the state-run vocational rehabilitation system. He found that each program had developed problems, sometimes unanticipated by the policymakers, sometimes emerging despite policymakers' attempts to avoid them. In proposing disability insurance, for example, the Social Security Administration had intended to establish a uniform national program administered by the federal government. Determination of applicants' eligibility was to be carried out by federal examining teams, thus avoiding the inconsistencies created by multiple disability boards and the overinvolvement of lawyers in the system. However, private insurance companies, physicians, and state governments lobbied against the plan. The American Medical Association, for example, feared federal disability insurance as an entering wedge for the creation of national health insurance. Political opposition led to a compromise program, Social Security Disability Insurance, in which states play an administrative role. Although the federal government establishes a basic definition of permanent disability, states have the authority to determine who fits the definition and is eligible for benefits. The strictness of the federal definition and the complexity of state eligibility systems have led to increased use of the courts to contest unfavorable rulings. Despite the original intentions of its creators, disability insurance has become a complicated and inconsistent program that frequently relies on attorneys and the courts.[15]

In reviewing the other disability programs, Berkowitz found similar problems within programs and a lack of coordination between them. The history of disability policy suggests that these problems have arisen because of the lack of a broad political following for disability programs; differences of philosophy between policymakers; conflicting political pressures from state governments, doctors, and other groups; and the difficulties in defining disability.

Berkowitz argues that the system needs reform and that historians can help in that reform. History is important, he argues, because it brings order to a complicated and confusing picture. Historical analysis shows the development of each disability program and the interactions between programs over time. Based on this overview, Berkowitz makes a variety of recommendations to policymakers. He notes, for example, the ongoing failure of disability policy to blend income maintenance and rehabilitation approaches. As a partial remedy, he suggests that the disability insurance program distinguish between individuals, often older, who should be helped to retire on a disability pension, and workers who are capable of returning to the workforce and would like to do so. Disability insurance, he suggests, could provide "independence initiatives" to the latter group in the form of vouchers for attendant care, modification of transportation and architectural barriers, and so forth. Using his historical training to develop a broad view of disability policy, Berkowitz thus makes an important contribution to the review and potential reform of current approaches.[16]

Historical Analysis of Agency Policy

Unlike the previous examples, the history of agency policy is often informal and unwritten. Yet awareness of an agency's development is an important tool for understanding current agency programs and policy. This awareness can help workers and administrators appreciate agency strengths and analyze and deal with agency shortcomings. In addition, social workers often find themselves in situations like the one described in our opening vignette on the mental health center, in which a current practice or regulation appears unusual and/or ineffective. Knowing something about the development of the policy and the key actors in that development can be an essential ingredient in getting it changed.

Methods of Policy History

How is policy history carried out? The preceding examples give some sense of the process of historical analysis. In this section, we provide more specific guidelines for carrying out that process.

One of the most important tasks in historical analysis is the formulation of hypotheses or guiding questions related to the issue or program to be studied. Historians differ somewhat on how structured this formulation should be. Those with a social science orientation tend to stress the development of formal hypotheses regarding what the historical data will reveal. Those with a humanities orientation find it more appropriate to draw up a number of questions, adding perhaps some hunches, to bring to the study of the evidence. In either case, the researcher needs to have a guiding framework for approaching a mass of detail. Without this framework, the study might be no more than a descriptive exercise, with little sense of pattern or meaning. The researcher would not know exactly what to look for in the data or how to organize the final document. As Jacques Barzun notes, the historian is like a traveler, who pieces together "the 'scenery' of the past from fragments that lie scattered in many places." To do this, the researcher soon develops "a guiding idea to propel [him or her] along the route, a hypothesis ahead of the facts, which steadily reminds [the traveler] of what to look for."[17]

In a study of the development of sexual harassment policies in social work agencies, for example, the researchers approached the data (interviews with agency administrators and staff as well as agency policy documents) with the following questions in mind: (1) How did the policies on sexual harassment in these agencies come about? (2) Why were these policies developed at the time they were? Were they the result of lobbying on the part of female administrators and staff? and (3) What is the past and present nature of these policies? Not only did these questions provide guidance for conducting the study—for example, helping the researchers decide what to ask in their interviews—but they also aided in the structuring and recommendations of the final report.[18] Another way to approach this study would have been to develop a specific hypothesis, such as "Sexual harassment policies are most likely to develop in agencies with women administrators at the top level," and to examine the histories of a number of agencies to see if that hypothesis made sense.

The next step in developing the history of a social welfare policy, practice, or organization is to gather evidence related to the major questions or hypotheses. Historians emphasize the use of primary data, that is, records made at the time an event occurs and by participants or direct observers of the event, rather than secondary sources that are reconstructions of an event by a person without firsthand knowledge of it. A letter from Jane Addams to a colleague regarding strategy for passing child labor legislation is a primary source; a chapter in a textbook on labor law describing Addams's involvement would be a secondary source. Primary sources include letters, diaries, oral histories (a special kind of interview described in Appendix B), board and committee minutes, testimony at congressional hearings, administrative records, newspaper articles about an event written at the time the event was taking place, and similar sources of direct data regarding events.

The best history relies on a variety of kinds of data. Secondary sources summarize and synthesize the historical material, giving you a good place to start. These sources, however, reflect the biases of the writer, both in terms of the selection of material to present and in its interpretation. Such biases are not always made clear to the reader. Although primary sources can also include bias (for example, firsthand reporters of political rallies are real people with their own ideological perspectives), by examining a number of different primary sources you can strive to develop a balanced picture of what actually occurred. The description of the development of a policy on confidentiality in the agency where you work would be incomplete, for example, if it relied only on the minutes of the committee drawing up the policy. You might also want to consult the written requirements on confidentiality put out by the state organization that funds the agency and to interview agency staff members and administrators who were present when the policy was constructed and implemented.

Sources of primary and secondary data for historical policy analysis and means of locating these sources are described in the appendixes on historical policy analysis and library research. This material should be useful as you pursue the story of how a policy or program developed over time.

As historical evidence is gathered, it must be evaluated and interpreted. The end product, or conclusions, will relate to the guiding questions or hypotheses with which you began your quest. A number of questions can be asked about the evidence, including:

- Is it authentic? (Was the policy written when it was dated, or was it inserted later in the agency files when the agency was involved in a legal case? Do the pages of the social worker's diary include material added by the diarist years later?)
- What was the condition of the witness of the event? (Was this person actually present when the committee debated the matter? Did the individual have strong prejudices regarding the issue? How long after the event did the witness make his or her report?)
- What was the intent of the document in question? (Was it simply to report or to persuade? Was it for an internal or an external audience?)

The use of multiple sources of evidence helps in weeding out inaccuracies and inconsistencies and in recognizing biases. In addition, all historical sources should be read with an understanding of the time and context in which they were written. One should be careful not to evaluate material from the past from a present-oriented point of view. For example, flowery, openly affectionate language between women was common in the late 1800s; Jane Addams's correspondence with women friends and colleagues should therefore be read with that understanding in mind. Similarly, social workers writing about African Americans in the 1920s rarely questioned the injustices of segregated social agencies. Although this appears overtly racist today, these writers reflected the very limited consciousness of racial injustices characteristic of many whites at the time.[19]

The final stage of the analysis is deciding what the evidence has to say in relation to the hypotheses or questions of the study. In history, as in any other research topic, interpretation of the data must be careful and systematic. As Barzun and Graff explain, the historian uses the evidence with "informed common sense" to demonstrate the probability that a certain event occurred for particular reasons and with particular results.[20]

A number of common errors can lead to misinterpretation of historical evidence. One is cross-cultural error, or the lack of understanding of values and customs of another culture. White social welfare historians, for example, have tended until recently to ignore the importance of self-help groups in the African American community as a form of social welfare organization. Similarly, one can make the mistake of assuming that the ideas and lifestyle of a particular group represent all of society. Those who have studied the domestic lives of middle- and upper-class women in the Victorian era have sometimes falsely concluded that it was typical for women of this period to stay at home providing a nurturing environment for husbands and children. In that same period, however, many poor and working-class women were employed outside the home, took in boarders, or did paid work in the home to help support their families. "Presentism" is yet another error in interpretation. This occurs when we read characteristics of our own time into the past. Historians have sometimes had difficulty, for example, in under-standing that the suffragists, while they promoted women's rights, had a different understanding of women's rights and roles in society from that of today's feminists.

Other types of misinterpretation can be demonstrated by looking at two important books on social welfare, Charles Murray's *Losing Ground* and Frances Fox Piven and Richard Cloward's *Regulating the Poor.* These works are not strictly histories; they might best be called sociological studies of past policies and events. They constitute policy analyses that use historical methods to attempt to make sense of current social issues. It is therefore useful to analyze them based on some of the same criteria one would use in assessing the accuracy and usefulness of a historical study.

As we discussed in Chapter 3, Murray's book was published during the Reagan era and gained immediate popularity among conservatives as a justification for reductions in government social programs. Murray is a former journalist and political scientist now associated with the Manhattan Institute, an organization that raises corporate money to support the work of conservative authors. His study focuses on this question: Why, after twelve years of greatly increasing expendi-tures on government social welfare programs, was the percentage of Americans in poverty in 1980 (13 percent) the same as it had been in 1968? Murray seeks to answer this question through a wealth of statistics, discussion of policy experi-ments, and reconstructions of the possible motives behind the actions of the poor. He concludes that government social programs did worse than fail to alleviate poverty; they were in fact responsible for creating poverty in the United States in the 1960s and 1970s.[21]

Murray argues that according to a variety of indicators, including the rate of poverty, poor people were becoming worse off in the late 1960s, just as the War on Poverty social programs were beginning to take effect. He describes the growth in federal spending on social welfare, the development of new programs such as job training and community action projects, and the loosening of regulations regarding who could receive benefits. He then details increases in crime, unem-ployment, divorce, and the number of households headed by single women, as well as the end to a previous decline in the poverty rate. He attributes these disturbing phenomena to increased spending, changes in programs, and ultimately to the fact that the "new rules" of welfare made it "profitable for the poor to behave in the short term in ways that were destructive in the long term." Using a fictitious low-income couple named Harold and Phyllis, who were unmarried and expecting a child, Murray describes a scenario in which the only reasonable choice for such individuals was to live together on what was then AFDC rather than seek employment and financial independence.[22]

At first reading, Murray's analysis seems convincing, especially to those who suspect a connection between welfare and dependency. Yet as numerous scholars have pointed out, he makes a number of errors in presenting and interpreting his data. The first of these is what Barzun and Graff call "generalizing beyond the facts." In other words, the writer produces a broad generalization based on limited facts and fails to test the generalization with negative examples. This occurs, for example, when Murray argues that welfare programs encourage marital breakup and the rise in female single-parent households. To make this generalization, he relies on the results of a social policy experiment: the implementation of a negative income tax program in several U.S. localities during the late 1960s and 1970s (the SIME/DIME experiments discussed in Chapter 3). Using a financial supplement, the program brought the income of selected groups of low-income individuals up to the poverty line for a three-year period; control groups received no supplement. In some areas, the divorce rate of the experimental group was much higher than that of the control group. From this finding, Murray generalizes that "welfare undermines the family." He thus equates the negative income tax with all welfare programs. He does not look for other examples (e.g., the rate of marriage dissolution among AFDC recipients in similar or other time periods) against which to test his findings. In fact, the bulk of research examining the relationship between welfare benefits and marital breakup has been inconclusive, with some studies showing no relation between the two and others reporting only a small impact of AFDC benefits on divorce. Interestingly, some studies show that women's participation in the labor force *also* increases marital dissolution.[23]

Murray comes to other misinterpretations through errors in his analysis of the data. Much of his argument regarding the negative results of War on Poverty programs rests on the observation that government welfare spending increased dramatically during the late 1960s and the 1970s. Yet the bulk of these expenditures was in programs for the elderly. Help to the nonelderly poor through means-tested programs showed only modest growth, much of which was in benefits to the disabled. Expenditures for AFDC expanded little in the 1970s; between 1972 and 1980, real benefit levels for AFDC recipients fell by about 30 percent. Thus Murray's linkage between rise in government expenditures for the nonelderly, nondisabled poor and the increase in poverty for this group makes little sense.[24]

Finally, Murray falls into the trap described by Barzun and Graff as reducing all the diversity of history to "one thing," such as characterizing the French Revolution as resulting solely from a conspiracy. "A true researcher," they observe, "shows the parts that make up the complexity." Yet Murray too often fails to examine this complexity or to explore the context within which trends like a rise in poverty or in marital dissolution rates occur. As historian Michael Katz notes, Murray tells us the story of federal social policy in a "contextual vacuum." He ignores factors such as changing occupational structures, rising unemployment, and transformations in U.S. cities during the 1960s and 1970s. To illustrate, if we look again at Murray's use of the negative income tax experiment, we note that he is content to present the evidence that divorces increased among some of the experimental groups. He does not question why this happened or what it was about the particular policy that encouraged or made divorce possible. Did increased financial resources, for example, allow women to escape from stressful marriages? Asking such questions might help us to understand more fully why divorces occur (rather than to pin them to the single cause of welfare policy) and perhaps even guide us in developing policies that would strengthen marriages.[25]

The idea of reducing a historical event to one thing is part of a discussion of the notion of causation and how it might be approached historically. Frances Fox Piven and Richard Cloward's study *Regulating the Poor* is similar to Murray's work in its attempt to trace the causes of a particular phenomenon, in this case increases in welfare benefits, over time. Although Piven and Cloward make comparisons of several historical periods rather than rely on data from only one or two decades and they provide more of the context of the situation they are studying, they nevertheless can be criticized for presenting an overly simplistic picture of the reasons behind government expansion in welfare programs.

Regulating the Poor was published in 1971; its authors had participated in welfare reform movements during the 1960s. Cloward was a sociologist and social worker; Piven is a political scientist and urban planner. As scholar–activists, the two combined social science theory and historical analysis in a study of the rise and fall of welfare rolls over time. The central thesis of the book is that public welfare exists primarily to control the poor. Piven and Cloward argue that "relief arrangements are initiated or expanded during the occasional outbreaks of civil disorder produced by mass unemployment, and are then abolished or contracted when political stability is restored. . . . Expansive relief policies are designed to mute civil disorder, and restrictive ones to reinforce work norms." In other words, public relief programs are based on the need to control dissension among the unemployed (by increasing welfare payments) and to regulate the labor market (by forcing people into low-income work when relief is cut back). This is a social control argument that attributes the development of social policies and programs to the desire of those in power to maintain order for their own advantage.[26]

To arrive at their conclusions, Piven and Cloward trace relief practices in Europe from their beginnings in the sixteenth century through the rise of capitalism. They then look at data on the relief rolls in the United States from 1930 through the 1960s. This approach is called historical trend analysis, or the examination of data over time in order to ascertain certain patterns. By comparing the patterns of welfare contraction and expansion to social and political events such as race riots and other unrest, Piven and Cloward conclude that changes in welfare policy were designed primarily by elites to regulate the poor.[27]

Piven and Cloward make a meaningful contribution to our thinking about social welfare policy by alerting us to the fact that the desire to keep low-income people from "causing trouble" can indeed influence the type and amount of welfare that society provides. This understanding prevents us from viewing the development of social policy simply as the story of an ongoing humanitarian march toward progress. Piven and Cloward also help us to appreciate the connections between the purposes of welfare, the political process, the occupational structure, and the market economy. Yet despite providing at least some of the context that Murray lacks, their analysis is problematic because in the end, it sees the social control motive as the primary factor in the shaping of public welfare.[28]

Their conclusion is troublesome on two counts: It stresses a mechanistic, single-factor explanation of a complex phenomenon and it encourages simple assumptions about cause and effect. A number of writers have criticized *Regulating the Poor* for reducing the growth and decline of public welfare to one element, social control, rather than seeing this factor as one among many. They have questioned whether the model developed can be accurately applied to other historical periods (similar to the argument that Murray neglected to find other examples against which to test his conclusions). If relief rolls do not exhibit the same pattern during the revolutionary period in American history, for example, this may cast doubts on Piven and Cloward's findings.[29]

In addition, Piven and Cloward's thesis raises questions about the search for causation in history. Have the two authors shown that the need for social control "causes" change in the welfare rolls? Here Piven and Cloward may have fallen into a dangerous trap, the prediction backwards from results to motives. True, policymakers and public officials may often seek to maintain order and the status quo. But we can't base our conviction that this is so solely on the outcomes of social programs. In addition, much can happen between the creation of a policy and its implementation. Budget committees, rules and regulations, and the actions and personalities of public welfare administration and staff intervene to affect the policy outcome. Given this complexity, the relationship between motives and results becomes unclear in either direction. Finally, we might ask whether it is reasonable to look to history for causes at all. Barzun and Graff have commented that what history shows about the past is not the "cause," but the conditions accompanying an event's emergence. Causation is really the picture of a long chain of events, rather than the notion of a single element, such as the motives of a group of policymakers.[30]

Clarke Chambers, a major social welfare historian, believes "the past is the most practical thing we can study."[31] This is a wise statement, yet not in the way that many think. Too often we expect history to provide us with neat formulas for avoiding past mistakes and with clear descriptions of what caused certain events. As our critique of Murray and of Piven and Cloward suggests, good history gives us context and a view of complex, interacting forces, rather than single-factor explanations of the past. What can we do with this history? We can analyze the failures and successes of past social programs for suggestions—but only suggestions—of what might work today. We can learn about the relationships between policy-makers' intentions, the evolution of policies, and the impact of those policies in the past to try to understand such relationships in the present. We can be alerted to the importance of social, political, and economic factors in policy and program development. Finally, we can try to fathom where we've been in order to understand where we are.

To give you a real-world sense of all this, we end this chapter with a policy history of a social agency in a middle-sized, Midwest community. This is the sort of history you might develop yourself as you begin to work at an agency. It is guided by the questions of how an organization developed its policies and programs and how that earlier development affects its operations today. The history is based on interviews with the agency's administration, staff, and board members; local newspaper articles about the organization over the past thirty years; and agency records, including a large scrapbook documenting staff training, retreats, and other activities.

The Benton Park Crisis Center

The Benton Park Crisis Center is located in a residential area of a Midwest city. It currently functions as a crisis and referral agency with a telephone hot line, out-reach mental health services, and educational programs for public school students on substance abuse and suicide prevention. It has a paid professional staff of six and a large body of volunteers. It is in some ways similar to, and in other ways quite different from, the center that was established more than thirty years ago.

The crisis center opened in the summer of 1970. At the time, the main city high school was located a block away. Because of overcrowding in the high school, the lack of after-school recreational facilities, and the general proclivities of teenagers, many young people hung around in the neighborhood before and after classroom hours. This was also a time of anxiety about drugs, rebellion, delinquency, and a "hippie element" among the young, and though many adult fears were exaggerated, real problems—bad trips, attempted suicides—did exist. Responding to the concerns of local residents and of businesspeople in the neighborhood, a handful of volunteers opened a recreational and drop-in center whose goal was to prevent drug abuse and provide alternative activities for teens. The initial group that backed the center included a juvenile court judge, a probation officer, and several local businesspeople and homeowners. The center was located in a building owned by the city and made available at a low rent; it had almost no funding other than some voluntary donations.

The drop-in center offered some rap and counseling groups and various recreational activities and was open to all on a twenty-four-hour basis. Perhaps not surprisingly, the facility was forced to close down almost immediately. The open-door policy and the small volunteer staff meant a lack of control; overnight "crashing," drinking in closets, and similar events were embarrassing signs that the center was perhaps encouraging rather than preventing problem behavior. However, the agency reopened shortly, this time with more structure and a federally funded worker from a program similar to today's Americorps to offer services and help coordinate the volunteers. Slowly, the center became a place to go and do particular things rather than a building in which to hang out.

Within the next two years, the center hired an executive director (paid, but on a minimal level), a substance abuse counselor with a professional degree, and a part-time workshop coordinator. Staff and programs were still funded by donations, and the reliance on community volunteers remained. Being close to the drug abuse problem and other crisis situations promoted a spirit of mutual dependence among volunteers, paid staff, and the young people who frequented the center. A sense of support was established that has lasted throughout the program's history.

Following the hiring of paid staff, the center received some state funding for substance abuse services through the local community mental health board. Staff had not vigorously sought this funding; rather, the mental health board, not too sure about what to do with these state funds, decided to give them to the one agency that had developed a reputation for working on the problem of drug abuse. Increases in funding helped encourage more structure in the organization. There was less reliance on volunteers and a larger program of counseling by professionals. A drug educator was hired to do preventive work in the schools. Still, an art workshop and other recreational programs remained, as well as a body of volunteers, although these now began to receive formalized training for their activities.

A major focus of volunteer activity was staffing a telephone hot line to answer crisis calls from the community. Initially, this had simply been a business phone for the center, but as the organization became recognized as "the place that knows about drugs and is willing to help," people facing drug problems themselves, or families and professionals involved at a secondary level, began to call the center for assistance. Gradually, the center again expanded its use of volunteers and developed the extensive system of volunteer screening and training that is one of its hallmarks today. The hot line developed into a twenty-four-hour crisis counseling and referral telephone service, handling not only drug-related problems but also the full range of human difficulties, from suicide calls to mental health problems to requests for information on welfare services and emergency housing. Calls now came from people of all ages.

By the mid-1970s, the recreational and art workshop programs were in decline, spurred by the relocation of the high school to the outskirts of the city. In response to occasional nighttime use of the center's building by individuals with mental illness looking for shelter, the staff reluctantly decided to lock the facility at night.

In the meantime, state funding increased, including some funding specifically for mental health services, and with the increase came more outside control over programming. Drug and mental health programs were emphasized by funding requirements; no special financial aid existed for activities such as the art workshop. In addition, state licensing had been developed for substance abuse services. Complying with the licensing brought new restrictions for the center, such as regulations about the sorts of staff needed and detailed rules about the format and content of notes on client contacts. New and innovative programs were harder to launch. Still, volunteers continued to work on the phone line, and an informality and sense of mutual support among staff remained.

Mental health funding led to the hiring of professionally trained "mental health screeners" who could respond to psychiatric emergencies. The fact that their outreach assessment work sometimes led to commitments of individuals to mental hospitals brought a value dilemma to the agency. Was the center, which prided itself on allegiance to the client and to the principle of self-determination, about to become identified with "the system" and with social control? Gradually, however, as emergency calls increased and taxed the skills and energies of volunteers, mental health screeners came to be seen as important backups for the work of the center. The fact that screeners tended to be individuals who were former volunteers with additional training helped in making this transition.

In the past ten years of its history, the Benton Park Crisis Center has added more staff, received additional funding from the local United Way, and shifted program priorities from substance abuse to mental illness, in part due to a change in the types of clientele seeking help. The consolidation of the county substance abuse and mental health planning agencies under a single human services umbrella has actually made adaptation of programs to client needs somewhat easier, as funds now come from a common source. For some time, the center had been part of an alcohol and substance abuse council; it recently became incorporated under a separate board of directors. This new autonomy helped formalize the move from a drug abuse services mission to a goal of dealing with a broad range of crisis problems in the community. There has been a resurgence of innovative activity in the organization. The phone line remains a strong asset, still staffed primarily by volunteers, including interns from a nearby university's undergraduate social work program. The visitor to the center today is impressed not only by the array of professional services but also by the cheerful camaraderie of the "phone room" and the comfortable informality of staff offices.

The crisis center thus combines innovation and standardization; volunteer and professional help; casualness and regulations concerning paperwork, staff screening, and the like. As a new worker, you might find these combinations confusing. In order to make sense of this milieu, you might seek out the sort of historical information we have presented. The history of the Benton Park Crisis Center would help you see how a variety of elements—the needs of the community and the clientele, the requirements of funding and licensing agencies, the social and economic conditions of the surrounding community, and the traditions embraced by the staff—have all shaped the direction and spirit of the agency.

Conclusion

To some, history may seem like a dry collection of facts and figures from the past. We hope, however, that you will see its importance in your work with individuals, groups, organizations, and communities. The history of an individual, family, or neighborhood will enable you to put current situations and issues into perspective. In addition, as in our example of the Benton Park Crisis Center, knowing what has happened in the past will help you respond in a knowledgeable way to current issues and increase your ability to carry out organizational change.

Notes

1. David Gollaher, *Voice for the Mad: The Life of Dorothea Dix* (New York: Free Press, 1995).

2. See the following for descriptions of a traditional "scientific" approach to social work research: Walter W. Hudson, "Scientific Imperatives in Social Work Research and Practice," *Social Service Review* 56 (June 1982), pp. 246–258; William Gordon, "The Professional Base of Social Work Research: Some Essential Elements," *Social Work Journal* 33 (1952), pp. 17–22; and William Reid, "Developments in the Use of Organized Data," *Social Work* 19 (September 1974), pp. 585–593. These ideas have more recently been challenged. See Martha Brunswick Heineman, "The Obsolete Scientific Imperative in Social Work Research," *Social Service Review* 55 (September 1981), pp. 371–397; Howard Jacob Karger, "Science, Research, and Social Work: Who Controls the Profession?" *Social Work* 28 (May/June 1983), pp. 200–205; and Karen B. Tyson, "A New Approach to Relevant Scientific Research for Practitioners: The Heuristic Paradigm," *Social Work* 37 (November 1992), pp. 541–556.

3. Jacques Barzun and Henry F. Graff, *The Modern Researcher,* 4th ed. (San Diego: Harcourt Brace Jovanovich, 1985), pp. 193–205; Robert Jones Shafer, *A Guide to Historical Method,* 3rd ed. (Homewood, IL: Dorsey Press, 1980), p. 34.

4. Michael Reisch, "The Uses of History in Teaching Social Work," *Journal of Teaching in Social Work* 2 (1988), p. 3.

5. Geoffrey Guest, "The Boarding of the Dependent Poor in Colonial America," *Social Service Review* 63 (March 1989), p. 95.

6. Guest, "The Boarding of the Dependent Poor in Colonial America," p. 93.

7. Guest, "The Boarding of the Dependent Poor in Colonial America," p. 95.

8. Eve P. Smith, "The Care of Children of Single Parents: The Use of 'Orphan Asylums' through the 1930's," presented at the Annual Program Meeting of the Council on Social Work Education, March 1990; see also Eve P. Smith, "Bring Back the Orphanages? What Policymakers of Today Can Learn from the Past," *Child Welfare* 74 (January/February 1995), pp. 115–142.

9. Smith, "The Care of Children of Single Parents," p. 1; Matthew A. Crenson, *Building the Invisible Orphanage: A Prehistory of the American Welfare System* (Cambridge, MA: Harvard University Press, 1998), pp. 17, 73–75, 78.

10. Smith, "The Care of Children of Single Parents," p. 1.

11. Clarke A. Chambers, "Toward a Redefinition of Welfare History," *Journal of American History* 73 (September 1986), pp. 407–433; Anne Firor Scott, *Natural Allies: Women's Associations in American History* (Urbana: University of Illinois Press, 1993); Susan L. Smith, *Sick and Tired of Being Sick and Tired: Black Women's Health Activism in America, 1890–1950* (Philadelphia: University of Pennsylvania Press, 1995).

12. W. Andrew Achenbaum, "The Making of an Applied Historian: Stage Two," *The Public Historian* 5 (Spring 1983), pp. 21–23.

13. Edward D. Berkowitz, *Disabled Policy: America's Programs for the Handicapped* (Cambridge, England: Cambridge University Press, 1987).

14. Berkowitz, *Disabled Policy: America's Programs for the Handicapped*, p. 1.

15. Berkowitz, *Disabled Policy: America's Programs for the Handicapped*, pp. 43–78.

16. Berkowitz, *Disabled Policy: America's Programs for the Handicapped*, pp. 226, 234–235.

17. Bogart R. Leashore and Jerry R. Cates, "Use of Historical Methods in Social Work Research," *Social Work Research and Abstracts* 21 (Summer 1984), pp. 24–25; Barzun and Graff, *The Modern Researcher*, p. 198.

18. Leslie Leighninger, Norma Jean Barrett, Michelle Ann Debie, Nancy Hallack, Lynn Krol, Clayton Maodush-Pitzer, Janet Richardson, Kathleen Smith, Lisa Vanderwel, Roger Vanderwoude, and Meg Wilson, "Sexual Harassment Policies in Social Service Agencies," Field Studies in Research and Practice, School of Social Work, Western Michigan University, June 1987.

19. Shafer, *A Guide to Historical Method*, pp. 149–170. Unfortunately, of course, that consciousness remains limited for a number of white Americans today.

20. Barzun and Graff, *The Modern Researcher*, pp. 163–191.

21. Charles Murray, *Losing Ground* (New York: Basic Books, 1984), pp. 3–9; Christopher Jencks, "How Poor Are the Poor?" Book review of Charles Murray's *Losing Ground*, *New York Review of Books* (9 May 1985), p. 41.

22. Murray, *Losing Ground*, pp. 9, 63, 154–162.

23. Barzun and Graff, *The Modern Researcher*, p. 156; Murray, *Losing Ground*, pp. 148–153; William Julius Wilson and Kathryn M. Neckerman, "Poverty and Family Structure: The Widening Gap between Evidence and Public Policy Issues," in Sheldon H. Danziger and Daniel H. Weinberg, Eds., *Fighting Poverty: What Works and What Doesn't* (Cambridge, MA: Harvard University Press, 1986), pp. 246–252.

24. David T. Ellwood and Lawrence H. Summers, "Poverty in America: Is Welfare the Answer or the Problem?" in Danziger, *Fighting Poverty*, pp. 84–86;

Jencks, "How Poor Are the Poor?" pp. 43–44; Michael Katz, *The Undeserving Poor* (New York: Pantheon Books, 1989), pp. 151–156. John E. Schwarz's book *America's Hidden Success* (New York: W. W. Norton, 1983) contains other findings at odds with Murray's presentation. Schwarz contends that Americans have a false perception of the failure of the economy and of social programs in the 1960s and 1970s and marshals data that indicate that poverty rates had been dramatically reduced by the second half of the 1970s. Government programs, rather than economic growth, were responsible for the bulk of that decline (Schwarz, pp. 1–36).

25. Barzun and Graff, *The Modern Researcher*, pp. 156–157; Katz, *The Undeserving Poor*, p. 155.

26. Frances Fox Piven and Richard A. Cloward, *Regulating the Poor: The Functions of Public Welfare* (New York: Vintage Books, 1971), p. xiii; Achenbaum, "The Making of an Applied Historian: Stage Two," pp. 38–39.

27. Piven and Cloward, *Regulating the Poor*, pp. xv–xvii, 3–41; David A. Rochefort, "Progressive and Social Control Perspectives on Social Welfare," *Social Service Review* 55 (December 1981), pp. 581–582.

28. John K. Alexander, "The Functions of Public Welfare in Late-Eighteenth-Century Philadelphia: Regulating the Poor?" in Walter I. Trattner, Ed., *Social Welfare or Social Control* (Knoxville: The University of Tennessee Press, 1983), p. 69; James T. Patterson, *America's Struggle against Poverty, 1900–1994* (Cambridge, MA: Harvard University Press), p. 134.

29. Raymond A. Mohl, "The Abolition of Public Outdoor Relief, 1870–1900: A Critique of the Piven and Cloward Thesis," in Trattner, *Social Welfare or Social Control*, p. 36; Achenbaum, "The Making of an Applied Historian," pp. 39–41; Alexander, "The Functions of Public Welfare in Late-Eighteenth-Century Philadelphia," pp. 15, 30.

30. Achenbaum, "The Making of an Applied Historian," pp. 30–41; Rochefort, "Progressive and Social Control Perspectives on Social Welfare," p. 586; Barzun and Graff, *The Modern Researcher*, pp. 185–191.

31. Clarke A. Chambers, "Doctoral Research and Dissertations on the History of Social Welfare and Social Work," Faculty Development Institute, Council on Social Work Education Annual Program Meeting, 3 March 1990.

Social/Economic Analysis

The Personal Responsibility and Work Opportunity Reconciliation Act of 1996 was due to be reauthorized by October 1, 2002. This did not happen, although programs supported by the bill, mainly the Temporary Assistance for Needy Families program (TANF), are operating under a continuing resolution until reauthorization is passed. In anticipation of the reauthorization debates, we have had conversations with a number of people who were familiar with the bill. Here is what a few had to say:

A member of a governor's office staff: We have been very supportive of the TANF program ever since its inception in 1996. We like that the states are given more leeway in designing programs that will reflect the economic and political realities in their own states. We do, however, have some concerns about some of the provisions of the reauthorization bills. We are particularly concerned with the increase in the work participation rate from 50 percent to 70 percent, with penalties to states that fall below the new level. With the downturn in the economy, we are having trouble meeting the 50 percent rate and the new level will be nearly impossible to meet. We are also very concerned with the House bill that increases day care funding by only $1 billion, an amount that won't even make up for inflation. If this version passes we will need to cut down on the amount of day care we can fund, and that will make the 70 percent work participation rate even more difficult to satisfy.

A community organizer: Both the House and Senate versions stink as does the original bill. The only thing that protects poor people and promotes social justice is national-level control of programs. You move control to the local level and the same bunch of good old boys who have run things for years will exert their power and do everything possible to save money. What we will see between the states is a race to the bottom to see who can develop the cheapest, most punitive welfare system possible.

A minister in a conservative Christian church: This bill places the emphasis of the welfare system on work, exactly where it should be. The former system rewarded people for staying home and doing nothing. After a few years, nothing becomes all you are able to do. Also, there was no "stick" to make people get off their duffs and become self-supporting and self-respecting. The new system helps people but tells them in no uncertain terms that they have only two years to get their lives together and they better get to it. I think this is great.

A city manager: I know everyone is putting their arms out of joint patting their own backs over the TANF program but, as for myself, I see problems. It's OK to encourage, even to force people to get jobs, but I'd like to see some concern about what type of jobs. It does little good to place a mother of three into a minimum-wage job with no benefits and no opportunity for advancement. She won't be able to afford day care, she won't be able to afford medical care, etc., so when these benefits expire she will be out on the street. The reauthorization bill, particularly the House version, is even stingier with benefits to support people transitioning to employment. What will we do when people without adequate jobs begin to be thrown off the rolls? These people are not elderly Eskimos who will go out on the ice to die. They'll set up house-keeping on the streets of our cities and then the same group of business owners who are now so enthusiastic about this bill will be in my office demanding that I get the street people away from the fronts of their stores.

These people are all talking about the same policy, they are all knowledgeable about its details and mechanics, yet they have very different interpretations about whether it is good or bad, what values it reflects, what its goals are, and whether its effects are likely to be positive, negative, or nothing at all. Answering these, and similar, questions is the task of the social/economic section of a social welfare policy analysis.

In this chapter, we look at those sections of the outline presented on pages 37–39 under the headings of Social Analysis and Economic Analysis. The basic task of social/economic analysis is fairly straightforward—to gain an in-depth understanding of what our society considers to be social welfare problems, how we seek to deal with these problems, why we deal with them in the ways we do, and what will be the probable consequences of dealing with them in one way versus another or, perhaps, of not dealing with them at all.

Delineation of the Policy under Analysis

Before the policy analysis process can begin, a critical first step is to specify care-fully the boundaries of the policy you intend to analyze. Policies have vague and overlapping boundaries that can easily shift over the course of an analysis unless the analyst has carefully specified them and is constantly aware of the need to maintain focus. For example, imagine that you have been hired as a social worker with a state child protective services agency and you wish to research the policy context of your new job. Before you begin, you must decide: Do you wish to an-alyze the overall topic of child welfare policy? Only policy that concerns child abuse and neglect? Only child abuse and neglect policy in your state? Foster care policy in your agency? Or one specific law such as the Keeping Children and Fam-ilies Safe Act of 2003? If your concern is protective services policy in your agency, are you going to limit your analysis to child protective services, or do you want to include adult protective services? You can, of course, look at several of these or all of them if you are willing to do the work. However, once you define the topic, you must stick with that definition.

Once you have defined your policy topic, the next step is to identify the pol-icy *realm* you are concerned with. Staying with the example of child welfare, you need to decide whether you are interested in only government-sector activities, such as state-financed foster care; enterprise-sector activities, such as for-profit therapeutic day care; or voluntary-sector activities, such as church-sponsored children's homes. Because of the interaction between the realms of policy, in most cases you will need to look at all three, although you will probably concentrate on only one.

The major problem we find with the work of student policy analysts is that they fail to specify the boundaries of their analysis clearly and therefore tend to change focus, often more than once, during the course of the analysis. In the case of one student's analysis we recently read, for example, when the social analysis was conducted, the focus was on public-sector child welfare in general, concentrating on the Adoption Assistance and Child Welfare Act of 1980. When the political analysis was done, the focus changed to adoptions policy of the voluntary sector, looking at changes in private adoption agencies since 1970. The economic analysis concentrated on the development of for-profit day care providers. The focus kept changing until the historical analysis, which dealt with church-sponsored child care institutions. Rather than doing one coherent policy analysis, the student had done one section of each of five separate analyses. The first rule of policy analysis is: Specify the policy you wish to analyze as carefully as possible and keep that specification before you all during the analysis. The purpose of this is similar to that of a scientist who states a research question and hypothesis or of a historian who draws up a list of questions in order to keep the research on one path throughout its course.

Social Problem Analysis

The next step in social/economic analysis is to clearly and completely identify and define the problem the policy addresses. Social welfare policies are hypothetical solutions to perceived social problems. For this reason, the definition of the problem is the heart of the policy, the key to understanding its logic. Gerry Brewer and Peter deLeon state that the policy process "begins when a potential problem . . . is first sensed, i.e., problem recognition or identification. Once a problem is recognized, many possible means to alleviate, mitigate, or resolve it may be explored quickly and tentatively."[1] Thus the first step in practitioner policy analysis is to decipher what problem the formulators of the policy under analysis had in mind when they designed the policy. The definition of the problem addressed by a social welfare policy may be vague and obscure, sometimes even misleading. The problem definition phase of a policy analysis is a critical step, the complexity of which should not be underestimated. Leslie Pal states that "There is universal agreement that the key factor [in policy analysis] is the problem or at least the definition of a situation considered problematic. . . . The reason problem structuring is so important is that policy analysts seem to fail more often because they solve the wrong problem than because they get the wrong solution to the right problem."[2]

Our initial inclination when faced with the task of defining social problems is to view them as objective conditions that a large number of people think we need to do something about. When problems are defined this way, the definitions seem obvious—a policy regarding homelessness deals with the problem of people who have no homes; an antipoverty policy deals with the problem of people without enough money. However, sociologists point out that objective conditions are not, by themselves, sufficient explanations of how we define social problems—the process of problem definition has other important dimensions. In a work that has come to be considered a classic in the social problem literature, Malcolm Spector and John Kutsuse define social problems as "the activities of individuals or groups making assertions of grievances and claims with respect to some putative conditions."[3] In other words, social problems are labeled, constructed, and defined by individuals and groups, and these labels are accepted or rejected by society based more on the power and skill of the individual or group than on any objective manifestation of the condition being defined. An extreme example of this perspective on social problems is a statement by sociologist Pierre van den Berghe, who argues that "there is no such thing as a social problem until someone thinks there is. Social problems have no more objective validity than ghosts. They exist only in the minds of those who believe in them. . . . It seems axiomatic to me that the solution to a 'social problem' is for people to stop defining it as such."[4] A number of influential people have proposed exactly this as the solution to the problem of abuse of marijuana—simply stop defining the use of marijuana as a problem and it will cease to be one.

The social construction of social problems is of critical import for understanding social welfare policies. Let's look, for example, at the problem of homelessness. The problem could be defined in terms of the large number of people who are suffering because they have no permanent and decent shelter. From this definition, the obvious policy response would be programs to provide an increased supply of low-cost housing and supportive services to enable people to take advantage of the housing. Using this definition, we can understand the policies of an organization such as Habitat for Humanity. But what of the policy of the city of Phoenix, where the city council dealt with the homeless by removing their support system, including closing shelters, alcohol treatment programs, and residential hotels, and ordering the public works department to spray kerosene on trash so as to render any leftover food inedible?[5] Obviously, the problem for the city of Phoenix was not that people were suffering due to lack of shelter and needed to be housed, but that homeless people were cluttering up the streets and needed to move elsewhere.

When attempting to define the problem being dealt with by a particular social welfare policy, it is helpful to ask, "For whom is this a problem?" and, "Who will benefit as a result of the policy?" In the case of Phoenix, the problem being dealt with by the policy is clearly not experienced by the people without any shelter. The intended beneficiaries of the policy appear to be businesspeople and property owners in the areas with large homeless populations, not the homeless people themselves.

It is also helpful to break problems down into primary problems and derivative problems. In the case of mental health policy, the primary problem is that there are a number of people who are suffering because of psychological illness of one sort or another. Derived from this are problems of employers who have employees who are not very productive, children in single-parent homes, people living on the streets of Phoenix, and the list goes on. Most social welfare policies deal with the derivative problems.

Finally, it should be noted that a policy is often a response to more than one problem, and this often creates tensions and inconsistencies in the policy. Financial assistance policy seeks to deal with a number of problems simultaneously, prominent among which are the facts that many people are unable to earn a living, that many poor children are not receiving adequate care, and that the level of family breakup is increasing. Some policy analysts argue that it also deals with the problem of regulating the labor market.[6] Aspects of the policy that address one of these problems may be in direct contradiction with those addressing others. For example, TANF policy requires that welfare recipients take jobs that may well result in a deterioration in the quality of care provided to the recipients' children. The reason for this is that the employed parent will not be home with the children but the job provided for the person most likely will not pay enough to purchase adequate child care.

Facts Related to the Problem

In this section of the policy analysis, we assess the information we actually "know" about a social welfare problem. Two major areas must be explored in this phase of a policy analysis. The first is an assessment of the completeness of the knowledge regarding the problem—how many facts do we know about it, and what is the state of knowledge regarding cause–effect relationships. The second area is the one in which we generally have quite a lot of knowledge regarding any social welfare problem—what do we know about the population affected by the problem?

Completeness of Knowledge Related to the Problem

One of the most important factors in understanding social welfare policy analysis, and in understanding any social welfare policy area, is the realization that there is a tremendous amount we really don't know about most social welfare problems. We have any number of theories, and we have a seemingly infinite number of discrete facts about any one problem, but when it comes to actually knowing why certain people are poor, why the rate of violent crime is increasing, how we can improve the school performance of inner city kids, our knowledge often is incomplete.

In some areas, the knowledge base is much more complete than in others. We know quite a lot, for example, about health care. We know that by increasing the availability of prenatal care, we can reduce the number of birth defects. We can even calculate how much money we need to spend to eliminate a certain number of birth defects and compare that to the cost of repairing or managing the defects that result from the lack of care. In mental health policy, by comparison, the degree of completeness of knowledge is fairly low. For years we have developed policies that provide psychotherapy to persons suffering from psychological disorders without much evidence that the provision of these services does any good.[7] Recently, in response to advances in knowledge of the biochemical basis of mental illness, we are establishing policies that provide pharmaceutical treatment to patients, but we are learning that the lack of supportive counseling greatly diminishes the effectiveness of prescribed medications.

Thus it must be recognized that most social welfare policies are actually experiments. Based on the completeness of the knowledge, we can state that some are more experimental than others. The primary questions in health policy revolve around what services we want to provide and how we want to deliver them. We have a pretty good idea regarding the results. In mental health, public assistance, and family policy, the primary questions are what services should we provide and will they work. In many cases, we really don't know.

Population Affected by the Problem

The one area about which we know quite a lot regarding most social welfare problems is the characteristics of the population affected by the problem. How large is the population? What are the population trends? We obviously tend to worry more about a problem that affects a large population than we do about a small one, but what probably worries us most is a problem that is rapidly growing. AIDS, for example, does not affect as large a population as cancer, but we were initially terrified because it was growing and the rate of growth appeared to be increasing. Now that the level of AIDS in the United States is stabilizing, the panic has subsided, although concerns about its growth worldwide have increased.

After we have established the population size and the growth trends of the problem under analysis, we then look at the defining characteristics of the population affected—the statistics on age, sex, race, family structure, geographic distribution, and so forth. These characteristics often lead to some interesting hypotheses about how we deal with the problem. Continuing with the example of AIDS, it is interesting that the level of concern, as indicated by the amount of money spent on AIDS research and treatment, began to increase dramatically when significant numbers of heterosexual, non–drug users began to show up in the statistics.

Theory of Human Behavior Undergirding the Policy

It is curious that we as social workers frequently overlook the obvious fact that the objective of many, if not most, social welfare policies is to effect some form of behavioral change. Public assistance policy seeks to increase recipients' labor-force participation, child welfare policy seeks to improve people's level of parenting, criminal justice and juvenile justice policy seek to decrease law-violating behavior, and so on. Thus every policy is based on some, rarely explicitly stated, theory of human behavior. To understand a policy, and to understand why many policies are ineffective, we need to determine what theory of human behavior the policy is based on and whether the theory is valid and applicable.

Most social welfare policies are based on some version of the rational choice perspective on human behavior. This perspective views people as rational beings who make choices based on self-interest. Rational choice theory assumes that people are purposive and goal oriented; that humans have sets of hierarchically ordered preferences (generally called *utilities* in this theory); and that in choosing lines of behavior, human beings make rational calculations with respect to the costs and benefits of various alternative behaviors.[8] The version of rational choice theory perhaps most familiar to social workers is social exchange theory. This theory is based on the minimax principle, which simply states that people will make choices based on an assessment of which course of action will minimize costs and maximize rewards. Behavior is explained using the simple calculus of rewards minus costs equals outcome. It is assumed that if the result of this calculation is positive, the person will choose the behavior; if it is negative, the person will avoid the behavior.[9]

Probably the clearest example of rational choice theory in social policy is in the area of criminal justice. We continue to increase the penalties for crimes based on the belief that people make rational choices regarding the commission of crimes. We envision a person saying to himself, "If I rob this store and get caught, the maximum penalty I'll get will be one year in prison. That's not so bad and I really need the money, so I guess I'll do it." We then enact legislation to increase the penalty and assume that the person's conversation with himself will change to "If I rob this store and get caught, I'm sure to get at least five years in prison. That's really a lot so I guess I'd better not do it."

Social workers know that although rational choice certainly plays a major part in people's behavior, many other factors also enter into the equation. Many policies fail, or are much less successful than they could be, simply because they are based on an inadequate understanding of the behavioral dimensions of the problem being addressed. One of the major contributions social workers can make to policy analysis is bringing a much more sophisticated, nuanced, and multidimensional understanding of human behavior to the table than is usual among policy professionals.

Social Values Related to the Problem

We have observed that the definition of social welfare problems is largely socially constructed and that the level of knowledge regarding most problems is incomplete. Based on these observations, it should come as no surprise that values constitute what is probably the most important dimension for understanding social welfare policy. David Easton's definition of politics as "the authoritative allocation of values for society" could just as well apply to social welfare policy.[10] In order to understand our society's response to social welfare problems, you must inquire as to what values support a policy and what values a policy offends.

What major U.S. values lead people to support or oppose various responses to social welfare problems? Probably the best analysis, although now a bit dated, is that developed by sociologist Robin Williams.[11] Williams identifies fifteen major value orientations in U.S. society.[12] These are discussed in the following paragraphs.

Achievement and Success

U.S. society is marked by a great emphasis on achievement, particularly occupational achievement. Ours is a competitive society, and people who don't measure up in the competition are looked down on. Social welfare policies deal with problems closely related to lack of success. Poor people have not achieved occupationally, people experiencing marital discord have not succeeded in their relationship, people with psychologically disturbed children are viewed as having failed as parents, and so forth. Thus almost any social welfare policy faces an uphill struggle for public support in that it generally deals with a problem that violates this basic value. A frequent response to this value by social welfare policymakers is to couch policies in terms that indicate that the policy will attempt to instill this value in its clients. A program started by the state of Alabama in response to the welfare reform act of 1988, for example, is entitled Project Success.

Activity and Work

Numerous observers, from Tocqueville up to the most recent, have noted that Americans place a high value on being busy. Even in our leisure activities, we emphasize some form of purposeful, action-oriented behavior. However, the primary manifestation of this value is in relation to work. Williams observes, "Directed and disciplined activity in a regular occupation is a particular form of this basic orientation."[13] Work has become almost an end in itself, valued even when it is not necessary for economic survival. Observe, for example, that the first thing most winners of large sums of money in lotteries are quoted as saying is some variant of the statement, "I'm not going to quit my job." Because many social welfare programs provide people with means of existence that are not tied to work, they are immediately suspect in the eyes of many Americans. The TANF program, passed as part of the 1996 Personal Responsibility and Work Opportunity Reconciliation Act, enjoys great popularity precisely because it forces people to go to work.

Moral Orientation

Americans generally view the world in moral terms—right and wrong, good and bad, ethical and unethical. The recipients of social welfare benefits are often suspected of having engaged in behavior that is morally bad or of having not engaged in behavior that is morally good. Some welfare mothers, for example, have had children without benefit of marriage, have dropped out of school, and are not working, all behaviors we are likely to condemn as bad, perhaps even sinful. This moral orientation has often led to differentiation between recipients of services and benefits as "worthy" or "unworthy."

Humanitarian Mores

Caring for one another, particularly those who are perceived as less fortunate and suffering through no fault of their own, is a key value in U.S. society. Williams points out that one manifestation of this value is the fact that fully one-third of the adult population participates in some form of voluntary service. This value serves, to a certain extent, to counter punitive social welfare policies that occasionally emerge out of our moral orientation.

Efficiency and Practicality

Our society places a high value on good stewardship of time and material resources. We feel a compulsion to continually seek the best means possible for achieving a certain end. This value has several important consequences for the social work profession. The first is a historic interest in developing better technical means to deal with social welfare problems. For years social workers have sought to develop a "science of social casework." Another way this value manifests itself is in our continual concern with accountability, that is, in demonstrating that social welfare programs are being run efficiently and are having the intended effects. It is ironic that the end result of this value is often antithetical to the value itself. For example, it has been estimated that as much as 40 percent of a social worker's time in public agencies is spent doing paperwork, mostly for the purpose of documenting that the agency is doing its job efficiently and effectively. During training sessions on procedures for completing time documentation forms, a frequent—and legitimate—question is "Where on this form do I put down all the time I spend filling out this form?"

Progress

Americans hold charter membership in what Williams has called the "cult of progress," believing that things can, and should, continually be getting better. The historian Henry Steele Commager has observed that "throughout their history Americans have insisted that the best was yet to be. . . . The American knew that nothing was impossible in his brave new world. . . . Progress was not, to him, a mere philosophical ideal but a commonplace of experience."[14] Because of this belief, U.S. society has never accepted the position of many other societies, both past and present, that social problems are simply a part of the natural order of things and that attempts to change social conditions are as useless as trying to change the ocean's tides. We are continually attempting to do something about conditions such as poverty, ill health, crime, violence, and so forth. An unfortunate side effect of this value is that if a policy or program does not demonstrate immediate results, we tend to grow impatient with it quickly and abandon it in order to try something else. Poverty, for example, has been around for thousands of years; when the War on Poverty didn't eliminate it in three years, Congress became disillusioned and began to dismantle the policy.

Material Comfort

The United States is an acquisitive and materialistic culture. This statement really requires no more justification than to look at the lifestyles of friends and acquaintances and at what is emphasized in TV commercials and magazine ads. We equate material possessions with happiness and success. The relevance of this value for understanding social welfare policy resides in the fact that people needing social welfare services generally, although not always, are people who are experiencing a low level of material comfort. This raises difficult questions concerning what level of material comfort they have a right to and what the rest of society has an obligation to provide. We also believe that a lack of material comfort can be a good thing because it will tend to spur people on to solve their own problems to gain the material comforts they desire. (The comedian Red Skelton once said, "I've got a solution to poverty—tax the poor; give them an incentive to get rich.") One of the major principles of financial assistance policy ever since the 1601 Elizabethan Poor Laws has been that of less eligibility. This is the notion that the level of material comfort of people receiving the highest level of welfare benefits should always be lower than the level of the least comfortable working person.

Equality

The value of equality constitutes a steady theme throughout U.S. history. Yet, as Williams notes, "few other value complexes are more subject to strain in modern times."[15] We express strong support for the idea of equality as a philosophical principle, but our society is characterized by a high degree of inequality, and most Americans believe this is as it should be. The explanation for this apparent discrepancy is that when most Americans speak of equality, they mean equality of opportunity, not of outcome. We believe people should have an equal chance in life and find elements such as ascribed social status, old boy networks, and the like to be deeply offensive. Social welfare policies that help achieve equality of opportunity, such as Head Start, are warmly supported by most people in the United States. Policies that smack of equality of outcome, whether this is the intent or not, such as guaranteed annual income, racial and sexual hiring quotas, and the like, always face strong opposition.

Freedom

As anyone who has taken a high school civics class is aware, the concept of freedom is complex and multidimensional. Obviously, freedom does not mean freedom from all external control. In the United States, *freedom* generally refers to a preference for control by diffuse social processes rather than by any definite social organization. For example, the practice of neighborhood segregation by race or religion has been made illegal because it violates the value of freedom by forcefully excluding people from certain residences by law. However, few people are totally free to live wherever they wish, simply because they can afford only certain neighborhoods. Thus, in the United States, freedom generally means freedom from excessive and arbitrary external restraint. This way of looking at freedom has resulted in "a tendency to think of rights rather than duties, a suspicion of established (especially personal) authority, a distrust of central government, a deep aversion to acceptance of obviously coercive restraint through visible social organization."[16] The value of freedom has important consequences for understanding almost any social welfare policy. Social welfare policies are often viewed as increasing the rights of one group and decreasing the freedom of another. Child protection laws increase the rights of children to a minimal standard of care but reduce the freedom of parents to rear children as they see fit without interference by government; financial assistance policies increase the rights of individuals to live with a certain degree of dignity but decrease the freedom of taxpayers to enjoy the fruits of their own labor; health care policy increases the rights of people to receive medical care but decreases the freedom of physicians to practice medicine as they wish, and so on.

External Conformity

Even though the U.S. self-image celebrates individualism, it has been frequently noted that we have a rather low tolerance for those who do not conform to accepted standards. Williams observes that "American 'individualism,' taken in broadest terms, has consisted mainly of a rejection of the state and impatience with restraints upon economic activity; it has not tended to set the autonomous individual up in rebellion against his social group."[17] By and large, we do not approve of those who vary too far from the norm in dress, behavior, manners, lifestyle, or whatever. Social welfare policies are often directed at people who do not conform to some important standard; they may be unmarried mothers, teenagers who don't go to school, people who use drugs, or adolescents who refuse to comply with adult authority figures. Social welfare policies directed at these groups are generally aimed at helping them but often have an underlying purpose of attempting to control, and sometimes eliminate, the nonconforming behavior.

Science and Secular Rationality

Americans have great faith that the methods of science will eventually solve all, or nearly all, problems of living in our physical and social world. We believe that even the seemingly intractable social problems addressed by social welfare policies will eventually succumb to the onslaught of scientific method. At the present time, however, we are still some way from good, useful knowledge applicable to most social welfare problems, and this causes much frustration among policymakers.

Nationalism–Patriotism

Every society is characterized by some degree of ethnocentrism—that is, the belief that membership in that group is preferable to membership in any other group. In the United States, this feeling is quite strong, although probably no stronger than in many other areas of the world. (In some traditional cultures, people outside the culture are not even considered to be human.) In the United States, nationalism–patriotism has one unique dimension: a sense of missionary zeal to spread U.S. economic and governmental institutions throughout the world, generally by nonmilitary means. Many nations have, in the past, sought to conquer other nations in order to dominate them and thereby gain wealth and advantage. The United States wishes for other nations to adopt our way of doing things not directly for our own advantage but because we feel they, and consequently the rest of the world, will benefit if they do so. Nationalism–patriotism is a value complex that does not have a great relevance for understanding social welfare policy, but it does have some. In Chapter 3, we discussed cross-cultural comparison as one approach to policy analysis. Cross-cultural comparisons often result in findings that are embarrassing to the United States because they show that we, who like to think of ourselves as world leaders, often rank below some developing nations on social indicators such as infant mortality. Appeals to the value of nationalism–patriotism can often be more effective in engendering sympathy for social welfare proposals than appeals to more obvious values such as humanitarianism.

Democracy

It goes almost without saying that one of the star positions in the U.S. constellation of values is a belief in the democratic process, that is, decision making with every person's preferences being weighed. Democracy, however, is sometimes problematic in social welfare policy. The reason for this is related to what Tocqueville referred to as the "tyranny of the majority." This means that if everything is done by majority rule, people, or groups of people, who are not part of the majority can suffer some harsh consequences as a result of never getting their way. African Americans, Hispanics, lesbians and gays, and migrant workers have all suffered because the majority has not been sensitive to their problems. Social welfare policies often face strong opposition based on the argument that they are undemocratic because they benefit a minority group against the will of the majority. School integration, not a social welfare policy as we are defining the term but certainly a social policy, is probably the clearest example of this.

Individual Personality

In the United States, we place an extremely high value on the worth and dignity of the individual. We also place a heavy load of responsibility on the individual in the form of credit for success and blame for failure. In many areas of the world—Japan is probably the most frequently cited example—the well-being of the group is the central value, and individuals are expected to defer their own wishes to the collective welfare of the group. This is not the case in the United States. Groups are viewed as collections of individuals formed for the purpose of facilitating the goals and promoting the welfare of individual members. The value of individual personality is critical for understanding social welfare policy in this country. By their very definition, social welfare policies involve collective provisions for the assistance of individuals. Thus they generally involve sacrifice by individuals for the good of the group. For example, public social welfare policies require individuals, sometimes against their will, to sacrifice part of their income, in the form of taxes, to finance provisions for people without enough money to live on. This is deeply offensive to many Americans and guarantees opposition to any proposed expansion of social welfare programs.

Racism, Sexism, and Related Group Superiority Themes

Although the United States is characterized by strong values of democracy, individualism, humanitarianism, and so forth, we have to recognize that there also are what Williams refers to as "deviant themes, contrary to the main thrust of American society," namely racism, sexism, and related prejudices. Because these themes run counter to so many of our other value clusters, we have attempted to resolve them through numerous pieces of legislation. However, we must recognize that they are still present to a much greater degree than we care to admit. Ugly as the value cluster of racism, sexism, and so forth may be, we must recognize its existence if we are to understand social welfare policies fully. The common perception is that the majority of beneficiaries of most social welfare policies are minorities and women, and thus these policies are often equated with these groups. On the one hand, social welfare policies often receive support from individuals and groups who support attempts to redress the effects of discrimination against minorities and women. In fact, many policies, such as affirmative action and minority scholarships, are often proposed specifically for this purpose. On the other hand, individuals and groups often oppose social welfare policies and, although they generally don't admit this, the reason for the opposition is often directly a result of racism and sexism.

Contradictions in the U.S. Value System

As you may well have figured out from thinking about the values discussed previously, they do not result in a uniform pattern but rather are shot through with conflicts and contradictions. We are motivated to help the poor by our value of humanitarianism, but this is mitigated by other values: *moralism*, which leads us to believe that poverty is somehow related to improper behavior; *individualism*, which places responsibility for problems and for their solutions at the feet of the individuals affected; and the value of activity and work, which causes us to suspect that welfare programs encourage nonwork behavior. Policies to assist groups who are victims of oppression, such as women, African Americans, and lesbians and gays, are encouraged by our belief in equality but are retarded by values of *democracy* and *freedom*, which lead us to suspect that by promoting the rights of one group we will be discriminating against another; and, below the surface, by *racism, sexism,* and *group superiority* themes. Thus our social welfare policies often appear to be illogical because they are attempting to balance numerous conflicting values.

Goals of the Policy under Analysis

In *Alice in Wonderland,* Alice has the following exchange with the Cheshire Cat:

> "Would you tell me, please, which way I ought to go from here?"
> "That depends a good deal on where you want to get to," said the cat.
> "I don't much care where—" said Alice.
> "Then it doesn't matter which way you go," said the cat.[18]

Unlike Alice, the designers of social welfare policies have fairly specific destinations, or goals, in mind. To understand a policy, it is necessary to understand just what these goals are. This task constitutes the next stage of the social analysis.

A policy goal is the desired state of affairs that is hoped to be achieved by the policy. As with many areas of policy analysis, the task of determining goals appears simple at the outset, but once you are into it you discover that it can be extremely complex and often misleading. There is a rich sociological literature on the subject of goals that deals with the topic in much greater depth than we need to here.[19]

Policies generally are directed toward more than one goal, and these multiple goals are often in conflict with one another.[20] This is a result of the conflicts in the value structure of U.S. society discussed previously, in combination with the political nature of policy making. Child welfare policy, for example, pursues two often incompatible goals. On the one hand, we seek to ensure that all children grow up in a safe home. On the other hand, we seek to ensure that a child can grow up in his or her own family. Ensuring the safety of children can involve removing them from their families; keeping families intact can involve putting children at risk. In a similar fashion, mental health policy has a goal of preventing mentally ill people from harming themselves and/or others, but also has a goal of putting people in the "least restrictive environment." Obviously, the less restrictive an environment becomes, the greater the risk of disturbed persons harming themselves or others. Financial assistance policy seeks to support people at an adequate level but also has a goal of motivating people to work. If the level of assistance ever becomes such that it truly could be defined as adequate, this presumably would lower the recipient's motivation to work.

In almost all cases, policies are directed toward different levels of goals, often distinguished as *goals* and *objectives*. The goal of a policy is a general and abstract statement of the state of affairs the policymakers seek to accomplish. A goal is generally difficult to measure and often is not even intended to be accomplished.

It is rather a benchmark, a statement that provides general direction to the activities of the programs set up under the policy. For example, the goal of a state policy regarding child welfare staffing was stated as: "To assure that all dependent and neglected children in the state receive the highest possible quality services from experienced, professionally trained social workers and allied personnel." Objectives are derived from goals and are specific, concrete, measurable statements. The objectives derived from the state child welfare personnel goals were:

1. Increase the number of competent, practice-ready BSW and MSW candidates applying for employment in child welfare in the Department of Human Resources (DHR).
2. Improve the retention of child welfare staff in DHR.
3. Increase the responsiveness and effectiveness of the State and Departmental Personnel systems in certifying qualified applicants for employment in DHR child welfare positions.[21]

The final, and probably the most important, aspect of goals we must understand in order to do a social analysis is that policies contain unstated, as well as stated, goals. Stated goals are sometimes referred to in the literature as official or manifest goals, and unstated goals are often called operative or latent goals. This is the single most important item in understanding why there are so many policies that seem to make no sense yet are never effectively reformed. High school teachers, for example, often express their frustration that they have difficulty teaching because so many of their students "have no business in school," in other words are not interested in learning and are not benefiting from being in the classroom. The teachers ask why the school system does not adopt a policy encouraging these young people to leave school, get jobs, and not return to school until they are ready to benefit from it. The reason school systems do not adopt this seemingly rational policy is that, although the stated (official, *manifest*) goal of school systems is to educate young people and prepare them for adult life, an unstated (operative, *latent*) goal of every public school system is to keep young people off the street and out of the full-time job market until they are eighteen years old. Therefore, dropout prevention is always a goal of schools, even though any teacher realizes that many prevented dropouts do not benefit in any way from their additional years in school and in fact often interfere with the education of other young people.

Another example of the difference, and often conflict, between stated and unstated goals, and one of more relevance to social workers, is public assistance policy. The public welfare system has been reformed again and again, but none of the reforms has ever had much of an impact on our country's dependent population. For example,

Temporary Assistance for Needy Families (TANF) is a block grant created by the Personal Responsibility and Work Opportunity Reconciliation Act of 1996, as part of a federal effort to "end welfare as we know it." The TANF block grant replaced the Aid to Families with Dependent Children (AFDC) program, which had provided cash welfare to poor families with children since 1935. Under the TANF structure, the federal government provides a block grant to the states, which use these funds to operate their own programs. States can use TANF dollars in ways designed to meet any of the four purposes set out in federal law, which are to: (1) provide assistance to needy families so that children may be cared for in their own homes or in the homes of relatives; (2) end the dependence of needy parents on government benefits by promoting job preparation, work, and marriage; (3) prevent and reduce the incidence of out-of-wedlock pregnancies and establish annual numerical goals for preventing and reducing the incidence of these pregnancies; and (4) encourage the formation and maintenance of two-parent families.[22]

As will be further discussed in the chapter on anti-poverty policy (Chapter 7), the authors are skeptical about this policy's potential to permanently reduce economic dependency. The reason for our skepticism has to do with our analysis of the unstated goals of the public welfare system. We argue that the primary operative goal of the public welfare system is to manage economic dependency in as efficient a manner as possible while preserving the social and economic status quo in the society. Thus, policies that significantly redistribute power and resources will not be considered. Without significant redistribution of power and resources, there is really no solution to the problem of economic dependency. In other words, the operative goal of the welfare system is not to eliminate dependency but rather to manage dependency while preserving the wealth and power of the rest of society.

Hypotheses Underlying the Policy

The next step in the analysis of a social welfare policy is to identify the hypotheses or theories on which the policy is based. In most areas of social welfare, the state of knowledge is incomplete; little is known about cause–effect relationships. Thus every social policy is in effect an experiment and, like all experiments, contains one or more hypotheses. The hypotheses and theories undergirding a policy are rarely explicitly stated and generally must be inferred from other statements.

A hypothesis is an if–then statement: If we do X, then Y will happen. A careful reading of a policy statement will reveal the hypotheses on which the policy is based. The TANF program, for example, hypothesizes that *if* we require welfare recipients to work in return for their grants, *then* they will learn work skills necessary for regular employment; *if* we provide basic education and job training, *then* recipients will find jobs and leave the welfare rolls; *if* we place a time limit on receipt of assistance, *then* people will be motivated to become self-supporting.

Behind every hypothesis is a theory that may be partially or totally incorrect. The theory behind TANF is that welfare dependency is a result of individual short-comings in the recipients and that if we address these shortcomings, we can reduce the welfare rolls. Social workers, sociologists, and economists have recognized for years that many of the problems behind the "welfare mess" reside mainly in the social and economic structure of society, not exclusively in the individual recipient. These are problems involving the number of jobs available, the amount these jobs pay, and the support infrastructure necessary for people to be able to take advantage of the jobs that are available. Social policies will continue to fail unless financial assistance policy begins to address hypotheses such as *if* enough decent-paying jobs are made available, and *if* adequate support services such as day care and transportation networks are put in place, *then* people will become self-supporting.

Economic Analysis

A central concept in the study of economics is that of scarcity. That is, economics is based on the assumption that there is not now, nor will there ever be, enough resources to satisfy all of our needs and wants. Thus, economics is concerned with the matter of choice: How do we choose to distribute scarce resources? Questions of choice in resource allocation revolve around questions of *effectiveness* (Do the measures we support work?), *efficiency* (How much benefit do we get for a given expenditure of resources?), and *equity* (Are resources divided fairly?).

Social welfare policies involve the expenditure of large quantities of money—money that could be spent for alternative social welfare policies or even for other things altogether. Probably the most volatile policy issue is that social welfare benefits are largely financed by tax money, which many people feel would be spent more effectively, efficiently, and equitably if it were left in taxpayers' pockets to spend as they wish. Thus the economic ramifications of social welfare policies are of critical interest.

As discussed in Chapter 3, economic analysis of social welfare policies can be extremely technical and complex, generally requiring a competence in higher-level mathematics. The economic analysis section of a practitioner policy analysis need not be so complex. What this section of an analysis should do is employ the general perspective of an economist to ask questions related to what the effect of a given policy, or policy proposal, might be on the distribution and consumption of scarce resources. In addition, economists have a certain perspective on individual behavior, one that is somewhat different from that of most social workers.[23] In the economic analysis section, we look at the macroeconomic ramifications of a policy, analyze the opportunity cost, and assess the implications of the policy for the behavior of individuals, using an economic style of interpretation.

Macroeconomic Analysis

Macroeconomic analysis is concerned with aggregate economic performance. It looks at questions of output, income, inflation, and unemployment. These are the main items of economic interest you view on the evening news—what is happening to the gross national product, the gross national income, the inflation rate, and the unemployment rate. Taken together these broad measures give us some idea of our collective economic health.

The macroeconomic analysis section of a social welfare policy analysis asks what the effect of an existing or a proposed policy is, or is likely to be, on aggregate economic performance. Will the policy increase or decrease productivity and, consequently, profits? What will the effects be on the rate of employment? Will the policy contribute to an increasing rate of inflation? Minimum wage legislation probably provides the clearest illustration of macroeconomic concerns with a social policy. Every time the minimum wage is increased, critics voice the concern that it will result in higher unemployment due to employers laying off employees they can no longer afford; business failures resulting from marginal enterprises failing under the burden of increased payroll costs; and inflation due to merchants increasing prices to cover the higher cost of doing business, which, of course, results in the value of the increased wage eventually being no more than the wage it replaced.

Macroeconomic analysis also asks what the effects of the larger economy are on the social problems the policies seek to redress. Loic Wacquant and William Julius Wilson, for example, assert that welfare reform initiatives have always been failures because they insist on incorrectly identifying the cause of welfare dependency as individual inadequacy. Welfare reform proposals "have paid too little attention to the broader economic and social-structural factors that are responsible for the crystallization of a large underclass and persistent welfare dependency." They argue that an effective welfare policy will need to deal with macroeconomic issues, mainly full employment at an increased minimum wage.[24]

Opportunity Cost

Because social welfare policies involve the expenditure of scarce resources, policy analysis inevitably involves some study of the costs. Cost accounting and auditing are, of course, important administrative functions, but they are not what we are concerned with here. Rather, we are concerned with how the cost of a certain policy, or proposed policy, compares to policy alternatives. This is referred to by economists as *opportunity cost*.

The opportunity cost of a policy consists of all the outcomes or benefits that must be sacrificed if that particular policy is adopted rather than an alternative policy. In other words, given finite resources, if we spend our money to implement one proposed solution to a social problem, we are not able to implement alternative solutions. Although advocates of prevention rarely use the term, opportunity cost is what they are talking about when they criticize social welfare policy in a number of areas. They point out that we spend so much money keeping people in jail that we can't afford community programs that might prevent a number of people from ever getting in trouble with the law; we allocate so many resources to foster care that we are not able to provide adequate family preservation services to prevent foster care being needed in the first place; we spend too much on law enforcement and drug treatment programs and too little on drug prevention education and counseling.

Opportunity cost is used to assess alternative social welfare policies, but it is also used by critics of the welfare system to argue that the money spent on welfare benefits could be better spent on something altogether different and that the poor would benefit most from this alternative allocation. Conservatives such as George Gilder, Martin Anderson, and Charles Murray argue forcefully that spending money on welfare benefits depresses the economy (a macroeconomic analysis) and that if the money were available for investment instead, it would result in economic growth, which would make jobs and opportunities for advancement available for the poorest Americans.[25] In other words, the opportunity cost of welfare programs is that businesses cannot expand and provide jobs that would be preferable to welfare.

Effects on Individual Consumer Behavior

The economist looks at behavior in a way that is somewhat different from other social scientists. The economic explanation of behavior is based on an assumption that Gordon Tullock refers to as the "90 percent selfish" hypothesis.[26] This means that while people may occasionally act in generous and selfless ways, in the overwhelming proportion of instances they will seek their own best interest. The economist will add the following disclaimer: Economic analysis of behavior makes no claims that it can explain the behavior of any one individual, only behavior in the aggregate. Thus the economist cannot explain the behavior of the individual physician who could make $60 per office visit treating private patients yet chooses instead to serve Medicaid patients at only a fraction of this amount. However, economists will predict with a high degree of confidence that, under the conditions just described, most physicians will treat as many private patients as possible and treat Medicaid patients only when they have no private patients available.

Historically, the economic analysis of effects of policy on individual behavior has been one of the driving forces behind financial assistance policy. This policy has been guided by what is known as the doctrine of less eligibility. This refers to the policy principle that a person living on welfare should always be worse off than the lowest paid working person. Guided by the 90 percent selfish hypothesis, this assumes that if people can do as well or better on welfare than they can by working, most people will choose to live on welfare. This was the foundation of critiques of welfare programs during the Reagan administration—that the welfare system had become too generous and the result was that it had sapped people's motivation to work and improve their lives. One author, for example, says,

> Expanded welfare programs [since the 1960s] made it economically rational for women to have children out of wedlock, for fathers to desert wives and children. By 1970, the package of welfare, food stamps, Medicaid and housing subsidies provided a gross income higher than many working people earned. Small wonder that a sizable number chose the world of welfare.[27]

The Temporary Assistance to Needy Families program enacted in 1996 is specifically designed to make life on welfare less secure so as to motivate people to work hard to get off the rolls.

A rather extreme example of an economic explanation of behavior regards the problem of homelessness. Lawrence Schiff says:

> In plain English, the welfare state is in essence providing, for a large percentage of the homeless, a lifestyle that would cost roughly $10,000 to $12,000 were it to be purchased in the open market, possibly a little less at some of the worst (read: city-run as opposed to private-contract) shelters. And the greater the monetary value of the benefits in kind—i.e., housing, food, clothing, medical care, etc.—the larger the number of people willing to consider homelessness as a viable option. For the question is not whether the homeless would really prefer to have permanent residences. Of course they would. They are simply subsidized to not obtain the skills and make the sacrifices necessary to obtain such housing, when substandard accommodation is available free.[28]

As will be discussed in Chapter 7, analyses of the actual behavior of welfare recipients casts doubt on this purely economic explanation of behavior.

Using the economist's perspective on behavior, the policy analyst asks what the effects of a policy are likely to be on individual behavior. The assumption is that people will be utility maximizers. That is, they will behave in the way that will result in the greatest benefit and the lowest cost to them.

Conclusion

In this chapter, we have looked in more detail at the social and economic analysis section of our policy analysis model. As should be obvious from the discussion, conducting a social welfare policy analysis is not a simple, straightforward project. Many areas are vague and poorly defined. Because the actual goals of many policies are not the same as the stated goals, and because policies often reflect values that we as a society do not care to admit we possess, the real goals and values of a policy will often be hidden and sometimes will not even be recognized by the people actually involved in formulating and implementing the policy. Also, policies seek to solve problems about which there is little agreement as to the definition of the problem or the desirable solution. Uncovering these vague and often highly emotionally charged aspects of a policy is the task of the social/economic analysis. It more often resembles an art than a science.

Notes

1. Gerry D. Brewer and Peter deLeon, *The Foundations of Policy Analysis* (Homewood, IL: Dorsey Press, 1983), p. 18.

2. Leslie Pal, *Beyond Policy Analysis: Public Management in Turbulent Times*, 3rd ed. (Toronto: Thomson/Nelson, 2006), p. 97.

3. Malcolm Spector and John Kutsuse, *Constructing Social Problems*, 2nd ed. (New York: Aldine de Gruyter, 1987) p. 75.

4. Pierre L. van den Berghe, "How Problematic Are Social Problems?" *Social Problems Theory Division Newsletter, The Society for the Study of Social Problems* 4 (Summer 1975), p. 17.

5. Michael Higgins, "Tent City: Struggling for Shelter in Phoenix," *Commonweal* (3 September 1983), pp. 494–496.

6. Frances Fox Piven and Richard A. Cloward, *Regulating the Poor: The Functions of Public Welfare* (New York: Vintage, 1971); Ken Blakemore, *Social Policy: An Introduction* (Philadelphia, PA: Open University Press, 1998), pp. 81–99.

7. Carol Tavris, "Mind Games: Psychological Warfare between Therapists and Scientists," *The Chronicle Review, The Chronicle of Higher Education* (28 February 2003), pp. B7–B9.

8. Jonathan Turner, *The Structure of Sociological Theory* (Homewood, IL: Dorsey Press, 1991), p. 354.

9. John Thibaut and Harold Kelley, *The Social Psychology of Groups* (New York: Wiley, 1959); Elizabeth D. Hutchison, *Dimensions of Human Behavior—Person and Environment*, 2nd ed. (Thousand Oaks, CA: Pine Forge Press, 2003), pp. 45–47.

10. David Easton, "Political Systems," *World Politics* 9 (1956–1957), p. 381.

11. Robin Williams, *American Society, A Sociological Interpretation*, 3rd ed. (New York: Alfred A. Knopf, 1970), pp. 454–500.

12. In a later work, Williams expanded his list to nineteen by separating some of the values into two or three. Tropman has taken Williams's list and condensed the values into seven value dimensions—work, mobility, status, independence, individualism, moralism, and ascription. We do not believe that either of these permutations improves on the 1970 version of the list used as the basis for this discussion. See Robin M. Williams, Jr., "Change and Stability in Values and Value Systems: A Sociological Perspective," in Milton Rokeach, Ed., *Understanding Human Values: Individual and Societal* (New York: Free Press, 1979), pp. 15–46; and John E. Tropman, *American Values and Social Welfare: Cultural Contradictions in the Welfare State* (Englewood Cliffs, NJ: Prentice-Hall, 1989).

13. Williams, *American Society*, p. 459.

14. Henry Steele Commager, Ed., *America in Perspective* (New York: Random House, 1947), pp. xi, xiv, quoted in Williams, *American Society*, p. 468.

15. Williams, *American Society*, p. 472.

16. Williams, *American Society*, p. 480.

17. Williams, *American Society*, p. 485.

18. Lewis Carroll, *Alice in Wonderland—Authoritative Texts of Alice's Adventures in Wonderland, Through the Looking Glass, The Hunting of the Snark,* Donald J. Gray, Ed. (New York: W. W. Norton, 1971), p. 51.

19. See, for example, Amitai Etzioni, *Modern Organizations* (Englewood Cliffs, NJ: Prentice-Hall, 1964); Petro Georgiou, "The Goal Paradigm and Notes toward a Counter Paradigm," *Administrative Science Quarterly* 18 (September 1973), pp. 291–310; Charles Perrow, "The Analysis of Goals in Complex Organization," *American Sociological Review* 26 (December 1961), pp. 856–866.

20. Dipak K. Gupta, *Analyzing Public Policy: Concepts, Tools, and Techniques* (Washington, DC: CQ Press, 2001), pp. 74–78.

21. Alabama Department of Human Resources, *Task Force on Staffing for Child Welfare Services, Final Report* (Montgomery: photocopy, March 1991).

22. Martha Coven, *An Introduction to TANF* (Washington, DC: Center on Budget and Policy Priorities, 3 October 2003), p. 1.

23. For an interesting, although irreverent, demonstration of how economic analysis can be applied to a number of social issues, see Steven D. Levitt and Stephen J. Dubner, *Freakonomics: A Rogue Economist Explores The Hidden Side of Everything* (New York: William Morrow, 2005).

24. Loic J. D. Wacquant and William Julius Wilson, "Poverty, Joblessness, and the Social Transformation of the Inner City," in Phoebe H. Cottingham and David T. Ellwood, Eds., *Welfare Policy for the 1990's* (Cambridge, MA: Harvard University Press, 1989), pp. 99–102.

25. Martin Anderson, *Welfare: The Political Economy of Welfare Reform in the United States* (Stanford, CA: Hoover Institution Press, 1978); George Gilder, *Wealth and Poverty* (New York: Basic Books, 1981); Charles Murray, *Losing Ground* (New York: Basic Books, 1984); Lawrence Mead, *Beyond Entitlement: The Social Obligations of Citizenship* (New York: Free Press, 1986).

26. Gordon Tullock, "Economic Imperialism," in James Buchanan and Robert Tollison, Eds., *Theory of Public Choice: Political Applications of Economics* (Ann Arbor: University of Michigan Press, 1972).

27. Eugene H. Methvin, "How Uncle Sam Robbed America's Poor," editorial review of Charles Murray, *Losing Ground, Readers Digest* (April 1985).

28. Lawrence Schiff, "Would They Be Better Off in a Home?" *National Review* (5 March 1990), pp. 33–35.

chapter **6**

Politics and Social Welfare Policy

In spring 1993, the Louisiana State Legislature passed six laws granting legal protections and redress to adult survivors of childhood sexual abuse. This package of legislation was enacted largely through the efforts of Carolyn Evans, a graduate student in social work. Evans's field internship experience in a recovery center for survivors of sexual abuse had helped convince her that current policies were inadequate for dealing with the problem. The legislation she helped create and pass is a comprehensive package that broadens the definition of criminal sexual activity with minors and extends the time limit for reporting the crime. Instead of a limit of three years past the age of majority, survivors can now initiate prosecution up until the time they reach age twenty-eight. The legislation also allows survivors to sue for damages (which can compensate for money spent on therapy and for earnings lost due to emotional problems) and requires those convicted of abuse to participate in a sex offender treatment program.

The journey toward enactment of the child sexual abuse legislation began with Evans's exploration of the topic in a social work Independent Readings course. As she studied what remedies were available for individuals like those at the recovery center, she realized that Louisiana law provided inadequate protection for sexually abused children and little recourse for people who did not fully recognize what had happened to them until they were adults. She also discovered that some states had developed legislation to fill these gaps. Perhaps Louisiana could adopt similar laws. On the advice of a law student acquaintance, she took her research and her recommendations to a state senator who had a record of concern about family and children's issues. When he expressed an interest in her project, she "gingerly handed him" her eight-inch-thick stack of research findings. At his request, she also summarized the major items she felt ought to be in a protective package. He turned her work over to a legislative aide, who set the recommendations into several bills to submit to the legislature. This package of bills was essentially the same as the final legislation, with one exception: In the bills initially proposed, no time limit was put on when survivors had to report the abuse.

What followed was a complex process of testimony, lobbying, negotiation, and collaboration with other state legislators. It began with Senate committee hearings on the bills. In consultation with the senator and his staff, Evans and several other supporters attended the hearings and provided written testimony. As the hearings were being held, she also had the chance to attend a "legislative luncheon" sponsored by the state chapter of the National Association of Social Workers. This is a yearly affair held at the state capital, attended by legislators sympathetic to social work issues. Evans presented her concerns and her legislative goals to the group and was later approached by several women legislators who promised their support if the bills were sent by the committee to the floor of the legislature.

The first bill to come before a Senate committee, and one that Evans regarded as key, was the bill abolishing the statute of limitations for reporting child sexual abuse; in other words, no matter how late in life people realized they had been abused, they could still initiate prosecution of the alleged abusers. This policy, Evans reasoned, would not only help adult survivors but would also deter people from committing abuse in the first place. The senator presented the bill to the committee in a calm and matter-of-fact manner. He had already secured the support of the committee chair. The only objection raised at the hearing was voiced by a representative of the insurance industry, who argued that insurance companies might have to bear the costs of successful suits for damages (as those sued might try to use their homeowners policies to cover their fines.) With no time limit on initiating suits, many more could be filed. However, this argument was not taken seriously enough to prevent the bill from being reported out to the legislature.

The bill was then introduced on the Senate floor. The senator's presentation was again calm and low-key, aimed in part at dispelling the concerns of the insurance industry and predictions of a rash of false accusations. The problem was defined as the need "to protect our women and children from sexual abuse"; this appeal, made by a male legislator to a mostly male Senate (often skittish about what they saw as "feminist issues"), was successful. The bill passed unanimously and proceeded to the House.

"Now," the senator told Evans, "your work really begins." The State House of Representatives presented a formidable challenge because it contained many powerful and philosophically divided factions. This often led to intense, even rowdy debates in committees and on the floor. Buoyed by the bill's success in the Senate but nervous about its fate in the House, Evans took advantage of the short period before the House committee hearings to "learn the lay of the land." She spent time observing proceedings on the House floor, determining state representatives' interests from their speeches. With this understanding, she was able to approach legislators individually to explain the importance of the child sexual abuse bills. In each encounter, she tried to tailor her talk to their particular legislative concerns (a tactic known as partisan policy analysis, which we discussed in Chapter 3). She found all but one willing to discuss the issues. She was "surprised and touched at their treatment of me. I had expected them to treat me like a nuisance. Instead, they were courteous and listened carefully to what I had to say." Legislators, she learned, appreciated the chance to hear directly from someone at the "grassroots level" who had observed a problem firsthand.

When the lead bill was introduced in the House committee by its Senate sponsor, it faced more opposition than in the Senate. One particularly adamant woman legislator opposed the bill on the grounds that giving adults the chance to prosecute for sexual abuse they thought they had suffered as children would lead to "a witch hunt" of innocent individuals. Another committee member seemed amused by the issue. This would not be the first time that legislators demonstrated skepticism over the seriousness of the problems faced by survivors of sexual abuse.

In the same hearings, however, one of the women legislators who had earlier promised support spoke favorably about the bill; she was backed by several male legislators. Evans and her supporters sat ready to present testimony, but the senator was able to handle the objections successfully and the bill received enough support to be reported out.

Evans and the senator then had to find a representative who could introduce and defend the bill effectively in the House. The senator originally asked a member of the influential legislative Black Caucus to present the bill. When it turned out that he was unable to do so, Evans was fortunate in locating a legislator from New Orleans who had already proposed legislation similar to hers. Like the senator, this was a man with strong interests in issues involving women and children. A close rapport quickly developed between Evans and the representative and his aides, and he agreed to introduce the bill.

By now, with Evans's help, a coalition was beginning to build around the legislation. The group included the women legislators who had heard her presentation at the NASW luncheon. A human services lobbyist also offered her advice and support. Several social work students and faculty members sat with Evans in the House gallery, waiting for the bill to come up. As they waited, they wrote personal notes to each representative, asking him or her to support this important legislation.

The New Orleans representative presented the bill in a manner similar to that of the senator, stressing its importance as a protection against sexual abuse of children. This time, as in the House committee, debate was spirited. Representatives rose to proclaim the ridiculous nature of a bill that would allow "a sixty-year-old woman to sue her eighty-year-old father." The possibility of such lawsuits could "destroy the family." While some cried "witch hunt," others remained unconvinced of the seriousness of the issue or the need for legislation. Questions arose about the implications for the insurance industry. The representative fielded questions knowledgeably; other legislators argued in support; and Evans and her student/faculty companions wrote feverishly from the gallery, sending notes to lawmakers about the importance of the issue. In the end, the bill was defeated by one vote.

When the bill was defeated, arrangements were made immediately by the sponsoring representative to have it brought up again before the close of the legislative session. In the meantime, one of the supportive women legislators gave Evans a list of all the lawmakers who had voted no, with the directive "now you really have to work hard." Evans lobbied individually with each one, speaking with great conviction about the problems of child sexual abuse and its effects on survivors. As she did so, she discovered that the lack of a limit on reporting time was particularly troubling to lawmakers; most were amenable to a compromise of a ten-year time period for filing a suit. When the bill was reintroduced with this change, Evans found she had won over almost every negative vote. The bill passed 98 to 1.

The other bills in the legislative package proceeded through a similar process, but this time with much less debate. With the major concern over an unlimited time period for prosecution of alleged abusers resolved, most legislators felt able to support a broadened definition of sexual abuse, the right to sue for damages, and court-mandated treatment for those convicted of abuse. Within six months of its development, this student-inspired package of policies became state law.[1]

We tell this story not only as a lesson that policy changes can indeed stem from the vision and work of one individual uniting with others but primarily as an example of how policy making takes place within a political context. Perhaps this seems obvious, since we are using an example of law making, which you would expect to involve politics and politicians. Yet politics permeates policy making in all areas, including social work agency regulations, personnel policies of large organizations, court decisions, and urban planning projects. An important school of thought in political science and history holds that "politics—the facts of power, the relations of domination . . . insinuates itself in the [very] tissue of reality."[2] The argument is that power and politics are everywhere and cannot be isolated in the glass case of congressional or state legislative proceedings.

We use this particular case, however, because the development of child sexual abuse legislation in Louisiana nicely illustrates the role of politics in various stages of policy creation. It also demonstrates, in a particularly dramatic way, a social worker's involvement in the politics of policy. Although this example may be somewhat unusual, social workers are constantly involved in political life in more subtle ways, beginning with their relationships with clients and including their positions in organizations and communities.

The political context of policy is first seen in the politics of problem definition. We have noted the inclination of a legislative body to define the sexual abuse survivor issue as part of a "feminist agenda," an agenda that some see as trivial, radical, or even vindictive. In this situation, both the student and supportive lawmakers were careful to frame the problem primarily in terms of children and the need to protect them from abuse and its potential effects. This is a good example of the way power is involved in language and in the structuring of arguments.

Politics influences the second stage, the development of a proposed policy solution to the problem, in various ways. In this case, the student brought her initial research, including examples of laws in other states, to a legislator; he in turn had it translated into language appropriate for legislation. This was a situation in which existing legislation served as a guide for the policy. In other instances of policy making, the choice and shape of the proposed policy is generally hammered out through debate and compromise.

A third stage in policy development is the enactment or legitimization of a policy; the current example suggests the importance of lobbying, compromise, and other political tools in achieving this goal. The power and interests of the various legislators and lobbies helped dictate what kind of legislation could be passed. Two other stages, which we did not touch on in this particular example but which are nonetheless of great importance, consist of the implementation and the evaluation of policy. Policy evaluation has already been discussed in Chapter 3. We will see later how politics affects the implementation stage.

Finally, our example of child abuse legislation indicates that each step in policy development involves a number of political players. In this case, they included advocates (the student and her supporters), professionals (NASW members), and lawmakers who represented a variety of interests and constituencies (including insurance companies, parents, women concerned about issues of abuse and exploitation, attorneys, people worried about the strength of families, and the legislative Black Caucus). Political scientists call such people and groups *stakeholders*. Stakeholders are all the actors interested in and potentially affected by a policy, such as interest groups, public officials, individuals and their families, civil servants, businesses and corporations, professional organizations, and labor unions. Important stakeholders in social welfare policy include the beneficiaries of those policies, such as public welfare recipients or people receiving Social Security checks. Each group has particular assumptions and concerns regarding policies and the problems to which they are intended to respond. As we will see, stakeholders play a major role in each of the stages of policy development.

This chapter aims at helping you understand the politics of policy making. It does this within a larger discussion of *process analysis* of policies. Process analysis looks at the development, enactment, and implementation of policies. All of these areas are influenced by politics in its broadest sense, not just the formal politics of the legislative process.

The chapter begins with an introduction to ideas about the political context of policy making. It then describes and critiques various models of policy development and social change. Finally, it examines political factors as they come into play during the various stages of the policy process: problem definition, the framing of policy solutions, policy enactment, and implementation.

The Politics of Policy Making

Politics is one of those words that is used often and with confidence, yet it is rarely defined in a concise manner. The *Random House Dictionary*, for example, gives a circular definition of *politics* as the practice of conducting political affairs. Perhaps the best single statement for our purposes is the general one that "politics has to do with who gets what, when, and how." As Talcott Parsons elaborates, the polity (or government) of a society is the organization of different collectivities for the purpose of attaining their goals. The political process, Parsons notes, "is the process by which the necessary organization is built up and operated, the goals of action are determined and the resources requisite to it are mobilized."[3] So politics is about how groups organize to try to get their needs met and to achieve their goals. Power is a central component of this activity.

The meaning of power has long been a subject of debate among philosophers, political theorists, and others. Many definitions have been offered. Robert Dahl, a political scientist, calls power the control of behavior, in which *A* gets *B* to do something that *B* would not otherwise do. Power has also been described as the ability to influence people through physical force, rewards or punishments, or propaganda and similar ways of shaping opinions. Power has been seen as being an attribute of individuals, or of groups, or of economic classes—or of all three.[4]

A number of theorists have pointed out the interactive nature of power, arguing that the dominated individual or group invests the dominant person with power. As philosopher Hannah Arendt explains, the person "in power" is put there, or empowered, by others. Stated another way, the power of command does not exist unless others accept the commander's authority. College students, for example, generally concede to professors the power to give out grades—even when these might not be the grades they would like. When power is not accepted or is not accorded to the powerful, people may not obey the commands. It has been argued that the common reaction of the powerful—coercion, violence—is no longer power but a way of responding when power has been lost.[5] The view of power as a relationship should make you think of the various ways in which those exercising power achieve their credibility or legitimacy, including position in an organization or government (CEO, chairperson, elected official), possession of specialized skills or knowledge (engineer, teacher, social worker, physician), or tradition and authority ("kings have always been obeyed").

Most of these conceptions of power have focused on powerful individuals or groups and their effects on those they dominate. Michel Foucault has developed a much broader view of power as something that circulates through society and is never in just one person's hands.[6] Foucault was a French philosopher whose works on power and the nature of knowledge have had a strong influence on political science, history, and other disciplines over the past thirty years. Foucault faulted modern political theorists for their reliance on an idea of power stemming from the development of an absolute monarchy in Europe from the Middle Ages through the sixteenth century. Power, Foucault reasoned, is no longer constituted in the relationship between a king and his subjects, a relationship that stressed laws, limits, and obedience. Although the modern state has assumed some of the power of the king, modern relations of power extend beyond the limits of the state. The state lacks total control and instead operates on the basis of already existing power relations. These power relations go beyond laws and are embodied in families, institutions, organizations, and bureaucracy.

In his examination of institutions such as the prison and the insane asylum, Foucault focused on the mechanics of power—the small-scale, immediate points at which power is carried out.[7] He came to think of power in terms of a universal surveillance, in which people are kept under constant scrutiny. In the prison and the mental institution, for example, doctors, wardens, chaplains, psychiatrists, and social workers possess the power to discipline, supervise, and socialize people into meeting "normal" expectations of behavior. This new kind of power, Foucault concluded, is everywhere.

The preceding paragraph presents only a few generalizations from a vast and complex body of work. But it points to at least two themes that are useful to think about: the universality of power and the shape it takes in the bureaucracies and institutions in which social workers are often employed. And though the lesson may seem depressing, Foucault points out that "there is . . . always something which in some way escapes the relations of power; something in the social body [and] in the individuals themselves which is not . . . reactive raw material . . . which responds to every advance of power by a movement to disengage itself."[8] Furthermore, Foucault saw a role to be played by intellectuals or professionals who join in the "everyday struggles" of those with little power at "the precise point where their own conditions of life or work situate them (housing, the hospital, the asylum, the laboratory, the university . . .)." Foucault's list of intellectuals included social workers.[9]

Other writers have also spoken about the positive aspects of power and particularly about the possibility that power is not a finite substance but one that can be multiplied. For example, when public officials create democratic institutions, they may fear losing power, but in fact by widening the circle of decision making they are increasing the power that circulates throughout the community. The discussion of social change and empowerment later in this chapter gives insight into the potential of sharing power rather than being bound up in a system with the powerful on one side and the powerless on the other.[10]

Models of Policy Making

Although there is universal agreement that policy making is a political process, there is a lively debate as to how this process works. The debate centers on the interrelated questions of who makes policy and how are policies made.

Who Makes Policy?

In light of the preceding discussion, this question concerns which individuals and groups have the power to get *their* policy goals, rather than the policy goals of others, adopted. The most important theories regarding this question are referred to as pluralism, public choice, and elitism.

Pluralism

Traditionally, political scientists have depicted policy as the output of government institutions. The study of policy therefore consisted of the study of governments and what they do. More recently, political scientists have developed other models of policy or decision making that introduce additional actors to the scene. One of the major models, established by Robert Dahl, Nelson Polsby, and others in the 1950s and 1960s, is the pluralist approach. Still a major approach to policy study in the United States, pluralism assumes a sort of "marketplace of ideas," in which numerous groups and interests compete for power and influence in making policy. Individuals are able to participate in decision making through membership in organized groups. These groups have relatively equal power. Some groups may have more power over particular issues than others, but the essential assumption in pluralism is that all voices will be heard. Power is widely diffused rather than centralized. A pluralist description of the development of health care reform would visualize physicians, allied health professionals, hospitals, insurance companies, businesses, labor unions, health reform advocates, and consumers joining in the debate over health care and each having some say in its resolution.[11]

The pluralist model has been subjected to important critiques. One of the most potent is the argument that not every voice manages to make it to the debate. Certain powerful persons and groups can prevent those with threatening or opposing ideas from reaching an audience and presenting their ideas in public. Those in power may manipulate existing values or use institutional procedures to stifle demands before they get to the relevant decision-making arena. For example, branding a policy proposal as "socialistic" (which happens regularly when people propose a national health care system for the United States like that in England or Scandinavia) is an effective way to discredit the proposal and prevent any serious discussion. Organizational rules can also be manipulated to suppress challenges to the interests of powerful decision makers.[12] In a case study of the difficulties faced by poor coal miners in Appalachia, John Gaventa tells how a group of miners and their families appealed to a state regulatory agency to deny a permit to a strip mine operator who planned to work close to their homes. To thwart their efforts, a state official mailed them information on the appeals process *after* the permit had been granted.[13]

Political scientist Robert Salisbury offers another example of the uneven playing field for political voices. In describing the attempts of various groups to influence public policy in Washington, Salisbury differentiates between interest-based groups with *personal* membership, such as consumer organizations that advocate for health care reform, and *institutions*, such as hospitals and insurance companies, that also seek to influence the reform process. Salisbury observes that institutions have long-time concerns, often with a variety of policies; these concerns tend to be represented by lobbyists. Institutions generally have more resources than interest groups to devote to policy making. They also have less obligation to consult with people other than top management in making decisions about policy issues. Membership groups, on the other hand, "must look far more carefully to the desires of their members, both to assure political legitimacy and to keep their supporters happy." Because of these factors, Salisbury notes, large institutions have come to dominate interest representation in the federal government.[14]

This critique of pluralism focuses both on who gets what—and how—and who gets left out—and how.[15] Powerful people are said to control the agenda of public discussion and to limit such discussion to relatively unimportant topics. Truly important topics are reserved for private negotiations among only those groups with the required power and influence. One might see this in a private psychiatric hospital for adolescents in which staff members try to raise the question of why patients get discharged when their private insurance runs out and get firmly redirected to what they "ought to be concerned with"—perfecting their therapeutic techniques.

Public Choice Theory

A somewhat different version of the pluralist model is public choice theory, which brings an economic dimension to the discussion. The traditional economist's view of marketplace behavior stresses individuals pursuing their own private interests. Public choice theorists apply this notion to the political arena and assume "that all political actors—voters, taxpayers, candidates, legislators, bureaucrats, interest groups, parties, bureaucracies, and governments—seek to maximize their personal benefits in politics as well." Public choice theorists offer a useful discussion of the separate interests of voters, politicians, and bureaucrats, explaining that the interests of politicians and bureaucrats are to win elections and to expand their power. Voters, in turn, are often concerned with how policies will affect them and what benefits they will receive.[16] This understanding of the difference in goals between public officials and voters will be helpful when we talk about policy development and implementation.

Elitist Model

The elitist model of policy development and social change contrasts with the pluralist approach. Rather than conceptualizing policy as the product of a multitude of groups and interests, this model sees it as reflecting the goals of an elite group of individuals—or what C. Wright Mills called the "power elite." The power elite represents the interests of wealthy citizens and the leaders of corporations and military institutions. It may also include the leaders of well-financed interest groups. Sometimes, the division between the powerful and the powerless is depicted as a class struggle between capitalists and workers. In the elite model, people on the lower rungs of society are viewed as powerless and therefore apathetic; even if they had strong opinions, they would rarely have the resources to organize as interest groups. As Thomas Dye notes, "Policies flow 'downward' from elites to masses; they do not arise from mass demands."[17]

In his study of Appalachian coal miners, Gaventa gives a vivid picture of the control exercised by a large mining company over a several-county area. Company men held offices in local government, miners lived in company houses and had to buy supplies at company stores, and the company hired the people who taught in the schools. Control was so thorough and far-reaching that miners in that area rarely protested low wages or dangerous working conditions. As Gaventa observes, the elite used their power "for the development and maintenance of the quiescence of the non-elite."[18]

Although the pluralist and elitist models seem at opposite ends of the spectrum, it is possible that both can be useful in analysis of policies. Perhaps each side is correct, depending on the situation. In the case of certain foreign policies, for example, some interests and groups—the leaders of the armed forces, the defense industry, and certain government officials and business interests, such as large oil companies—have between them enough power to make the crucial decisions. Yet in other cases, such as policy to protect the rights of those with disabilities, many different and opposing groups can enter fairly equally into the debate.[19]

How Are Policies Made?

The models described in the previous paragraphs focus on *who* makes policy or influences social change. The remaining models seek to address the issue of *how* change comes about. Major theories include rational decision making, incrementalism, and conflict theory.

Rational Decision Making

The rational decision-making approach presents this process in a nice, neat package: Concern over an unmet need or social problem leads to development of first informal and then formal groups of concerned persons, who gather information about the problem. These organized groups develop general policy solutions and lobby for change. Decision makers review the range of existing and proposed policies, identify all the relevant social goals and values, and study the consequences of each policy alternative. On the basis of all this information, an operational policy is then formulated, enacted, and, finally, carried out.[20] The rational decision-making model views the policy process as occurring in a manner similar to the problem-solving approach used in social work practice.

Incrementalism

Many observers of policy development have questioned the seeming logic of the rational decision-making version of how policies come about. In the real world, they argue, policy making is messy. It is not just a simple matter of the problem driving forward the political process. Generally a problem becomes politically significant only when it is attached to a "politically imaginable solution."[21] For example, in the Middle Ages, poverty seemed an unchangeable fact of life. It was only when governments and economies were more organized, and more capable of tackling the problem, that antipoverty policies began to develop.

One of the best-known alternatives to the rational decision-making model is presented by political scientist Charles Lindblom. Lindblom describes policy change as "an untidy process" rather than a neat series of steps. It is rarely possible for decision makers to review all policy alternatives and research their costs, benefits, and "fit" with social goals. In addition, the rational model does not take into account people's reluctance to undertake major change. Lindblom proposes an alternative model, the incremental approach, which views change as occurring in small steps, based on a series of compromises. Because rapid change can upset the status quo and shift the balance of power, policymakers tend to do the politically feasible—they propose incremental modifications and variations of existing policies and programs. Lindblom concludes: "Many policymakers . . . see policy making as a never-ending process in which continual nibbling substitutes for the good bite that may never be offered."[22] This model fits with the colloquial definition of politics as the "art of the possible." What is possible is generally a very small change from current policy, even if all rational logic and data indicate that a much larger change is called for. Rather than depicting policy development as rational decision making, Lindblom describes it as "muddling through."

Conflict Theory

Although Lindblom's formulation makes a lot of sense, it fails to explain why sudden and major change does occasionally occur. Conflict theorists attempt to deal with the difficult issue of how and why such change takes place. They stress the existence of conflicts and contradictions that are built into society. When these erupt, the result can be major changes in the system. Marxist social theorists describe these conflicts as occurring along class lines, between an oppressed working class and a dominant elite. When conflict builds, and its sources are recognized by those who are exploited, violent revolution can occur, as in Russia in 1917. However, change may also come through nonviolent means, as in Mahatma Gandhi's movement for independence in India.

Some conflict theorists use a political economy perspective. This perspective focuses on political policies and economic processes, on the relations between the two, and on their mutual influence on social institutions such as the family and social welfare. The political economy approach is essentially an offshoot of Marxism, adding a political and social dimension to Marx's stress on class struggle. Feminist writers have used a political economy perspective to describe what they see as the oppression of working women. They assert that under a capitalist system, men have the power to control women's labor both in the home and in the labor market, where women face occupational sex segregation in the form of less prestigious and lower-paying jobs. They also argue that welfare policy has been used to reinforce a whole social system of women's subordinance.[23]

Policy analysts don't often talk about revolution (there are relatively few references to oppression, conflict theory, or political class struggle in standard policy texts).[24] However, U.S. history yields a few examples of policy changes that were influenced, at least to some degree, by antagonism between oppressed and dominant groups. Franklin Roosevelt's New Deal programs after 1935 were justified in part by a rhetoric focusing on political conflict—the people against elite economic groups. The Community Action initiative of Lyndon Johnson's Great Society included a clause mandating the "maximum feasible participation of the poor" in program development, which had the potential of giving people at the bottom rung of the economic ladder some power in making policies. An understanding of conflict theory is helpful in examining these policy developments as well as responses to the student uprisings and the revolts in the African American ghetto in the 1960s.

As in the relationship between pluralism and elite theory, the incremental and conflict models of policy development, although often contradictory, might each be seen as useful in explaining particular instances of social change. Conflict theory helps us to understand periodic occurrences of large-scale structural change, whereas incrementalism sheds light on a society's ongoing policy shifts.

During the 1960s, social workers talked much more about broad-scale social change than they do today. Awareness of the problems of oppression and powerlessness took a different shape starting in the 1990s, emerging in a stress on "empowerment." This can be defined as "a process of increasing personal, interpersonal, or political power so that individuals can take action to improve their life situation."[25] It can include a union organizer's attempt to bring people together in groups to push for better working conditions and a school social worker's commitment to helping parents gain more say in school policies. There has been a tendency lately to turn *empowerment* into a buzzword and to use it so widely that the original strength of the concept has been lost. Social workers and others have equated empowerment variously with peer counseling, a focus on client strengths, and enhancing people's self-concepts—all worthwhile endeavors but none capturing the significant power gains implied by the concept. The ultimate in misleading and superficial uses of the term is a billboard (seen by one of the authors) in which a large hospital advertised itself as "The Place Where Empowerment Begins." A complex and powerful hospital setting is one of the last places one would expect people to develop control over their lives.

Nevertheless, empowerment can be an important goal for social workers as they seek to gain more control over their own lives and to assist clients in doing the same. Once people who feel powerless achieve some success in this attempt, they tend to increase their activity in political and other areas. They become involved in an active, self-creative process in which "they are able to do things collectively that they could not have done alone."[26]

Phases in the Policy Process

Having discussed broad ways of thinking about policy development, we now move to a more concrete description of how policies come about. At the risk of sounding like the rational decision-making school of policy development (whose sense of precision does not seem to us to accurately reflect the policy process), we have organized the following discussion in terms of separate phases. This is simpler and easier to follow than a portrayal of several steps in policy making going on at the same time. However, in reading this section, you should bear in mind that these different parts of the policy process frequently overlap.

Problem Definition

All policies relate to some sort of perceived problem or issue. How does this issue or problem get defined? For whom does it represent a difficulty? In Chapter 5, we discussed some of the social aspects of problem definition. Here, we need to look at the political dimension by explaining the role of stakeholders in problem definition and discussing the ways in which definitions get publicized and accepted by a broad audience.

Heffernan describes problem definition as arousing the passion of stakeholders. "From a political perspective," he notes, "a problem is one that touches a significant number of people or a number of significant people and about which a case has been made that a change by the government [or a nongovernmental organization] will improve things."[27] Social problems are defined by particular individuals and groups, and acceptance of these definitions by society is based largely on the power of the definers. For example, the rapid rise of Mexican immigration to the United States in the last few years has become an increasingly contentious issue among politicians and elected officials at the local, state, and national levels, as well as among employers, immigrant rights organizations, anti-immigrant groups, social agencies, law enforcement personnel, and the general public. Each of these groups, along with the newcomers themselves, has played a role in defining the problems and issues of today's immigration. However, as in the example at the beginning of this chapter, some stakeholder groups have had more influence and power than others in that definition and in developing responses and "solutions" related to the latest wave of immigrants.

The number of Mexican immigrants arriving in the United States has been rising rapidly in recent years. Almost all of these are considered "illegal" or unauthorized immigrants because they have not gone through a legal process that would eventually lead to U.S. citizenship. As we will explain later, however, that process is not open to every foreigner who wishes to live here.

For residents of Mexico, coming to the United States generally means making their way across the Mexican–American border, often by foot, through the states of Texas, New Mexico, Arizona, or California. Most come through Arizona's 390-mile border, much of which is desert. Although Mexicans constitute the largest group crossing the border, unauthorized individuals from other South American countries and even countries such as Korea cross there as well. Once the immigrants make the crossing, they disperse to various parts of the country. Some stay in Arizona, but others fan out to a number of other states, including California, Texas, Florida, New York, New Jersey, Illinois, and North Carolina. Although it is hard to calculate how many Mexican immigrants cross the border, we do know that there were about six million unauthorized Mexican immigrants living in the United States in March, 2004. Altogether, unauthorized and authorized Mexicans make up 30 percent of all immigrants in the United States. Almost 80 percent of unauthorized immigrants coming here in 2005 were from Latin America, and 56 percent of those were from Mexico.[28]

Coming to the United States from Mexico can be very dangerous. Many immigrants are brought through the desert by immigrant smugglers, or "coyotes," who charge fees to guide people to the United States. Fees for bringing an individual across can be as high as $800 to $1800. Sometimes the immigrants are locked into crowded and dirty drop houses, with limited bathroom and bathing facilities, until the fees are paid. Immigrants can also be abused while crossing the desert. Women are often raped. Sometimes pregnant women make the crossing. Lilia Ortiz tells the story of being in a group that included an eighteen-year-old woman who went into labor during the crossing. The smuggler and other migrants disappeared when the mother screamed with labor pains. Ortiz, who had a child of her own, delivered the baby and snipped the mother's umbilical cord with nail clippers. The women were apprehended by the U.S. Border Control, which sent the mother to a hospital in Tucson, where she and the baby were treated. Mother and baby were then sent back to Mexico. So was Ortiz, who went to a shelter in Nogales. She intends to try the crossing again, in hopes of a better life for her own daughter, who lives with an aunt in Mexico.[29]

Why do people emigrate from Mexico? By and large, they are driven by the lack of jobs, low wages in available jobs, and poverty in Mexico. Jesus Alonzo Camacho, age forty-four, came through the New Mexico border with six other men because "We can't support ourselves at home; we need the money from the other side." In Mexico, they made about $6 a day working in the fields. His plan was to walk north until he found someone who would give him work. "Anyone," he said. "Anywhere."[30]

Although the migration is predominately male, with immigrants sending money home to their families, women and children also come. Often fathers come to join their families that are already living here. Nearly two-thirds of their children are born in the United States. These children are automatically U.S. citizens.[31]

A recent study by the Pew Hispanic Center found that 38 percent of recent immigrants were high school graduates or had some junior college or even university education, compared to 27 percent of those who came fifteen years ago. Once they arrive, they quickly find jobs working in agriculture, factories, construction sites, and in retail stores. Whatever their education levels, most work in low wage occupations. A much higher percentage of men work than women. About 20 percent of unauthorized workers work in construction (as opposed to 6 percent of native workers), 15 percent in "production, installation, and repair," and 4 percent in farming. The largest percentage (31 percent) are in the service occupations, including restaurant and hotel work. In Phoenix and other areas of the Southwest, immigrant men are particularly visible as lawn and garden crews, immigrant women as cleaners of people's homes. In Iowa, many work in the meatpacking plants. In North Carolina, they slaughter hogs. A community of Mexicans has even been established in the chilly state of Minnesota, where immigrants work in landscaping and the food industry. In addition to involvement in these occupations, 10 percent of unauthorized workers are in management, business, and professional positions.[32]

Immigrants and their families often live in poorer city neighborhoods with a high concentration of Hispanics, often called *barrios*. Others, particularly in border areas such as Tucson, live in *colonias*—separate settlements such as the Old Nogales Highway Colonia, a cluster of manufactured homes "plopped down in a desert area with dirt roads, no sewer or water lines, sidewalks, or streetlights." Since the community is in a floodplain, on some rainy, muddy days, children can't get out to school and parents can't go to work. However, when they can, many Hispanics move out of ethnic communities into areas with quiet streets and good schools. In Arizona, about 54 percent of Latinos lived in non-Hispanic neighborhoods in 2000. These residents are mostly bilingual and English speakers, "with higher incomes and lower poverty rates than Latinos living in ethnic enclaves." This has been the classic pattern for immigrants to the United States over the last hundred years or so.[33]

Employers are another major stakeholder group. According to one analyst, "employers feel very strongly about maintaining access to immigrant workers." Wal-Mart was recently found to have hired undocumented immigrants to clean floors at stores in twenty-one states. Landscapers, construction companies, restaurants, and other businesses often hire unauthorized workers in their businesses.

Farmers need people to work in the fields. Ed Curry, who grows chiles on a large farm, hires undocumented workers during the harvest season. This year, because of border patrols, he has only about 60 workers instead of his usual 120. He is now three weeks behind schedule for his harvest. In another example, construction booms in Long Island, New York, have created a strong need for more workers, many of whom are undocumented immigrants.[34]

Thus, because of worker shortages, many employers support laws that would allow those who cross the border to work legally in the United States. Kevin Rogers, president of the Arizona Farm Bureau and a fourth-generation farmer says, "The reality is we need access to foreign pools of labor within a legal system. . . . Without access to foreign labor, we are quite literally out of business." Putting it more colorfully, the owner of a plant nursery in Phoenix says that without access to immigrant workers "we'd be screwed."[35]

In 2004, legislation was proposed in Arizona to "crack down" on employers of the undocumented. The bill would have suspended the business licenses or permits of those employers who hired undocumented workers. Many business owners were understandably upset. Although the bill did not become law, a spokesman for the Arizona Chamber of Commerce described the potential effect on his own business: "It would be the equivalent of a death sentence." The bill failed, and similar legislation the following year, which would have included a requirement that business owners certify the citizenship status of their workers, met the same fate. However, the state legislature has not given up on the issue, and by spring of 2006, Arizona's business community appeared resigned that the state would impose penalties against those businesses who hired undocumented immigrants.[36]

Immigrant workers obviously have a major stake in the type of work they do, what they are paid, and the quality of their work environment. Often all of these areas are problematic. First of all, the workplace can be a dangerous place for unauthorized immigrants. One reporter noted that the workplace is deadlier for Mexican workers. A nationwide study found an especially high level of injuries among immigrant day laborers. Death rates for Mexican immigrants as a whole (not just day laborers) are higher than those of U.S.-born workers in southern and western states. In those states, a Mexican worker is four times as likely to die while working than the average U.S. worker. Sometimes this is because employers fail to follow basic safety rules. Such rules were ignored when eighteen-year-old Carlos Huerta fell to his death while building low-income housing in North Carolina. His bosses put him in a trash container that wasn't firmly attached to a forklift. It soon toppled, taking Huerta with it.[37]

Immigrant employees also face wage violations. Employers sometimes don't pay them on time. In a recent survey of day laborers, more than half of the respondents reported that employers had "cheated them" on wages in the previous two months. Those who conducted the survey were particularly surprised by the "pervasiveness of wage violations and dangerous conditions that day laborers faced."[38]

The founders and staff of day labor centers are another important group of stakeholders. These centers were developed to respond to the following difficulties faced by laborers, as well as to concerns of the general population. People who are hired for day labor don't sit at home waiting for a phone call from an employer. They stand out by the street or in the parking lots of Home Depot and other businesses, waiting for contractors, people who run gardening businesses, and other potential employers to stop, pick them up, and take them to a worksite for the day. As you can imagine, people shopping at Home Depot, Home Depot personnel, and folks living near an informal pick-up station are none too happy to have a group of workers standing around their homes and businesses. Laborers on the street had little access to bathrooms, occasionally trampled grass, and sometimes left food wrappers and cups around (although we should note that often there were insufficient trash cans for them to use). The idea of day labor centers is to provide a clean and organized place where workers can wait and be matched up with employers. As an example, the tax-funded Macehualli Work Center in the Scottsdale area of Phoenix was created at the request of area businesses and residents "to give workers a safe place to wait for day work" and to eliminate the problems of workers standing by the street. The center has a raffle system to determine who will get jobs that day. Coordinators draw ten tickets so ten people are always available for work. Potential employers come to the center and negotiate for painters, landscapers, and other workers. One Scottsdale resident frequently hires workers to paint her house or lay bricks. She says she feels safe, "like the people have been screened. . . . I would rather help people like this, and I don't feel I'm getting ripped off." While workers wait, they have access to bathrooms and food, and play games and sing.[39]

Other stakeholders in the immigration issue include advocacy groups, social agencies and anti-immigrant groups, human service professionals, the general public, and politicians and legislators. The National Council of La Raza, for example, was originally inspired by Cesar Chavez's work in organizing Mexican agricultural workers in California. La Raza, which has $90 billion in assets, concentrates on "giving a voice to Hispanics in urban areas." The League of United Latin American Citizens (LULAC) promotes education, organizes political forums, and advocates for immigrant communities. There are also local groups, such as the Workplace Project in Long Island, which advocates for better working conditions for day laborers.[40]

Social agencies and social workers are also involved in the immigration issue. Chicanos por La Causa is a large agency in Arizona, with branches in Phoenix and other communities. It offers Mexican immigrants help with housing and employment and also provides counseling and other social services. The organization recently established a loan program through its credit union, which allows newcomers who are not eligible for a Social Security number but have other forms of legally acceptable identification to apply for loans. The Friendly House, a settlement house/community center in Phoenix, was originally established in the 1920s to work with a growing Mexican community. Now, as it did then, the settlement offers English classes, financial literacy services, and help with immigrant children in school. Both of these agencies hire social workers. Social workers also work with immigrants in child welfare, schools, hospitals, and other settings.[41]

The National Association of Social Workers, at the national and state levels, has also promoted better understanding and responses to the needs and issues of Mexican immigrants. In the words of Dr. Ann Nichols, a social work professor at the Tucson branch of the Arizona State University School of Social Work, "There is a small group of people who believe all of our social problems are caused by illegal immigrants.... They believe that immigrants are 'draining' our money from education and social welfare, and they cause crime and that we need to somehow stem this tide of illegal immigration." Nichols believes that "U.S. policy has to change in order to address the problem.... Until and unless we do something about promoting economic development in Mexico and allowing a more reasonable policy, we're going to continue to have these problems."[42]

Groups opposing immigration are also a part of the picture. Most visible are the vigilante groups that come to the border to harass immigrants and try to prevent them from crossing. Chris Simcox is head of the Minuteman Civil Defense Corps, which has "armed 'citizen' border patrols in Arizona, California, New Mexico, and Texas." Members of these patrols carry guns and stand near the official border control agents. Krysten Sinema, a social worker who is a member of the Arizona State House of Representatives, describes the Minutemen and other vigilantes standing in front of incoming migrants and brandishing guns in their faces. Sinema is part of a group of people who go to the border regularly to "bear witness" to the situation.[43]

Finally, members of the public are also stakeholders. Polls of public opinion on the issue bring mixed results. One national poll found that people saw immigration as a growing concern, and another that immigrants were a burden. Yet a third poll reported that most Americans would let immigrants stay in the country.[44]

As you know, much legislation has been proposed at the national and state levels to deal with immigration issues. A chronicle of this legislation from 2004 is a daunting task and would add even more pages to this chapter. Legislation at the state and federal level has focused on such "remedies" as building a permanent wall across the border, increasing the numbers of federal troops and state border forces patrolling the barrier, penalizing businesses that hire migrants, making English the country's official language, and, in Arizona, requiring that all voters in state elections show official identification at the polls. This law was put in place to assuage the fears of some people and groups in Arizona that large numbers of immigrants were voting in these elections.[45]

Federal bills have included a "Border Terrorism and Illegal Immigration Control Act" that called for 700 miles of fencing along the border, imposing sanctions on those assisting or hiring undocumented immigrants, and declaring undocumented felons. Another bill proposed blocking states from issuing standard drivers licenses to illegal immigrants and making it easier for judges to expel people seeking asylum (which is a specific category of immigrant status that has long been honored in the United States).[46]

Probably the most controversial proposal in the U.S. Congress so far is the idea of creating a guest worker program which includes what some term an "amnesty provision" for immigrants already living here. Such a program was first presented by President George W. Bush, who has a sympathy regarding the situation of Mexican immigrants, no doubt based on his closeness to the issue in his home state of Texas. But although at least one poll showed over 75 percent of Americans favoring a guest worker plan, dissension within Congress made it impossible to develop and pass a compromise bill by spring 2006.

A widely accepted policy regarding a fair and realistic approach to "illegal" immigration has yet to be found, although no doubt federal lawmakers and other groups are still working behind the scenes on a reasonable solution acceptable to lawmakers and the various stakeholders who elect them. In the meantime, new legislative proposals have sent immigrants and their supporters to the streets to protest against immigration restrictions. They were particularly incensed by a bill passed by the House of Representatives (but not heard in the Senate before both branches of Congress went into a two-week recess) that would speed up deportations, tighten border security, and criminalize illegal immigrants. On April 10, 2006, huge numbers of immigrants, their employers, and other supporters rallied in Washington, New York, Los Angeles, Phoenix, and other cities. In Phoenix, where about 50,000 people were expected to march, well over 100,000 people marched through city streets to a rally near the state capitol. Among them were immigrants and their families (with small children pulled in wagons and pushed in strollers), representatives of immigration rights groups and labor unions, church groups, social workers (including one of the authors of this text), and other professionals. The headline of the article on the first page of the *Arizona Republic* read "March of Strength, Over 100,000 Rally in Phoenix for Immigration Reform." This was by far the largest march in Phoenix history.[47]

By now you have probably realized just how complex the immigration issue is, with its large number of stakeholders. All of these stakeholders participate in some way in defining the problem and potential solutions.

Legitimation

In this phase, a generally formalized policy solution or set of solutions is formally enacted or legitimized. In the process, the proposed policy receives further refinement and definition, largely through negotiation and compromise. Individuals and groups seek to influence the decision makers in the final shaping of policy. This often occurs through the formation of coalitions, as in the child sexual abuse legislation. As public choice theory suggests, the personal agendas of policymakers, including reelection or reappointment considerations, come into play along with concern for other stakeholders and for the public interest. After the final details of the policy are decided—for example, how much will be budgeted for a particular program or initiative and which organizations or departments will carry it out—the policy is enacted through the legislative process or other legitimizing procedure.

Ironically, although one would expect this last phase of policy making to stress the practical aspects of how the policy will be implemented, frequently these details are not given the attention they deserve. The need to respond quickly to demands to "deal with the problem" often takes precedence over figuring out whether the proposed solution can be successfully carried out.

The policy legitimation process is essentially the same for agency policies as it is for federal or state legislation. Suppose that in a family and children's counseling center, for example, the issue of providing evening hours to accommodate the schedules of working parents is raised. A group of newer staff members has proposed the change, based on feedback from clients. They suggest the agency curtail some of its daytime hours in order to accommodate the new system. Some of the senior staff, long accustomed to daytime work, oppose the idea. Each group has developed its position and presented it in staff meetings. The agency administrator is highly sensitive to public perceptions of her organization, which affect both funding and also her reputation as an agency head. She appears to be leaning toward establishing evening hours in order to show the agency's sensitivity to client needs. The opposing staff members, seeing the writing on the wall, start talking to the other workers about limiting these hours to two nights a week and rotating them among all agency personnel. Because neither the newer staff nor the administrator relish the idea of a disgruntled group of senior workers, the compromise seems reasonable. After consulting with workers at the agency's weekly staff meeting, the administrator proposes a policy of Monday and Wednesday night hours to the board of directors. They concur and the policy is made official.

Policy Implementation

The final stage of policy making is called implementation. Many people think that once a policy is enacted, the process of alleviating a problem is well under way and implementation is simply a matter of carrying out a clearly specified program or initiative. This is far from the truth. Policies on both the governmental and private levels are often broadly stated—long on mission and short on detail. The implementation phase is generally a time of filling in the detail through regulations, personnel procedures, program guidelines, and other specifications, all of which further shape the policy. This administrative process is often referred to as "secondary legislation." Heffernan describes it as a phase in which people "strive to translate abstract objectives and complex procedural rules to the street-level reality where the problems are encountered." Flynn observes that in both the government department and private agency, the details of implementation constitute the closest part of the policy world for social work practitioners. Here are the memos, manuals, rules, and verbal directives to which workers must respond. It is also an important area for worker discretion and influence.[48]

There are political as well as organizational aspects to the implementation of the programs or actions called for in a policy. Sometimes the politicians or officials who enacted a policy do not really want it carried out; their activity was intended to convey attention to a problem, and they may care less that the proposed solution is actually implemented. Often the proposed approach is impractical, complicated, or capable of creating hardships that could eventually lead to negative publicity. For example, in the past, state legislators have created the appearance of cracking down on "welfare loafers" by passing legislation imposing stiff regulations that limited eligibility for benefits. Yet these same legislators sometimes looked the other way when state officials interpreted the regulations to allow for a number of exceptions. Even the strict federal welfare reform act of 1996 included certain exceptions. For example, although the legislation instituted a five-year lifetime limit on cash assistance, states are allowed to exempt 20 percent of their caseload from this limit.

Factors such as agency capabilities, such as worker skills and computer capacity, and agency resources, such as budget and staff size, also affect policy implementation. In addition, an agency's ideology may color the way in which a program or approach is set up and administered. Martha Derthick, who has written extensively on the administration of government programs, argues that a major problem in implementation is the lack of policymakers' attention to such agency characteristics. She contends that legislators and even presidents tend to attach low priority to administration and are often unable to foresee the administrative consequences of their policy choices. Presidents, particularly early in their terms of office, are often eager to bring about dramatic transformations in domestic policy. As they pursue the "big fix," they do not want to hear that the solution will take time and necessitate changes in organizational mission or structure. Members of Congress must also play to their constituencies and often have little time to attend to the details of administration. In our federal system of government, both the executive and legislative branches of government are supposed to give guidance to administrative agencies; this guidance is sometimes contradictory. Consequently, government agencies must work in an unpredictable environment, often with little concrete direction and with demands for immediate results.[49]

In the case of legislative responses to the issue of undocumented immigrants, no national legitimation of any proposal had been reached by May of 2006. The complexity and difficulty of the issue has helped lead to a hardening of stances on either side of the immigration issue, particularly in the U.S. Congress. Since lawmakers have been unable to resolve their differences, analysts are predicting that immigration is likely to be a huge issue in the 2008 presidential race.

The details of the implementation process can also be seen in an analysis of administration of a "quality assurance" program in a county social services agency in California. Concerns over high welfare costs in the late 1970s led many states to institute "quality control" systems aimed at reducing both client fraud and worker error in determining benefits. In California the state welfare system imposed a quality assurance program that involved a massive audit of the grant computation process. In the agency described here, the program succeeded in lowering error rates from 34 to 15 percent, although the side effects of its implementation included major shifts in the work of middle managers and problems with worker morale.

The state gave county offices leeway in the actual administration of the quality assurance initiative. In the particular office studied, the method selected for identifying errors in benefits was a continuous audit of the case records of all eligibility workers, to be carried out by their supervisors. Choice of this approach over analyzing a smaller sample of worker records and spending time on error prevention planning was due largely to the intense anxiety instilled by federal and state threats to limit the funding of "high error" offices. Long-range planning for error prevention took a backseat to the perceived need for masses of data that would impress the state office and let agency management and workers know immediately where they stood in terms of errors. In addition, top agency management decided to report the data separately for each of four eligibility divisions in the agency.

These administrative decisions led to two unanticipated consequences. First, supervisors found themselves devoting an inordinate amount of time to auditing records, often duplicating eligibility worker efforts by recomputing all their figures. Second, the reporting of error rates by division led to intense competition within the agency. The struggle to avoid being seen as the "worst division" undercut worker morale and diminished agency cohesion around common goals. The decision to use a quality assurance system for immediate error reports, in the expectation that this alone would "shock" workers into being more accurate, did in fact lower the error rates. But in addition to the reported side effects, this particular form of implementation of error control prevented planning for long-term error prevention approaches, such as improved worker training and lower case loads.[50] A more thoughtful implementation process might have brought about more meaningful and lasting change.

Conclusion

Using the issue of immigration as an example, this chapter has indicated the importance of political elements in all stages of the policy-making process, including problem definition, the proposal of a policy solution, and legitimatization of the policy. Even in the implementation phase, in which it appears that the major task is the technical one of transforming agreed-upon goals into action, political considerations come into play. Stakeholders such as elected officials, advocacy groups, social agencies, individuals and groups opposing the policy, members of the public, and the people to be affected by the policy all help to shape the implementation process and, ultimately, the policy itself. Successful policy creation, implementation, and revision thus demand an understanding of what's at stake, for whom, and why.

Notes

1. Karen Martin, "La. Can Thank Woman for Strides against Child Sexual Abuse," *Baton Rouge Sunday Advocate* (11 July 1993), p. 3H; Sally T. Kuzenski, "Social Work Student Guides Six Bills through Legislative Session," *LSU Today* (Louisiana State University News Service) (30 July 1993), pp. 1, 7; Interview with Carolyn Evans, December 9, 1993.

2. Charles Chatelet, "Recit," in Meaghan Morris and Paul Patton, Eds., *Michel Foucault: Power, Truth, Strategy* (Sydney, Australia: Feral Publications, 1979), p. 24.

3. A paraphrase of Harold Lasswell in Peter Bachrach and Morton S. Baratz, *Power and Poverty: Theory and Practice* (New York: Oxford University Press, 1970); Talcott Parsons, "Power and the Social System," in Steven Lukes, Ed., *Power* (New York: New York University Press, 1986), p. 96.

4. Robert Dahl, "Power as the Control of Behavior," pp. 37–58, and Steven Lukes, "Introduction," pp. 1–18, in Lukes, *Power.*

5. Bertrand Russell, "The Forms of Power," pp. 59–74, and Hannah Arendt, "Communicative Power," pp. 19–22, in Lukes, *Power.*

6. Michel Foucault, "Disciplinary Power and Subjection," in Lukes, *Power,* pp. 229–242.

7. "Truth and Power," interview with Michel Foucault by Alessandro Fontano and Pasquale Pasquino, in Morris and Patton, *Michel Foucault,* pp. 38–39; Charles Taylor, "Foucault on Freedom and Truth," in David Couzens Hoy, Ed., *Foucault: A Critical Reader* (Oxford, England: Basil Blackwell, 1986), pp. 74–77.

8. "Powers and Strategies," interview with Foucault by the Revoltes Logiques Collective, in Morris and Patton, *Michel Foucault,* p. 52.

9. "Truth and Power," in Morris and Patton, *Michel Foucault,* pp. 41–47.

10. We are indebted to Matt Leighninger for his contribution to this discussion.

11. Thomas R. Dye, *Understanding Public Policy,* 7th ed. (Englewood Cliffs, NJ: Prentice-Hall, 1992), pp. 21–23; B. Guy Peters, *American Public Policy: Promise and Performance,* 2nd ed. (Chatham, NJ: Chatham House, 1986), pp. 42–43.

12. Bachrach and Baratz, *Power and Poverty,* pp. 6–51.

13. John Gaventa, *Power and Powerlessness: Quiescence and Rebellion in an Appalachian Valley* (Urbana: University of Illinois Press, 1980), pp. 230–235.

14. Robert H. Salisbury, "Interest Representation: The Dominance of Institutions," *American Political Science Review* 78 (March 1984), pp. 64–76.

15. Bachrach and Baratz, *Power and Poverty,* p. 13.

16. Dye, *Understanding Public Policy,* pp. 39–42.

17. Bruce S. Jansson, *Becoming an Effective Policy Advocate: From Policy Practice to Social Justice,* 3rd ed. (Pacific Groves, CA: Brooks/Cole, 1999), pp. 278–279; Dye, *Understanding Public Policy,* p. 28.

18. Gaventa, *Power and Powerlessness,* p. 4.

19. Jansson, *Becoming an Effective Policy Advocate,* pp. 278–279.

20. Beth Huttman, *Introduction to Social Policy* (New York: McGraw-Hill, 1981), pp. 10–12; Dye, *Understanding Public Policy,* pp. 30–33.

21. Daniel T. Rodgers, *Atlantic Crossings: Social Politics in a Progressive Age* (Cambridge, MA: Belknap Press of Harvard University Press, 1998), p. 7.

22. Charles E. Lindblom, *The Policy-Making Process,* 2nd ed. (Englewood Cliffs, NJ: Prentice-Hall, 1980), pp. 4–5, 38.

23. Patricia Yancey Martin and Rosyln H. Chernesky, "Women's Prospects for Leadership in Social Welfare: A Political Economy Perspective," *Administration in Social Work* 13 (1989), pp. 118–119; Mimi Abramovitz, *Regulating the Lives of Women: Social Welfare Policy from Colonial Times to the Present* (Boston: South End Press, 1988); Barbara Nelson, "The Origins of the Two-Channel Welfare State: Workman's Compensation and Mothers' Aid," in Linda Gordon, Ed., *Women, the State, and Welfare* (Madison: University of Wisconsin Press, 1990), pp. 123–151; Linda Gordon, *Pitied but Not Entitled: Single Mothers and the History of Welfare* (New York: Free Press, 1994).

24. Notable exceptions to the neglect of conflict theory in analysis of policy include Frances Fox Piven and Richard A. Cloward (see *Regulating the Poor: The Functions of Public Welfare,* New York: Vintage, 1971); Theda Skocpol (e.g., *The Politics of Social Policy in the United States,* Margaret Weir, Ann Shola Orloff, and Theda Skocpol, Eds., Princeton, NJ: Princeton University Press, 1988, "Introduction," pp. 13–16); W. Joseph Heffernan, *Social Welfare Policy: A Research and Action Strategy* (New York: Longman, 1992); and Howard J. Karger and David Stoesz, *American Social Welfare Policy: A Pluralist Approach,* 2nd ed. (New York: Longman, 1994).

25. Lorraine Gutierrez, "Working with Women of Color: An Empowerment Perspective," *Social Work* 35 (1990), pp. 149–153. See also Steven P. Segal, Carol Silverman, and Tanya Temkin, "Empowerment and Self-Help Agency Practice for People with Mental Disabilities," *Social Work* 38 (1993), pp. 707–712.

26. Kathy Ferguson, *The Feminist Case against Bureaucracy* (Philadelphia: Temple University Press, 1984), p. 103. See also Frances Fox Piven and Richard A. Cloward, *Poor People's Movements: Why They Succeed, How They Fail* (New York: Vintage, 1979); and Lawrence Goodwyn, *Democratic Promise: The Populist Movement in America* (New York: Oxford University Press, 1976).

27. Heffernan, *Social Welfare Policy,* pp. 36–39.

28. Jeffrey S. Passel, "Unauthorized Migrants: Numbers and Characteristics," Pew Hispanic Center, online at www.pewhispanic.org, p. 4; John M. Broder, "Immigrants and the Economics of Hard Work," *New York Times* (2 April 2006), p. 3.

29. Daniel Gonzalez,"Prosecutors Go After Immigrant Smugglers," *The Arizona Republic* (5 September 2004), p. 1; "Woman Forgoes U.S. to Aid Laboring Migrant Mom," *The Tucson Citizen* (28 April 2006), p. 17; "An Awful Industry, Our Stand: We Can't Continue to Ignore Slave Trade in Migrants," *The Arizona Republic* (19 February 2004), p. B10.

30. Passel, "Unauthorized Migrants," p. 11; Passel, "Background Briefing Prepared for Task Force on Immigration and America's Future," Pew Hispanic Center, pp. 2–3, 17; "Immigrant Flow to U.S. to Increase," *Arizona Republic* (3 December 2005), p. 10; Kevin Sullivan, "Desperate Moves," *The Washington Post National Weekly Edition* (14–20 March 2005), p. 9.

31. Stephen Ohlemacher, "Families a Big Part of the Picture," *The Arizona Republic* (8 April 2006), p. 21.

32. Passel, "Background Briefing," pp. 23, 26–28; William Grimes, "In This Small Town in Iowa, the Future Speaks Spanish," *New York Times* (14 September 2005), p. B6; Lance Compa and Jamie Fellner, "Meatpacking's Human Toll," *Washington Post National Weekly Edition* (8–14 August 2005), p. 26; Eduardo Porter and Elisabeth Malkin, "Way North of the Border," *New York Times* (30 September 2005), pp. C1–2.

33. Susan Carroll, "Restricting 'Colonias,'" *The Arizona Republic* (23 January 2006), p. 1; Yvonne Wingett, "More Latinos Opting out of Barrios," *The Arizona Republic* (21 January 2005).

34. Eduardo Porter, "The Search for Illegal Immigrants Stops at the Workplace," *New York Times* (5 March 2006), p. 3; Chuck Bartels, "Wal-Mart Fined $11 Million," *The Arizona Republic* (19 March 2005), p. 6; Susan Carroll, "Who Will Work the Fields?" *The Arizona Republic* (3 November 2005), pp. 1, 20; Roben Farzad, "The Urban Migrants," *New York Times* (20 July 2005), p. C1.

35. Kevin Rogers, "Unskilled Labor," *The Arizona Republic* (18 March 2005), p. B7; Yvette Armendariz and Mary Jo Pitzl, "Crackdown Could Trigger Gap in Labor, Workers Say," *The Arizona Republic* (26 February 2006), p. D5.

36. Elvia Diaz, "Bills Worry Migrants, Employers," *The Arizona Republic* (18 February 2004), p. 1; Mary Jo Pitzl, "Businesses Accept Bill on Hiring," *The Arizona Republic* (23 April 2006), pp. D1, 7.

37. Justin Pritchard, "Workplace Deadlier for Mexican Workers," *The Arizona Republic* (14 March 2004), pp. 1, 12; Steven Greenhouse, "Broad Survey of Day Laborers Finds High Level of Injuries and Pay Violations" *New York Times* (22 January 2006), p. 17.

38. Steven Greenhouse, "Day-Labor Issue Widespread in U.S.," *The Arizona Republic* (22 January 2006), pp. 1,5.

39. Yvonne Wingett, "Day Labor Center Brings Calm," *The Arizona Republic* (5 June 2003), p. B1.

40. Thomas Crampton, "After 30 Years, Hispanic Leader is Retiring from Advocacy Group," *New York Times* (6 October 2005), p. 10; Yvonne Wingett "2 Lulac Leaders Toppled," *The Arizona Republic* (12 January 2005), p. B1; Patrick O'Gil Healy, "In This Corner, a Fighter for Immigrant Laborers," *New York Times* (1 March 2005), p. B4.

41. Yvette Armendariz, "Loan Program Helps Migrants," *The Arizona Republic* (22 August 2002), p. D1.

42. Lyn Stoesen, "Social Workers Fighting for Safe Borders," *NASW News* (February 2006), p. 4.

43. "The Little Prince," *Intelligence Report*, The Southern Poverty Law Center (Winter, 2005), pp. 21–24.

44. Marjorie Connelly, "In Polls, Illegal Immigrants Are Called a Burden," *New York Times* (1 April, 2006); Susan Carroll, "Most in Poll Would Let Immigrants Stay," *New York Times* (19 October 2005), pp. 1, 19.

45. Elvia Diaz, "Officials OK Prop. 200 Vote Rules," *The Arizona Republic* (18 August 2005), pp. B1, 2.

46. "Ask Your Senators to Support Comprehensive Immigration Reform," www.socialworkers.org/advocacy/alerts/2006/041206.asp; David D. Kirkpatrich, "House Passes Tightening of Laws on Immigration," *New York Times* (11 February 2005), p. A11.

47. Daniel Gonzalez, Mel Melendez, and Pat Flannery, "March of Strength: Over 100,000 Rally in Phoenix for Immigration Reform," *Arizona Republic* (11 April 2006), p. 1.

48. John P. Flynn, *Social Agency Policy: Analysis and Presentation for Community Practice*, 2nd ed. (Chicago: Nelson-Hall, 1992), p. 8; Robert Pruger, "The Good Bureaucrat," *Social Work* 18 (July 1973), pp. 26–40.

49. Martha Derthick, *Agency Under Stress: The Social Security Administration in American Government* (Washington, DC: Brookings Institution, 1990), pp. vii, 51–65, 68–92.

50. Leslie Leighninger and Erica Baum, "Is QA Amiss?" Unpublished study, School of Social Welfare, University of California at Berkeley, April 1977.

part

III

The Framework Applied

Regardless of how focused on individual practice a social worker is, he or she is often sharply brought back to the realization that practice occurs within a policy context and that practitioners will experience problems and provide inadequate services if they do not understand this context. Consider the following conversations the authors had with former students at an alumni gathering several years ago (names have been changed).

Samantha Bowen received her B.S.W. degree four years ago and works as a social worker in the Temporary Assistance to Needy Families (TANF) program in a large northern state. Sam told one of the authors:

> I've been working since graduation as a financial assistance social worker. I feel very confident of my social work skills in helping my clients problem solve. However, now that I'm considered a senior social worker in the county office I'm being called upon more and more often to do things like address civic groups about the Temporary Assistance to Needy Families (TANF) program; to serve on community committees and boards related to services to poor people; and I've just been assigned as the practice representative to my department's state office committee charged with the responsibility of monitoring the welfare reform plan in our state. My knowledge and expertise in social work practice is of little use to me in fulfilling these tasks. These tasks all require knowledge of laws, regulations, economics, program effectiveness, and stuff like that. After four years I'm beginning to realize that there is a lot about my job that I simply don't understand. Also, I'm really tired of people buttonholing me at a party, asking my opinion about this or that welfare program, and then looking at me like I'm some sort of a fool because I don't know much, if anything, about it.

Beth Stapleton reported on her job as a social worker with a large hospital:

I really love my job, particularly dealing with families in crisis. It is so exciting and so satisfying helping them sort out issues, come to grips with the reality of their situations, and make plans for managing in the future. I really feel good when I receive cards or visits from former clients who tell me that they didn't even know what a social worker was before their hospital experience, but that the presence of me and my colleagues was the thing that enabled them to survive the crisis. But it's so depressing that I may not be able to do this much longer. With all the health care reform proposals and the implementation of managed care, it looks like social workers are going to be relegated to doing discharge planning with no clinical work at all. I wish I had a better grip on where health care reform is going and how social workers will fit into it.

Janice Kozinski stood out from her colleagues at the reunion largely due to the fact that she arrived driving a Lexus GS 430 and was wearing a $600 suit. She told a group of classmates from the M.S.W. program:

Being a social worker doesn't mean you can't prosper. After working in community mental health for three years, I got together with two of my colleagues and we went into private practice. After we became familiar with government and insurance company policy, we opened an outpatient phobic disorders clinic and an inpatient substance abuse clinic. Within four years we had clinics in twelve locations. Last year we were bought out by a national health care corporation. As part of the deal I received a large block of stock in the parent company and the job of Vice President of Clinical Operations. I find that the efficiency inherent in the profit-making sector results in far more good for clients than the bureaucratic nonsense I had to put up with in community mental health.

Following the reunion, Janice offered one of her classmates, Raphael Ramirez, a job as director of social services at one of her clinics. He called one of the authors and said:

I'm really conflicted about the offer. It's a great job by all of the standard criteria, but I really worry about profit goals interfering with treatment goals. The reputation of Janice's outfit is that every client referred to their clinics is assessed as needing twenty-one days of inpatient treatment, no more and no less. The reason for this is, of course, that twenty-one days is generally the maximum that most managed care plans will cover for this type of thing. It also concerns me that when I told Janice I'm a family therapist and have little expertise in either phobic disorders or substance abuse it didn't really concern her. Her response to my concern was to say, "You're fully licensed, aren't you? Then what's the problem?"

Bill Bouchet had been working for a state child protective services program as a child welfare worker for three years since earning his B.S.W. He told a group of classmates about a discussion he had with a state senator at a political rally:

> When I told the senator about my job, the senator said, "Tell me, Bill, do you believe in the philosophy that seems to be dominant now in your department that it is nearly always best to leave a child with the natural parents? This seems unconscionable to me and many of my fellow legislators. Parents who do some of these things to their kids should lose their right to be parents. Surely we can do better by this state's kids than to leave them in unwholesome and often dangerous home environments. All this stuff about family preservation seems to me to be so much liberal pap designed to mask the unpleasant fact that evil does exist, is irreparable, and is present in many of these parents." Fortunately we were interrupted before I could reply because I was stunned. I work in the Families First unit and believe in it. But I feel I should write the senator a letter explaining the approach and correcting his misrepresentations. However, I'm really not sure where to start.

Mustafa Alleem works as a social worker in a large senior citizens center. He told a group of his classmates:

> The elderly people who are members of various groups I lead at the center are all feeling really uneasy. It seems like every week one of them comes in with some new rumor about what is going to happen to their entitlements. One week it was the matter of privatizing social security benefits, another it was increasing the co-pay for Medicare services, another time it was lowering the income for eligibility for Medicaid. They were really panicked a while ago when a group of them went to the community center to hear a congressional candidate who advocates the total elimination of entitlement programs and replacing them with means-tested programs, which he estimated would reduce the number of beneficiaries by 40 percent. I spend a lot of time processing these folks' feelings, but I really wish I could give them more concrete information on how real these threats to their security are. I suspect that some of the rumors are just that—rumors. However, some may be real and I feel a responsibility to separate facts from rumors so we could begin to develop strategies to deal with the true threats.

The situations described here are all very different in terms of the people involved, the fields represented, the levels of sophistication, as well as a number of other differences. They have one thing in common, however—they all involve social work practitioners who find themselves in the position, whether they would describe it this way or not, of needing to conduct a policy analysis.

The first thing most social workers who find themselves in this situation will do is go to the library to look up policy analyses in the area they are concerned with. What they will find are studies conducted by professional policy analysts of various types. These are fine, but they have two major shortcomings. The first is that—given the time it takes to do a policy study, write, edit, and finally publish a book reporting the findings—much of the material will be dated before it reaches the library shelf. By the time a study reaches the hands of a library patron or a bookstore customer, the data are at least four years old. Four years may not seem like too long a time until you consider that it represents two sessions of Congress, one presidential term, four United Way fund-raising and planning years, and so forth. As dynamic and fluid as the social welfare policy field is, a four-year-old study may well be completely out of date.

The second shortcoming of analyses by policy professionals from the perspective of the social work practitioner is that they almost always deal only with what we identified in Chapter 2 as macrolevel policy. In addition, they almost always deal exclusively with public policy. Mezzo- or agency-level policy and private-sector policy are rarely dealt with, even though this may be the most important information for the social work practitioner to have.

The solution to the problem of gaining access to current information regarding policies that affect social work practitioners is to become skilled in what we refer to in Chapter 3 as practitioner policy analysis. There is nothing esoteric or complex about conducting a practitioner policy analysis. It is really nothing more than taking a basic framework for analysis, such as the one presented at the beginning of Part II, and filling in the information regarding a specific policy or policy area mainly using library research skills (see Appendix A). Sources of information for practitioner policy analysis and skills for accessing these sources are discussed in the appendixes.

In the following chapters, we demonstrate how our policy analysis framework might be applied by the social workers described in the preceding vignettes. Each chapter involves either the major program or the hottest current issue in five broad social welfare policy arenas. In the economic assistance arena, we look at Temporary Assistance to Needy Families and current welfare reform efforts; in the area of aging, we discuss entitlement programs, mainly Social Security; in mental health, we look at the rapid expansion and increasing influence of managed care and the profit-making sector; in substance abuse, we review several policies; and in child welfare, we direct our attention to family preservation.

As you read the following chapters, you will notice that our policy analysis framework provides a guide but not a rigid template for our analyses. Some of the outline sections are important for some of the areas but not for others. For example, economic analysis is central to any discussion of the TANF program, which has replaced AFDC, but of only minor importance for understanding family preservation; enterprise sector analysis is important for understanding current trends in mental health policy but is not central to welfare reform. We do, however, believe that historical analysis is central to any policy analysis. There are several reasons for this. The first is our belief that it is virtually impossible to understand any current situation without studying its antecedents. The problem with many current social welfare policy proposals is that the people instigating them have no knowledge or understanding of history. President Reagan's effort to return much of the responsibility for social welfare to private charity, an idea also supported by the current president, is a good example. The assumption seems to be that the public sector assumed responsibility for social welfare out of some misguided liberal desire to extend the scope of government. In reality, the public sector assumed responsibility for social welfare only when the Great Depression bankrupted private charitable agencies and thus demonstrated the inability of a private system to deal with the massive social and economic disruptions characteristic of a modern urban industrial state. The government assumed responsibility not because it wanted to but because it *had* to. Thus historical policy analysis reveals that proposals to privatize large portions of the welfare system are not only wrongheaded but also just plain foolish.

The second reason we emphasize the historical dimension in practitioner policy analysis is that historical research is manageable for most social work practitioners. Elements of policy analysis such as economic analysis and evaluation are so complex that a complete job generally cannot be done unless one has extensive specialized training and adequate resources. Historical analysis can be successfully done by anyone with a good general education, training in some basic principles as laid out in Chapter 4 and Appendix B, and a willingness to do some careful detective work to uncover the best sources. This is not to say that historical analysis can be done sloppily or that most historical analysis is well done. It cannot and it isn't. It constantly amazes us how many people who attempt historical analyses are ignorant of the basic principles discussed in Chapter 4 and Appendix B or too lazy to apply them.

We conclude each chapter with a look at current proposals for policy reform. We include this section even though we realize that by the time this book is off the press this section will have become part of the history section—the proposals we describe will have been acted on and been killed, adopted, modified, or simply abandoned. This brings us back to the reason we are spending so much time discussing how to analyze policy rather than simply providing analyses and leaving it at that. Social welfare policy changes so fast that even the very first person to read this book will have to read our Current Proposals section as the last part of the history section and will have to go out and do his or her own analysis to find out, as one of our favorite reactionaries, Paul Harvey, says, "The rest of the story."

chapter 7

Fighting Poverty: Temporary Assistance to Needy Families

Welfare reform, always a hot-button issue, has been center stage in the political arena since Bill Clinton, as a candidate, promised to "end welfare as we know it." When the Republican party seized control of the 104th Congress, they made the reform of welfare a key plank in their Contract with America. After a protracted fight that included one presidential veto of a welfare reform bill, President Clinton, on August 22, 1996, signed H.R. 3734, the Personal Responsibility and Work Opportunity Reconciliation Act (PRWORA) of 1996. This act replaced the basic architecture of the public assistance system that had been in place since the 1935 signing of the Social Security Act by replacing the Aid to Families with Dependent Children (AFDC) program with a new program called Temporary Assistance to Needy Families (TANF). This new act leaves us facing an uncharted landscape in public assistance. As President Clinton noted when he signed the act, "This is not the end of welfare reform; this is the beginning. We have to fill in the blanks."[1]

As we have noted elsewhere, the term *welfare* conceptually refers to a wide range of programs.[2] Included in the category are programs such as Social Security, Worker's Compensation, Supplemental Security Income, and a number of others. However, it is clear that when speaking of welfare, or welfare reform, only one program is being referred to—public assistance, which used to be the AFDC program and is now TANF. Public assistance is the public program designed to aid the very poorest members of our society. Although it is true that men and married couples could technically qualify for AFDC and are eligible for TANF, in reality beneficiaries of public assistance have always been, and will continue to be, almost entirely women and their children.

Although the trend throughout the twentieth century was to move welfare programs to the federal level, programs for women and their children have remained under tight state control. AFDC was run through a joint federal–state partnership, with the federal government providing a set of regulations governing the operation of the program and approximately 75 percent of the funding. The individual states provided the additional 25 percent of funding and set their own eligibility and benefit levels. Under the TANF program, the states have even more control of the program, with the federal government providing only the most general guidelines. States are allowed to use TANF funding in any manner "reasonably calculated to accomplish the purposes of TANF." This situation has resulted in wide variations in the program, with average monthly benefits for a family of three ranging from a low of $170 in Mississippi to a high of $923 in Alaska. This lack of uniformity between states was considered a weakness of the AFDC program. Under TANF it is defined as a strength because the theory is that each state will experiment with different approaches, increasing the likelihood that for some work will be found.

To qualify for public assistance, a person must be very poor. Under AFDC, total liquid assets for a family could not exceed $1,000; if the family owned a car, its market value was limited to $4,000. Under TANF these figures vary from state to state, with most allowing $1,000 to $1,500 in cash and some increasing the value of a car an applicant can own. If a family has assets exceeding state guidelines, they are required to spend these before qualifying for aid. Generally, benefits come in a package that includes food stamps and Medicaid. These additional benefits theoretically provide a family sufficient resources to survive. Benefits under TANF are even stingier than under AFDC because the federal regulations require only that states spend an amount equal to at least 75 percent of their historic spending level (called maintenance of effort, or MOE) and provide options for the additional 25 percent to be spent for purposes other than direct assistance.

A number of scholars have observed that a major thrust of welfare reform during the later half of the twentieth century was an effort to separate programs believed to be for the "deserving poor" out of the welfare category and to define them as social insurance, a nonstigmatizing category. Donald Norris and Luke Thompson note:

> First many elderly were covered under Social Security. Later the number of elderly who were covered was expanded. Subsequently, many people with disabilities were given aid through the vocational rehabilitation acts, and later, through Supplementary Security Income. Many of the unemployed were covered under systems of unemployment compensation, either through companies or through state governments. Gradually, these groups of "deserving poor" recipients became isolated from AFDC recipients.[3]

Feminist scholars such as Linda Gordon and Theresa Funiciello have argued that we have systematically separated programs used by men and whites out from programs used largely by women and minorities and defined the former as social insurance, a category with little stigma, and the latter as welfare, a highly stigmatized category and one always considered in need of reform.[4] The new TANF program reinforces this stigmatization process through its institutionalization of the idea that remaining home to rear children is not a legitimate social role for poor women.

With the passage of the Personal Responsibility and Work Opportunity Reconciliation Act of 1996, we began a new era in public assistance policy. For the prior sixty years, the receipt of financial assistance by the needy was considered a right of citizenship; the federal government cast itself in the role of leading the states toward more progressive and humane social policies; staying home and parenting children was defined as a legitimate social role for the mothers of small children; and the reality that work was not available for all people was at least implicitly accepted. This has now all changed. Financial assistance is now to be granted only on a temporary basis; the federal government has abdicated its leadership role and now seeks only to get out of the way of the states; women are expected to be in the labor market; and it is assumed that jobs are available for all people if they will just look hard enough and accept whatever comes along. In the following sections, we look at the factors that have led to the current situation, attempt to make some sense of the situation, and make some projections about where the nation will go from here.

Much of the study of public assistance relies on historical data. The most important questions involve trends in numbers of recipients, length of time on assistance, number of recipients who become employed, number who leave the welfare rolls and stay off, and number who leave but then return. The PRWORA passed in 1996 and implemented in 1997 makes this analysis difficult for two reasons. First, the federal government has changed the data-collecting procedures and this makes comparisons to data prior to 1997 difficult. Second, as the law has been in effect for less than ten years, trends within the new program are harder to discern. The fact that the years since passage of the law have been ones of extraordinary economic growth makes assessment of the effects of the new program even harder to calculate. Now that the economy is slowing down, we will get a better idea of the true impact of the TANF program. As a result of these factors, some of the data in this chapter refer to the now-defunct AFDC program. Although we may not be comparing apples and oranges, we realize that we are comparing tangerines and oranges—similar things but not really an exact comparison. This is not the most desirable policy analysis situation, but it is, unfortunately, unavoidable.

Historical Analysis

The idea of public assistance, defined as the obligation of the government to provide an economic safety net for people, and of people's right to expect such a safety net based simply on citizenship, has a very short history in the United States. As recently as the end of the nineteenth century, this idea was considered absurd and offensive by most people. The great philanthropic leader of the nineteenth century, Josephine Shaw Lowell, stated the opinion of many people involved in the early development of social work in this country when, at the 1890 National Conference of Charities and Correction, she said:

> Every dollar raised by taxation comes out of the pocket of some individual, usually a poor individual, and makes him so much the poorer, and therefore the question is between the man who earned the dollar by hard work, and the man who, however worthy and suffering, did not earn it, but wants it to be given to him to buy himself and his family a day's food. If the man who earned it wishes to divide it with the other man, it is usually a desirable thing that he should do so, and at any rate it is more or less his own business, but that the law, by the hand of a public

officer, should take it from him and hand it over to the other man, seems to be an act of gross tyranny and injustice. . . . The less that is given [of public assistance] the better for everyone, the giver and the receiver.[5]

Based on this belief that government had no right to levy taxes in order to provide financial assistance to people, there was really no such thing as a large public assistance system until the twentieth century. Throughout the nineteenth and the early years of the twentieth centuries, poverty and related social problems were dealt with primarily through local voluntary organizations, with gifts from wealthy donors (such as Mrs. Lowell) providing most of the financial support. The little public support provided was mostly through a means known as *indoor relief*. This meant that assistance was provided to people only through institutions such as poorhouses, orphanages, mental hospitals, schools for the deaf and blind, and so forth. The provision of direct cash benefits to people, a practice known as *outdoor relief*, was frowned on as it was believed to encourage indolence and dependency. If direct cash relief was provided, it was thought that it should not come from tax revenues and that only a voluntary organization was capable of the level of scrutiny and supervision of recipients that prudence required.

As the twentieth century dawned, the rapid growth of urbanization, industrialization, and immigration resulted in a level of poverty and related social problems that threatened to swamp private charities. Many people were becoming concerned with the number of children who were residing in orphanages due not to parental desertion or death but to parental poverty. These were generally the children of widows who could not earn enough money to support their children and so placed them in orphanages because it was the mother's only option. In response to this problem, developments early in the century began to reestablish financial assistance as a public responsibility. The first development was the establishment in a number of cities, Kansas City being the first in 1908, of boards of public welfare to carry out "duties of the city toward all the poor, the delinquent, the unemployed, and the deserted and unfortunate classes in the community, and to supervise the private agencies which solicited money from the public for these purposes."[6] The second development was the 1909 White House Conference on Children convened by President Theodore Roosevelt. A major recommendation of this conference was that children should not be separated from their parents simply for reasons of poverty. A system of outdoor relief was strongly endorsed as being preferable to institutional placement.

Following the White House Conference on Children, advocates for the poor began to lobby successfully for state welfare laws that became known as "mothers' pensions." This rather strange term was borrowed from the powerful and popular industrial insurance movement, which was successfully lobbying for worker's compensation, unemployment insurance, and retirement programs as measures to insure workers against the risks of industrial employment. The perspective implied in the name "mothers' pension" was that women with children were productive workers of a sort and had a right to insurance against widowhood, the primary threat to their livelihood, just as men had a right to insurance against industrial accident. The first mothers' pensions laws were passed in Missouri and Illinois in 1911. Within two years, similar laws were passed in seventeen additional states, and by 1919 thirty-nine states had mothers' pensions programs.

There are two aspects of the mothers' pensions movement that are particularly important for understanding the history of public assistance. The first is that these programs were aimed, to quote President Theodore Roosevelt, at "children of parents of worthy character."[7] This meant women who were widowed or who had disabled husbands. A small percentage of recipients were divorced mothers, but these were considered worthy only if it could be demonstrated that the divorce was no fault of the women, primarily instances in which the husband had deserted the family. The programs were never intended for the children of unwed mothers, and very few such children received aid. The second important aspect of these laws is that they were based on a traditional model of the family in which the mother was expected to stay home and care for her children. The very name "mothers' pensions" implied that being a wife and mother was analogous to a career and widows were entitled to support when this career was disrupted. There were no work provisions, or even expectations, contained in these laws.

Although mothers' pensions programs established an important precedent in the development of public assistance, it was not until the Great Depression of the 1930s that state and federal government actually began to play a major role. Mothers' pensions programs were always quite small; in 1930, for example, fewer than 3 percent of female-headed households received benefits under these programs.[8] Private agencies, with substantial local government support, continued to provide the bulk of financial relief. The central role of private agencies was strongly endorsed by social workers and leaders in philanthropy, who questioned the morality of government providing assistance and doubted the ability of government to provide efficient and effective professional social services. This situation began to change rapidly with the onset of the Depression in 1929 and its increasing severity into the 1930s.

The Depression shocked the nation in general, and social workers in particular, into the realization that local programs supplemented by private relief agencies were not adequate for dealing with the massive economic problems of an urban industrial society. When the Depression hit, private agencies almost immediately ran out of money and began to rely to a much greater extent than previously on state and local governments for assistance. The state and local governments in turn got into financial peril and turned to the federal government for assistance. The realization that private agencies and state and local governments could not cope with the economic crisis, along with the fear that if something dramatic was not done revolution might well occur, resulted in the passage of the Social Security Act in 1935. This act was the first national framework for a social welfare system. The Social Security Act, as it finally emerged after many compromises, was designed to alleviate financial dependency through two lines of defense: contributory social insurance and public assistance. One of the public assistance programs was Aid to Dependent Children (ADC), a program established to serve single mothers with small children, basically the same group targeted by state mothers' pensions laws. This is the program that later was called Aid to Families with Dependent Children (AFDC) in recognition of the fact that mothers as well as their children were receiving assistance.

It is not surprising that AFDC has become more and more controversial over the years, because evidence indicates that its designers did not really understand what they were passing and certainly could not predict what the program was going to become. Scholars often romanticize New Deal programs and characterize their designers as humanists and liberals with a far-reaching vision of a just society and a realistic plan for achieving it.[9] Yet evidence indicates that the designers of the AFDC program supported it only because they believed that the program was temporary and would wither away as social insurance came into effect. Further, the designers of AFDC never imagined that the program would support the children of unwed mothers. Franklin Roosevelt characterized welfare as "a narcotic, a subtle destroyer of the human spirit" and argued that federal job creation was far preferable to welfare.[10] Edith Abbott, a social worker and prominent social reformer, advocated for AFDC with the assurance that it would support only "nice" families.[11] Social worker and Secretary of Labor Frances Perkins supported the program under the misunderstanding that the term *dependent mother* referred only to women who were widows, married to disabled workers, or divorced due to no fault of their own. It never occurred to her that unwed mothers would be included in the definition of *dependent*.[12] Historian Linda Gordon states,

> The authors of the New Deal welfare programs, often thought of as spiritual allies of contemporary liberals, would severely disapprove of what the New Deal programs have subsequently become with liberal encouragement: a source of more-or-less permanent support for single mothers who, in many instances, are not white and "not nice."[13]

By the 1950s, policymakers began to realize that the AFDC program was not going to wither away and was in fact providing benefits to a number of people considered "undesirable." The fact that the program did not wither but instead grew, often at an alarming rate, led to calls for welfare reform. Reform strategies can be lumped into two large categories. The first category is attempts to limit the number of people eligible for the program. These policies have taken the form of "suitable home" and "man in the house" rules and residency requirements. The suitable home and man in the house rules stated that aid would not be given to children who were living in immoral environments, generally defined as home situations in which it appeared that the mother was having a sexual relationship with a man to whom she was not married. These rules were struck down by the Supreme Court in 1968 in *King v. Smith.* Residency requirements denied assistance to any person who had not resided in a locale for a certain period of time, sometimes as long as five years. These requirements were declared unconstitutional by the Supreme Court in the case of *Shapiro v. Thompson* in 1969.

The second group of reform strategies have been efforts to move people off welfare and onto self-sufficiency through rehabilitating the recipient or else removing environmental barriers. There has been a series of these efforts, beginning in the mid-1950s and continuing to the current reform efforts. The one element that unites all these efforts is their uniform lack of effectiveness. Major strategies have been:

Social Service Strategies

Amendments to the Social Security Act in 1956 and again in 1962 facilitated the provision of social services to welfare recipients. The idea was that social workers would help recipients solve the problems that were preventing them from being self-supporting. This approach lost credibility when welfare rolls did not decline but actually increased at a rapid rate following full implementation of the strategy in the 1960s.

Institutional Strategies

First tried in the 1960s as part of Lyndon Johnson's War on Poverty, these attempted to empower individuals and neighborhoods. These programs were based on a "blocked opportunity" thesis that attributed poverty to environmental variables. These programs rapidly ran into political problems, welfare rolls did not decline, and they were discontinued after a very short life. In the 1980s, a few institutional strategies were implemented, namely enterprise zones and public housing "ownership" initiatives, but these have also met with little success.

Human Capital Strategies

In the 1960s, as the social service and institutional strategies were losing popularity, the argument was advanced that a more direct approach to poverty was called for. This approach simply said that people were poor because they could not get good jobs, and they could not get good jobs because they did not possess valuable skills. Economists refer to a person's saleable skills and attributes as human capital. To address this problem, a series of job training programs has been attempted, beginning in the early 1960s with the Manpower Development and Training Act (for the disadvantaged in general) and the Community Work and Training Programs (specifically for welfare recipients). In 1967 the WIN (Work Incentive) program was implemented, which was a joint effort of state welfare departments and employment service offices. This program required all AFDC recipients without preschool age children to participate. As will be discussed in the next section, the human capital approach continues to be popular, its latest manifestations being the 1988 JOBS (Job Opportunity and Basic Skills) program, basically an extension and expansion of WIN, and the work and training requirements that are central to the TANF program that replaced AFDC in 1996.

Job Creation and Subsidization Strategies

One of the major criticisms of the human capital approach is that there are not jobs available for most of the participants. Various attempts have been made to counter this criticism by creating public service, or publicly subsidized, private-sector jobs. The Works Progress Administration and the Civilian Conservation Corps of the Depression era serve as models for this approach. In recent years, the most popular version of this approach has been providing subsidies to employers to offset the costs of creating new jobs for low-skill workers. The Targeted Tax Credit and the WIN Tax Credit are two examples. A popular, if somewhat perverse, twist on this approach has sometimes been to require welfare recipients to perform unpaid community service in return for their grant.

Child Support Strategies

This approach was developed in response to the changing composition of AFDC caseloads, where the majority of cases were children with living fathers who did not provide support. In the mid-1970s, the federal Office of Child Support Enforcement was created to assist states in efforts to gain and enforce child support from absent fathers. Federal legislation in 1984 and 1988 strengthened child support provisions. When a woman applied for AFDC, she was required to identify the father of her children and file for a child support order if she hadn't already done so; if she had and the father was delinquent, she was required to swear out a warrant for collection.[14] This policy has continued under TANF.

Recent Welfare Reform Efforts

In the 1980s, with the election of Ronald Reagan to the presidency and the beginning of a long conservative trend in society, pressure for substantial welfare reform began to mount. The first major effort climaxed in 1988 with passage of the Family Support Act, viewed by many as a major reform of welfare and one that would quiet the calls for reform for many years. This was not to be. Almost before the ink was dry on the Family Support Act, critics began to complain that it had not gone far enough and to demand even more drastic reforms. These efforts resulted in the passage, and subsequent veto by President Clinton, of the Personal

Responsibility Act of 1995. Following the veto of this act, the 104th Congress modified the bill slightly and passed the Personal Responsibility and Work Opportunity Reconciliation Act of 1996. In what many viewed as a crass example of political opportunism, President Clinton signed the bill into law on August 22, 1996. These recent welfare reform efforts have been examples of what Thomas Corbett labels the "make work pay" strategy and the "make 'em suffer" strategy.[15] The "make work pay" strategy is based on the idea that people make rational choices and thus, if we want people to choose work over welfare, we need to provide work opportunities that will enable them to be substantially better off than they are while receiving assistance. The "make 'em suffer" strategy is based on the same basic idea but comes at it from the opposite direction. Rather than attempting to provide options more attractive than welfare, these strategies impose penalties on a range of behaviors that are seen as counterproductive to becoming self-sufficient. Welfare recipients are required to attend school, participate in work training, immunize their children, and similar things. If recipients do not accept these responsibilities, they are penalized by reductions in their welfare grants.

The 1988 Family Support Act, primarily a "make work pay" effort, had as its centerpiece an employment and training program called Job Opportunities and Basic Skills (JOBS). The purpose of this program, commonly called "workfare," was to provide the necessary resources (education, training, and child care) to enable welfare recipients who were capable of working to do so, and it included provisions requiring them to take advantage of these resources.

This attempt at welfare reform was not a success. The AFDC rolls continued to rise, and by 1996 no state had come anywhere close to meeting the goal of having 20 percent of recipients in jobs or job training.

Due to the apparent failure of the 1988 Family Support Act to meet its initial goals, and to conservative concern that the bill was too soft on recipients, welfare reform was attempted again in the 104th Congress. In 1996, H.R. 3734, the Personal Responsibility and Work Opportunity Reconciliation Act of 1996, was passed and signed into law by President Clinton. Major provisions of H.R. 3734 are:

- The Aid to Families with Dependent Children (AFDC) program has been replaced by the Temporary Assistance to Needy Families (TANF) program.
- Under TANF, states receive a block grant in an amount calculated to be the highest of (1) the average payment they received under AFDC in fiscal years 1992 through 1994; (2) the amount they received in fiscal year 1994; or (3) the amount they received in fiscal year 1995. (AFDC was an uncapped entitlement program. The states had a right to reimbursement from the federal government for 75 percent of the cost of AFDC grants up to an unlimited amount, as long as they followed regulations.) States have much more freedom

regarding how to spend TANF money than they had under AFDC, but when it is spent they will have no right to additional funds from the federal government. A contingency fund has been established to help states that exceed their block grant amounts, but this is available only under specific and limited conditions (i.e., an exceptional increase in unemployment).

- Adults receiving cash benefits are required to work or participate in a state-designed program after two years or their payments will be ended. This work requirement is defined as one individual in a household working at least thirty hours per week.

- States must have at least 50 percent of their total single-parent welfare caseloads in jobs by 2002. States that fail to meet this requirement will have their block grant reduced by 5 percent or more in the following year.

- States are allowed to sanction, through a reduction or termination of cash benefits, people who fail to fulfill the work requirement.

- Payments to recipients using federal funds must end after a maximum of five years for all spells (times receiving assistance) combined, thereby requiring that families become self-supporting at that point.

- Persons immigrating to the United States after the passage of H.R. 3734 will be ineligible for most means-tested programs, including TANF, food stamps, and Medicaid, for their first five years of residence.

- Illegal aliens will be barred from all means-tested programs.[16]

President Clinton expressed reluctance to sign this bill, saying, "You can put wings on a pig, but that still does not make it an eagle." He also expressed the belief that the 105th Congress would repeal or soften significant portions of the legislation. However, Senator Daniel Patrick Moynihan, probably the leading expert on social welfare policy in the Senate at the time, strongly asserted his belief that the votes simply would not be there to modify this law. As predicted by Senator Moynihan, there have as yet been no major modifications to soften this law.

Social Analysis

From the previous section, it is apparent that public assistance in this country has always been controversial, generating many strong feelings about what the problem is and about the character of those benefiting from the program. In this section, we attempt to provide an accurate description of the problem, the population affected, the state of our knowledge regarding these, and the social values that shape our public assistance programs. Because the TANF program did not go into effect until July 1997, some of the data available relate to the AFDC program.[17]

Problem Description

At the heart of our chronic dissatisfaction with our welfare programs is the fact that public assistance addresses two different problems, and the solutions to these problems are inherently contradictory. On the one hand, public welfare deals with the problem of child poverty. The solution to child poverty is fairly simple and straightforward—the provision of cash and other benefits to poor children in levels sufficient to lift them out of poverty. On the other hand, public assistance is concerned with the problem of adult dependency, people who are perceived as not doing the things necessary to be fully functioning, contributing members of society. The solution to this problem is also fairly straightforward—reduce or completely eliminate benefits in order to force people to support themselves. The difficulty is, of course, that it is not possible to pursue these two goals simultaneously. If we raise benefits in order to reduce child poverty, we risk encouraging adult dependency. If we become harsh and stingy in order to reduce adult dependency, children will inevitably suffer. Because it is not possible to maximize two divergent goals at the same time, we address them serially, first paying attention to one and then to the other.[18] Thus a round of welfare reform that reduces child poverty by increasing benefits will be perceived as increasing adult dependency and will lead to a reform effort to counteract this. The reform effort will attempt to reduce dependency by cutting benefits, which will increase child poverty and lead to calls for reform because of this. The process will go round and round ad infinitum. This partially explains why a TANF reauthorization bill, due in 2001, has (as of May 2006) still not been passed.

Population

A large part of the unpopularity of public assistance has to do with the public's perception of characteristics of the recipients and of the program. The stereotype of the typical recipient is a never-married minority-group woman living in the inner city of a large urban area, having her first child at a very young age, having a large number of children, and receiving assistance on a more or less permanent basis. In addition, the public perceives the size of the population and cost of the program as being huge and growing at an ever-increasing rate. Like most stereotypes, this one contains a seed of truth but is highly oversimplified. The following is a description of the TANF population based on the most accurate and recent data available.

Size

In 2002, there were an average of 2,060,300 families averaging 2.5 members receiving TANF, for a total of 5,964,000 recipients (Table 7.1). This sounds like a

Table 7.1 Characteristics of the TANF Population, 2002

Monthly average number of TANF families	2,060,300
Average number of persons in TANF families	2.5
Average number of children	1.9
Average monthly grant	$355.00
Distribution of number of children in TANF families	
One	47.0
Two	28.0
Three	14.2
Four	8.9
Distribution of cases by ethnicity	
White	31.6
African American	38.3
Hispanic	24.9
Asian	2.5
Native American	1.3
Other	1.4
Marital status of TANF parents	
Single	66.6
Widowed	0.7
Married	11.5
Divorced	8.2
Separated	13.0
Education	
No Formal Education	2.4
1–6 years	3.2
7–9 years	11.5
10–11 years	28.1
12 years	51.4
More than 12 years	3.3
Employment status	
Employed	25.3
Unemployed	74.7

Source: Adapted from data in U.S. Department of Health and Human Services, TANF Sixth Annual Report to Congress, November 2004, 2004 *Green Book. Characteristics and Financial Circumstances of TANF Recipients,* www.acf.dhhs.gov.

large number, and indeed it is, but it is only 1.8 percent of the population in the country. As shown in Table 7.2, the size of the AFDC caseload rose at a truly alarming rate between 1960 and 1975, but the rate of growth slowed considerably until 1990, when it once again began to grow at a rapid rate. In 1999, two years

Table 7.2   AFDC/TANF Caseload Size, 1960 to 2003

Year	Recipients	Families	U.S. Population	Percentage of Population
1960	3,005,000	787,000	180,671,000	1.7
1965	4,329,000	1,039,000	194,303,000	2.2
1970	8,466,000	2,208,000	205,052,000	4.1
1975	11,165,185	3,498,000	215,973,000	5.2
1980	10,597,445	3,642,380	227,726,000	4.7
1985	10,812,625	3,691,610	238,466,000	4.5
1990	11,460,382	3,974,322	249,913,000	4.6
1995	13,652,232	4,876,240	263,034,000	5.2
1996	12,648,859	4,553,339	265,284,000	4.8
1997	10,936,298	3,946,304	267,636,000	4.1
1998	8,770,376	3,179,167	270,029,000	3.2
1999	6,889,315	2,535,824	272,878,000	2.5
2000	5,964,000	2,269,000	281,400,000	2.1
2001	5,488,616	2,124,726	284,800,000	1.9
2002	5,187,006	2,080,862	287,984,799	1.8
2003	4,963,771	2,039,917	290,850,005	1.7

Source: U.S. Department of Health and Human Services—Administration for Children and Families.
Fact Sheet—Welfare, www.acf.dhhs.gov/programs/opa/facts/tanf.htm.

before the passage of TANF, the welfare population began to decline. Following the passage of TANF, the welfare population continued to decline. The decline accelerated until by 2002 the caseload was at the lowest level since 1960.

Cost

Although the welfare rolls were growing until 1994, the expenditure, adjusted for inflation, has declined since 1976. In 1976, total payments (in 1990 dollars) came to approximately 22 billion dollars. By 1990, this amount had shrunk to about 18.5 billion dollars. The cap for total federal cost of the TANF program is set at 16.5 billion dollars, which was the actual 1994 federal government expenditure on the AFDC program. The reason for this decline in expenditures is that, although the number of AFDC families expanded until 1994, the average size of these families declined and the size of the average AFDC grant also declined at a rapid rate (Table 7.3). Adjusted for inflation, the average AFDC payment dropped from $676 in 1970, to $434 in 1990, and to $381 by 1993.[19] The average TANF payment in 2000 was only $349 per month. More detail regarding the cost of the AFDC and TANF programs is provided in the section on economic analysis.

Table 7.3 Average AFDC/TANF Family Size and Monthly Benefit

Year	Average Family Size	Average Monthly Benefit (in Constant Dollars)
1970	4.0	676
1975	3.2	576
1980	3.0	483
1985	3.0	443
1990	2.9	434
1995	2.9	373
2000	2.6	349
2002	2.5	355

Source: Committee on Ways and Means, U.S. House of Representatives, *Overview of Entitlement Programs: 1995 Greenbook* (Washington, DC: U.S. Government Printing Office, 1995), p. 325; *Characteristics and Financial Circumstances of TANF Recipients,* www.acf.dhhs.gov.

Race of Recipients

The racial composition of the TANF program is only slightly changed from that of the AFDC program. Slightly more than 68 percent of TANF recipients are minority group members. Thirty-eight percent are African American, 25 percent are Hispanic, 2.5 percent are Asian or Pacific Islanders, and 1.3 percent are Native American. The racial and ethnic differences in the TANF population are even more apparent when the composition of the total population is considered. About 81 percent of the total population of the United States is white, while whites constitute only about 32 percent of the TANF population. About 7 percent of white mothers receive aid. African Americans make up about 12 percent of the total population, but account for 38 percent of TANF caseloads. About 25 percent of African American mothers receive aid. These factors account for the popular stereotype of TANF being a minority program even though one-third of the recipients are white.

Family Size

Another popular stereotype of the TANF program is that welfare recipients have very large families. Actually, welfare families are not particularly large. Data from 1995 indicate that mothers on AFDC gave birth to an average of 2.5 children, compared to an average of 2.1 children for mothers not on AFDC (Figure 7.1) and that fertility rates for welfare recipients are declining. Fertility rate figures for TANF mothers are not yet available, but they will probably be similar. In 2004 nearly half of TANF families had only one child and about one-third had two children. Only one-tenth of the families had more than three children.[20] These figures are very close to those for all families with mothers of childbearing age.

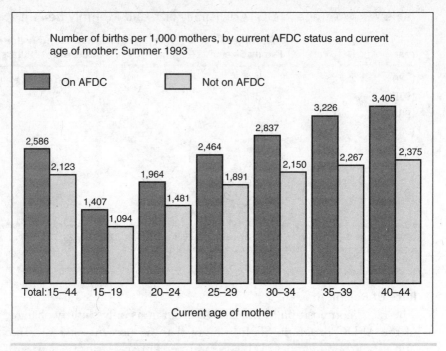

Number of births per 1,000 mothers, by current AFDC status and current age of mother: Summer 1993

Figure 7.1   Fertility Rate of AFDC and Non-AFDC Mothers

Source: Bureau of the Census Statistical Brief, *Mothers Who Receive AFDC Payments—Fertility and Socioeconomic Characteristics* (Washington, DC: U.S. Government Printing Office, March 1995).

Age of Mothers

TANF mothers are younger than those not receiving TANF, averaging thirty years of age, compared to thirty-four years old for mothers not receiving TANF. Six percent of TANF parents are teenagers, and 19 percent are forty years or older.

Education

The number of years of schooling is significantly less for TANF recipients than for the general population. Over half (54 percent) of TANF recipients never completed high school, compared to only 14.5 percent of nonrecipients. It is interesting that the educational level of TANF recipients is lower than it was for AFDC recipients. This is probably a result of the large number of recipients who have recently left the rolls. It is reasonable to guess that those with the highest educational levels are those finding employment and exiting the program.

Length of Time on Welfare (Spells)

Policy analysts refer to the length of time a person is on assistance as a *spell*. The major concern of policymakers, as well as of the general public, about public assistance programs is their belief that recipients get on the rolls and never leave. It is precisely this concern that is behind the TANF time limit of two years for any one spell and five years for the total of all spells. This is a somewhat troublesome area to discuss because the terms can be confusing and the same data can be presented in ways that create different impressions. For example, critics of AFDC asserted that 65 percent of recipients of AFDC received assistance for eight or more years, while defenders of the program said that nearly 60 percent of people were on AFDC for less than two years. Both are, in fact, using the same data, and what both say is equally true. How can this be?

The answer is that statistics regarding welfare spells look quite different depending on whether by "time on welfare" you are referring to everyone who has ever had a welfare spell or to the length of the spell of people currently on the rolls. Let us explain by way of the following example:

> Imagine you are asked to compile statistics on average length of room rental in a small apartment motel in your town. The motel has ten units, and you find that eight of the units have been occupied by the same people for the entire previous year. The other two units have been rented by different people each month. Thus the motel has had a total of thirty-two tenants (the eight year-long tenants and twenty-four who each rented one of the other two rooms for a month). If someone were to ask you, based on your analysis, what the typical tenant in the apartment/motel is, you could answer one of two ways. You could say that the typical tenant was a long-term renter because at any one time 80 percent (eight of the ten) were long-term renters. However, you could just as honestly answer that the typical tenant was a short-term renter because over the past year, 75 percent of all guests (twenty-four short-term renters out of a total of thirty-two) rented a room for only a month.

As can be seen by inspection of Table 7.4, the situation with welfare spells is similar to the motel example. Of all the persons who ever began a welfare spell,

Table 7.4 Length of Time on Welfare (Spells) (in Percentages)

Years	Persons Beginning a Spell	Persons on Welfare at a Point in Time (Current Spell)	Persons on Welfare at a Point in Time (Total Spells)
1–2 years	59.25	15	7
3–7 years	27.75	36	28
8+ years	13.00	49	65
Totals	100.00	100	100

Source: Adapted from Greg J. Duncan and Saul D. Hoffman, "The Use and Effects of Welfare: A Survey of Recent Evidence," *Social Service Review* 62 (June 1988), p. 243. Used with permission of the University & Chicago Press.

59.25 percent received assistance for less than two years. So for the majority of people who used the AFDC program, it worked exactly as it was intended. Almost 60 percent of people who received assistance used it to help them over a temporary life crisis (death in the family, divorce, illness, job layoff, etc.), and then they got back on their feet and continued life as productive, tax-paying citizens. Few people in our society begrudge the program as it worked for these people.

However, of the people on the program at any one time, the current spell for 49 percent of them was longer than eight years. If all the spells of the people on the program at any one time were added together, 65 percent of the recipients had spells totaling eight or more years. Thus, 65 percent of the people on AFDC at any one time were clearly stuck in the program. They became dependent on it and for some reason, be it personal limitation or lack of opportunity, they were unable to escape. Nearly everyone agreed that something different was needed for this segment of the population. This is the challenge for the TANF program. The rolls have been falling rapidly, but most likely many, probably most, of those leaving are those who would have been short-term recipients under the AFDC program. The question now as we deal with the two-year spell limit under TANF is: Will the former long-term recipients be able to become self-sufficient? In the likely case that many will not, what will society's response to them be?

The Onion Metaphor.   As should be apparent from the preceding information, the welfare population is much more diverse than the popular stereotype. Corbett developed a useful metaphor relating the various parts of the welfare population to layers of an onion.[21] The outer layer consists of recipients who receive assistance for two or fewer years. These people generally enter welfare due to a discrete and easily observable event in their lives—illness, job loss, divorce, or the like. They generally have comparatively high education, ability, and motivation and, with a few supports, will reenter the labor market in a short time. The only thing this group needs is short-term financial help and some assistance in regaining entry into the labor market.

The middle layer of the onion is composed of people who receive assistance for two to eight years and are often on-and-off-again recipients. These people have limited options. They generally have some basic skills and education, but the employment opportunities do not exist to elevate them out of poverty on a permanent basis. Their fortunes are highly related to the functioning of the economy. When the economy is doing well, members of the middle layer will have opportunities available to them that allow them to escape welfare, if perhaps not poverty. When the economy is doing poorly, because of their relatively low level of education and skills, people in this layer will be the first to be laid off. Appropriate interventions for members of this layer are educational/vocational preparation to help them be more competitive and measures to strengthen the economy.

The core of the onion is composed of recipients who remain on assistance for eight or more years, sometimes referred to as being systems dependent. This is the group we usually picture when discussing public welfare. In addition to low earning capacity brought on by lack of education, training, and job experience, this group also faces barriers to self-sufficiency such as drug abuse, psychological problems, health problems, abusive personal relationships, and so on. This group is also often suspected of lacking basic motivation and of possessing values that are not conducive to work. This group requires far more extensive interventions to achieve self-sufficiency than do members of the two outer layers.

Finally there is the very inner core. These people are permanently functionally limited due to severe physical or emotional impairment. For these people, self-sufficiency is simply not a realistic objective. The response to this group should be to recognize that they will never be totally self-sufficient and to develop non-stigmatizing ways of providing income support. Corbett believes, "An expanded disability program (e.g., a liberalization of Supplemental Security Income) seems an appropriate vehicle through which to assist this group."[22] All of this has clear implications for the reauthorization of TANF.

TANF Time Limits.   One of the centerpieces of the TANF program is the sixty-month lifetime limit on receipt of assistance. According to Corbett's typology there are two groups, those he calls the core and the inner core, most of whom will not be able to achieve self-sufficiency. What will happen to these people? This has, from the beginning been one of the big questions of the TANF program. As it turns out, the sixty-month time limit is not inflexible. States are allowed to extend up to 20 percent of their caseload beyond the federal limit. States also may elect to continue additional recipients on benefits by paying for them out of state funds. A study by the Manpower Development Research Corporation (MDRC) found that, as of December 2001, about 54,000 families had reached the sixty-month time limit. Of these, only 8,000 (about 15%) lost their benefits. The others remained on assistance either under the 20 percent allowable federal extension or by having their benefits covered by state funds. As noted in the MDRC, report, "In reality, the federal time limit is not a limit on individual families but, rather, a fiscal constraint that shapes state policy choices."[23] These are, of course, very preliminary findings representing only a small fraction of the families who will eventually reach the time limit.

Relevant Research

There is a vast amount of research relevant to welfare reform, most of which is systematically ignored by policymakers. In Chapter 3, we briefly mentioned the New Jersey, Seattle, and Denver Income Maintenance Experiments, the largest and most ambitious attempts to test an alternative approach to public assistance. We will only tangentially mention these studies here, even though they are considered landmarks, because the approach they tested, known as a guaranteed annual income or negative income tax, is a liberal welfare reform approach no longer in the public assistance policy arena.* The largest body of research relevant to welfare reform consists of numerous studies being conducted for the purpose of evaluating current reform efforts. These will be discussed in some detail in the section on evaluation. There is also a good deal of research on the economics of welfare, some of which will be reviewed in the economic analysis section. In this section, we review research that studies one of the greatest concerns of welfare policymakers—whether the receipt of welfare promotes undesirable behavior among recipients.

A constant feature of welfare policy is the fear that by giving people assistance we will somehow damage their moral character by, in the terminology of economics, exposing them to moral hazard. Major concerns are that receipt of public assistance will promote family instability by enabling women to leave their husbands or to have children without ever being married; that receipt of welfare will damage the recipient's spirit of independence (i.e., will make the person permanently dependent); and, finally, that children who grow up in welfare households will think being on welfare is a normal state of affairs and will hence be more likely to turn to welfare for their own support when they become adults.

David Ellwood and Mary Jo Bane have studied the relation of welfare receipt to family formation. They looked at a list of family structure variables and, using several databases, analyzed the effects of welfare receipt on these variables. The data indicated no effect of welfare receipt on births to unmarried mothers and only a small effect on divorce, separation, or the establishment of female-headed households. Interestingly, the one really significant effect of welfare they found was that in states with low benefit levels, welfare mothers were more likely to live with their parents than they were in high-benefit states. Their conclusion was that they found little evidence that receipt of welfare was a primary cause of variation in family structure.[24]

---

*It is interesting to note that although this approach has been abandoned as a public assistance alternative, it has with almost no fanfare been adopted as the approach of choice for helping the working poor. The Earned Income Tax Credit, first employed in the 1970s, was greatly expanded in 1993. Under this program, workers can deduct job-related expenses, such as child care, from taxes. If the credits exceed taxes due, a refund is paid. In other words, an employed individual can get back from the IRS more than he or she paid in. Refunds from this program now total over 22 billion dollars, making it the largest antipoverty program in the United States.

The effect of more generous welfare payments on family stability was also one of the major questions in the Income Maintenance Experiments. Findings from the experiments in Gary, New Jersey, and the Rural studies were inconclusive. However, the findings from Seattle and Denver indicated that the more generous negative income tax benefit was strongly related to increased marital dissolution rates for both blacks and whites. Rates for Hispanics also increased, but increases were smaller and not statistically significant. These data were reanalyzed in the late 1980s, using more sophisticated statistical techniques, and the positive relation between the program and increased rates of marital dissolution was found to be spurious. However, by the time the reanalysis was released, the damage to the idea of a negative income tax as a welfare approach had been done, and the topic was no longer in the policy arena.[25]

Lerman has reviewed the first five years of TANF data looking for effects on family structure. Consistent with the findings of Ellwood and Bane, he found that the policy changes had no effect. In fact, the proportion of married recipients has continued to decline, as has the rate of married parenthood generally.[26]

A popular stereotype of public assistance is that children who grow up in welfare households will be much more likely than nonwelfare children to become welfare-dependent adults themselves. This is related to the "culture of poverty" idea referred to earlier, that children who grow up on welfare will be taught values that are positive toward welfare receipt and therefore will not have the aversion to welfare that people who did not grow up in welfare households generally have. Consequently, the argument goes, when times get tough, these people will be more likely to turn to welfare for support than will people who grew up in nonwelfare households. Using fourteen years of data from the University of Michigan's Panel Study of Income Dynamics, Martha Hill and Michael Ponza looked at the intergenerational transmission of welfare dependency. They found that welfare children typically did not become welfare-dependent adults. Only 19 percent of the children from African American welfare families and 26 percent of children from white welfare families were heavily welfare dependent in their own homes. In terms of intergenerational transmission of welfare dependency, there were no statistically significant differences between African Americans who grew up in welfare-dependent homes and those who did not. For whites, the only significant difference was for people who grew up in homes with the very highest level of parental welfare dependence, and even these differences were not consistent across all of the models tested.[27]

It should be noted that questions concerning the relationship between welfare receipt and the behavior/character of recipients are extremely complex and the research results are not clear to the point of being unassailable. However, as Greg Duncan and Saul Hoffman state,

The fact that several million individuals are persistently dependent on welfare raises questions of whether welfare itself promotes divorce or out-of-wedlock births, discourages marriages, or instills counterproductive attitudes and values in recipients. Sparse evidence on the effects of welfare on the attitudes of recipients fails to show any such links.[28]

Has welfare policy making been affected by relevant research? The evidence does not indicate that it has. Why is this so? The answer is that the research evidence is in direct conflict with some very deeply held U.S. values.

Values and Welfare Reform

As is the case in most areas of social welfare policy, in public assistance deeply held values supersede empirical knowledge. Public assistance exists at the intersection of two conflicting sets of values, one supportive of welfare and one deeply antagonistic to it. The values that are antagonistic to welfare are:

The United States as the Land of Opportunity

Most of us sincerely believe that in this country there is opportunity for everyone, if only a person looks for it. Anyone with a good heart and a willing spirit can find work and get ahead. The idea that in our post-industrial, international economy there is no place for many workers offends this belief. Public welfare is seen as an accusation that the economy does not work well and, as such, is seen as almost un-American. The booming economy of recent years has reinforced this belief.

Individualism

Americans believe that individuals are autonomous and have control over their own destinies. We believe that people should get full credit for their successes and take full blame for their problems. We are still fascinated by, uplifted by, and—more important— believe in the rags-to-riches American success story. We reject the notion of collective responsibility for individual problems. As public welfare is, by definition, collective re- sponsibility, we think it is a bad thing. Individuals should support themselves and not rely on their neighbors.

Work

Work is considered important because it provides the means for survival. However, we also think of work as a moral virtue, valuable for its own sake, not just for its contribution to our material well-being. Laziness and idleness are viewed as evidence of weak moral char- acter. Because welfare allows people to survive without working, we tend to suspect that it is a contributor to immorality. As such, public welfare is viewed as more of a moral prob- lem than an economic one.

The Traditional Nuclear Family

The nuclear family—husband, wife, and children—is viewed as the main pillar of a stable, moral society. This type of family is considered a moral virtue, and the more a family deviates from this ideal the greater the degree of social disapproval. As the welfare population is primarily composed of female-headed families with a high proportion never married, the morality of these families, and by extension the whole program, is suspect.

In support of public welfare are the following values:

Humanitarianism

Although some of our values may be rather harsh, at the core the American people believe that it is wrong, even sinful, to allow other people, especially children, to suffer when we have it in our power to help.

Sense of Community

David Ellwood has stated, "The autonomy of the individual and primacy of the family tend to push people in individualistic and often isolating directions. But the desire for community remains strong in everything from religion to neighborhood. Compassion and sympathy for others can be seen as flowing from a sense of connection with and empathy for others."[29]

Thus our values regarding public welfare amount to what Lloyd Free and Hadley Cantril have referred to as a "schizoid combination of operational liberalism with ideological conservatism."[30] On the one hand, strongly held values lead us to conclude that providing financial assistance to people is a bad thing. Assistance leads, in the public mind, to people giving up individual responsibility for their lives; it allows people to live without working, which encourages the development of sloth and laziness, major character flaws; it allows women to live without husbands, which is seen as contributing to family breakdown. On the other hand, we feel driven out of a sense of compassion and desire for community to help people who are suffering. This value conflict over public assistance is really not hard to understand. The different values relate to the different objectives of the program discussed earlier. The objective of doing something about the problem of child poverty is addressed by our values of humanitarianism and desire for community. The objective of discouraging adult dependency is addressed by the values of individualism, work, and family. Ellwood asks, "Can we design social policies that are consistent with all these values or that at least minimize the conflicts between them?" He concludes, and we agree, that "the conflict is inevitable."[31]

Economic Analysis

Although we generally classify public assistance as social welfare policy, we must recognize that at its core it is *economic* policy. The need for public assistance results from a failure in our economy to provide a place for everyone. Thus, probably the most important questions about public assistance are economic questions. The major macroeconomic questions are: How much does welfare cost? Is the cost growing? and What are the employment prospects of welfare recipients in the market economy? The major microeconomic concern is whether welfare receipt serves as a work disincentive: Is the total package of benefits so great that a person is better off on assistance than he or she would be working, thus leading to a rational economic decision to favor welfare over work? A second microeconomic concern has to do with the economic effects of welfare receipt on family formation. A final microeconomic concern, one that has not been given much attention but deserves more, is: What are the behaviors that welfare recipients actually engage in in order to survive on the minimal grants they receive?

Macroeconomic Issues

Listening to politicians and to the popular media leads to the conclusion that public assistance is tremendously expensive and is driving our economy into ruin. It is also frequently alleged that the cost of public assistance has been increasing at a rapid rate and has been a major contributor to past federal budget deficits,[32] although this concern has lessened after the implementation of TANF.

How Much Does Public Assistance Actually Cost?

The surprising answer is that in terms of the total government budget, not very much. The total combined spending of federal and state governments on TANF in 2001 was a little more than 25.5 billion dollars, 60 percent from federal revenues and 40 percent from the state treasuries. In absolute terms, of course, this is a lot of money, and presented with nothing to compare it to, it does seem like a reason for major concern. However, when viewed in context, the amount seems small. The 2005 federal budget alone amounted to more than 2.4 trillion dollars. The federal share of TANF was less than 1 percent of this figure. Between 1996 and 2001, the amount states spent on TANF (in constant dollars) declined from $15 to $9.7 billion. By way of comparison, in 2005 the Department of Defense received 401.7 billion dollars, and 130 billion dollars was spent on the savings and loan bailout.[33] Thus it can be seen that public assistance is not a major contributor to either federal or state deficits, and cutting costs for the program by replacing AFDC with TANF has not resulted in a great savings, although states are somewhat better off.

Is the Cost of Public Assistance Growing?

The other common macroeconomic concern regarding public assistance is that its cost is growing at a rapid rate and is, in fact, out of control. This is also not true. As we noted earlier, the cost, in constant dollars, has actually declined since 1976. The reason for this perception of the growth of public assistance probably has to do with the fact that data on the cost of AFDC were generally lumped in with general social spending, which has, as can be seen in Figure 7.2, increased significantly since 1980. However, the lion's share of the increase is accounted for by Social Security, Medicare, and Medicaid. AFDC and food stamps have increased at modest levels, and the cost was declining even before the implementation of TANF in 1997. Even when looking at total social spending, many economists argue that the rate of growth has been very moderate. Richard Sutch, for example, has analyzed social spending and concludes, "Since the mid-1970s, social spending, has been stable. . . . The impact of recessions in 1975–76, 1982–83, and 1991–92 can be seen, but overall, social spending has been growing at about the same rate as the economy for twenty years."[34] As can be seen in Figure 7.3, the cost of TANF has actually declined since 1996.

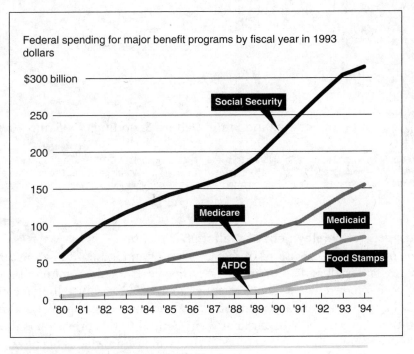

Figure 7.2 Entitlement Spending

Source: Congressional Budget Office, Office of Management and Budget.

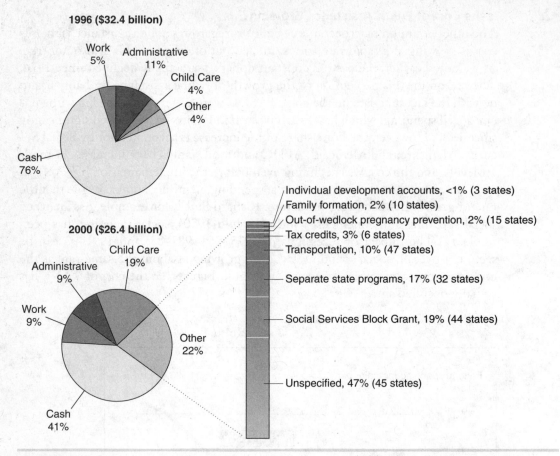

Figure 7.3   Distribution of Federal and State Welfare Spending, 1996 and 2000
(in 2000 Dollars)

Source: Sheila R. Zedlewski, David Merriman, Sarah Staveteig, and Kenneth Finegold, "TANF Funding and Spending across the
States," in Alan Weil and Kenneth Finegold, Eds., *Welfare Reform: The Next Act* (Washington, DC: Urban Institute Press,
2002), p. 234. Original source note: 1996 data collected from federal sources on individual spending on programs replaced by
TANF; 2000 data from the ACF. Reprinted by permission.

Prospects for Employment of Welfare Recipients

One of the major provisions of the TANF program is a limit of two years for any
one welfare spell and a lifetime limit of five years for the total of all spells. This
has been referred to as a "shock therapy" approach, basically telling recipients that
they have only a limited amount of time to get their lives together and then they,
and their children, will be on their own. Central to this provision is the assumption that there is work for everyone if they will just do what is necessary to obtain
it. Thus a key research question for public assistance policy is whether this assumption is true.

An interesting opportunity for a natural experiment on this shock therapy approach occurred in Michigan when the state terminated its general assistance (GA) program in 1991. General assistance is a state-financed welfare program intended to benefit people who look very much like the TANF population but are not eligible for TANF for one reason or another, generally because they do not have children at home. Sandra Danziger and Sherrie Kossoudji looked at former GA recipients in Michigan two years after their termination from the program to see how they had fared. They found that about one-half of former recipients with a high school diploma or GED were working, but fewer than one-quarter of those lacking these credentials were employed. Among those who were working, very few were earning enough money to elevate themselves over the poverty line. This study "suggests that welfare recipients who reach the time limit, but are not offered work opportunities, will have difficulty obtaining and holding jobs."[35]

Prior to the implementation of TANF, a number of scholars predicted that the labor market would not be able to absorb the inflow of former welfare recipients.[36] Their gloomy predictions, at least initially, turned out to be incorrect. Early data indicate that people exiting welfare are generally working and are enjoying incomes much greater than they had as recipients.[37] A study of labor markets in twenty large metropolitan areas concludes that the markets have been able to absorb the new workers without increasing the unemployment rate.[38] However, it should be noted that the implementation of TANF has occurred in what Brauner and Loprest refer to as "stellar labor market conditions."[39] Now that the economy is slowing and TANF caseloads are beginning to rise in many states, the employment picture for people leaving welfare, as well as for those who have recently left, may be quite different.[40]

The conclusion from an analysis of the macroeconomic aspects of public assistance is that the cost is so small in relation to other parts of the economy that its effects on the economy are minimal. Neither substantial reductions nor increases in welfare benefits will have any great effect on aggregate measures of the performance of the economy.

Microeconomic Analysis

Is Public Assistance a Work Disincentive?

The major microeconomic concern with public assistance is that it serves as a work disincentive. The argument goes that people given a choice between living on welfare or working for a living will choose to work only if they will be significantly better off as a result of doing so. As Sar Levitan and Frank Gallo note, the total package to which a welfare recipient is entitled (cash grant, food stamps, Medicaid, and in some cases subsidized housing) often exceeds the compensation available from low-wage work. They note that in 1991 the average nonworking mother with two children received almost $7,500 in combined AFDC/food stamp benefits, compared with $8,900 earned income from a minimum wage job.[41] If the person received subsidized housing, or if the job did not include free medical coverage, the total welfare package would exceed the minimum-wage job by a good margin.

The evidence regarding the degree to which welfare acts as a work disincentive is mixed and generally finds less of an effect than logic would predict. Frank Levy and Richard Michel conducted a longitudinal comparison of AFDC benefits as a proportion of the average wage of workers in the retail trade industry. Their hypothesis was that the higher the ratio of welfare to wages, the more likely it would be that people would choose welfare over work. Thus, if welfare benefits were increasing relative to wages, the size of the welfare rolls should show an increase; if welfare benefits were declining relative to wages, the welfare rolls should shrink. Analyzing twenty-five years of data, they found that this relationship did not hold. Although the ratio of welfare to wages declined during this period, the welfare rolls expanded.[42] After conducting a thorough review of the literature, economist Robert Moffitt came to a different conclusion. He found that "the available research unequivocally indicates that the AFDC program generates nontrivial work disincentives." The researchers whose work Moffitt reviewed found that the amount of work reduction was small, however, ranging between 1 hour to 9.8 hours per week.[43] The Income Maintenance Experiments that tested the more generous negative income tax approach to welfare assistance also hypothesized that the approach would result in a reduction in the hours of work by members of the experimental groups. Like the researchers reviewed by Moffitt, they found that this was indeed the case, but that the reductions were small. Husbands in the experimental group worked 119 hours per year (7 percent) less than control group husbands, wives worked 93 hours (17 percent) less, and female family heads worked 113 hours (17 percent) less.

In any case, with the implementation of TANF, this concern becomes moot. In passing TANF, policymakers accepted the assumption that public assistance is a work disincentive and structured the program in such a way as to enforce labor market participation.

Economic Survival Strategies of Welfare Recipients

States determine the level of welfare benefits based on a concept called "level of need." Level of need is what the state determines as the minimum amount families of various sizes need to survive. The state then sets a percentage of this amount, usually around 50 percent, as the public assistance grant level. Now, the question the authors have often pondered is this: How in the world do we expect people to survive when, by our own calculations, we provide them with one-half of the minimum amount necessary for survival? Sociologist Kathryn Edin and anthropologist Laura Lein have now researched this question and have come up with an answer: People can't and don't survive on welfare benefits alone.

In order to study the question of how welfare mothers survive economically, Edin interviewed a sample of fifty women in Chicago in 1989, and she and Lein interviewed several hundred more in Massachusetts, South Carolina, and Texas between 1990 and 1994.[44] They invested considerable time developing relationships of trust with the women in their sample; based on these relationships, the women were willing to reveal candid details of their economic lives. Edin and Lein collected detailed data on the women's household budgets and on their sources of income. What they found is that the women were not able to come anywhere close to making ends meet on the amount they received from the combination of welfare and food stamps. In the Chicago sample, for example, the women had average monthly expenses of $864 and average income from welfare and food stamps of $521. Thus their average monthly shortfall was $343.

With an average monthly shortfall of $343, how did these mothers survive? The answer found by Edin and Lein is that virtually all of the women had additional sources of income they did not report to the welfare department (reported income would result in a reduction of the welfare grant, although generally not dollar for dollar). The women's sources of income varied. Some income was obtained from family and friends, some from the absent fathers of the children, some was earned in the regular economy and hidden from authorities by means of false Social Security numbers, and some (a very small amount, averaging only $38) was earned in the underground economy through activities such as drug dealing and prostitution. The average family income from the Chicago sample was $897, $521 obtained from welfare and food stamps, and $376 obtained from unreported sources. Through these means, the women were able to cover their basic monthly expenses with an average of $33 of discretionary income left over.

The Effects of Public Assistance on Family Structure

It has long been a major concern of public assistance policy that by allowing women to have children without being married, welfare assistance encourages single parenthood. This concern intensified as the proportion of AFDC children who were born out-of-wedlock grew from 38 to 60.4 percent between 1979 and 1994.[45] One explanation for this increase is that it simply reflected changes in U.S. mores, which now define unwed parenthood as acceptable when only a few years ago it clearly was not. Another explanation, however, is that the increase in the proportion of welfare recipients who are unwed mothers is, at least partially, due to perverse economic incentives not to marry, created by welfare programs. The argument, nicely summarized by economists Levy and Michel, is based on one long-advanced by black writers, first W. E. B. Du Bois in 1899, later by E. Franklin Frazier in 1939, and most recently revived by Harvard University sociologist

William Julius Wilson. The idea is that if a man does not have an adequate job and has few prospects for finding one, he will not be viewed as an acceptable prospect for marriage. In inner city areas, the number of men who have jobs that pay more than a woman can get on public assistance is decreasing. "Thus if welfare benefits are higher than the incomes of a significant portion of men, it may provide an incentive to create more female-headed families."[46]

Levy and Michel analyzed this theory using data from the *Current Population Survey* conducted on an ongoing basis by the Census Bureau. They found that in 1960, 69 percent of black males aged twenty to twenty-four and 83 percent aged twenty-five to thirty-four had incomes above the average AFDC grant of $1,269. By 1983, only 38 percent of black males aged twenty to twenty-four and 71 percent aged twenty-five to thirty-four had incomes greater than the average AFDC grant, which was $4,741. They conclude that this data confirms Wilson's findings that the increase in female-headed families in black inner city areas is due to the decrease in the number of men who are able to provide an income large enough to support a family at above-welfare levels. It is important to note that Levy and Michel do not conclude that rising welfare benefits are responsible for the decline in two-parent families. Indeed, as noted previously, in constant dollars the actual amount of welfare benefits has been declining. Rather, the culprit appears to be the lack of employment opportunities available to people with low education, little experience, and few job skills.

The concern that public assistance may be a contributor to the formation of single parent families was central to the 1996 welfare reform legislation that replaced AFDC with TANF. Three out of four legislated purposes of TANF specifically address family formation objectives: (1) end the dependence of needy parents on government benefits by promoting job preparation, work, and marriage; (2) prevent and reduce the incidence of out-of-wedlock pregnancies and establish annual numerical goals for preventing and reducing the incidence of these pregnancies; and (3) encourage the formation and maintenance of two-parent families.[47] These objectives have been pursued through two primary means. The first is the Healthy Marriage Initiative that has provided grants totaling over $25 million in 2002–2004 to support "a range of activities to increase access to marriage strengthening services and awareness about the values and benefits of healthy marriage for children, adults, and communities." The most prominent of these activities has been a widely distributed compendium providing basic facts and information from research studies on marriage and its benefits, as well as examples of existing programs, curricula and promising practices. Other frequent activities include grants to support the development and implementation of an array of marriage and relationship skills classes and related marriage strengthening services. Current legislation (H.R. 240 and S. 667) increase the amount of money available for this program to $100 million annually. There is currently no hard evidence that these programs have any effect on either promoting marriage or on reducing the number or rate of out-of-wedlock births.

The second means of addressing out-of-wedlock births specifically concerns the belief that teenagers were having children as a means of setting up their own households and thus escaping parental control. Rebecca Blank has named this the "independence effect" of welfare and has found some evidence supporting its existence.[48] Under TANF policy, mothers under 18 years of age must live with a parent or guardian and must be enrolled in high school in order to receive welfare benefits, thereby eliminating this supposed benefit of pregnancy for young teenagers. There is some early evidence that this policy may be contributing to a reduction of the fertility rate of 15- to 17-year-old girls.[49]

Evaluation

For the thirty years prior to its end, the primary goal of the AFDC program was to get recipients into jobs and thereby off the rolls. Before 1967, it was generally accepted that AFDC was intended to allow deserving mothers to remain home with their children. Work was, undoubtedly unintentionally, discouraged through a policy that reduced the amount of a recipient's grant dollar for dollar when that person had earned income. In 1967 the policy of AFDC officially changed to encourage work through the passage of the WIN (Work Incentive) program. The WIN program employed a carrot-and-stick approach, the carrot being a formula that decreased a recipient's grant at a rate equal to only a portion of earnings so she would always be better off working than not. The stick was a provision that allowed states to drop people from the rolls who declined to participate in employment or training "without good cause." Various iterations of the WIN program remained in effect until the program was replaced in 1988 with the JOBS (Job Opportunities and Basic Skills) program, the centerpiece of the Family Support Act.[50] The TANF program emphasizes employment even more heavily, with the new twist of time limits. Recipients are now eligible to receive assistance for only two years for any single welfare spell and for a lifetime total of five years for all spells combined. The TANF program adopted a new philosophy of welfare known as "Work First." This philosophy holds that training is preferable to idleness, but work, regardless of the type, is preferable to training. Under the AFDC program, a recipient could enroll in a registered nurse training program even if nurse's aides jobs were available. Under TANF and Work First, the recipient is required to take the job as a nurse's aide, even if at minimum wage.

Thus the most important evaluation questions currently facing public assistance policymakers relate to the effectiveness of employment training and placement programs for TANF recipients. The most critical questions are: Do recipients who are provided with these services actually get jobs? Do those who get jobs earn enough to get them off the welfare rolls and out of poverty? What is the relationship between the jobs obtained and the quality of life of former recipients? Do job programs result in cost savings for the programs? Fortunately, there has been significant effort expended to evaluate employment programs for welfare recipients.

Most evaluations of welfare-to-work programs have found positive results for the programs, but in all cases the results have been slight. The WIN program had very poor results. As summarized by James Patterson, evaluations of WIN found that

> of the 2.8 million welfare recipients eligible for WIN in 1967, only about 700,000 were deemed by local authorities to be 'appropriate for referral.' The rest were ill, needed at home, considered untrainable, or without access to day care. Of the 700,000, only 400,000 were actually enrolled in WIN as of mid-1972, four years after the program got under way. Around a quarter of these completed training, and only 52,000, or less than 2 percent of the total pool, actually were employed— at an average wage of around $2 an hour.[51] (Minimum wage in 1972 was $1.60 per hour).

Ronald Reagan's work-oriented welfare reform program in California, passed in 1971 when he was that state's governor, has often been cited as a model for national welfare reform efforts. However, an evaluation of that program found that although the stated goal of the program was to place 30,000 welfare recipients in jobs, at its peak it managed only 1,000 placements.[52]

The poster child for welfare-to-work programs is the GAIN program in Riverside, California. This program, started under the JOBS program, has demonstrated the largest measured impacts to date. Judith Gueron summarizes the evaluation results as "double digit increases in the share of AFDC recipients working, a 50 percent increase in average earnings, a one-sixth reduction in welfare payments, impressive effects on long-term recipients." However, she notes that this is an exceptional program, and the difference between it and more typical programs is wide. She concludes, "The more typical program, while achieving positive results, remains severely strapped for funds, does not reach most of the people who could theoretically be subject to its mandates, and has not dramatically changed the message of welfare."[53] Moreover, Theresa Amott reports that although the California program has achieved significant results, the actual earnings of the average participant were only $785 greater over a two-year period than the earnings of members of a control group who did not participate in the program.[54]

Levitan and Gallo reviewed thirteen experimental studies (evaluations that included a treatment/experimental group and a control group) that were conducted on employment programs between 1978 and 1993. They found that the employment rate of the treatment group subjects was statistically higher in five studies, the same or lower in six studies, and unknown in the remaining two. In eleven of the thirteen studies, the experimental group members had statistically higher earnings than the control group. However, once again, although earnings increased significantly, the amount was small—ranging for one year from a low of $12 to a high of $1,607.

A review of welfare-to-work evaluations reveals that the basic assumption of these programs may be false. This assumption is that welfare recipients do not want to work and that to get them to work requires two things. The first is a stern motivator, such as a time limit on welfare, to scare them into seeking self-sufficiency. The second is the provision of a few resources such as brief education, training, and job counseling programs to help them capitalize on their motivation to become self-sufficient. But virtually every evaluation prior to the passage of the Personal Responsibility and Work Opportunity Reconciliation Act found no real problem in recipient willingness to work. The problems that have been found all are related to the fact that the programs seriously underestimate the barriers to employment for most long-term welfare recipients. On the one hand, the level of problems that recipients have with health, drug abuse, low ability level, low intelligence, lack of job experience, child care, transportation, and so forth contribute to very low employability of many recipients. On the other hand, the number of jobs available that require few skills and a generally low ability level is inadequate in all but the best economic times. To mount a really successful welfare-to-work program would require two changes. First, many more services and resources would need to be put at the service of clients than is currently the case. Second, the government would need to intervene in the job market and create jobs of last resort to prevent former recipients from having to return to the welfare rolls during periods of economic downturn. Levitan and Gallo argue: "Society's work is never done. There is no shortage of useful work that could be performed to fulfill needs unmet by the market economy. The limited skills of AFDC recipients would dovetail well with child care, long-term care, and other services that already rely heavily on unskilled low-wage labor."[55]

Is TANF Succeeding?

To answer the question of whether welfare reform is succeeding, we first must ask what is meant by success. Public policy makers, and much of the public in general, seem to define the success of welfare programs by the single criterion of reduction in the number of recipients. We argue that success must be measured not only by this but also by the criterion of whether the new program improves the lives of the poor. The evidence gathered to date on the TANF program indicates that it has succeeded by the first criterion, but there is considerable concern about the second.

TANF and the Welfare Rolls

In 1996, Congress passed the Personal Responsibility and Work Opportunity Reconciliation Act, the legislation that set up the TANF program, in spite of the negative results of evaluations of prior programs that mandated work for welfare recipients. The opinion of much of the country at that time was that the growth of the welfare rolls was out of control and some hard-nosed measures were needed in order to stop the alarming increase. Little noted by policymakers or the general public was that the rolls had actually been declining for two years, dropping from 5 million to 4.5 million between 1994 and 1996, the year the Personal Responsibility and Work Opportunity Reconciliation Act became law.

The general perception of TANF, based exclusively on the criterion of reduction in the number of recipients, is that the program has been an unqualified success. As can be seen from inspection of Figure 7.4, the number of cases has declined from 4,533,000 at the beginning of the program in 1996 to 2,029,751 in 2002. This represents a decrease of more than 53 percent, a truly remarkable number. This figure would indeed be cause for celebration if all the people leaving the

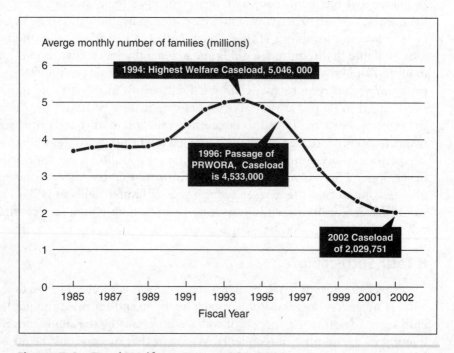

Figure 7.4   Total Welfare Cases, 1985–2000

Source: Adapted from Alan Weil and Kenneth Finegold, *Welfare Reform: The Next Act* (Washington DC: Urban Institute Press, 2002), p. xx. Original source note: Administration for Children and Families (1988–1997), Office of Planning, Research, and Evaluation (2000), and Administration for Children and Families (2000a, 2000b, 2001a, 2001b); 2002 data from TANF Sixth Annual Report to Congress. Reprinted by permission.

welfare rolls had achieved self-sufficiency and a better life, but this is not the case. Studies of families that have left the TANF rolls show that at any point in time about 60 percent are employed and 40 percent are not.[56] Several factors account for the number of people who have left TANF without being employed. One is that a number of applicants have been placed in diversion programs rather than being certified for TANF benefits. There are two types of diversion programs. In the first, the state agency administering TANF offers an applicant a one-time cash payment, in return for which the person gives up her eligibility for assistance for a specified period of time. The idea is that the one-time payment will solve the immediate problem, or problems, that are preventing the person from working and being self-sufficient (car repair, work wardrobe, back rent, and the like). If the person spends the money and still is not in a position to work, she is out of luck until the period for which she has agreed expires. In the second type of diversion program, a number of states require applicants to look for work for a specified period of time before their application for TANF will be accepted. Many do not find work but become so discouraged by the bureaucratic hassle that they never return to complete the application process.

The second factor that explains why so many people have left TANF without being employed is that they have been sanctioned (read "kicked out of the program") for failing to comply with program rules.[57] A recipient can be sanctioned for something as minor as failing to respond to a letter directing her to attend a meeting. Inspecting various government reports, Lens concludes that sanctions have increased by 30 percent nationally since 1994 and that in any given month approximately 5 percent of a state's total welfare caseload is under sanction. In addition, records indicate that sanctions are often incorrectly applied. In Wisconsin, for example, it was found that 44 percent of the penalties imposed on recipients in a five-month period were later found to have been erroneous.[58]

So, if the welfare rolls have declined by 2,503,249 cases since 1996, and if 40 percent of these have left for reasons other than getting a job, this means that approximately 1,001,300 poor families have been abandoned to fend for themselves without any government assistance. We don't know exactly what is becoming of these families, but a reasonable guess is that they are turning to family and friends, people who probably have few extra resources themselves, or they are living on the streets or in shelters. Lens concludes, "In sum, disentitling otherwise eligible people by diverting them from the rolls or by terminating assistance cannot be equated with the individuals achieving self-sufficiency."[59]

TANF and the Quality of Life of the Poor

The second criterion that must be assessed in judging whether TANF is successful is the effect of the program on the lives of those it is intended to help. This is the question asked by those concerned with an ethical evaluation of TANF, and the results give ample reason for concern. Obviously, for the 40 percent of people who have left the TANF rolls but are not employed, the effect of TANF has been negative. But what of the 60 percent who have managed to enter the labor market? Are they, as frequently stated by President George W. Bush, on the first step of the American ladder of success, or are they just squeaking by? Although we are sure that there are a number of former TANF recipients whose lives are steadily improving, the evidence coming in suggests that for many the program has not led to a better life.

Wages of Former Recipients.   The first problem for former TANF recipients is that most are making very low wages. Using data from the National Survey of American Families, Loprest found that the median wage (50th percentile) of former welfare recipients in 1999 was $7.15 per hour; those at the 25th percentile were earning $6.05, and those at the 75th were earning $9.00 per hour.[60] In addition to low wages, few of the jobs held by former recipients provide good benefits. Only about one-third of the jobs include health insurance, and only about one-third provide paid sick leave.[61] Even these low wages result in incomes considerably in excess of welfare grants for those who are working full time. However, a large number of former welfare recipients have jobs that are only part time. As a result of these factors, about 52 percent of those who left the welfare rolls for jobs in 1999 still had incomes below the poverty level.[62]

Upward Mobility of Former Recipients.   The theory behind welfare reform is that once people enter the labor market they will begin to get raises and promotions. Thus the fact that many former recipients are in very low-paying, scant-benefit jobs is not seen as a major problem. Backers of TANF believe that this is a problem every working person faces; we all start off in the mail room, so to speak. Does it appear that their current employment will be the first step on the road to success for most former TANF recipients? There is not yet good data on this question. Analysts have, however, expressed concern over the prospects for former recipients. This concern is based on analyses of the twenty-first-century job market that conclude that skills and education are essential for upward mobility. The work first philosophy of TANF requires that a person choose work over education and training, regardless of the situation.* Lens has reviewed the research

---

*The difference between the old AFDC approach and the TANF Work First approach can be illustrated with the following example. Let us say that there is a woman who completed three years of a four-year nursing degree. She left school to raise a family and now finds herself in the position of being without any income when her husband suddenly dies. Under AFDC the woman and her social worker could work out a plan for support from AFDC for the one year it would take to complete her nursing degree, with the prediction that upon graduating she could find a job paying around $18.00 per hour with full benefits. Under the TANF work first approach, if a job is available as, for example, an assistant in a nursing home paying $5.15 per hour with no benefits, she will be required to take it, even if it prevents her from ever returning to school.

literature on the relation of level of education to income and to the likelihood that a person will exit and stay off welfare. The data revealed a clear relationship between education and income level and a link between high school graduation and not returning to welfare. The link between earning a college degree and permanently exiting welfare was even stronger. Lens concludes that

> far from ensuring self-sufficiency, . . . an approach [such as work first] relegates welfare mothers to the low end of the labor market, a vulnerable place in good and bad economic times. It also ensures that the gap in wages based on educational level will persist and endure as poor women, forced to choose between losing their benefits or feeding their families, are trapped in low-paying jobs.[63]

Are Adequate Support Services Available?   As anyone in the labor market knows, holding down a job can be expensive. Good-quality child care can cost well over $100 a week. In an urban area that lacks a good public transportation system, a reliable car is essential to steady employment. A car involves not only the expense of purchase but also substantial operating expenses for gas, repairs, and insurance. Do the math. A person earning the median post-TANF wage of $7.15 per hour cannot afford expenses such as these. The designers and administrators of the TANF program are aware of this problem, and in response states have been spending 18 percent of their TANF budget on child care, 2 percent on transportation, and 11 percent on other work supports.[64] There is concern that even this may not be enough. There are time limits on child care subsidies for women who leave TANF. As this benefit runs out, a number of former recipients may be forced to return to the program because they cannot afford to purchase child care at full cost. The transportation problem is also serious, and solutions appear to be far off. After an analysis of the transportation problem for former TANF recipients, Lens concludes, "none of [current transportation reform] attempts really address the root of the problem, and transportation problems persist. To get welfare recipients to work, no less than a radical restructuring of public transportation systems may ultimately be needed."[65] A former recipient who has been placed in a job far from her home, without reliable transportation resources or involving a bus trip requiring three transfers and two hours, is soon going to be back on the welfare rolls.

Welfare Reform and the Well-Being of Children.   Because TANF requires parents to work rather than stay home with their children, possible adverse effects of the program on children has been a major concern. To address this concern the Administration on Children and Families contracted with Abt Associates, Child Trends, Manpower Demonstration Research Corporation, and Mathematica Policy Research, Incorporated, to assess the impact of welfare reform on the lives of children. The research was called the Project on State-Level Child

Outcomes and data was collected in Connecticut, Florida, Indiana, Iowa, and Minnesota. The primary data source for each State study was a survey that focused mainly on children who were between the ages of five and twelve at the time of the survey. The children were surveyed and then a follow-up survey was conducted at intervals varying from 2.5 to 6.5 years, depending on the state. The main findings from the five states were summarized in the *TANF Seventh Annual Report to Congress* as:

- There is little evidence that these programs resulted in widespread harm or benefit to young school-age children.
- In two states positive impacts on children's functioning appear to be related to increases in family income. In a third state, increased family income had a neutral effect.
- In two states the programs had the most favorable impacts on children in the most disadvantaged families, such as those with a longer history of welfare receipt or less work experience. In the three other states there was little difference in the pattern of impacts on young school-age children by the level of family disadvantage.
- The programs increased children's participation in child care.
- While the studies mainly focused on young children, data on a limited number of measures on outcomes for adolescents were collected. This data indicated that the programs sometimes had negative effects on adolescents' school performance.

Basically the studies did not find strong evidence that TANF is having strong effects on children's lives in either a positive or a negative direction.[66]

Problems Facing the TANF Program.   In the county of one of the authors, the director of the local office of the Department of Social Services goes around to civic groups giving a PowerPoint presentation on how the department's Work First TANF program is going to end poverty in the county within ten years. It's a nice dream, but it's not going to happen and, if he doesn't stop giving this presentation, soon he is going to look foolish. There is evidence that the early, spectacular, reductions in the welfare rolls are beginning to disappear—the decline between 2001 and 2002 being only 73,413 families, about one-third of one percent of the total caseload. There are a couple of reasons why the caseload decline is coming to an end.

TANF Caseloads Are Not Reaching the "Inner Core of the Onion."   Earlier in the chapter, we discussed Corbett's onion metaphor that illustrated different types of poverty. Burt has presented a similar idea specifically related to problems of TANF recipients. She observes that recipients can be classified into three different groups based on their barriers to self-sufficiency. The first group, similar to Corbett's outer layer of the onion, comprises recipients with barriers that resources can overcome quickly. These are people who in most cases need simple resources such as child care, transportation, or job search assistance. Removing these barriers and getting the recipient to work is a simple matter of providing services or resources, and the services and resources needed are obvious. The second group, similar to Corbett's middle layer and core, are recipients with barriers that are treatable, controllable, or reversible with adequate and appropriate resources. The barriers for this group include physical and mental illnesses or disabilities, addictions, illiteracy, lack of basic work-related skills, inability to speak or understand English, lack of work experience, and recent release from a correctional institution. To get this group to work, the TANF agency must provide support during a period of treatment that may last for a number of months and then be prepared to provide intensive and lengthy postemployment support. The final group, analogous to Corbett's inner core, face permanent conditions. These are people with permanent and severe physical disabilities, chronic mental illness, or learning or developmental disabilities.[67]

Data on recipients who have left TANF and on those who have not reveal that the majority of the leavers are those with less serious barriers to self-sufficiency. Data from the National Survey of American Families have been used by Zedlewski and Alderson to look at six potential barriers to work by welfare recipients: (1) poor physical or mental health, (2) less than high school education, (3) having a child under the age of one, (4) having a child on SSI,* (5) low proficiency in English, and (6) lack of work experience. They found that 56 percent of recipients with no barriers were working, but only 20 percent of those with two or more barriers were working.[68] Some of these recipients with serious barriers may be eligible for Supplemental Security Income on the basis of their disabilities, but many are not because of the extremely restrictive eligibility requirements that exclude all but the most seriously disabled. Increasing the work participation rates is going to become more and more difficult for states in the coming years as a greater percentage of the pool of recipients consists of those with a serious barrier or several barriers.

Welfare Reform Has Been in a Virtuous Cycle.   This is a term coined by Weil and Finegold to describe the years since the PRWORA was passed in 1996. These have been years ideal for the implementation of work-oriented welfare policies because they have been characterized by an exceptionally strong economy, healthy state budgets, the federal requirement that states maintain their AFDC spending

---

*In order for a child to be on Supplemental Security Income (SSI), that child must have a serious mental or physical disability.

levels, and the block grant structure that has required the federal contribution to the states to stay constant even when the number of recipients has been falling. These last two factors have resulted in state social service departments having extensive resources to provide support services for recipients seeking employment and for those who have recently left the welfare rolls to help them make the transition to work. Weil and Finegold say,

> Yet this virtuous cycle could just as easily become vicious. Low unemployment and sustained economic growth have contributed to the recent decline in welfare caseloads. A recession will reverse these trends while straining state budgets. . . . The new structure of welfare may make the highs and lows of policy more extreme than they were in the past. The United States has been living through the highs; it has yet to experience the lows.[69]

The economy has recently been sputtering, although a full-scale recession has been avoided. Many economists are predicting that the virtuous cycle may be over. We may well soon see a stunning reversal in the trend in caseload size.

Conclusion

We have presented a large amount of data in a fairly brief space regarding the public welfare system in the United States. Much of this information may seem contradictory and confusing. However, based on the data presented, we think it is possible to come to several conclusions. These are outlined in the following sections.

American Values Related to Welfare Have Permanently Changed

When Aid to Families with Dependent Children, the first national welfare program in the United States, was passed in 1935, the value on which it was based was clear. What's more, there was a national consensus regarding this value. This value was that women with children, especially small children, should be able to stay at home with them. Over the next sixty years, this value slowly and steadily eroded. This was due to several factors, the first being a general change in the role of women in society, resulting in many self-supporting women working rather than caring for children full time. The second is the growth of the AFDC program until its cost became a great concern for many people who began questioning whether we could afford for poor women to stay at home rearing children. The third factor is that the composition of the AFDC recipient population changed. When the program was enacted, it was thought that the recipients would be widowed white women. By the 1960s, the typical recipient was an unmarried minority group mother. Racist though it may be, this factor resulted in a major loss of support for the idea that welfare mothers should be able to stay at home rather than work.

The TANF program that replaced AFDC is based on a different core value. This value is that work and self-support is a person's primary obligation to society. Hence the term *personal responsibility* in the legislation that created TANF. The key result of this value change is that the research reviewed above showing that employed former recipients have undesirable jobs, receive low pay, have few benefits, and often remain below the poverty line is pretty much beside the point. There is a near national consensus that it is *always* better for a person to be working than to be supported by public welfare.

The conclusion we draw from this is that if we as social workers want to improve the lives of the poor, we will be far more effective if we seek to improve work and supporting services than if we agitate to loosen the work requirements for recipients.

Welfare Is Not the Problem; Poverty Is the Problem

It is an obvious, but too often ignored, truism that welfare is a response to poverty. The welfare reform debates in recent years have almost ignored the evidence that poverty in our country is increasing. The distribution of income has become rapidly more unequal in recent decades. Summarizing the data, Danziger and Gottschalk found, "In 1989, the real income of a family at the 20th percentile was 5 percent below the 1969 level, while that of a family at the 80th percentile was 19 percent higher."[70] Both the number and the percent of people below the poverty line decreased at a steady rate between 1959 (when we first started counting) and 1978. This population then increased, rising from 24.5 million people, 11.4 percent of the population in 1978, to 36.9 million people, 14.5 percent of the population in 1992. In 1994 the poverty population began to decline until 2001, when the poverty rate was 11.7 percent, or 32.9 million people. As the economy has begun to deteriorate, the poverty rate is again increasing, rising to 12.7 percent, or 37 million people, in 2004. The reasons for these fluctuations are numerous, complex, and not fully understood. We will not go into them here. Suffice it to say that solving the welfare problem is not the answer to solving the poverty problem, as policymakers often imply. Rather, solving—or at least dealing with—the poverty problem is the answer to solving the welfare problem. It is, however, apparent that TANF is directed much more at the welfare problem than at the poverty problem.

Public Assistance Is a Social Condition, Not a Social Problem

In the classic book *The Unheavenly City*, Edward Banfield made a useful distinction between urban problems and urban conditions. He defined an urban problem as something that could be fixed, such as potholes and broken water mains. Urban conditions are things that are permanent, or very nearly so, and simply must be managed as well as possible. Banfield identified poverty as an urban condition.[71]

We think Banfield's observation is a useful conclusion to the discussion of welfare reform. Many things about the welfare system can be improved. However, we need to recognize that in a large, rapidly changing, urban, postindustrial society, we will always need a large welfare system. In other words, welfare is simply a condition with which we should make peace. Leo Perlis, a union organizer, hit the nail on the head when responding to an earlier welfare reform initiative:

> The current somewhat apologetic emphasis on rehabilitation [of welfare recipients] seems almost obscene—as if rehabilitation would not cost more (at first at least), as if rehabilitation is always possible (in the face of more than 4,000,000 jobless among other things), as if rehabilitation is a substitute for relief for everybody and at all times. I think we all need to make a forthright declaration that direct public assistance in our competitive society is unavoidable, necessary, and even socially useful.[72]

Selected Web Sites on Welfare Reform

Administration for Children and Families

www.acf.dhhs.gov

Provides information on this major branch of the U.S. Department of Health and Human Services. Includes data, reports, news, program descriptions, and links to other major federal Web sites.

American Public Human Services Association

www.aphsa.org

Contains information on the former American Public Welfare Association, the largest and oldest organization in the country devoted to government antipoverty programs. Site includes news of state activities, publications, policy analyses, job listings, conference announcements, and links to related sites.

Electronic Policy Network

www.epn.org

This network of policy and research institutions deals with a wide range of policy issues, including welfare reform.

Urban Institute

www.urban.org

This site includes reports from the Assessing the New Federalism project of the Urban Institute. This is a multiyear project to monitor and assess the devolution of social programs from the federal to the state and local levels. The project analyzes changes in income support, social services, and health programs and their effects.

Welfare Watch

www.welfarewatch.org

This site developed by the Annenberg School of Communication at the University of Southern California provides summaries of current media reports related to welfare reform.

Notes

1. "Clinton Signs Controversial Welfare Bill," *Dallas Morning News* (23 August 1996), sec. A, p. 32.

2. Philip R. Popple and Leslie Leighninger, *Social Work, Social Welfare, and American Society*, 5th ed. (Boston: Allyn and Bacon, 2002).

3. Donald F. Norris and Luke Thompson, Eds., *The Politics of Welfare Reform* (Thousand Oaks, CA: Sage, 1995), p. 4.

4. Linda Gordon, "How We Got 'Welfare': A History of the Mistakes of the Past," *Social Justice* 21 (1995), pp. 13–16; Theresa Funiciello, "The Poverty Industry: Do Government and Charities Create the Poor?" *Ms.* (November/December 1990), pp. 33–40.

5. Josephine Shaw Lowell, "The Economic and Moral Effects of Public Outdoor Relief," in *Proceedings of the National Conference of Charities and Correction, 1890* (Boston, 1890), pp. 81–82.

6. L. A. Halbert, "Boards of Public Welfare: A System of Government Social Work," *Proceedings of the National Conference of Social Work, 1918*, pp. 20–21, cited in Roy Lubove, *The Struggle for Social Security, 1900–1935* (Pittsburgh: University of Pittsburgh Press, 1986), p. 94.

7. Roy Lubove, *The Struggle for Social Security, 1900–1935*, p. 98.

8. Joel F. Handler and Yeheskel Hasenfeld, *The Moral Construction of Poverty: Welfare Reform in America* (Newbury Park, CA: Sage, 1991), p. 71.

9. For example, see Terry Mizrahi, "The New 'Right' Agenda Decimates Social Programs, Devalues Social Work and Devastates Clients and Communities," *HCSSW Update* (School of Social Work, Hunter College of the City University of New York) (Spring 1996), p. 1.

10. Sar Levitan and Frank Gallo, "Jobs for JOBS: Toward a Work-Based Welfare System," *Occasional Paper 1993–1*, (Washington, DC: Center for Policy Studies, The George Washington University, 1993) (March 1993), p. 1.

11. Linda Gordon, *Pitied but Not Entitled: Single Mothers and the History of Welfare, 1890–1935* (New York: Free Press, 1994), p. 299.

12. G. D. Reilly, "Madame Secretary," in K. Louchheim, Ed., *The Making of the New Deal: The Insiders Speak* (Cambridge, MA: Harvard University Press, 1983), p. 175.

13. Gordon, *Pitied but Not Entitled*, p. 299.

14. Thomas Corbett, "Child Poverty and Welfare Reform: Progress or Paralysis?" *Focus* 15 (Spring 1993), pp. 4–5.

15. Corbett, "Child Poverty and Welfare Reform," p. 5.

16. U.S. House of Representatives, "The Conference Report on the Personal Responsibility and Work Opportunity Reconciliation Act of 1996," 31 July 1996.

17. Data for this section, unless otherwise noted, is from Administration for Children and Families, Office of Family Assistance, *Temporary Assistance for Needy Families (TANF), Sixth Annual Report to Congress*, November 2004. Online at www.acf.hhs.gov.

18. R. M. Cyert and J. G. Marsh, *A Behavioral Theory of the Firm* (Englewood Cliffs, NJ: Prentice-Hall, 1963).

19. U.S. Department of Health and Human Services, *Characteristics and Financial Circumstances of AFDC Recipients, FY 1993* (Washington, DC: U.S. Government Printing Office, 1995), p. 1; Kenneth Jost, "Welfare Reform," *CQ Researcher* 2 (10 April 1992),

p. 316; Committee on Ways and Means, U.S. House of Representatives, *1995 Green Book* (Washington, DC: U.S. Government Printing Office, 1995), p. 325.

20. Jane Lawler Dye, "Fertility and Program Participation in the United States: 1996," *Current Population Reports, P70–82* (Washington DC: U.S. Census Bureau, 2001), pp. 2–3; Administration for Children and Families, Office of Family Assistance, *Temporary Assistance for Needy Families (TANF), Sixth Annual Report to Congress,* November 2004, Table 4. Online at www.acf.hhs.gov.

21. Corbett, "Child Poverty and Welfare Reform," pp. 9–12.

22. Corbett, "Child Poverty and Welfare Reform," p. 12.

23. Dan Bloom, Mary Ferrell, Barbara Fink, with Diana Adams-Ciardullo, *Welfare Time Limits, State Policies, Implementation, and Effects on Families— Executive Summary* (New York: Manpower Development Research Corporation, 2002), p. 2.

24. David T. Ellwood and Mary Jo Bane, *The Impact of AFDC on Family Structure and Living Arrangements* (Cambridge, MA: Harvard University Press, 1984).

25. David Greenberg, Donna Linksz, and Marvin Mandell, *Social Experimentation and Public Policymaking* (Washington, DC: The Urban Institute, 2003), p. 127.

26. Robert Lerman, "Family Structure and Childbearing before and after Welfare Reform," in Alan Weil and Kenneth Finegold, Eds., *Welfare Reform: The Next Act* (Washington, DC: Urban Institute Press, 2002), pp. 33–52.

27. Martha S. Hill and Michael Ponza, "Does Welfare Dependency Beget Dependency?" Videographed (Ann Arbor, MI: Institute for Social Research, 1984) and "Poverty across Generations: Is Welfare Dependency a Pathology Passed from One Generation to the Next?" (Paper presented at the Population Association of America Meeting, Pittsburgh, March 1983), cited in Greg V. Duncan and Saul D. Hoffman, "The Use and Effects of Welfare: A Survey of Recent Evidence," *Social Service Review* 83 (June 1988), pp. 38–257.

28. Duncan and Hoffman, "The Use and Effects of Welfare," p. 254.

29. David Ellwood, *Poor Support: Poverty in the American Family* (New York: Basic Books, 1988), p. 16.

30. Lloyd A. Free and Hadley Cantril, *The Political Beliefs of Americans: A Study of Public Opinion* (New York: Simon & Schuster, 1967), p. 37.

31. Ellwood, *Poor Support,* p. 18.

32. Richard Sutch, "Has Social Spending Grown out of Control?" *Challenge* (May–June 1996), p. 12.

33. Mimi Abramovitz and Fred Newdom, "Fighting Back! Challenging AFDC Myths with the Facts," photocopy prepared for the Bertha Capan Reynolds Society.

34. Sutch, "Has Social Spending Grown out of Control?" p. 12.

35. Testimony of Sheldon Danziger, Professor, School of Social Work and School of Social Policy, University of Michigan, before the Senate Finance Committee (29 February 1996), p. 6.

36. Danziger, Testimony, p. 6; Katherine S. Newman, "Job Availability," *National Forum: The Phi Kappa Phi Journal* 76 (Summer 1996), pp. 20–24.

37. Norma B. Coe, Gregory Acs, Robert I. Lerman, and Keith Watson, "Does Work Pay? A Summary of the Work Incentives under TANF," *New Federalism: Issues and Options for the States* (Washington, DC: Urban Institute, 1998).

38. Robert I. Lerman, Pamela Loprest, and Caroline Ratcliffe, "How Well Can Urban Labor Markets Absorb Welfare Recipients?" *New Federalism: Issues and Options for the States* (Washington, DC: Urban Institute, 1999).

39. Sarah Brauner and Pamela Loprest, "Where Are They Now? What State Studies of People Who Left Welfare Tell Us," *New Federalism: Issues and Options for the States* (Washington, DC: Urban Institute, 1999).

40. Pamela J. Loprest and Sheila R. Zedlewski, *Making TANF Work for the Hard to Serve,* No. 2 in series, *Short Takes on Welfare Policy* (Washington, DC: Urban Institute, 2002), online at www.urban.org/publications/310474.html.

41. Levitan and Gallo, "Jobs for JOBS."

42. Frank S. Levy and Richard C. Michel, "Work for Welfare: How Much Good Will It Do?" *American Economic Review* 76 (May 1986), pp. 399–404.

43. Robert Moffitt, *Incentive Effects of the U.S. Welfare System: A Review* (Madison: Institute for Research on Poverty, University of Wisconsin, March 1990).

44. Kathryn Edin, "Surviving the Welfare System: How AFDC Recipients Make Ends Meet in Chicago," *Social Problems* 38 (November 1991), pp. 462–474; Kathryn Edin and Laura Lein, "Work, Welfare, and Single Mothers' Economic Survival Strategies," *American Sociological Review* 62 (April 1997), pp. 253–266; Christopher Jencks, "What's Wrong with Welfare Reform," *Harper's* 288 (April 1974), pp. 19–22.

45. Administration for Children and Families, U.S. Department of Health and Human Services. *Healthy Marriage Initiative: Activities and Accomplishments 2002–2004* (Washington, DC: U.S. Government Printing Office, 2005).

46. Levy and Michel, "Work for Welfare," p. 403.

47. Administration for Children and Families, *Healthy Marriage Initiative.*

48. Rebecca Blank. *It Takes a Nation: A New Agenda for Fighting Poverty.* (Princeton, NJ: Princeton University Press, 1997).

49. Leonard M. Lopoo and Thomas DeLeire, "Did Welfare Reform Influence the Fertility of Young Teens?" *Journal of Policy Analysis and Management* 2 (2006).

50. James T. Patterson, *America's Struggle against Poverty, 1900–1994* (Cambridge, MA: Harvard University Press, 1994), pp. 175, 231.

51. Patterson, *America's Struggle against Poverty,* p. 175.

52. David L. Kirp, "The California Work/Welfare Scheme," *Public Interest* (Spring 1986).

53. Judith M. Gueron, "The Route to Welfare Reform," *Brookings Review* 12 (Summer 1994), pp. 14–15.

54. Teresa Amott, "Reforming Welfare or Reforming the Labor Market: Lessons from the Massachusetts Employment Training Experience," *Social Justice* 21 (1992), pp. 33–37.

55. Levitan and Gallo, "Jobs for JOBS," p. 51.

56. Martha Coven. "An Introduction to TANF" (Washington DC: Center on Budget and Policy Priorities, 2002).

57. Coven, "An Introduction to TANF," p. 3.

58. Vicki Lens, "TANF: What Went Wrong and What to Do Next," *Social Work* 47 (July 2002), pp. 280–281.

59. Lens, "TANF: What Went Wrong and What to Do Next," p. 281.

60. Pamala Loprest, "How Are Families Who Left Welfare Doing over Time? A Comparison of two Cohorts of Welfare Leavers," *Economic Policy Review* (Federal Reserve Bank of New York) 7 (Sept. 2001), pp. 9–11.

61. Gregory Acs and Pamala Loprest. "Synthesis Report of the Findings from ASPE's 'Leavers' Grants" (Washington, DC: U.S. Department of Health and Human Services, 2001).

62. Demetra Smith Nightingale, "Work Opportunities for People Leaving Welfare," in Alan Weil and Kenneth Finegold, Eds., *Welfare Reform: The Next Act* (Washington, DC: Urban Institute Press, 2002), pp. 103–120.

63. Lens, "TANF: What Went Wrong and What to Do Next," p. 284.

64. Coven, "An Introduction to TANF," p. 1.

65. Lens, "TANF: What Went Wrong and What to Do Next," p. 285.

66. TANF Research and Evaluation, in *TANF Seventh Annual Report to Congress,* www.acf.hhs.gov.

67. Martha R. Burt, "The 'Hard to Serve': Definitions and Implications," in Weil and Finegold, *Welfare Reform: The Next Act,* pp. 163–178.

68. Sheila Zedlewski and Donald Alderson, "Do Families on Welfare in the Post-TANF Era Differ from Their Pre-TANF Counterparts?" *Assessing the New Federalism,* Discussion Paper 01–03 (Washington, DC: Urban Institute, 2001).

69. Weil and Finegold, *Welfare Reform: The Next Act,* pp. xxii–xxiii.

70. Sheldon Danziger and Peter Gottschalk, "Introduction," in Sheldon Danziger and Peter Gottschalk, Eds., *Uneven Tides: Rising Inequality in America* (New York: Russell Sage Foundation, 1993), p. 6.

71. Edward C. Banfield, *The Unheavenly City: The Nature and Future of Our Urban Crisis* (Boston: Little, Brown, 1970).

72. Leo Perlis, Statement, January 29, 1962, AFL-CIO Community Services Activities papers, folder 78, Social Welfare History Archives, University of Minnesota–Twin Cities, quoted in Patterson, *America's Struggle against Poverty, 1900–1994,* p. 133.

chapter 8

Aging: Social Security as an Entitlement

MORE SECURITY FOR
THE AMERICAN FAMILY

THE SOCIAL SECURITY ACT AS AMENDED
OFFERS GREATER OLD-AGE INSURANCE
PROTECTION TO PEOPLE NOW NEARING
RETIREMENT AGE.

FOR INFORMATION WRITE OR CALL AT THE NEAREST FIELD OFFICE OF THE
SOCIAL SECURITY BOARD

Edith Chavala, seventy-five years old, lives alone in a mobile home near Silver City, New Mexico, on $703 a month—$161 from a small pension and $542 from Social Security. She jokes about being poor but is quick to point out that she still has her health. As she observes the debates over changing Social Security, she has come to one conclusion: She is not at all happy about proposals to put part of the funds, now invested in Treasury securities, into the stock market. It doesn't matter to her whether it's the federal government doing the investing or individuals investing part of their Social Security taxes themselves. "I'm not a gambler," she says. "It seems like they want to gamble with our retirement money."[1]

Foster Jones and Heather Breaux are having cappucinos in the coffeehouse across from the bank where they work. When their conversation turns to earmarking money for personal investments, Foster declares heatedly, "What irks me is that I have to put in so much for Social Security—I think President Bush has the right idea—we should all get to keep at least some of that money to invest so we can build our own retirement nest eggs."

Maggie, a thirty-four-year-old working on her income tax return, comments to her mother, "You know, a lot of money from my paycheck goes for Social Security—but I figure Social Security probably won't be around when I'm older." Her mother, who teaches social work and social policy, is horrified. How could her daughter be so convinced by the scare tactics of people who want to dismantle the Social Security system?

Agnes and Jesse Moorhead have a small apartment and two cats. Mr. Moorhead retired from his custodial job ten years ago. The couple lives modestly, but they go out to dinner and a movie with friends few weeks and take a short vacation at a nearby lake each summer. Mr. Moorhead has only a small pension, so they rely chiefly on Social Security for their income. "It's not a huge amount," Mrs. Moorhead says, "but it's enough to keep us going. And it certainly gives me peace of mind to know that check will come every month."

Most Americans today, with only dim memories of the Great Depression, cannot recall the extraordinary social and economic conditions that led to the creation of Social Security. However, U.S. society, although far wealthier than it was then, still features the inequities and abrupt dislocations that led to the creation of Social Security. This protective system—which some have called the bedrock of the U.S. welfare state—will it still be there when those now in their early thirties begin to retire? If it does exist in the 2030s, will it be in the same form? Will people be able to choose between participating in Social Security and investing their own money toward retirement? Will methods of financing benefits be different, and will they be available only to certain groups of people, such as the needy? Will we still think of it as the major entitlement program in our country's social welfare system? Alarmists talk about the need to fix Social Security before the baby boomers start retiring "and bust the federal budget." Others, based on their belief in the basic strength of the U.S. economy, are confident that universal social programs such as Social Security can be shored up by federal surpluses and will continue to be entitlements that we can depend on.[2]

The term *entitlement* has been talked about a good deal in the past few years. It has been applied not only to the old-age insurance part of the Social Security Act but also to the many other programs making up the U.S. "safety net." In the late 1990s, ideological conflicts between a Democratic president and Republican majorities in Congress led to close scrutiny of our social welfare system and its costs and benefits and to a national debate over "who's entitled" and to what. Welfare clients, as we saw in Chapter 7, have not fared well in this debate; their "entitlement" to ongoing public aid was dashed by the federal welfare reform legislation of 1996.

Some of the participants in the discussion of entitlements have taken the issue to extremes. Robert J. Samuelson, for example, calls our belief in a network of entitlements a fantasy. In his book *The Good Life and Its Discontents: The American Dream in the Age of Entitlement*, Samuelson pictures postwar America as a time when we expected all social problems to be solved; poverty, racism, and crime to recede; and a "compassionate government" to protect the poor, the old, and the unfortunate. "We not only expected these things," Samuelson notes, "after a while, we thought we were entitled to them."[3] Thus, Samuelson recasts the notion of a mutual obligation in our society to achieve security for all into the image of a childish "wish list" in which all of us want gifts and candy that we don't truly "deserve."

Defenders of entitlements view them as the expression of society's obligation to the poor, the elderly, and the unemployed. Some argue that all citizens have a right to economic security, whereas others stress that certain entitlements, such as Social Security, are in fact earned benefits. Discussions of Social Security thus become inextricably tied up in contemporary debates about the purpose and desirability of entitlements.

This chapter analyzes the Social Security program within the larger context of these debates. It describes the development of Social Security as the first comprehensive effort by the federal government to meet the economic needs of a wide variety of citizens. The chapter concentrates on the social insurance portion of the Social Security Act, the major U.S. policy dealing with the common needs of the elderly. It also touches on the program's provisions for the poor elderly, people with disabilities, and disadvantaged children. We provide a detailed discussion of President George W. Bush's attempt to add a private investment component to the Social Security system and responses to this proposal. The chapter also discusses the current state of employee pensions, which have traditionally been an important part of economic security for many retirees.

The Problem That Social Security Was Developed to Solve

In any society in which the vast majority of people depend on wages for their income, old age will present an economic problem. Once people have stopped working, they must find another source of revenue to pay the rent or mortgage, the grocery bill, and the doctor's bill. Wealthier members of society will have built up savings and acquired other assets for this occasion, and some workers will receive good pensions from the companies where they worked. But many will enter retirement and old age with only small savings and pension funds and perhaps a paid-off mortgage—or no assets at all.

Today, almost all people age sixty-five and over (and in some cases, age sixty-two) have another source of income: their monthly Social Security benefits. Before the Social Security Act was passed in 1935, the only public old-age pensions that existed were limited to certain groups of people—veterans, federal civil service employees, and employees of some state and local governments. Some workers received help through the private pension program of their unions or places of employment. Most elderly people depended on savings, help from their families, assistance from public and private charity (which was generally quite limited), and, as a last resort, the local poorhouse. Not surprisingly, a large proportion of the elderly worked as long as possible to forestall the poverty of old age. In 1930 almost 60 percent of men over sixty-five were still employed.[4]

The Great Depression decimated most of these sources of income. Bank closures wiped out lifetime savings; unemployed children could not help elderly parents; older people lost their jobs at even higher rates than younger workers; failing companies closed down their pension plans; and the coffers of both private charities and local public assistance programs quickly dried up. Describing the crisis, economist (and later Senator) Paul Douglas declared that the Depression "increasingly convinced the majority of the American people that individuals could not themselves provide adequately for their old age and that some sort of greater security should be provided by society."[5]

The Social Security Act of 1935

The economic crisis of the Great Depression brought about a recognition of fundamental economic insecurities in U.S. society. In response, President Franklin D. Roosevelt and his advisors crafted and won passage of the 1935 Social Security Act. This act, perhaps more than any other major social policy, has been subject to continued change and expansion. We detail those changes in the historical section of this chapter, presenting here a basic description of the legislation signed by Roosevelt on August 14, 1935.

The 1935 act is a broad piece of legislation that includes two social insurance programs and three "welfare," or public assistance, programs, along with several smaller programs such as vocational rehabilitation and child welfare services. Although social insurance benefits were to be made available to people of all income levels, public assistance payments would be made only to those determined by states to be financially needy. The two programs of direct relevance to the elderly are described in Titles I, II, and VIII. Under Title I, "Grants to States of Old-Age Assistance" (OAA), the federal government would reimburse states for 50 percent of the amount they spent on public (cash) assistance to poor people over the age of sixty-five. Each state was required to have a statewide plan for old-age assistance, and its system of administering the grants would have to be approved by the federal government.

Title II, "Federal Old-Age Benefits," contains what most consider is the program synonymous with the term *social security*—a federal system of old-age insurance. The program created a federal trust fund, the Old-Age Reserve Account, to which funds would be appropriated each year to provide monthly payments to retired people sixty-five and over. Excluded from the program were farm laborers, domestic servants, U.S. government employees, state and local government employees, and workers in nonprofit agencies. Old-Age Benefit payments would begin in 1942. For workers whose total wages between the start of the program and the time they reached sixty-five were $3,000 or less, monthly benefits would amount to one-half of one percent of these wages. For a person who reached sixty-five in 1942 and who had worked for the previous five years at fifty dollars a month, for example, this would amount to the munificent sum of fifteen dollars a month. As a mild measure of income redistribution, workers making higher salaries would receive a much lower percentage of their salary for all wages in excess of $3,000. No retired worker could receive more than eighty-five dollars a month.[6]

Title VIII detailed the source of funding for the old-age insurance program: federal taxes to be paid by both employers and employees. For the first few years of the program, workers and employers would each pay the federal government 1 percent of the first $3,000 of the worker's annual wage. The percentage paid would rise every three years thereafter, to a final level of 3 percent in 1949. Then, as now, workers with lower wages paid proportionately more of their income into Social Security than did people with higher wages.[7]

The other social insurance program of the Social Security Act is a joint federal–state unemployment compensation system detailed in Titles III and IX. Under these titles, the federal government was authorized to appropriate funds to help states administer benefits to unemployed workers. States would collect a payroll tax from employers of eight or more individuals and would give these revenues to the federal government. The federal government would keep the revenues in a central fund for each state; that fund would be used to pay unemployment benefits to workers. Employers would be given federal tax credits to offset most of their payroll taxes. Each state would enact its own unemployment insurance law, which would determine levels and duration of benefits. These laws would have to be approved by the federal government, but the criteria for approval related to administrative matters rather than to the amount or length of payments.

The Social Security Act also brought into existence joint state–federal programs of public assistance for dependent children and the blind. Title IV, "Grants to States of Aid to Dependent Children" (ADC), established a system in which the federal government covered one-third of a state's expenditures for the support of needy children in families with one caretaker (usually a widowed or divorced mother). As in unemployment compensation, state plans were to be approved by the federal government, but approval was again limited to administrative procedures and did not include minimum levels of benefits. A similar program for public assistance payments to needy blind persons was included in Title X, with funds provided half by the federal government and half by the state. In both the ADC and Aid to the Blind programs, the percentage paid by the federal government was calculated on benefits up to a certain amount; if states paid more than that amount to beneficiaries, they would have to cover the excess.

Finally, the act established a new federal entity, the Social Security Board, to administer the old-age insurance system and the federal portions of the other programs. The board was also responsible for approval of state program plans for unemployment compensation, old-age assistance, and aid to children.

Historical Development of Social Security Programs in the United States

Although the 1935 Social Security Act may have seemed a bold policy innovation on the part of the Roosevelt administration, each program established by the act drew on precedents dating back at least to the early 1900s. A complex set of social, political, and economic factors influenced the development of the social insurance and public assistance provisions elaborated in 1935. A thorough history of this development, and of the subsequent implementation and amendments of the act, would run to hundreds of pages. We present a brief analysis here, concentrating primarily on programs related to the elderly.

Precedents of the Social Security Act

The creation of federal old-age insurance is often viewed as a watershed in U.S. social welfare history. Historian Mark Leff describes the program as "both the pearl and the pillar of the American welfare state, a political marvel that has beaten the ideological odds and has allowed Americans to receive government checks without stigma."[8] In developing this "political marvel," the architects of the Social Security Act built on a patchwork of existing programs. The idea of old-age pension plans was not new in the 1930s. The public sector had taken the lead in establishing such programs. The federal government established public pensions for U.S. war veterans after the Civil War. While at first these applied only to financially needy and disabled veterans, by 1912 old age alone could qualify former soldiers to receive benefits. Veterans' pensions had become a broad and generous system of social provision, including payments to many widows and dependents. In addition, at the turn of the century most major U.S. cities provided pensions for firefighters and police officers. The majority of states had retirement plans for schoolteachers by 1916, and in the early 1930s a number of states established mandatory pension laws for their residents. In 1920 a federal Civil Service Retirement System was established.[9]

Businesses and corporations had also developed pension plans as one part of a private social welfare system that emerged in the United States in the 1880s. Based both on moral arguments and the desire for a more efficient and docile workforce, employers created a variety of social welfare amenities, including retirement programs. At the same time, some trade unions established pension plans. However, union and corporate programs together covered only about 14 percent of U.S. workers in 1932.[10]

Nor was the idea of social insurance new in the 1930s. Beginning in the Progressive era, reformers such as Isaac Rubinow, Abraham Epstein, and Jane Addams promoted programs based on those developed in Germany and England, in which the government used tax money to protect people against the inevitable hazards of an industrial state: industrial accidents, disability, ill health, and unemployment. To the reformers, social insurance represented a source of public funds that could spread the cost of dealing with such risks across a large number of people. It also allowed for some redistribution of income from the wealthy to the less well-off. To further these goals, Rubinow helped form the American Association for Labor Legislation. The association provided research and model bills to states experimenting with various programs to aid unemployed and retired workers.[11]

Despite such activity, the idea of a national public system of old-age insurance was slow to catch on. Americans held fast to ingrained beliefs in self-help and private responses to need. Even the developing labor movement did not initially back public old-age benefits, preferring to trust the union's ability to improve wages and provide security.

Creation of the Social Security Act

Forces let loose during the Depression changed all this. The 1929 stock market crash led to unprecedented levels of unemployment and was particularly devastating for the elderly. A relatively small and scattered array of private, state, and local social welfare programs quickly proved inadequate to deal with rising levels of need. Traditional beliefs in independence and self-reliance were badly shaken.

When Roosevelt took office in 1933, he faced the challenge of coping with the country's deepening crisis. Although at first pursuing temporary relief measures such as those provided by the Federal Emergency Relief Administration, the president was loath to simply replace the traditional poor law system with federal funds. His belief that more permanent relief should stress jobs over handouts led to the creation of vast public works programs; his commitment to "rebuilding many of the structures of our economic life and reorganizing it in order to prevent a recurrence of collapse" led to a program of social insurance.[12]

Political forces helped shape this move toward social insurance, particularly where it pertained to the problems of old age. The desperation of the elderly was portrayed in numerous letters to the White House. One citizen noted,

> I am about 75 or 76 years old and Have Labored Hard all My Days until depression Came on and I Had No Job in three years. . . . Please Sir do what you Can for me I am to old to be turned out of doors.[13]

Older people like these formed a major support for increasingly popular flat-rate pension plans, such as that proposed by Dr. Francis Townsend, a retired California physician. Starting in his home state, Townsend built a national movement for a program that promised to end the Depression by giving everyone over age sixty a pension of $200 a month. Financed through federal taxation, the plan would bolster the economy by requiring recipients to spend the entire $200 within thirty days. By 1934, Townsend claimed 5 million supporters. Other utopian schemes included Louisiana Senator Huey Long's proposal to give thirty dollars a month to every poor person over age sixty and to finance this "Share Our Wealth" program through income, inheritance, and other taxes. Long, who had originally supported Roosevelt, was beginning to emerge as a potential political rival. In addition, a bill supported by the Communist party and a number of social workers, other professionals, and unemployed workers was introduced into Congress in 1935 and received wide support. The Lundeen bill would have guaranteed to all persons willing to work but unable to find a job an income equal to the average wages in their district and would have provided a social insurance scheme for the elderly. Calls for action, especially to deal with unemployment, came also from social work organizations and increasingly powerful unions representing unskilled workers.[14]

Clearly, Roosevelt needed to maintain his political support and to keep control of the reform agenda. In June 1934, he responded to political pressures and to the country's continued economic distress by announcing to Congress his intent to find a sound means for providing "security against several of the great disturbing factors in life—especially those which relate to unemployment and old age." He proceeded to create the Committee on Economic Security (CES) to make recommendations for a broad program of legislation to ensure that security.[15]

The committee was chaired by Frances Perkins, Secretary of Labor, and included other cabinet members and Federal Emergency Relief Administrator Harry Hopkins. Both Perkins and Hopkins were social workers. Two University of Wisconsin labor economists played important roles in the legislative drafting process. One, Edwin E. Witte, served as executive director of the CES, while the other, Arthur J. Altmeyer, chaired an accompanying Technical Board. Experts (government officials and academics) on the Technical Board and on the CES staff did much of the actual work in formulating the legislation and presenting major policy issues to CES members for their review.[16]

Thus a large group of people with different skills and perspectives came together to develop a social insurance program. In their decision making, CES members brought to bear not only their own points of view but also their sense of the general thinking of the president. In addition, they were sensitive to issues of constitutionality, as previous Supreme Court decisions had cast doubt on how far the federal government would be allowed to go in enacting social legislation. Administrative feasibility, public and congressional reactions, and technical problems in financing and implementation were further factors to be considered. The committee's expert advisors, while tuned in to technical issues, were less concerned about constitutionality and congressional acceptance. Perkins referred to working with them as similar to "driving a team of high-strung unbroken horses." In a good example of the messy world of policy making, academics, politicians, and top officials in the Roosevelt administration all plunged together into uncharted waters to develop a politically, economically, and administratively feasible national economic security program.[17]

To complicate matters, as historian Andrew Achenbaum has noted, there was not a clear consensus about the major thrust of an economic security plan. Although some New Deal scholars have portrayed the development and implementation of the Social Security Act as following a set ideology, it seems more accurate to view the process as reflecting a fundamental ambivalence and lack of clarity about goals. Achenbaum describes two potentially conflicting social policy objectives related to Social Security: social adequacy and equity. *Adequacy* referred to assisting people based on their actual need, *equity* to giving assistance based on what people had put into the system. The former was sometimes called welfare and included a redistribution of income; the latter emphasized principles of self-reliance and fairness: Recipients would receive benefits based on what they had contributed.[18]

Roosevelt himself seemed to have had both approaches in mind when delivering his economic security message to Congress. The president spoke of "the security of home, and the security of livelihood" as constituting "a *right* which belongs to every individual and every family *willing to work* [italics added]." This ambivalence between a program that based benefits on citizens' rights and one that rewarded people for contributions based on work was ingrained in the U.S. Social Security system from the beginning.[19]

The work of the CES and its staff led to a broad program that combined the two approaches. The bill that emerged contained old-age insurance and unemployment compensation tied to wage contributions (the equity approach) as well as more traditional public assistance measures (the social adequacy approach). The social adequacy/income redistribution goal even played some part in the old-age insurance program because low-income workers got a larger percentage of their wages back in benefits than did higher-income workers.

The bill also drew on existing U.S. values and systems. Wage-based old-age insurance and unemployment compensation programs supported the work ethic. A neighborly sense of compassion for deprived children helped justify the ADC proposal, which at the time was considered a rather minor part of the Social Security Act. The same sense of compassion undergirded extra assistance for the poor elderly; in addition, this aid was seen as a justifiable benefit for folks who "deserved help" in their later years. Most parts of the new system fit the U.S. brand of federalism, with its stress on states' rights. Whereas old-age insurance broke new ground as a large, nationally administered program, unemployment compensation was shaped by the individual plans of each state, and the federal government was given relatively minimal control over the assistance programs for children and the elderly. For example, states had complete say in determining the level of benefits in the ADC program, leading to a wide range in benefits that still exists in public welfare today.

Two important issues raised during the bill's development concerned the scope of coverage and financing. For a number of reasons, two groups were excluded from participation in the old-age insurance plan: domestic servants and farmworkers. CES staff visualized the plan as particularly important for industrial workers who had relatively low salaries. Because these workers tended to have a stable relationship with a single employer, it would be easy to administer a payroll tax on them and their employers. Farmworkers and servants might receive in-kind benefits in addition to their wages, such as room and board, and because they were seen as having many employers, collection of a payroll tax might be difficult. An argument could thus be made to exclude these groups, at least for the time being. Yet the fact that many of these workers were African American farm laborers and female domestic servants adds another, more sinister dimension to their exclusion—the influence of southern legislators anxious to control their workforce and the apathy of many of the policy-makers regarding the plight of African Americans in the United States. As a result, half of the African American workforce was excluded from benefits.[20]

Financing the old-age insurance portion of the Social Security Act through payroll deductions drew fire from progressives and radicals in the 1930s, and as we will see later, that criticism still surfaces today, although from other types of groups and for other reasons. Detractors asserted that tying benefits to income levels maintained a system of economic inequality and failed to produce the re-sources needed to give a meaningful amount of aid to all the elderly. The usual in-terpretation for this financing decision by the bill's creators is that Roosevelt and his policymakers needed to cast social insurance as an earned benefit, rather than a handout, in order to get it passed. Although this was an important factor, other considerations played a part as well. The social insurance systems of European countries were financed out of general tax funds. Roosevelt and the other archi-tects of old-age insurance rejected this approach in part because federal tax rev-enues at the time were quite low—less than 5 percent of the population paid federal income taxes in the 1930s. In addition, both the president and the expert staffers of the CES were leery of future attempts by Congress to change appropriation levels for social insurance. While we think of old-age insurance as the linchpin of the Social Security Act, the program actually had little support in Congress and was almost dropped when the bill went through committee. To safeguard the pro-gram from politicians in the future, it seemed necessary to create a separate, more easily protected trust fund. Thus for ideological, political, and economic reasons, the opportunity to use general taxes to create substantial income redistribution and a more reasonable level of aid to the elderly was lost.[21]

The bill drew both praise and criticism as it went through Congress. Those supporting the plan included national women's organizations, the American As-sociation of Social Workers, organized labor, liberal politicians, and even the U.S. Chamber of Commerce. However, many businesspeople and Republican politi-cians opposed it, focusing most of their disapproval on the provisions for old-age insurance. Detractors called this "the worst title in the bill . . . a burdensome tax on industry" that would establish "a bureaucracy in the field of insurance in com-petition with private business." Fears of the oppressive hand of "big government" were added to this strenuous defense of the private market system. From the other end of the political spectrum, radical critics argued that the plan did little to change the negative effects of the market system. Despite these criticisms, Roosevelt and the CES succeeded. Through compromise, careful management in the legislative system, and popular demand for change, the bill passed by wide margins in both the House and Senate.[22]

The Social Security Act, for all its flaws, was a milestone in the history of U.S. social welfare programs. It cleverly joined welfare and insurance programs, state and federal levels of financing and implementation, and the often conflicting U.S. values of mutual responsibility and self-reliance. Although the old-age insurance portion did not attack income inequalities the way some had hoped, it nevertheless included a slightly redistributive measure that paid the poorest workers a higher percentage of their income (note that because this percentage was figured on a lower income, they still got less money than better-off workers). Moreover, as the following section shows, the act created a program capable of slow and steady expansion and reform.

Changes in Social Security

The Social Security system has proved a remarkable example of incremental policy change. Before the first old-age insurance benefits were even distributed, a set of amendments had begun to alter the act's balance between equity and social adequacy. Through the years, subsequent changes have broadened the bill's scope and liberalized its benefits.

The first changes, made in 1939, were largely a response to political pressures. Because the first old-age benefits were not due to be paid until 1942, there was a long period before the advantages of the new system would be felt. In the meantime, workers' deductions were piling up in a reserve fund, which was, at least in theory, not to be used for anything else. (In reality, the government bought U.S. treasury bonds with the funds, thus loaning itself money with which to finance current operations.) Workers experiencing their first payroll deductions wondered where their money was going. They also lost some spending power, which hurt the economy. Those who were already elderly had to wait for five years to receive aid; this put pressure on the Social Security Act's state-administered old-age assistance program (OAA). The Social Security Board worried that expanding the assistance program would make politicians less likely to support future growth in social insurance. At the same time, older people's groups pressed for programs with broader coverage, and politicians criticized the social insurance financing arrangements.[23]

Roosevelt and the Social Security Board responded with rhetoric that expressed one thing and a set of amendments that did another. In order to keep old-age insurance from being overshadowed by OAA, defenders sharpened the distinction between social insurance and welfare and promoted insurance as an effective alternative to welfare. But in order to mollify critics of the program, they proposed a liberalization of social insurance benefits that in fact diminished the work-related aspects of the insurance program and moved it more toward the social adequacy, or "welfare," approach.[24]

A major change was the addition of family benefits. Monthly benefits were established for the survivors of both active and retired workers and for the dependent children of retired workers. By emphasizing care of widows and children who were likely to be needy, the amendments suggested a more paternal role for the government as provider of family support. Encouraging a continued fuzziness regarding the program's actual goals, the new benefits were still couched in the language of work-related insurance. This was not *entirely* misleading, because the new beneficiaries qualified through their relationship to a wage earner who had contributed to the system.

In addition, the 1939 amendments allowed benefit payments to begin in 1940 and lowered the combined worker–employer taxes from 3 to 2 percent. These changes, all voted into law, at the same time liberalized benefits and lowered taxes, not necessarily a winning formula for long-term financing of the program. After 1939 the Social Security program continued to grow incrementally. Extensions in benefits were approved relatively easily in the periods of economic expansion up through the early 1970s. A part of the motivation continued to be the goal of expanding social insurance at the expense of public assistance programs. In 1950, benefits were raised substantially, bringing old-age insurance to a parity with OAA. Four years later, regularly employed farmworkers and domestic workers were finally brought into the system, along with people who were self-employed.[25]

Financing was still not satisfactorily addressed, however. Although the Social Security Administration recommended that increased benefits be funded by general revenues, Congress chose a plan of gradually rising payroll tax rates, even though it had failed to implement such mandated tax rises in previous years.[26] The continued reliance on payroll deductions to finance the Social Security program reinforced the notion that workers were setting up their own "private savings accounts" for help in old age. Many people did not understand that their deductions were being used to support current retirees.

In 1956, social insurance was extended to workers with permanent disability aged fifty and over; once they reached sixty-five, recipients could receive regular old-age insurance benefits. The initial Social Security Act did not include a basic disability insurance program. It did provide for those who were blind, but only through a federal–state program of means-tested assistance. The changes in 1956 were made acceptable by linking disability with retirement (reflecting the equity, or work-related, approach to social insurance). Benefits were promoted as payments "to unfortunate individuals who had to 'retire early, because of mental or physical impairment.'" In 1960 the "social adequacy" goal undergirded an amendment to extend benefits to disabled workers of all ages and their dependents. (Today over eight million nonelderly disabled workers and their dependents receive Social Security benefits.) What was now Old Age, Survivors', and Disability Insurance (OASDI) also received further boosts in benefits. By 1961, all workers were allowed to retire, with reduced benefits, at age sixty-two. Congress also allowed increases in payroll taxes, to 3 percent, in 1960.[27]

The rediscovery of poverty during the Kennedy and Johnson years brought dramatic changes in Social Security programs for the elderly, changes that an expanding economy seemed well able to support. Three OASDI benefit increases were authorized in five years. In addition, an elusive quest for a federal health care program, which had been proposed intermittently since the 1920s but always rejected as politically insupportable, was finally partially realized through the creation of Medicare and Medicaid in 1965. Medicare provided acute-care health benefits to all old-age insurance recipients over sixty-five. Medicaid gave health care coverage to those in the Social Security assistance programs, including old-age assistance. By now, social insurance had become one of the country's most popular social programs, with a large number of stakeholders.

In 1968, Republicans bent on recapturing the presidency found it politically advantageous to include expansion of the Social Security system in the party platform. Once Nixon was elected, competition between a Republican president and a Democratic Congress to retain the "elderly vote" led to significant reforms and expansion in OASDI. In the presidential election year of 1972, a plan was adopted to tie benefits received after 1975 to rises in the cost of living. This automatic, annual "cost-of-living adjustment" (COLA) was based on the assumption that wages, and concomitant payroll taxes, would continue to rise. The COLA thus seemed feasible and affordable. Other changes included extending Medicare coverage to the disabled and transforming the jointly funded state–federal OAA into a federally funded Supplemental Security program (SSI). And, most spectacular of all, Congress passed a 20 percent increase in OASDI benefits. But Nixon did not raise the level of the payroll tax. This, along with the stagnation of wages in the mid-1970s, encouraged a crisis mentality regarding the Social Security insurance programs that persists today.[28]

The first crisis came in the 1980s, when—due in part to the serious inflation of the preceding decade—benefit payments threatened to exceed incoming tax revenues. Congress and the Reagan administration responded to the depletion of the reserve fund with a series of mostly incremental adjustments to the Social Security program. These included advancing the age at which people became eligible for benefits (to reach sixty-seven in 2017), increasing the payroll tax paid by workers, and initiating taxation of the benefits received by people with incomes above certain levels. These changes created large surpluses in the reserve fund, which, it was hoped, would prepare the country to handle the retirement of the baby boomers in the twenty-first century.[29]

Contemporary Analysis of Social Security

Thanks to the continued expansion of Social Security (as the old-age/disability insurance program is now popularly called), the economic position of older citizens has vastly improved. Much of the change occurred in the 1960s. At the beginning of the decade, 35 percent of the elderly were poor despite Social Security benefits; at its end, only 25 percent lived below the poverty line. The figure had dropped to 15 percent by 1979. This demonstrates the great success of the Social Security program. Yet the consensus supporting the program is beginning to unravel. Issues regarding Social Security's goals, coverage, and financing are raised by politicians, beneficiaries, and the public. In the following policy analysis, we pursue these historically based issues as they are played out in contemporary society.

Social Analysis

Social Security coverage is now almost universal for U.S. workers. Currently, about 47 million people (retirees and their dependents, underage survivors of deceased workers, and the disabled) receive a Social Security check each month. The average stipend is $1,184 a month, or $14,000 a year. For almost half of elderly women, Social Security benefits constitute 90 percent of their income. Many of these are single African American and Hispanic women. A third of African American retirees live on Social Security alone. Some of those receiving Social Security also have pensions from their jobs, but as we will see later, the traditional employment pension system is rapidly deteriorating in the United States.[30] See Figure 8.1 for recent information about sources of income for elderly persons. The poverty rate for older Americans has continued to decrease, declining to 10.1 percent in 2001. As Figure 8.2 indicates, Social Security has in the past played a notable role in reducing poverty for the elderly.

This is the good news. The bad news is that Social Security remains a supplement to income from other sources for many Americans. When these other sources don't exist, Social Security benefits are too low to lift all recipients out of poverty or to help the 6.5 percent of the elderly who are classified as "near-poor." Furthermore, the burden of poverty is unevenly spread among those over sixty-five. Nine percent of older whites were poor in 2001, compared to 22 percent of elderly African Americans and 22 percent of older Hispanics.[31]

Women face particular problems in the Social Security system. Because they were not seen as the primary wage earners in the early years of the program's development, it was expected that their benefits would most likely come through their positions as wives or widows of male beneficiaries. This turned out to be the case because many women either did not work for wages at all or

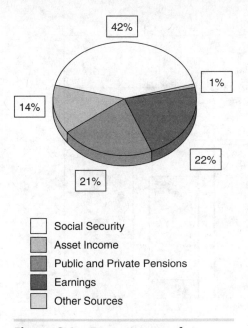

Figure 8.1 ■ Percentages of Aggregate Income of Elderly Persons from Various Sources

Source: Allan Sloan, "Social Security, A Daring Leap," *Newsweek* (14 February 2005), pp. 41–42.

did so sporadically. Their lower salaries led to lower contributions to the system, so their own pensions were less than those afforded to them through marriage. However, benefits established for elderly wives and widows were not generous either—50 percent of a husband's pension for a wife, and 75 percent for a widow. Apparently, women were expected to have lower expenses. In fact, widows have disproportionately high rates of poverty. For the past thirty years, these rates have been three to four times higher than those of elderly married women.[32]

Although some policymakers began to recognize women's problems in the 1950s, to date only small changes have been made, such as the provision of benefits to elderly divorced women in 1965. Due to lower salaries and the more intermittent work histories of wives and homemakers, the average monthly benefit for women was $722 in 2001, compared to $961 for men. If an older couple is living on the man's checks alone, a women will get less when her husband dies. Economists currently estimate that the surviving spouse's cost of living is about 80 percent of what the couple's was. However, the Social Security payments decline to about 65 percent.[33]

Percent of persons

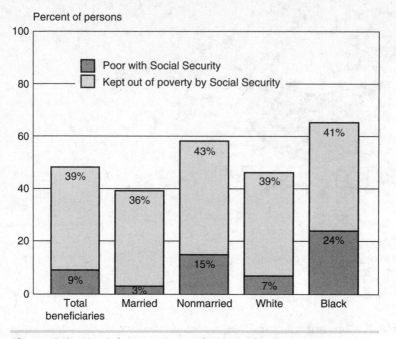

Figure 8.2   Social Security's Role in Reducing Poverty, 1998

Source: Annual Statistical Supplement to the Social Security Bulleting, 1999 (Washington, DC: U.S. Department of Health and Human Services, Social Security Administration, 1999), p. 20.

Lower salaries may account for racial disparities reported in 1998 data. In that year, African American women averaged $604, African American men $730. Widows as a whole received an average of $790; the figure drops to $640 for African Americans. Wives of retired workers averaged $370 a month. Whereas more than half of all retired men receive pension benefits in addition to Social Security payments, only about a quarter of retired women do. Finally, Social Security is the only source of income for 2.5 million older single women.[34]

Social Security's inequities and its inability to provide a firm safety net for lower-wage workers reflect competing social values. As shown in the discussion of the program's history, both the larger social security system and the social insurance plan drew on ideas of equity and social adequacy. *Equity*, as you recall, refers to a sense of fairness in the distribution of benefits based on contributions that workers made into the system. The U.S. work ethic undergirds this approach. *Social adequacy*, in contrast, stresses provision of a "basic floor of protection," or level of income to all who need it, unrelated to contributions. Social Security can be considered an intergenerational commitment or a collective responsibility "to provide at least a subsistence income to the most vulnerable of citizens." Thus an additional outcome of social adequacy measures is redistribution of income from the better-off to those with fewer resources.[35]

Sometimes social adequacy is equated with welfare, which may be confusing. Welfare as it exists today provides inadequate benefits, often not lifting recipients above the poverty line. In addition, when it involves people other than the poor elderly, public assistance carries a good deal of stigma. Some critics argue that welfare's main intent is to change behavior, not to protect the poor. Thus our current welfare system is only a partial step toward the goal of social adequacy. To achieve that goal, the system would have to provide higher benefits and promote the legitimacy of recipients' claims to them.

The conflict between equity and social adequacy boils down to the simple question: Do you deserve help because you are poor or because you worked hard and contributed to the system? Of course, even this question isn't really simple— poor people may work hard and still get low salaries; others, such as homemakers, may do unpaid labor and not get the chance to pay anything in. And we also need to remember that Social Security isn't like an individual savings account; the contributions of current workers support the older generation.

In the United States, people generally rank self-reliance over interdependence, thus finding equity a more "legitimate" basis for providing aid. When Social Security began, then, policymakers prudently portrayed the old-age insurance plan in the language of work and contributions. However, the notion of helping the less fortunate, particularly those, such as the elderly, whose poverty seems no fault of their own, still has a place in the U.S. value system. Thus the Social Security Act combined assistance and insurance programs, and both the act and subsequent changes brought an element of social adequacy into the old-age insurance program. Our ambivalence over the relationship between those two goals continues to complicate the debate over how to reform Social Security.

The question of who "deserves" help is closely connected to current discussions of entitlement. Attacks on the growth of entitlements bring up the same issues of who should be given government assistance and why. Although it is becoming popular to portray almost all public assistance and social insurance programs as entitlements, that concept had a more limited meaning when our modern social welfare system began in the 1930s. The architects of the Social Security Act did not even include the term in the act, stressing instead the right of wage earners to benefits. As Roosevelt explained, "We put the payroll contributions there so as to give contributors a legal, moral and political right to collect their pensions." While social insurance was justified as an "earned right," developers of the Social Security Act based the public assistance titles on a different conception of right: a poor person's "statutory right" to assistance, "even though that assistance was conditioned on need." The official rhetoric supporting the act and its later modifications suggests that this was a two-tier model of rights, with earned rights constituting the more legitimate ones.[36]

The use of the term *entitlement* probably originated in legal discussions of welfare in the 1960s. In a 1965 *Yale Law Journal* article, Charles B. Reich used *entitlement* to describe the idea that "when individuals have insufficient resources to live under conditions of health and decency, society has obligations to provide support, and the individual is entitled to that support as of right." Legal scholars fleshed out this idea further as they argued that entitlements could be construed as property rights, which could not be denied or cut off without notice and a fair hearing. They contended that ownership could be seen in terms of two different sets of property rights, involving either control over something tangible that one owns or control rights over income or other resources, such as welfare and social insurance benefits, needed for personal autonomy. This new interpretation of property as something intangible as well as tangible means, for example, that professionals have a constitutionally protected property right regarding licenses that affect their ability to practice. Such licenses cannot be denied, just as tangible property cannot be taken away or confiscated, without due process. Using similar reasoning, the Supreme Court ruled in 1970 that welfare recipients had certain constitutional rights to their entitlements and that the government could not cut these off without due process. The Court argued that it had become realistic "to regard welfare entitlements as more like 'property' than a 'gratuity,'" or charity.[37]

Such sophisticated legal arguments are not in most people's minds when they discuss entitlements today. Neither, probably, are such definitions as "services, goods, or money due to an individual by virtue of a specific status" *(Social Work Dictionary)* or "the state of meeting the applicable requirements for receipt of benefits" (Social Security Administration, 1995). Instead, people tend to think of a two-tiered system that includes "earned entitlements," such as Social Security, and "income-based entitlements," such as AFDC, and often tend to perceive the former as much more legitimate than the latter.[38]

Critics on the left argue that both kinds of entitlement are perfectly legitimate. However, there is a growing movement on the right to lump all types of entitlement together and to characterize the whole notion of entitlement as a false one, which has subtly "subverted personal and institutional responsibility." Under titles such as "Escaping the Entitlement Straitjacket," conservatives label entitlements "a problem" and question whether "popularly accepted 'rights'" should be "allowed to destroy the economy." The denigration of entitlements and the claims that they are no longer affordable can be seen as a smoke screen used by those wishing to divert attention from other ways to manage the budget. These ways include increasing taxes, especially for corporations and people with high incomes, and/or decreasing tax breaks, such as the waiver of local property taxes for some businesses and the use of home mortgage interest as a tax deduction. Just as in the equity versus social adequacy debate, confusion and ambivalence over the meaning and role of entitlements cloud public discussion of potential changes and improvements in Social Security.[39]

Political Analysis

As we have seen, the notion of entitlements is politically charged. Now, as at the beginning of Social Security, there are a number of stakeholders concerned about the system and its possible reform. These include current retirees, disabled workers, and their dependents; low-income workers; the children of aging parents; organized groups representing the elderly; current wage earners; employers; labor unions; the public at large; members of Congress; members of the executive branch of the federal government; politicians running for office; think tanks of all ideological persuasions; program administrators; private pension companies; and human service professionals such as social workers.

As Social Security has expanded, both the numbers and categories of beneficiaries have increased. One of the program's greatest protections is the sheer number and potential voting power of those assisted by it. The elderly in particular represent a large percentage of the electorate, and they vote in greater numbers than any other age group. However, there are subsets within this group with different agendas and needs. For example, many of today's retirees experienced the Depression and often have different views of the role of government in social provision than do the baby boomers, who are getting closer to retirement and who lived through several decades of cutbacks in social spending. Then, too, people receiving Social Security because of disabilities may have another set of concerns.

While elderly beneficiaries cast a good proportion of the votes on election day, a more concentrated type of power is exercised through the various citizen and professional organizations that make up the "Gray Lobby." By far the strongest of these is the American Association of Retired Persons (AARP), with a membership of more than thirty-five million people. The association is one of the biggest and most politically powerful organizations in the country. It has opposed most attempts to make cuts or other changes in Social Security that it believes would disadvantage older Americans.[40]

Conservative politicians have wielded a good deal of power in questioning the stability of Social Security funding, discussed in the next section, and in casting doubt on the desirability and legitimacy of entitlements. From the other side of the floor, liberal Democrats have generally defended the system. Think tanks, such as the conservative American Enterprise Institute and the Cato Institute, and the liberal Urban Institute, help provide the fodder for politicians' positions.

The general public has been somewhat ambivalent about support for Social Security and other entitlements, particularly when the federal government plays the dominant role in their financing and administration. Older voters, however, have been swinging away from Republican reform plans to shrink the federal government and putting more trust in the Democrats' traditional commitment "to protect the Social Security system." They are also leery of changes that might negatively affect their benefits. Younger workers may fear the demise of Social Security before they can benefit from it. Some may long for the chance to put at least part of their Social Security payroll taxes into the stock market, where they might get a greater return than if the money remained under government control. Younger workers may also resent the fact that their payroll deductions support current retirees, although a number of workers, especially middle-aged ones, are cognizant of the fact that Social Security helps to support their aging parents.

What most stakeholders are concerned about today is how to maintain a viable Social Security system, with good benefits, in light of the coming wave of baby boomer retirements. We turn now to the debates over how best to do this.

Economic Analysis and Proposals for Reform

When we wrote the first edition of this text in 1997, we noted that "the major issue regarding Social Security . . . is the solvency of the reserve fund." By the mid-1990s, projections had indicated that the system's income from payroll taxes would be greater than payments to beneficiaries up until the year 2013. At about that time, analysts predicted, the retirement of the baby boomers would cause a rise in beneficiaries that might engulf the system. This could lead to complete depletion of the trust fund in 2029. Pronouncements of a "Social Security crisis" received a great deal of publicity, causing politicians and policy analysts to rush to develop solutions.[41]

During the Clinton administration, worries about the future solvency of the system seemed less pressing. In 1998 the annual forecast by the trustees of the Social Security program extended the deadline for the depletion of the fund to 2032, an effect connected to a continuing economic boom. A still cautious Clinton put "saving Social Security for the twenty-first century" at the top of his agenda in his 1999 State of the Union Address and pledged to use budget surpluses to shore up the program before taking any other actions or cutting taxes. However, in his address a year later, Clinton spent far less time on the issue, concluding, as one reporter put it, that "times were good enough to call for [modest] tax cuts and more social spending."[42]

Five years later, claims that the Social Security system was in crisis suddenly reappeared. In his State of the Union address in February 2005, President George W. Bush warned the nation that without changes, the country's largest and costliest social program was headed for bankruptcy. Government actuaries had recently projected that the system's trust fund would have exhausted its reserves by the year

2042. In order to "strengthen and save" the program, Bush proposed adding individual, private investment accounts to the traditional system. These changes would not affect people fifty-five and older, reflecting the president's promises not to change Social Security for current or near retirees. But beginning in 2009, according to the proposal, those under fifty-five could enroll in private accounts. These enrollments were to be phased in over three years, with workers born in 1979 or later offered the chance to add investment accounts by 2011. Once the program was established, workers could choose to invest 4 percent of their current 12.4 percent Social Security payroll tax in private accounts. The president did not say how the plan would cover the "transition costs" during the shift, which were estimated at $2.2 trillion over the first 10 years.[43]

Republican members of Congress rose and cheered the president's proposal for personal savings accounts. Democrats "sat in stony silence." Unlike Franklin Roosevelt, who had worked carefully with members of both political parties, cabinet members, government experts in a special committee on economic security, and university economists, Bush made his proposals with much less consultation and political groundwork, other than the establishment of a panel on Social Security in 2001. Although Bush made a reference to "a better deal for 'younger workers,'" described by one analyst as a "clever allusion to the New Deal" of Franklin Roosevelt, Democrats were not impressed.[44]

After the State of the Union address, the president embarked on a tour through five states to promote his shift from the New Deal to the "ownership society." These tours had mixed results. In early February, Bush traveled to Montana and North Dakota. His message at his first stop in Fargo, North Dakota, acknowledged "all the complaints . . . [about] how this is going to ruin Social Security," but he told the crowd, "Forget it, it's going to make it stronger." He received a "rapturous reception from a carefully screened crowd of ticket holders." Yet both his approval ratings as president as well as polls measuring support for the changes in Social Security were simultaneously declining. By the end of March, support for individual accounts was lower than when he had proposed them a month earlier, and his own approval rating was in the mid-40 percent range. A month earlier, Senator Charles E. Grassley of Iowa, Chairman of the Senate Finance Committee, had warned that if public opinion didn't swing in favor of the president's proposal soon, it would be "an indication that the plan was in trouble."[45]

Further trips did not improve things. In West Virginia in early April, the president tried to refocus attention on the "accelerating problem" of Social Security, but by then various public opinion polls were indicating a large amount of concern about his proposals among Americans of varying ages and backgrounds. As early as mid-January, a *USA Today* poll found that although 55 percent of those younger than thirty called the addition of private accounts a "good idea," 63 percent of people over fifty found it a bad one. A poll of adults age thirty and over, conducted by the American Association of Retired Persons (AARP) reported 66 percent favoring keeping Social Security "as close to the present system as possible," with the figure rising to 79 percent among those sixty and older. Support for the plan weakened further when people learned the details. For example, almost half of those supporting private accounts changed their minds upon learning how much the transition would cost them. Other polls indicated that while 52 percent of Republicans favored the president's plan, only 7 percent of Democrats did so, and 56 percent of all respondents saw investing their Social Security money in the stock market as "too big a risk." A *Washington Post* survey reported that almost half the respondents felt the government should be mainly responsible for ensuring at least a minimum standard of living for retired elderly people (upholding the basic tenet of the Social Security Act), while 35 percent felt individuals themselves should be responsible.[46]

Members of Congress supporting the plan also had difficulties convincing constituents of its value. Senator Rick Santorum, for example, found his constituents in Pennsylvania skeptical about the proposed changes. Retirees and near retirees were the most critical. About half of the attendees at a forum held at Widener University were over fifty. They asked the senator many questions, and most were negative.[47]

Public responses to the Social Security overhaul became more negative in the following months. A *New York Times* poll in late March found that only 30 percent of Americans "approved of the way Mr. Bush was handling Social Security." In April, results of a *New York Times*/CBS News survey detailed the generation gap in responses to the president's plans. Respondents aged eighteen to forty-four were more likely to fear that the Social Security reserves would have disappeared by the time they retired and were more positive about the chance to invest in private accounts (although only half felt this was a good idea). Almost half of the younger group and 52 percent of the older group favored increasing Social Security taxes to keep the program going. Over three-fourths of people in both groups agreed that they lacked information about the president's proposal.[48]

By June, the public's support for the president's approach was falling rapidly. Sixty-three percent of respondents to a national poll felt his proposals would not improve the long-term financial stability of the Social Security system. Eighty percent said it was the government's responsibility to provide "a decent standard of living for the elderly." A strong majority approved of raising the amount of income subject to the Social Security payroll tax above the current level of $90,000. Basically, the public was not rallying around the vision of a new Social Security system.[49]

Groups representing the elderly, professional organizations, and unions also weighed in on the president's proposals. AARP warned that the private accounts plan would cause basic retirement income to be based partly on stock market ups and downs rather than on steady government guarantees. An AARP advertisement proclaimed "IF YOU have a problem with the sink, YOU DON'T tear down the entire house." The group also took out a full page ad in the *New York Times*, encouraging members to call their legislators and urge them to oppose private accounts. Members of the National Association of Social Workers participated in rallies across the country to express their concern about the privatization of Social Security and held a rally of several thousand people near the Capitol in Washington. The A.F.L-C.I.O staged demonstrations against the president's plan in New York, Washington, San Francisco, and seventy other cities on April 1st.[50]

Interestingly, many polls showed that seniors' real worries were the rising cost of health care, rather than the state of Social Security. An AARP survey found that three of four respondents aged fifty and over were "'very concerned' about the availability and costs of health care."[51]

Clearly, most of the president's proposals to "save the system" did not resonate with various constituencies or make sense to economists and other experts. The idea of private accounts is a good example. As Robert Greenstein, executive director of the Center on Budget and Policy Priorities, explains, while some Americans could reap windfalls, "you'd likely also have a significant number of losers," due to the ups and downs of the stock market. Another analyst presents this scenario: Suppose you set aside $1,000 a year for forty-three years and earned 4.6 percent annually on your investment. Your account would grow to $221,552 in today's dollars. This money would be yours on retirement, and would probably be paid out to you in increments of about $16,000 a year. But since Social Security's *guaranteed* benefits would be reduced by about $151,900 (the amount you could have contributed to Social Security but instead contributed to your personal account, plus 3 percent interest), your annual gain would only be about $5,000. And, due to the normal risks of the stock market, if you earned less on your investments, you might not have any gain at all.[52]

In addition to figuring out whether the changes in Social Security would be good for individuals, it is also important to ask if these changes would actually "save the system"—as the president set out to do. There are good arguments that they would not, and that there are other ways to approach the problem. Unlike an insurance policy, in which you pay premiums to cover your own benefits, in the Social Security system each generation of workers pays taxes to finance the retirement payments for the previous generation. There is nothing to prevent Congress from increasing the size of these benefits. Where would the money come from, you ask? Well, all tax monies go into the same pot in the U.S. treasury and are spent at the discretion of Congress. Sometimes Congress has used excess Social Security taxes to pay for other government programs.[53]

But you may also ask, how do we handle possible future deficits in the Social Security funds? For one thing, we could raise the income ceiling for Social

Security taxes. Currently, these payroll taxes are levied on salaries up to $90,000 (in other words, if you are lucky enough to make over that amount, no payroll taxes are deducted from the rest of your salary). Raising the taxable level would obviously bring more money into the system. In addition, although this would take a strong political movement, the tax cuts that Bush put into place earlier in his presidency could be rolled back. As one analyst notes, the cost of making these tax cuts permanent is about "three times the size of the Social Security shortfall over the next seventy-five years." Finally, as another expert weighs in, extending the life of the system's trust fund into the twenty-second century, with no change in benefits, "would require additional revenues equal to only 0.54 percent of GDP. That's less than 3 percent of federal spending." In fact, that is less than we are currently spending on the war in Iraq.[54]

In the end, Bush's proposal failed to make it through Congress. As early as mid-March 2005, one observer predicted no better than a one-in-four chance that some type of Social Security reform would be passed in that year. The president's drive for changes in the system ran into a solid wall of public opposition and quickly collapsed. In his State of the Union address in 2006, Bush said that "Congress did not act last year on my proposal to save Social Security." Democrats responded with a standing ovation.[55]

Pensions

Uncertainty among some Americans about the future shape of Social Security has now been joined by an awareness of the growing erosion in the U.S. system of public and private pensions. According to one commentator, "until recently, a pension seemed like a sure thing. If you worked long enough, you could count on a predetermined stream of income upon retirement, backed by the federal government." Currently, about thirty-six million working people in the United States are "planning on a fixed pension, funded by their employers and paying a monthly benefit for life." Now they're wondering if that benefit will be there when they retire. Representative Nancy Pelosi, House Democratic leader, recently noted that these failures of private pension plans drive home "the importance of a guaranteed pension" in Social Security.[56]

Dramatic stories about pension plan failures appear regularly in the national news media. A good example is the New York City transit workers strike in December 2005, which quickly brought the city to a standstill. The walkout occurred largely because the New York Transit Authority proposed that all new transit workers contribute 6 percent of their wages toward their pensions, an increase from the 2 percent that current workers paid. The proposal was an attempt to cover pension costs which had tripled over three years to a total of $453 million. During negotiations, New York Transit Authority representatives suggested that in exchange for an end to the strike, the Transit Authority would scale back its plan for cuts in pensions. Union representatives, in turn, said they would consider having their members pay more for health insurance. The transit workers returned to their jobs several days after the strike began, but as a sign of the intransigence of the pension issue, negotiations were still proceeding in April 2006.[57]

The New York Transit Authority is not the only entity cutting back on pensions. Many private companies are doing so as well. The Verizon communication company plans to save billions by freezing (not adding to existing amounts) the guaranteed pensions of managers. General Motors, facing slumping demands for its cars and strong global competition, recently instituted the same policy for its white-collar employees.[58]

Many companies have been replacing their traditional pension or "defined-benefit" plans (which guarantee a predetermined monthly income after retirement, usually based on the numbers of years that you worked and how much you were paid) with "defined-contribution" investment plans such as 401(k)s. In the latter, employees put aside a portion of their pay for retirement tax-deferred, and the company contributes a partial match. Whatever is in the investment account when employees retire is what they get; thus this type of retirement money is tied to the ups and downs of the stock market. Furthermore, there is no restriction against companies reducing or ending contributions to their employees' 401(k)s if times get tough. By 2003, only 45 percent of workers covered by a company retirement plan had a traditional defined-benefit pension. Put another way, in 2005, only 20 percent of all U.S. workers were covered by traditional pensions. Although the newer defined-contribution plans have the advantage of allowing employees to bring their retirement investments with them when they change employers, these plans are generally not worth as much money as the employee would have accrued in a traditional pension.[59]

The traditional pension was widely available to U.S. workers up until the 1980s, but since then it has been vanishing from the U.S. workplace. In 1983, more than two-thirds of households headed by people age forty-seven to sixty-four had someone earning a pension. By 2001, less than half did. Some companies, like Sears, have simply stopped providing pensions. Starbucks, Home Depot, and Dell have never provided them at all. Other companies have eliminated pensions for new workers. Due to bankruptcies, companies such as Bethleham Steel have canceled or reduced the pensions of many or all of their retirees. IBM has frozen its pension plan as of 2008, meaning that no new money will be added to employee's pension accounts after 2007. Janet Krueger, retired from IBM after twenty-three years, was told that she would no longer be eligible for the monthly checks of one-third of her salary, and "would instead receive a one-time lump sum equal to about two-thirds of my yearly salary—and nothing more than that."[60]

The recent bankruptcies of large companies, particularly in the airline industry, have made the situation worse. United Airlines is the best example. When the company went into bankruptcy in 2003, due to declining passenger travel, increasing jet fuel costs after 9/11, and rising pension and health benefits costs, it won the right in bankruptcy court to terminate its four employee pension plans. This move released the corporation from $3.2 billion in pension obligations for the following four years, shifting the payments to the federal agency in charge of guaranteeing pensions, the Pension Benefit Guaranty Corporation (PBGC), created in 1974.[61]

The following discussion is a bit complicated, but we hope it will help you understand the magnitude of the problem of failing pension systems. The PBGC is the U.S. government's "pension insurer." It collects premiums from corporations and uses this money to help workers when companies cannot fulfill their pension obligations. In recent years, the premiums have been at levels that have been insufficient to take over the pension systems of failing companies and those that declare bankruptcy. Often employees' pensions under PBGC are worth less than their original pensions would have been; for example, Jim Huber, a worker at a Bethleham Steel plant, found that his expected pension went from $2,800 a month to $1,300. By late 2005, the PBGC was $23 billion in the red, due to the number of large companies filing bankruptcies.[62]

These companies include other airlines, such as US Airways, Delta, and Northwest. In 2004, due to financial difficulties, US Airways sought U.S. government permission to stretch the $68 million in contributions it owed for the pensions of its mechanics and flight attendants over a five-year period. The company had already terminated its pilots pension plan as it moved to emerge from bankruptcy in 2003. In 2006, the pilots union at Delta Airlines voted to authorize a strike if Delta was successful in persuading an arbitration panel to void its contract with pilots so that it could impose as much as $325 million in long-term pay and benefit cuts. When Northwest Airlines went into bankruptcy in spring of 2006, its pensions were underfunded by $3.7 billion. One analyst predicted that once the airline emerged from bankruptcy, it might find that its workers, "bitter over the size of concessions and the way Northwest extracted them, could become more difficult to manage as the airline tries to improve customer service and efficiency."[63]

Other industries, such as automobile manufacturers and steel mills, have also been changing or shedding pensions. In 2006, General Motors sought to slash costs by dismissing hundreds of white-collar workers and reducing the benefits of those who remained. In 2002, the chief executive of Bethleham Steel shut down its pension plan, leaving the federal Pension Benefit Guaranty Corporation to meet the company's $3.7 billion in unfunded obligations to retirees. As one analyst notes, this has become an attractive option for companies in financial difficulty.

"Terminating a pension plan significantly lightens a company's balance sheet: the business instantly becomes more valuable."[64]

The status of pension funds for public sector employees is also becoming precarious. Generally, teachers, policemen, and other public employees have been guaranteed retirement benefits far richer than private pensions, but elected officials have often failed to set aside enough money to cover promised benefits. Facing a $2.6 billion bill for state workers' pensions, Governor Arnold Schwarzenegger tried to control costs by switching workers from traditional pension plans to 401(k) style plans. The state governments of Michigan and Virginia had been successful in making such a change, but in California, Schwarzenegger was forced to withdraw his plan after loud protests from public employees unions.[65]

Republicans in the U.S. Congress looked at possible pension reforms in the spring 2006 session. The bill they had proposed focused on making it more attractive for workers to put money into 401(k) accounts. However, they failed to complete their work before Congress adjourned in April.[66]

Many of you reading this chapter may be saying at this point, "Why did I have to wade through all that material on pensions and government bailouts?" Probably most of you are not currently in the full-time work force, so you don't spend much time thinking about pensions and retirement benefits. But many of you will soon be in that work force. In addition, the lack of adequate pensions for your parents could mean that you will have to help them when they retire.

One other important issue for today's worker is the availability of adequate health care benefits. For decades most U.S. workers have counted on their employers for health insurance. Now, based largely on ballooning health care costs in the United States, companies are rapidly pulling back from this commitment to their workers and retirees. As this occurs, medical benefits have become a central issue in major labor disputes across the country. For Michael Blake, an aircraft company employee who has cancer, a contract proposal that would force him to pay more for his health care has become a fight "worth taking to the street."[67]

The amount of money employers pay for their share of employees' health insurance increased by about 11 percent between 2000 and 2001 and almost 15 percent between 2002 and 2003, before it leveled out to a 9 percent increase from 2004 to 2005. Chrysler has seen its annual health care expenses for white-collar employees rise 100 percent since 2000. Chrysler's overall health bill was $2.3 billion in 2006, the equivalent of $1,400 per car. General Motors spent over $5.2 billion for 1.1 million workers in 2004.[68]

J.C. Penney, the Pfizer drug company, and Lucent Technologies are among the many other large companies that have canceled or reduced health benefits for retired employees. Overall, 12 percent of large companies terminated all retiree benefits for future retirees in 2005. "Coupled with countless frozen or terminated pension plans," one observer notes, "health benefit cutbacks make plain the growing transfer of economic risk and responsibility from employers and government to workers." To many retirees, these decisions feel like broken promises[69]

Some companies have not canceled their health benefits but have instead moved workers and retirees into managed care plans and plans with high "deductibles" in which current and retired employees have to pay for their care before their health insurance kicks in. Many businesses have also increased the copayments. One J.C. Penney's employee paid $43 a month out-of-pocket for himself and his wife before he took early retirement at age fifty-six. Once he retired, these costs rose to $690 a month. Workers and retirees with these kinds of plans often put off needed medical care for themselves and their families until health conditions worsen, generally leading to higher costs when they finally seek medical help.[70]

Job-based health insurance took hold during World War II, when companies used health benefits to attract scarce workers. These benefits, supported by federal tax breaks to companies, became the foundation of the U.S. health-care system and eventually covered over two-thirds of the population. But now that foundation is crumbling, with profound effects on citizens' lives and the country's health care system. A former secretary of the U.S. Department of Health and Human Services has recently called for reforms in Medicare and Medicaid and "government assistance to help employers provide insurance." This suggests an inching back toward the New Deal vision of national and comprehensive Social Security and health-care programs for all citizens.[71] Employment-based pensions can be an important supplement to these programs.

Conclusion

Is it fair to tax higher-income people at a greater rate than middle- and lower-income earners so as to redistribute resources? Is it reasonable to privatize the Social Security system in a way that would jeopardize poorer people's chance at a reasonable retirement income? Issues of equity and adequacy undergird the debates about Social Security reform. The various factors of choice analysis—how and to whom benefits are allocated, what benefits are provided, how benefits are delivered, and the method of financing—all relate to the desired balance between fairness and adequate provision, independence and mutual responsibility, and government and private market approaches. Values and ideology play a crucial role in Social Security policy choices.

One example of this relates to both fairness and adequacy of coverage for women in the present Social Security system. A number of working women contribute but end up receiving a benefit based on their husband's deductions because this is higher than their own pension would have been. This can seem unfair; women ask, "Where has *my* money gone?" In addition, women (or men) who do unpaid work as homemakers are not given the chance to contribute to the program. They are thus unable to build up their own pensions, which might, in fact, be higher than those available to them as a spouse. As a way of expanding the scope and amount of coverage in these situations, proposals have been made to give unpaid homemakers "earnings credits" toward Social Security. These credits would be financed out of general revenues. Another approach, "earnings sharing," would divide the total annual earnings of a married couple equally between them and calculate contributions accordingly. This would level off inequities between men's and women's salaries in awarding pensions. It would also give a spouse coverage for time spent working in the home.[72]

These provisions promote equity, and they also improve Social Security's ability to diminish poverty among older women. Yet the Social Security system could go much further to achieve social adequacy, as in the creation of a reasonable flat grant for all elderly people, coupled with a secondary pension based on contributions. Or coverage of the system could be dramatically widened—social insurance in the United States might be refashioned to include grants for all families to bring them up to a reasonable standard of living or to include universal children's allowances.

You are now probably asking, "How could we afford to do this? How would we do it? Why should we do it?" Beneath all social welfare questions lie our value preferences and our conceptions of the good society. If we chose to put more emphasis on social adequacy as a value, we might reach consensus on enlarging the Social Security system to include children and families and supporting it through general taxation. Taxes, including corporate taxes, would most likely have to be increased to do this. We would, however, have spread the burden of support in a fairer way across a broad social base.

The U.S. system of old age security combines public and private provisions for older Americans through Social Security and employment-based pensions. However, at present, both Social Security and private pensions are often inadequate in providing an economically secure future for all citizens. It is also important to recognize that Social Security has demonstrated significant progress in reducing poverty among the elderly. It also has a broad base of political support because the vast majority of Americans are eligible for benefits. The challenges to the program are basically small compared to the good the system accomplishes or could be expected to accomplish. We encourage social workers to be champions of Social Security and its potential to reduce poverty among all Americans. We also urge social workers to join with organizations for current and retired workers, such as labor unions, in promoting a fair and adequate private pension system.

Selected Web Sites on Social Security and Pensions

Administration on Aging, U.S. Department of Health and Human Services

www.aoa.dhhs.gov

Includes research on Social Security reform, information on retirement and financial planning, and links to other sites on aging.

American Association of Retired Persons (AARP)

www.aarp.org

Covers a variety of issues regarding people fifty and older, including private pensions and Social Security. See also www.aarp.org/socialsecurity.

National Senior Citizens Law Center

www.nsclc.org

Provides information on a broad range of legal issues affecting the security and welfare of older persons of limited income.

The Pension Benefit Guaranty Corporation

www.pbgc.gov

Pension Rights Center

www.pensionrights.org

A nonprofit consumer organization that works with the Administration on Aging's network of free pension clinics.

Social Security Administration

www.ssa.gov

Provides a wealth of information on Social Security, including how to estimate your future Social Security benefits by obtaining a Personal Earnings and Benefits Statement (PEBES).

The U.S. Department of Labor

www.dol.gov/ebsa

Notes

1. Fred Brock, "Why Roll the Dice?" *New York Times* (7 February 1999), sec. 3, p. 12.

2. Allan Sloan, "Books, Cooked D.C. Style," *Newsweek* (2 February 1998), p. 42.

3. Robert Samuelson, "Great Expectations," *Newsweek* (8 January 1996), pp. 24–26.

4. W. Andrew Achenbaum, *Social Security: Visions and Revisions* (New York: Cambridge University Press, 1986), pp. 14–15; Ann Shola Orloff, *The Politics of Pensions: A Comparative Analysis of Britain, Canada, and the United States 1880–1940* (Madison: University of Wisconsin Press, 1993), pp. 269–283.

5. Quoted in Achenbaum, *Social Security: Visions and Revisions*, p. 16.

6. Eveline Burns, *Toward Social Security* (New York: Whittlesey House, 1936), pp. 244–245.

7. Burns, *Toward Social Security*, pp. 246–247.

8. Mark H. Leff, "Historical Perspectives on Old-Age Insurance: The State of the Art on the Art of the State," in Edward D. Berkowitz, Ed., *Social Security after Fifty: Successes and Failures* (Westport, CT: Greenwood Press, 1987), p. 29.

9. Orloff, *The Politics of Pensions*, pp. 134–135, 269–270; Theda Skocpol, *Protecting Soldiers and Mothers: The Political Origins of Social Policy in the United States* (Cambridge, MA: The Belknap Press of Harvard University Press, 1995), pp. 1–2; Achenbaum, *Social Security: Visions and Revisions*, p. 15.

10. Edward D. Berkowitz and Kim McQuaid, *Creating the Welfare State: The Political Economy of 20th Century Reform*, rev. ed. (Lawrence: University Press of Kansas, 1992), pp. 1–4, 11–30; Orloff, *The Politics of Pensions*, p. 278.

11. Berkowitz and McQuaid, *Creating the Welfare State*, pp. 38, 112–113; David Stoesz, *Small Change: Domestic Policy under the Clinton Presidency* (White Plains, NY: Longman, 1996), p. 176.

12. Quoted in Edward D. Berkowitz, *America's Welfare State: From Roosevelt to Reagan* (Baltimore, MD: Johns Hopkins University Press, 1991), p. 15.

13. Quoted in Achenbaum, *Social Security: Visions and Revisions*, p. 17.

14. Jerry R. Cates, *Insuring Inequality: Administrative Leadership in Social Security 1935–54* (Ann Arbor: University of Michigan Press, 1983), pp. 22, 50–51; Achenbaum, *Social Security: Visions and Revisions*, pp. 17–18; Arthur J. Altmeyer, *The Formative Years of Social Security* (Madison: University of Wisconsin Press, 1968), pp. 30–31; Burns, *Toward Social Security*, pp. 136–137.

15. Quoted in Achenbaum, *Social Security: Visions and Revisions*, p. 19.

16. Altmeyer, *The Formative Years of Social Security*, pp. 7–8.

17. Altmeyer, *The Formative Years of Social Security*, pp. 14–15; Berkowitz, *America's Welfare State*, pp. 15–16; Frances Perkins, foreword to Edwin D. Witte, *The Development of the Social Security Act* (Madison: University of Wisconsin Press, 1963), p. vi.

18. Cates argues that Altmeyer, Witte, and other key figures in the development and implementation of the Social Security Act followed a conservative approach to social insurance that strongly emphasized self-reliance over redistribution of incomes (Cates, *Insuring Inequality*). Achenbaum, Coll, and others describe a broader set of goals. See Achenbaum, *Social Security: Visions and Revisions*, p. 3 and *Shades of Grey: Old Age, American Values and Federal Policies since 1920*

(Boston: Little, Brown, 1983), pp. 42–43; Blanche Coll, "Public Assistance: Reviving the Original Comprehensive Concept of Social Security," in Gerald D. Nash, Noel H. Pugach, and Richard F. Tomasson, Eds., *Social Security: The First Half Century* (Albuquerque: University of New Mexico Press, 1988), pp. 221–241.

19. Achenbaum, *Social Security: Visions and Revisions*, p. 19.

20. Berkowitz, *America's Welfare State*, p. 25; Orloff, *The Politics of Pensions*, p. 294; Linda Gordon, *Pitied but Not Entitled: Single Mothers and the History of Welfare* (New York: Free Press, 1994), pp. 275–276; Jill Quadagno, *The Transformation of Old Age Security* (Chicago: University of Chicago Press, 1988), pp. 115–116.

21. Altmeyer, *Formative Years of Social Security*, pp. 11, 34; Anthony Badger, *The New Deal: The Depression Years 1933–40* (New York: Hill and Wang, 1989), pp. 102–104, 231–234; Berkowitz, *America's Welfare State*, pp. 20–21.

22. Altmeyer, *Formative Years of Social Security*, pp. 32–33, 37–42; Witte, *The Development of the Social Security Act*, pp. 87–90; Berkowitz, *America's Welfare State*, p. 14.

23. Berkowitz, *America's Welfare State*, pp. 40–46; Achenbaum, *Social Security: Visions and Revisions*, pp. 26–30.

24. Berkowitz, *America's Welfare State*, pp. 46–48; Achenbaum, *Social Security: Visions and Revisions*, pp. 32–37.

25. Altmeyer, *The Formative Years of Social Security*, p. 283.

26. Berkowitz, *America's Welfare State*, pp. 25–61.

27. Achenbaum, *Social Security: Visions and Revisions*, pp. 43–44; Social Security Administration, *Basic Facts* (Washington, DC: Author, March 1998), p. 5.

28. Achenbaum, *Social Security: Visions and Revisions*, pp. 57–60; Bruce Jansson, *The Reluctant Welfare State: A History of American Social Welfare Policies*, 3rd ed. (Pacific Grove, CA: Brooks/Cole, 1997), p. 250; "Social Security," *Washington Post National Weekly Edition* (24–30 January 2005), p. 24.

29. Wilbur J. Cohen, *Social Security: The Compromise and Beyond* (Washington, DC: SOS Education Fund, June 1983); Achenbaum, *Social Security: Visions and Revisions*, pp. 61–99.

30. Roger Lowenstein, "A Question of Numbers," *New York Times Magazine* (16 January 2005), pp. 42, 72; U.S. Department of Health and Human Services, Administration on Aging, *A Profile of Older Americans: 2004*, pp. 1, 11 (online at www.aoa.gov/prof/statistics/profile/2004/2004profile.pdf); Thomas N. Bethell, "The Gender Gap," *AARP Bulletin* 46 (July–August 2005), p. 11.

31. *A Profile of Older Americans: 2004*, p. 11; Bethell, pp. 8–11.

32. *A Profile of Older Americans: 2004*, pp. 1, 11.

33. Kate Sernike, "The Bell Tolls for the Future Merry Widow," *New York Times* (30 April 2006), sec. 4, p. 1.

34. http://ideas.repec.org/p/mrr/papers/wp065.html

35. Martha Ozawa, quoted in John E. Tropman, *Public Policy Opinion and the Elderly, 1952–1978* (Westport, CT: Greenwood Press, 1987), p. 39; Richard W. Stevenson, "Squaring Off, at Last, on Social Security," *New York Times* (29 November 1998), p. 5.

36. Witte, *The Development of the Social Security Act*, p. 146; Philip R. Popple and Leslie Leighninger, *Social Work, Social Welfare, and American Society*, 6th ed. (Boston: Allyn & Bacon, 2005), pp. 618–619; Altmeyer, *The Formative Years of Social Security*, p. 22.

37. Cited in Daniel Patrick Moynahan, "The Case Against Entitlement Cuts," *Modern Maturity* 37 (November–December 1994), p. 14; John Brigham, *Property and the Politics of Entitlement* (Philadelphia: Temple University Press, 1990), pp. 4–6, 35–36; John Christman, *The Myth of Property: Toward an Egalitarian Theory of Ownership* (New York: Oxford University Press, 1994), pp. 171–173; Charles Reich, "The New Property," in G. B. Macpherson, Ed., *Property: Mainstream and Critical Positions* (Toronto: University of Toronto Press, 1978), pp. 177–198.

38. Jerry R. Cates, "Social Security: United States," in John M. Herridk and Paul H. Stuart, Eds., *Encyclopedia of Social Welfare History in America* (Thousand Oaks, CA: Sage Publications, 2005), pp. 355–358; *Annual Statistical Supplement to Social Security Bulletin 1995*, p. 374; Robert L. Baker, *Social Work Dictionary* (Silver Spring, MD: NASW, 1987), p. 49.

39. Samuelson, "Great Expectations," p. 27; Norman Ornstein, "Escaping the Entitlement Straitjacket," *Washington Post Weekly Edition* (7–13 March 1994), p. 25. Note that Ornstein is connected with the conservative American Enterprise Institute.

40. Walt Duka, "Watch Out: They're After You, Older Voters Loom Big as 2000 Target," *AARP Bulletin* 41 (February 2000), pp. 3–4.

41. "The Growing Need for Social Security," *AARP Bulletin* 46 (June 2005), p. 23.

42. Peter Passell, "Can Retirees' Safety Net Be Saved?" *New York Times* (18 February 1996), sec. 3, p. 1.

43. Amy Goldstein, "Forecast Brightens for Social Security," *Washington Post Weekly* (29 April 1998), p. A2; "The Text of the President's State of the Union Address to Congress," *New York Times* (20 January 1999), p. A22; Marc Lacey, "Clinton Claims Bragging Rights to Nation's Prosperity: Asks Tax Relief for Struggling Families," *New York Times* (28 January 2000), p. A1. Terence Hunt, "Bush: 'Save Social Security,'" *New York Times* (3 February 2005), pp. 1, 9–10.

44. Hunt, "Bush: 'Save Social Security,'" pp. 1, 9; Allan Sloan, "Social Security: A Daring Leap," *Newsweek* (14 February 2005), p. 41.

45. Russ Wiles, "Social Security: Bush to Make Case," *The Arizona Republic* (2 February 2005), p. 1; Albert Crenshaw, "Upping the Ante on Retirement: In Bush's 'Ownership Society,' You've Got to Play to Win," *The Washington Post National Weekly Edition* (24–30 January 2005), p. 18; Richard W. Stevenson, "Bus, On Road, Pushes Warning on Retirement," *New York Times* (4 February 2005), pp. 1, 15; Tom Raum, "Despite Long Odds, Bush Touts Private Retirement Accounts," *The Arizona Republic* (31 March 2005), p. 6; David E. Rosenbaum, "Public View on Social Security Needs to Swing Soon, Senator Says," *New York Times* (1 March 2005), p. 14.

46. Anne E. Kornblut, "Bush Renews Focus on His Plan For Revamping Social Security," *New York Times* (6 April 2005), p. 16; Barbara Basler, "What Do Americans Think About Taking Money Out of Social Security for Private Accounts?" *AARP Bulletin* 46 (February 2005), pp. 10, 13; Howard Fineman, "Special Report," *Newsweek* (14 February 2005), p. 38; Richard Morin and Dale Russakof, "Is Social Security in Crisis?" *The Washington Post Edition* (14–20 February 2005), pp. 19–20.

47. Robin Toner, "Appeal to Young on Pension Plan Gets the Attention of Their Elders," *New York Times* (23 February 2005), pp. 1, 16.

48. Daniele Gross, "Social Security as Dramamine," *New York Times* (20 March 2005); Marjorie Connelly, "A View that Changes with Age," *New York Times* (12 April 2005), p. 10.

49. "War Clouds: Bush's Poll Numbers Drop as Americans Lose Patience with Iraq and Social Security," *Washington Post National Edition* (13–19 June 2005), p. 11; "Survey Detects Pessimism on Social Security Payouts," *New York Times* (19 June 2005), p. 7; Robin Toner and Marjorie Connelly, "Poll Finds Broad Pessimism on Social Security Payments," *New York Times* (19 June 2005), p. 18; Robin Toner and Marjorie Connelly, "Bush's Support on Major Issues Tumbles in Poll," *New York Times* (17 June 2005), p. 1.

50. "Social Security: Where We Stand," *AARP Bulletin* 45 (December 2004), p. 15; *New York Times* (9 January 2005), p. 18; *New York Times* (20 February*

2005), p. 18; "Privatization Fought," *NASW News* 50 (6 May 2005), p. 1; Steven Greenhouse, "Unions Protest Against Bush's Social Security Proposal," *New York Times* (1 April 2005), p. 19.

51. Susan Stranahan, "The Big Fix," *AARP Bulletin* 45 (4 December 2005), p. 1.

52. Stranahan, "The Big Fix"; Jonathan Weisman, "The White House Explains Further," *Washington Post Weekly Edition* (14–20 February 2005), p. 17.

53. Rosenbaum, "At Heart of Social Security Debate, A Misunderstanding," *New York Times* (8 March 2005), p. 16.

54. Jane Bryant Quinn, "Social Security Isn't Doomed," *Newsweek* (29 March 2004), p. 47: E. J. Dionne, "Sheer Social Security Nonsense," *Arizona Republic* (8 February 2005), p. B7; Paul Krugman, "Inventing a Crisis," *Liberal Opinion Weekly* (20 December 2004), p. 5.

55. David Brooks, "Here's the Obituary, A Bit Early, for Social Security Reform," *Arizona Republic* (18 March 2005), p. B11; Paul Krugman, "The Great Revulsion," *New York Times* (21 April 2006), p. 23; Krugman, "State of Delusion," *New York Times* (3 February 2006), p. 27.

56. Mary Williams Walsh "Taking the Wheel before a Pension Runs into Trouble," *New York Times* (30 January 2005), sec. 3, p. 8; Jane Bryant Quinn, "Fresh Worries on Pensions," *Newsweek* (23 May 2005), p. 51; Robin Toner with David E. Rosenbaum, "Lawmaker May Hold Key to Bush Social Security Plan," *New York Times* (12 May 2005), p. 19.

57. Jennifer Steinhauer, "Citywide Strike Halts New York Subways and Buses," *New York Times* (21 December 2005), pp. 1, 30; Steven Greenhouse, "Transit Strike Reflects Nationwide Pension Woes," *New York Times* (24 December 2005), pp. 1, 16; Steven Greenhouse and Sewell Chan, "60-Hour Transit Strike Ends, and New York Cheers," *New York Times* (23 December 2005), pp. 1, 24; Thomas J. Lueck, "New York Labor Leaders Criticize Anti-Strike Law," *New York Times* (31 March 2006), p. 19; Nahal Toosi, "New York Transit Workers Return to Jobs without New Contract," *Arizona Republic* (23 December 2005), p. 3; Thomas J. Lueck, "Transit Union Leader Sentenced to 10 Days in Jail for Strike," *New York Times* (11 April 2006); Thomas J. Lueck, "Judge Fines Transit Union $2.5 Million over Strike," *New York Times* (18 April 2006), p. C14.

58. John Challenger, "Rethinking Older Workers," *AARP Bulletin* 47 (January 2006), p. 19; Jeremy W. Peters, "G.M. Lays Off Hundreds of White-Collar Employees," *New York Times* (29 March 2006), p. C5;

Ken Belson and Matt Richtel, "Verizon to Halt Pension Outlay for Managers," *New York Times* (6 December 2005), pp. A1, C5; Micheline Maynard, "G.M. Freezes Pension Plan of Its Salaried Workers," *New York Times* (8 March 2006), p. C3.

59. Albert B. Crenshaw, "All This Talk about Pensions," *Washington Post Weekly Edition* (18–24 October 2004), p. 21. Mary Williams Walsh, "Healthier and Wiser? Sure, but Not Wealthier: As Pensions Slip Away, Retirees May Take a Fall," *New York Times* (13 June 2004), Section 3, pp. 1, 9; Quinn, "Fresh Worries on Pensions," p. 51; Mark McSherry, "Alcoa Eliminates Pension for New Salaried Workers," *US News Today* (17 January 2006), p. 20; Eduardo Porter, "Reinventing the Mill: Can Steel Workers Provide a Road Map for Other Ailing Industry Giants?" *New York Times* (22 October 2005), p. B1; Christine Dugas, "Pension Cutbacks to Expand in U.S.," *USA Today* (11 November 2004), p. D1; Russ Wiles, "Traditional Pensions Vanishing," *Arizona Republic* (27 March 2005), p. D1; Mindy Fetterman, "Facing Cash Woes in Retirement?" *USA Today* (13 January 2006), p. B3.

60. Russell Wild, "Now You See It, Now You Don't," *AARP Bulletin* 46 (November 2005), pp. 12–14.

61. "United's Pension Debacle," *New York Times* (12 May 2005), p. 26; Michelin Maynard, "United Air Wins Right to Default on Its Pensions, *New York Times* (11 May 2005), p. 1; Rachel Beck, "Corporate Pension Troubles Show Signs of Worsening," *Arizona Republic* (3 September 2004), p. D2.

62. Roger Lowenstein, "The End of Pensions?" *New York Times* (30 October 2005), pp. 56–90.

63. Beck, "Corporate Pension Troubles"; Tim Gray, "Pension Roulette," *AARP Bulletin* 46 (July–August 2005), p. 14; Harry Weber, "Unions Gain Influence in Bankruptcies," *Arizona Republic* (8 April 2006), p. D6; Jeff Bailey, "Northwest Muscle May Leave Deep Bruises," *New York Times* (24 March 2006), p. C3.

64. Michael Ellis and Jennifer Dixon, "G.M.'s Top Executive Soothes," *Arizona Republic* (9 April 2006), p. D2; David Runk, "GM Begins Making Cuts: Pensions, Dividends, Health Costs Targeted," *Arizona Republic* (8 February 2006), p. D1; Mary Williams Walsh, "Whoops! There Goes Another Pension Plan," *New York Times* (18 September 2005), pp. 1, 9.

65. Dennis Cauchon, Pension Funds Fall Short of Guarantees," *USA Today* (17 January 2006), p. 7A; James Dao, "'55 and Out' Comes Home to Roost," *New York Times* (1 May 2005), sec. 4, pp. 1, 4: "The Terminator Takes Aim at State Pensions," *AARP Bulletin* 46 (April 2005), p. 6.

66. "The Trojan Pension Bill," *New York Times* (13 April 2006), p. 26.

67. Amanda J. Crawford, "Health Care's Foundation Crumbling," *Arizona Republic* (15 January, 2006), p. 6; John Christoffersen, "Fighting against Health Care Cuts," *San Francisco Chronicle* (26 February 2006), p. D7; Reed Karaim, "Broken Promises," *AARP Bulletin* 47 (April 2006), p. 18.

68. Jon Gabel, et al., "Health Benefits in 2005: Premium Increases Slow Down, Coverage Continues to Erode," *Health Affairs* 24 (September/October 2005), p. 1274; Micheline Maynard, "Chrysler's Salaried Workers to Pay More for Health Care," *New York Times* (16 March 2006), p. C3; effrey H. Birnbaum and Sholnn Freeman, "Just Don't Call It a Bailout," *The Washington Post National Weekly Edition* (12–18 December 2005), pp.19–20.

69. Karaim, "Broken Promises," p. 18.

70. Jane Bryant Quinn, "Health Care's New Lottery," *Newsweek* (27 February 2006), p. 47; Karaim, "Broken Promises," p. 19.

71. Crawford, "Health Care's Foundation Crumbling," pp. 6, 8.

72. Achenbaum, *Social Security: Visions and Revisions*, pp. 133–141.

chapter

Mental Health: Managed Care

Stewart Moskovitch's son Nitai was receiving psychiatric care for his severe depression at Danbury Hospital in Connecticut. But then Mr. Moskovitch's HMO stopped paying for hospital treatment and arranged for the young man to be transferred to a drug treatment center. While there, Nitai hung himself. Mr. Moskovitch sued his managed care company for medical negligence, saying, "I felt that the HMO in this case had to be held accountable. I do believe, and know in my heart, that they killed my son by making a medical decision for profit."[1]

Shirley McNamara is a clinical social worker with a private practice. Although she used to operate on a fee-for-service basis, like many of her colleagues she now has contracts with several managed care companies. When she talks about the way her work has changed, she says she likes the managed care stress on the outcomes of her sessions with clients. "It's extra work and effort to think about what I want to accomplish with each client and to document whether this has occurred," she notes, "but it keeps me on my toes and makes me think very precisely about what I'm trying to do. On the other hand, some of the other aspects of working in managed care drive me absolutely crazy—like the fact that none of the companies I deal with will approve more than six counseling sessions, at most, with a client, unless I convince them that the person is going to go right out and jump off a bridge. And I can spend an hour on the phone, trying to get through to the company's authorization person to get permission to start working with a client in the first place. So it's really a mixed bag, and social workers are going to have to learn to live with it if we want to keep doing therapy."

Jack Prevost is a social worker in the Planning Department of his state's Office of Mental Health. The office has recently created a public managed care program in mental health and converted its Medicaid program into a managed care system. Jack finds himself ambivalent about this new course. He worries that under the state's contract with a private managed care organization, the needs of the severely mentally ill may not be met. "What do private, for-profit companies know," he asks, "about working with a chronically ill population that needs frequent hospitalization? And what experience do they have in dealing with people of low incomes and all kinds of practical problems like poor housing and limited job possibilities? How will they cut costs and still do a good job of helping such people?" Jack is aware that, so far, not much is known about the quality of mental health services under Medicaid managed care arrangements. Yet he also finds himself getting excited about the prospect of change. Managed care companies seem to stress outpatient services and prevention and to have the flexibility to try new approaches. Maybe, with enough direction and controls, he muses, they could be made to work.

Managed care is now the major form of administration and financing of health care in the United States. Today, more than half of all Americans who have health insurance are enrolled in some type of managed care plan. Well over half of all

Medicaid beneficiaries were enrolled in some form of managed care in 2003. Although mental health managed care initially lagged behind similar arrangements for physical illnesses, managed care organizations (MCOs) have now become the chief administrators of mental health services in the United States. In 1999 78 percent of those with private or public health insurance were enrolled in some form of mental health managed care. Overall, the managed care industry is one of the nation's largest economic sectors, with managed mental health care alone constituting more than a $4-billion-plus industry.[2]

Yet, as the preceding vignettes indicate, all is not rosy in the world of managed care. Recent newspaper, newsmagazine, and professional association reports document continuing concerns about the managed care approach. Backlash against the restrictions involved in managed care has spurred a push for a patients' bill of rights. Worker frustrations with limited choice of physicians in most employee plans have led many employers to move to less-restrictive preferred provider organizations, or PPOs. Ironically, the resulting decrease in control over medical services has contributed to the return of rising health costs, which many employers have passed along to workers. Consumer groups also criticize managed care. In the field of mental health managed care, for example, the National Alliance for the Mentally Ill and the National Mental Health Association have fought for accountability of managed care companies to families of the mentally ill and to the recipients of services. Finally, physicians and hospitals have won suits against managed care giants Cigna and Aetna, which they accused of cutting payments to doctors and interfering with patient care. Social workers, too, have joined the fray, successfully contesting cuts in their reimbursement rates and the termination of mental health providers for activities such as appealing a decision of a managed care company.[3]

What is managed care—and the backlash against it—all about? What are its major goals, its promises, and its pitfalls? Is it, as one reporter has suggested, the "Wal-Mart of health care"—the ultimate marriage of business and health care?[4] Is it a cost-cutting mechanism that can also deliver high-quality care, or is it a profit-making scheme that causes health services to deteriorate? What (or whom) does it really manage—care, costs, clients, or the professionals who provide services? As managed care expands in the field of mental health, is it a blessing or a nightmare?

The following policy analysis explores the many questions surrounding the use of managed care in the mental health arena. It looks at both general trends as well as the great variation among managed care programs. Particular attention is paid to the criticisms and promised benefits of the approach. Because this is a policy that now has major significance for the way social workers practice, this chapter explores managed mental health care's effects on that practice and the variety of ways in which social workers can in turn affect the managed care movement. The chapter concludes with current proposals for managed care reforms.

The Problem That Managed Mental Health Care Was Developed to Solve

The first thing to note is that there is some controversy over *which* problem managed mental health care is meant to deal with. That controversy reflects different ideological perspectives on the appropriate financial support, structure, and goals of health care systems. Is the major problem the rising—some say exorbitant—costs of treatment for mental difficulties? Or is it the need to improve the current state of care for people with emotional problems and mental illness? Perhaps the "problem" is really the perceived need of companies in the health care business to expand into new market areas.

The goal of improving services, expressed most often by consumers of mental health care, their families, advocacy groups, and at least a certain proportion of mental health professionals and policymakers, reflects an expectation that comprehensive, sound, and adequately funded mental health services should be an important priority in our society. Unfortunately, this is not the predominant factor behind the move to managed care. Instead, the problem driving the managed care revolution appears to be widespread concern over costs. These costs are borne not only by individuals but also by businesses and government. Although most of us would agree that high costs can be a legitimate problem, the persistent focus on the "financial drain" of mental health services suggests that spending money on good treatment for mental problems is not necessarily a high priority either for the private sector, taxpayers, or the government. The possibility, as some observers suggest, that growth in mental health managed care systems stems from the health industry's search for profits underscores the idea that improvement in mental health care is not the primary issue being addressed. The same questions about priorities, costs, sources of revenue, and issues of quality have been raised for some time in the larger discussion of general health care reform in the United States.[5]

The Costs of Mental Health Care

It would be hard to find an American today who doesn't know that U.S. health care costs have risen precipitously over the last several decades. Between 1980 and 1990, national health care expenditures rose an average 11 percent a year, continuing at the rate of 8.7 percent into the early 1990s. As employers turned to managed care to contain costs, annual spending increases dropped to about 5 percent. However, costs are again on the rise, with an increase of 8.7 percent in 2001. We now spend almost 19 billion dollars on health care, topping the national defense budget.[6]

Of the nation's huge health care bill, about 10 percent goes to mental health services. The movement to managed care in the mental health field was spurred largely by the fact that the amount spent on mental health care doubled in the 1980s, making it the fastest growing portion of health expenditures in that decade. One-third of current mental health expenses goes to treatment of the severely mentally ill, who are mostly covered by the public mental health system. The less severely ill, who account for the remaining expenditures, are generally covered by employer-provided insurance. Most of the increases in mental health spending go to this group of patients, so employers have had a particular interest in controlling these costs.[7]

Incidence and Treatment of Mental Health Problems

One of the difficulties in planning for and funding mental health services is that, in the eyes of many insurers and employers (among others), mental illness is characterized by the four "uns"—it is "undefinable, untreatable, unpredictable, and unmanageable." In addition to such factors as lack of precision in diagnosis, it is much harder to calculate the number of people with mental illness than of those with physical ailments. Nevertheless, broad generalizations can be made about prevalence rates. About 5 to 7 percent of adult Americans have a mental disorder in any one year, and 12 percent of American children suffer from mental and emotional disturbances. Phobias and major depression account for the largest percentages of major mental difficulties in the United States.[8]

The costs of mental problems to individuals, families, and employers are high. The National Institute on Mental Health estimates the annual cost of untreated mental illness to be more than 300 billion dollars. This is due primarily to productivity losses (e.g., missed days of work), emergency health care costs, and inappropriate increased use of the criminal justice system. Compared with heart disease, diabetes, and back pain, depression generally leads to the longest average length of disability time. In addition, 10 percent of all permanently and totally disabled people have been diagnosed with schizophrenia. Although our discussion so far has focused largely on serious mental illness, it is important to remember that most of us have or will encounter at some point in our lives the kinds of problems—mild depression, anxiety, or stress in our marriages or relationships with parents—that make it difficult to function in our jobs or other areas of daily life.[9]

Despite the aura of unreliability and unchangeability, mental illness *can* be dealt with. On the one hand, the rehospitalization rate among persons with severe mental illness is quite high, and treatments for mental difficulties may take longer than those for other health problems. On the other hand, for example, the National Institute for Mental Health reports that 60 percent of those medicated for schizophrenia improve. Studies have shown that psychiatric rehabilitation services for adults with mental illness can reduce time spent in a psychiatric hospital, raise earning power, and increase the individual's level of independent living. Relatively low-cost outpatient treatment is often effective in helping people with phobias and other anxiety disorders.[10]

Managed Mental Health Care

The managed care movement in health and mental health has brought a whole new vocabulary to health care discussions. In order to understand the new approach and its application to mental health services, one needs to master certain terms. *Managed care* itself is a somewhat slippery term, as there are variations in managed care programs and the concept itself continues to evolve. One definition states, "Managed Care is the private regulation and financing of the delivery of health care with the goals of controlling costs while assuring quality." This definition is already outdated in its focus on the private sector; as we will see, managed care has now emerged in public forms as well. The focus on cost reduction and quality is, however, a common theme, as in the description of managed care as "a system used by groups to manage costs while maintaining high-quality health and medical services." The National Association of Social Workers adds a further dimension in its statement that managed care plans "cut costs by *monitoring access to* and the quality of medical care" (emphasis added). Here the NASW pinpoints a major approach to cost reduction—limiting the amount and type of services rendered. Sometimes the easiest way to identify managed care is to look for particular mechanisms in the health insurance plan, such as use of a specific set of providers, a contract with a customer based on capitated payments, preauthorization for services, specific guidelines and limits on services, and utilization review.[11]

"That's great," you say, "here's a definition with a whole bunch of additional jargon." We will attempt to demystify the situation by explaining some of the major terms now and clarifying others later. First, most managed care programs refer to the people delivering health or mental health services, such as physicians, social workers, psychologists, and even entire agencies, as "providers." Although you might think of "customers" as the people receiving the services, this term actually refers to the businesses or other bodies, such as state health or Medicaid departments, that contract with a managed care organization (sometimes abbreviated as MCO). These entities pay for the managed care plan through a system of *capitation*. In the traditional fee-for-service approach, the insurance plan pays health care professionals for each specific service they perform, such as a surgical procedure or an eye exam, that is covered in the plan. In capitation, the MCO pays a fixed, per-person amount to its providers for a given time period, regardless of the number of services rendered. The providers assume some or all of the risk in this arrangement. If they've figured correctly, the services they actually give to their clientele in a given month or year will balance the prepayment. The MCO has in turn been given a fixed amount by the customer (private employer or public entity) to arrange for care. Fewer services overall will mean an excess in payment, or profit, for the MCO; more services, a monetary loss.[12]

We've used the words *clientele* and *client* to identify people receiving health or mental health care. Other terms are *consumer, patient,* and in public systems such as Medicare, *beneficiary.* Under managed care, service to these individuals often requires a "preauthorization review," in which the provider seeks approval from an insurer or other entity before delivering a particular type of care. Care deemed unnecessary will not be authorized. MCO staff people who carry out preauthorization reviews have various titles, including *gatekeeper, primary physician* (in physical health managed care programs), and *case manager.* Many managed care programs also include *utilization reviews.* These are evaluations of the "necessity, appropriateness and efficiency of the use of health services, procedures, and facilities." Reviews of the appropriateness of hospitalizations and of length of stay, for example, might be conducted to evaluate the ongoing work of the provider. Finally, even "mental health services" have been given a new name by many MCOs. Mental health treatment is now often part of "behavioral health care," which also includes treatment of substance abuse.[13] In this chapter, we use the term *mental health managed care* unless the broader term is specifically called for.

To confuse things further, there are several kinds of MCOs. In health maintenance organizations (HMOs), the consumer must choose a provider from within the system. In preferred provider organizations (PPOs), the client has the option of choosing a practitioner from outside the system as well but at a higher cost. We describe the variety of MCOs further in the history section of this chapter. Note that throughout the chapter, we use the abbreviation MCO unless a specific kind of MCO is being referred to.

You now understand many of the rudiments of managed care policy. We focus next on the basic context, principles, and structure of managed care plans in general and then outline the specifics of managed care in the field of mental health.

Managed care in mental health is the latest manifestation of a general revolution in the way health care is financed and structured in the United States. Managed care organizations, particularly HMOs, grew exponentially during the country's recent debate over health care reform. As one analyst wrote in 1994, "Washington may be in gridlock on health care, but Wall Street is in high gear. A private-sector revolution is transforming the nation's medical system." By the end of this revolution, managed care seems firmly entrenched on the national scene.[14]

Federal legislation has promoted the spread of managed care approaches to physical and mental health issues. The Medicare Prescription Drug, Improvement and Modernization Act of 2003 created the Citizen's Health Working Group to provide "an informed national public debate" that would enable people to make choices about the services they wanted covered and how health coverage should be financed. As one part of this initiative, a Citizen's Health Care Working Group was established to present interim recommendations for making the country's health care system more effective and affordable. The meetings organized by this group included a discussion with a panel of mental heath experts that was held in Boston, Massachusetts, in August 2005. The panel included the director of a regional managed behavioral heath care organization based in the Northeast. The director explained that her organization contracted with doctors and hospitals for mental health services, set payment rates, and "made sure" that there were "good quality providers in the system." A major focus was improving the quality of mental health services and ensuring that claims were paid. She noted that public sector entities often hired managed behavior health organizations "to assist them with the goals of balancing costs, quality, and access" to services.[15]

The director described how some managed care organizations "bid low" in order to get business from an organization or governmental unit. In other words, they promise to work cheaply, which could lead to a low quality of service. Such situations, she pointed out, "can give managed care a black eye." She stressed that HMOs needed to be properly funded, as there are "no bargains" in health care. On the other hand, the privatization of what was formerly public mental care can lead to troubling issues regarding profits. In Arizona's Maricopa County, for example, which includes the city of Phoenix, the private organization Value Options was hired to provide mental health services to the area's poor and uninsured. Between 1998 and 2004, Value Options made a total before-tax profit of $84 million. As one state legislator noted, "you have to have a safety net, but that's kind of like building the whole boat."[16]

The most important impetus for the managed care revolution is the desire to contain costs. The movement aims to lower costs through managing (1) access to services, (2) the amount and types of services delivered, and (3) the choice, characteristics, and activities of health care providers. A managed care organization assures its public or corporate customer that, for a set fee based on the number of clients covered over a specific time period, it will provide cost-effective and high-quality health care to enrollees. The assumption is that management of care will make possible reasonable fees for customers and a profit margin for the MCO.

How does this work in the mental health arena? Let's say your employer has contracted with an MCO, American HealthCare, that provides both physical and mental health benefits to employees. American HealthCare in turn subcontracts with a behavioral health MCO, Majestic, to deliver mental health and substance abuse services. This type of arrangement, in which behavioral health care is handled separately from physical care, is called a *carve-out*.

You have been experiencing a lot of pressure on the job lately, which has led to feelings of anxiety, loss of appetite, and difficulties in concentrating on your work. You call the American HealthCare number listed in your policy and are referred to Majestic. Your call to this number is answered by a gatekeeper, who asks you a number of questions about your problems and what's been going on in your life lately. The gatekeeper then gives you the names of two therapists in your area from whom to choose; one is a social worker, the other a licensed counselor. She also explains that you will be expected to make a co-payment of thirty dollars for each session with the therapist. As in most MCOs, you won't have to pay a deductible.

You choose the social worker and make an appointment with him. This first session allows him to assess your situation and suggest an appropriate treatment approach, or way in which you and he can work together to deal with your difficulty. He explains that the Majestic gatekeeper will probably authorize six sessions over the next three months and that, in his experience, this will be enough to help you learn to understand and manage your anxiety. He outlines the specific goals that the treatment should accomplish, including a substantial decrease in your level of anxiety and the ability to work on job tasks for specified periods without losing concentration.

Several weeks later the social worker phones to tell you that authorization has been granted for the six appointments, and you proceed with the therapy. At the end of the three-month period, you both feel that the initial treatment goals have been met, although you're a little concerned that the problem will come back. The therapist encourages you to "try it on your own for a while" but explains that if you later feel the need for more therapy, he can seek authorization for another set of sessions. He also alerts you to the fact that Majestic will be sending you a questionnaire in another month to ask about your satisfaction with the treatment sessions.

This is how managed mental health care can look from the client's perspective. The following interviews with two of our colleagues give you a sense of what it's like from the provider's point of view. The first gives an example of contract work with an HMO as a private practitioner; the second details the experience of practice within a social work agency that contracts with an HMO.

How Does Managed Mental Health Care Work?

Interview with a Social Work Provider

Barry Daste is a professor in a school of social work and also engages in a small private clinical practice. Ten years ago he was invited to work in a managed care setting. Having heard of his strong skills as a therapist, the regional director of a new mental health component of a large HMO called Daste and asked him to direct a mental health clinic for the organization. In that geographical area, the freestanding clinic was then a common model for the delivery of managed care mental health services. Although Daste declined the directorship, he helped the company set up and staff the clinic, which hired two recent school of social work graduates, a substance abuse counselor, and several other clinicians. Daste became a part-time provider at the clinic.

The clinic's clients were all employed by local companies that had contracted with the HMO to provide health and mental health care. Employees or their family members with mental health problems who called the HMO were referred to the clinic for help. In these early days, clinic workers, including Daste, acted as both gatekeepers and providers. They assessed clients' problems and carried out the appropriate treatment. This generally consisted of short-term therapy, a model that Daste had long used successfully in his own practice. Group or individual therapy sessions were limited to approximately twenty to thirty a year; clients made a co-payment of ten dollars to twenty dollars a session, and the employer covered the rest through yearly fixed payments to the HMO.

After five years, in an attempt to lower its costs and to remain competitive with other MCOs, the HMO began downsizing. It closed a number of its mental health clinics, including the one where Daste worked. Daste and other staff became part of the HMO's network of private practitioner providers who practiced in their own offices. Some were full time; others, like Daste, worked part time. One clinic remained, functioning as a central office to manage the HMO's mental health services for the entire state. Soon that too closed, and the coordination function was handed over to a regional office three states away. Now when clients need services, they call a 1-800 number and are given their choice of a number of providers in their area. Although this is clearly less personalized than the original clinic system, the regional office staff person (called a *utilization review technician*) knows a fair amount about each provider and thus is generally effective in matching client and therapist. The price providers pay for this effectiveness match is the completion of lengthy paperwork about their credentials and treatment approaches.

When the client calls Daste or another therapist, he or she generally receives two sessions for assessment and the development of a treatment plan. If the caller appears to be in the midst of a crisis, Daste can get the person into a psychiatric hospital right away. If an immediate consultation with a psychiatrist seems necessary, for example in a case of serious depression necessitating medication, that also can be arranged. Otherwise, Daste sends the treatment plan to the central office for approval. He notes that the social worker has a lot of control over this first phase of the work.

In Daste's company, as in most other mental health managed care systems, the client's condition must fit one of the diagnoses in the American Psychiatric Association's *Diagnostic and Statistical Manual IV* (the *DSM IV*) in order for treatment to be covered. (Authors' note: Although the *DSM IV* includes mental problems that are affected by environmental factors, the manual tends to stress a medical model of mental illness. Thus help for situations such as "marital difficulties" may not be covered by an MCO unless the therapist can make a convincing case that the situation represents a crisis.)

Daste describes a typical treatment plan as follows: The diagnosis, such as simple phobia, is stated, followed by the treatment goals, such as patient's management of the phobia so it doesn't interfere with normal functioning. The outcomes are operationalized—for example, "Mr. Jones will be able to return to a manageable level of functioning. Treatment will be designed to enable him to perform his duties at work. This will also involve his being able to drive, both locally and on the highway." Daste feels the specification of how success in treatment will be measured is one of the great benefits of managed care. Finally, the plan includes a description of the treatment to be used, such as systematic desensitization therapy, and a justification of why this particular approach was chosen. The provider may also include "community resource referrals" as part of the treatment; if, for example, Mr. Jones has had difficulties in getting a job, Daste might also refer him to a local job training program. Finally, the treatment plan includes the provider's request for a specific number of sessions; Daste generally asks for six to eight and specifies when therapy will start and finish. Daste shares all the details of the plan with the client before sending it off to the regional office.

In this and most MCOs, the major authorization issue tends to be the number of sessions approved by the utilization review manager. Daste reports that he generally receives the number he asks for, or a few less (e.g., six if he asked for eight). If after the initial series of sessions is completed he feels more are warranted, he submits a new plan to the central office justifying continued treatment. The plan also indicates which therapy goals have already been achieved. If the review manager has questions about the request, he may call Daste for further details. Generally, Daste receives approval for additional sessions. The client is usually allotted a total of twenty sessions a year and would have to pay out of pocket for any additional therapy.

Daste is generally satisfied with the managed care system in which he works. He is comfortable with the emphasis on short-term therapy models and appreciates the fact that the company keeps its providers current with the latest treatment innovations (although he misses the frequent face-to-face in-service training sessions that were carried out in the clinic). He approves of the company's frequent quality control checks with clients, such as client satisfaction surveys and the detailed closing summaries in which therapists document outcomes of treatment. He is impressed by the thoroughness with which the MCO assesses potential providers, even though the review system creates a lot of paperwork. Overall, he feels, these factors "drive good treatment." Therapists must be competent, up-to-date, and accountable in order to remain on provider panels.

The system does have its drawbacks, however. Although there is careful screening of clinicians, the reviewers rarely know the providers; patient–therapist matches can suffer. The vast amount of paperwork and the need for frequent authorization and reauthorization requests can be tiresome. In addition, Daste points out, there are no built-in pay raises, because reimbursements for services are not regularly increased. In the future, in order to get into the provider pool, some therapists may agree to work for less, potentially lowering the rates for all. It is a system, Daste concludes, in which providers need to be assertive in order to deliver the best services to clients and to protect their own practice.

Daste has seen both the pitfalls and strengths of managed care in the private sector. As he watches its movement into the public mental health field, he ponders how the approach will work with the chronic mentally ill, including people who need prolonged hospitalization. How will MCOs handle individuals who refuse to take their medications? Will they be able to do outreach work with groups such as the homeless mentally ill? These and other questions mark the next stages of the managed care revolution.

Managed Care in an Agency Setting

Interview with a Social Work Staff Member

Judith Kolb Morris has many years of experience working with children and their parents, first as an early childhood educator and now as a social worker. She is currently employed at a private, nonprofit child and family services agency in a small city in Massachusetts. Until recently, this 150-year-old agency could be described as a typical example of a traditional social work practice setting: a community agency offering a variety of services to children and families; interacting and consulting with other organizations such as schools and public welfare offices; and supported by the United Way, clients' fees, private insurance, and Medicaid. In the past seven years, however, Morris's place of work has become part of the managed care revolution.

The agency has long offered outpatient counseling for people of all ages, adoptions and foster care services, a big brother/big sister program, and various mental health outreach activities. Many of its clients receive welfare and are covered by Medicaid. In the early 1990s, it became clear to the director that the usual sources of funds for these services were changing. The United Way and other charitable organizations had become less able to support social work programs and to compensate for cutbacks in federal and state funding. In addition, private employers were shifting their insurance systems from fee-for-service to managed care. Most significant, the state of Massachusetts had decided to convert much of its Medicaid system to a public managed care approach. A private MCO called Mental Health Management of America (MHMA) contracted with the state to cover the health and mental health needs of Medicaid recipients.

The agency board saw two basic choices: to try to resist managed care funding as long as they could, perhaps jeopardizing the existence of the agency, or to join in the new approach, seeking as much agency control over the process as possible. It chose the latter, and the agency signed a contract as a provider for MHMA. Morris recalls that when she was interviewed for her job as a clinical social worker, the director asked her views about managed care. Being a savvy interviewee, she said she saw it as the wave of the future, "like it or not." The director later told her that if she'd complained about MCOs, she wouldn't have been hired.

Although Morris sees a number of current or potential problems with the managed care system as it has developed at her agency, she notes that the director has done much to make it feasible for staff to work within it and to bring out its positive aspects. One of the agency's first steps was to develop an in-house Quality Management System to monitor therapists' clinical decisions, numbers of counseling sessions, and quality and timeliness of paperwork. The agency's clinical director runs the management system. MHMA saw early on that through this mechanism the agency worked efficiently and was able to offer clients good service in as short a time as possible. Essentially, the agency took on many of the monitoring and quality assurance functions usually carried out by MCO staff. In return for its effectiveness in this arena, MHMA gave the agency more leeway in decision making about client treatment.

MHMA was generous in what it would authorize for services to clients. New or returning clients could receive sixteen hours of counseling or other help in the first month. This allotment was based on research that indicated that "multiproblem families" (which constitute much of the agency's clientele) benefit from a strong dose of immediate and concentrated assistance. Clients could usually get another thirteen hours of treatment over the next thirteen weeks (sixteen for children). This help was not limited to individual or family counseling; it could include hours spent in vital social work interventions such as consultation with teachers and other people or organizations with whom clients interact. In managed care language, these traditional social work functions of brokerage, advocacy, and case management become "collateral contacts."

If the social worker felt it was warranted, he or she could ask the MCO to authorize another thirteen-hour/thirteen-week stretch. This was generally approved. After seven months, clients were put "on maintenance," a system of one session every two weeks, with no collaterals. Although no limit was put on the number of sessions in a given year, MHMA encouraged social workers to end their intervention after a year and a half.

Although the MHMA system offered a good amount of flexibility, Morris still saw problems. The first (and the one most providers point out) is "all those forms! Every time you turned around, you were filling out another one." Forms requesting authorization for treatment had to be sent a month in advance, but there was no guarantee they would be back in time for the sessions to start. In addition, the agency used to wait until services were authorized and payment made by the MCO before it would in turn pay the clinicians. The practice was stopped after staff banded together to protest it.

Another problem was the fact that although the agency held the overall contract with the MCO, staff members also had to contract individually with the organization. MHMA could refuse to certify certain clinicians, particularly if they worked with "unreliable" populations such as people who abuse drugs or alcohol. To the MCO, work with clients who often didn't show up for appointments did not fit with managed care's standards of efficiency.

Despite these drawbacks, MHMA was a reasonably flexible managed care system. It recognized the importance of environmental or collateral work, and its stress on quality control was positive. Although quality was measured largely by assessing the appropriateness of therapists' clinical decisions, the potential existed to use the extensive paperwork on each client to track reduction of symptoms and changes in behavior.

After several years, however, Morris's agency recently entered a new phase in its involvement with managed care. Perhaps because of its flexible benefits, MHMA lost its contract with the state. The company taking its place contracted with the agency as a provider under more stringent rules. Clients were now eligible for an initial set of only twelve sessions per calendar year; clinicians had to request additional services. This essentially eliminated the initial intensive treatment approach, leaving less time to do collateral work. Morris had to cut back on this important function in order to have the time to work with clients directly. She and other staff were also critical of the new MCO's forms, which were lengthier and more complicated. All in all, Morris notes, managed care can present basic ethical conflicts to practitioners. Refusing treatment to people who need it conflicts with both the social work code of ethics and her agency's own policies. "It's a real dilemma," she says, "when you want to help people and do good work and are told that you have to cut your services."

Managed Mental Health Care in the Public Sector

The agency in which Judith Kolb Morris works deals with a managed care plan for Medicaid clients. This is an example of a relatively recent venture in managed care: the expansion into services financed by governmental bodies rather than by private employers. The most typical of these are Medicaid managed care plans developed by state governments. Massachusetts was in fact the first state to implement a comprehensive privatized public sector health and mental health program for Medicaid beneficiaries. By 2004, all but 3 states had some form of behavioral health managed care plan to serve Medicaid and other populations eligible for publicly financed health care. Over half of all Medicaid recipients were eligible for behavioral health services under a managed care plan in 1999.[17]

While Medicaid managed care plans have a number of similarities with private employer plans, they also face some specific challenges. These include the need to serve people who are severely and chronically mentally ill and who have traditionally spent long periods of time in mental hospitals. The Medicaid population includes the poor elderly, public welfare clients, and, in many states, people just above the poverty line—groups that lack basic resources and who often have employment, housing, and transportation problems. Some are homeless. These difficulties exacerbate mental illness and make treatment more challenging. Many mental health practitioners and advocates believe that such problems call for an emphasis on outreach and community-based services.

The move to managed care Medicaid programs came about mostly because of the great increases in Medicaid costs in the late 1980s and early 1990s. Largely due to the cost-control strategies of managed care approaches, including reducing payments to providers, using gatekeepers, and relying more on psychoactive drugs than on psychotherapy, Medicaid costs did indeed diminish sharply in many states. Massachusetts, for example, saw a 30 to 40 percent decline in mental health expenditures between 1991 and 1995.[18]

It is as yet unclear, however, whether quality of mental health services has improved under Medicaid managed care programs. As we have noted, dealing with the mental health needs of low-income, often chronically ill individuals with few resources is a new challenge for MCOs. For their part, states have had difficulty in monitoring the quality of care. Problems have emerged in a number of places. In Tennessee the behavioral health managed care organizations under contract to deliver services to Medicaid recipients have been criticized for poor management and failure to provide needed services. A major behavioral health MCO terminated its contract with the state of Montana after the state accused the company of poor performance. On the other hand, managed care Medicaid programs tend to offer a wider mix of services than traditional Medicaid programs.[19]

Of particular interest to mental health advocates and to many mental health planners is the ability of managed care in Medicaid and other public programs to reduce reliance on psychiatric hospitalization and to increase the development and use of community mental health services. In Massachusetts, one study shows, the shift to managed care resulted in about a 25 percent decline in inpatient care for people with schizophrenia. The study did not report whether adequate alternative community services were developed. As mental health policy analyst David Mechanic notes, "The challenge is not simply to reduce inpatient utilization but to develop a balanced system of care with alternative care of appropriate quality." Medicaid managed mental health care thus has many challenges—cutting costs, maintaining or increasing quality of care, and creating an effective system of community resources for those with mental illness. The current decline in the states' and national economies makes meeting these challenges even more difficult.[20]

The History of Managed Care

The concept of managed health care has been around, in one form or another, for the last sixty years. Health maintenance organizations (HMOs) were first developed in the 1930s; these were prepaid medical services, provided initially at a specific clinic or medical center. Fixed monthly fees, usually paid by employers, covered all services provided. HMOs generally gave more comprehensive coverage than existing medical or insurance plans, including preventive services such as annual checkups. One of the best-known examples is the Kaiser-Permanente health plan, established by industrialist Henry J. Kaiser in California in 1942. By the 1950s, the Kaiser plan had a growing network of its own physicians, hospitals, and clinics and an enrollment of half a million people. Twenty years later an alternative type of HMO appeared, in which health organizations contracted with private physicians to deliver services in their own offices rather than in company facilities.[21]

The Nixon administration passed legislation supporting HMO growth in 1971, and the HMO Act of 1973 required all businesses with more than twenty-five employees to offer at least one federally qualified HMO plan as an alternative to conventional insurance programs, if such a plan was available in their locality. President Reagan continued the stress on HMOs as a way to contain costs in the 1980s. Yet while some HMOs were quite successful, particularly on the West Coast, the movement on the whole grew slowly. Prepaid plans lessened physicians' autonomy and were fought by groups such as the American Medical Association. AMA opposition and problems with support in Congress led to various restrictions on HMOs, which initially made it difficult for them to compete with conventional insurance.[22]

As medical costs continued to explode, however, HMOs became more and more attractive to businesses coping with their health care budgets. The growth of for-profit HMOs, generally using the private physician network approach, increased steadily toward the end of the 1980s. By 1991 more than 38 million people were enrolled in six hundred HMOs. Generally, these restricted enrollees to the use of specific providers (those of you with such plans are familiar with the list of physicians from which you must choose—either through careful research or by throwing a dart).

As HMOs have evolved and diversified in form, they have become subsumed under the broader rubric of "managed care organizations" or MCOs. MCOs include various types of HMOs; preferred provider organizations (PPOs), which offer discounted rates for using providers in a preselected group; and managed mental health firms. This last group provides services such as utilization review and management of provider networks to insurance companies or other MCOs. The commonality to look for in deciding whether to describe a program as managed care is whether it is designed to "generate cost savings through the restriction and management of access to health care."[23]

President Clinton included a form of managed care in his massive health care reform plan introduced in 1993. The Clinton proposal called for the administration of health insurance through large purchasing alliances. These alliances would offer several insurance options to consumers, including managed care plans. The alliances would operate under state control, with a national health board setting pricing standards. Yet health reform has never been an easy task in the United States due to the large number of powerful stakeholders in the health care system and to the tendency to dichotomize the issue into an either–or debate over the merits of the market system versus the government in dealing with social and economic problems. Bitterly fought by Republican politicians, much of the business community, and the AMA, the president's national health care program was declared "officially dead" in Congress in September 1994.[24]

While Washington and the rest of the country were caught up in the great health care reform debate, insurance companies, corporations, HMOs, and large hospital chains were quietly but steadily creating a private-sector, managed care revolution. With the demise of the Clinton health reform initiative, these forces were able to bring about dramatic and rapid change in how health care was financed and delivered in the United States. HMOs and insurance companies merged and grew larger, and hospitals and doctors banded together in alliances and networks of their own. One in six Americans was enrolled in an HMO by September 1994, and countless others had joined other variations of managed care programs. At the same time, as we have seen, several states were turning entire Medicaid programs over to private MCOs. For now, at least, private-sector managed care is becoming the "only show in town" when it comes to delivering health care.[25]

Although managed care in the mental health services developed somewhat later than in physical health care, it is now rapidly catching up. Historically, treatment for people with mental illness has been largely the responsibility of the public sector, particularly through state mental hospitals. Only individuals who could afford it saw private therapists or were treated in private mental hospitals. Although commercial health care insurance became available in the 1920s, insurance coverage for mental disorders or substance abuse did not appear until the 1950s. Unlike insurance for physical problems, which covers specific services deemed medically necessary for treatment, mental health benefits are based on duration of treatment. In other words, in the case of cancer, an insurance company generally covers the particular treatment methods necessary to cure or control the cancer, without a time limit; in the case of a condition such as manic–depressive disorder, benefits are limited to a specific number of sessions with a therapist or days in a mental hospital. As one health policy analyst comments, "This discrimination is 'justified' on the grounds that severely mentally ill people would consume 'unmanageable' (or 'unpredictable') amounts of service," as opposed to the physically ill, whose care presumably can be both managed and predicted. Thus a major problem with insurance for mental illness is that it "has remained limited, expensive, and not equivalent to coverage for other medical disorders."[26]

HMOs began to cover mental health and substance abuse services in the 1970s. The 1973 HMO Act required that in order to become a federally qualified HMO, a program had to offer not only basic services for physical disorders but also short-term outpatient evaluation or crisis intervention mental health services and referral services for alcohol and drug abuse. Employers became more and more interested in the managed care approach to mental health in the 1980s because of an unprecedented expansion in mental health services in that decade and a concomitant rise in the insurance costs borne by businesses. By 1986, due to employer interest and federal initiatives, nearly all MCOs offered mental health coverage. At first these benefits were organized by a department within the MCO, but soon managed care companies began to subcontract with specialized mental health managed care organizations to provide services. Specialized behavioral health care MCOs have now become a huge industry.[27]

The managed care approach has generally not led to expanded mental health benefits. If anything, as we have seen from the interviews with Barry Daste and Judith Kolb Morris, benefits are more tightly controlled under the new structure. The average MCO limits benefits to thirty hospital days and twenty outpatient visits a year.[28]

The most recent chapter in the story of managed care is the move into public managed care systems. The impetus for states to move into managed care was the same as that for private businesses—rising costs. Through most of the 1980s, combined state and federal spending on Medicaid grew over 8 percent a year. Between 1988 and 1992, due to expanding numbers of beneficiaries and spiraling health care costs, Medicaid expenditures exploded. Some states were spending as much as one-third of their resources on the program. State governments began to turn to managed care as a primary tool for controlling expenses, and MCOs were eager to exploit their desires to lower costs. As the private managed care market became saturated, companies saw the public system as "the next sales frontier."[29]

Managed care has actually been allowed under Medicaid since the 1970s, but it was voluntary for Medicaid beneficiaries and few chose to enroll. The major shift to Medicaid managed care systems by the states would not have been possible without the development of a federal waiver system in the 1980s. Under Section

1915(b) and 1115 Medicaid waivers, states can waive various program requirements, such as freedom of choice of providers. The 1115 waiver allows for many different types of changes to Medicaid, including development of statewide managed care plans with mandatory participation of the Medicaid population. States' use of waivers to establish managed care programs has grown rapidly.[30] As in the private sector, experimentation with many varieties of managed care has taken over following the demise of proposals for a more centralized and cohesive national health care system.

The Economics of Managed Care

One of the major issues in the economics of managed care is whether it does, in fact, save money and if so, whether cost reductions are a short-term or ongoing phenomenon. It will be helpful to begin this discussion with a recap of the mechanisms MCOs employ to curtail health expenditures.

Managed care's major device for cost cutting is a change in the incentive system for providers. Under the traditional fee-for-service practice, doctors and hospitals could pretty much set the going rate for each service they rendered. Thus there was no economic disincentive for performing many services for each patient, ordering expensive tests, or keeping people in the hospital for lengthy stays. Early attempts at changing incentives included the Diagnostic Related Groups (DRGs) regulations of the Reagan era, in which Medicare began to pay hospitals a set fee for treating each illness based on the average cost of treating that particular condition. But savings from the DRG approach were short-lived and applied only to publicly reimbursed care. The capitation system of managed care has proved much more successful in restricting rises in payments to providers. Because doctors, therapists, and health/mental facilities are prepaid a set amount for treating a given number of clients, it is in their interest to limit services as much as possible within whatever quality controls are set by the MCO. Mental health managed care further restricts costs through the use of gatekeepers to regulate the amount and type of therapy provided.

There is a good amount of evidence that managed care cuts health costs, at least at first. As the system expanded in the early 1990s, costs decreased dramatically. According to one survey, employers' insurance premiums rose only 2.1 percent in 1995, compared to 11.5 percent in 1991. A study of more than 2,500 companies indicated that during 1992, employers with traditional insurance coverage averaged a cost of $4,080 per employee, up 14 percent from the year before. Companies using MCOs paid an average of $3,313, an 8 percent increase. When large corporations contracted with mental health MCOs, they saw striking changes. IBM, for example, went from almost 105 million dollars in mental health spending in 1989 to 59 million dollars in 1993. Doubtless, managed care systems helped contribute to these changes.[31]

From 1993 through 1998, health care expenditures and consumer medical costs continued to show a relatively low rate of increase. National health spending growth was only 4.8 percent in 1997, the lowest rate in three and a half decades. Yet spending accelerated slightly in 1998, with a 5.6 percent growth. Health care costs had begun to rise, particularly in the areas of prescription drugs and use of new medical technology. Experts on health costs began voicing concerns; one warned as early as 1997 of "disquieting signs that the recent pause in health-care inflation is about to end." By 2000, national expenditures on health rose 7.4 percent, and in 2001, they rose 8.7 percent. In 2004, health spending rose 7.9 percent.[32]

The next ominous sign was the increase in health insurance premiums, beginning with the announcement of a 10 percent increase in premiums for federal employees in 1999. Premium rises for employees in the private sector also began surfacing in 1999, becoming sharper and more widespread in insurance plans for the year 2000. By 2002, health insurance premiums had increased by 12.7 percent. One health economist predicts that there will be double-digit health insurance increases for the next decade. Generally, employers pass at least some of these increases on to employees.[33]

Why, now that much of our health services are being delivered through managed care, is the nation facing a return to rising health costs? One possible answer is that the kinds of savings managed care can bring have already been achieved. With insured Americans now in the system, the nation has already gotten the "one-time savings" of a switch to less expensive medical arrangements. In addition, MCOs are moving out of a period of fierce competition among themselves to expand their markets (a situation in which premiums are kept down in order to attract new customers). Now, with fuller enrollments, the industry can focus on increasing profits by raising premiums. Companies are willing to risk losing some customers in order to increase their earnings. Finally, soaring prices for prescription drugs are responsible for an important share of increases in health care spending. Managed care pharmacy costs increased by about 17 percent in 1999, total managed care costs by only about 6 percent. Expensive new drugs have come on the market; drug companies have advertised these widely to consumers, rather than just to physicians; and the increased enrollment of Medicare recipients in managed care plans has added an older group of patients with greater pharmaceutical needs.[34]

A final consideration in the economics of managed care is the effect of corporate structures and practices on health care costs. Whereas some MCOs are nonprofit organizations, managed care is largely a for-profit enterprise. The expanding role of the stock market in the health care sector has been characterized as "Wall Street's Love Affair with Health Care." Investment advisors see opportunity, for example, in the aging of U.S. citizens because older people use many more health services than those under age sixty-five. For this reason, one business columnist noted, investors should keep health care "at the core of any well-formed portfolio." In the interest of improving their market share, many MCOs have merged with or bought other companies. Typical of such consolidation is managed care giant Aetna's acquisition of U.S. Healthcare in 1996 and Prudential Healthcare in 1999, creating what was at that point the largest provider of health care in the country. While investors look for greater profitability from such mergers, critics warn of the ability of huge health care companies to cut back services, raise premiums, and force doctors and other providers to accept lower reimbursement rates. By 2003, the ten largest managed care companies accounted for over half of the total health care enrollments in the United States.[35]

The same situation exists in managed mental health care, with one critic commenting that "managed behavioral health care is a financial, or Wall Street issue, not a health care issue" and another describing the "corporatization of mental health services." Magellan is currently the nation's largest managed behavioral health company, providing managed behavior health, wellness, and employee assistance programs to over 55 million members, or one in five Americans. The company is responsible for one/third of all behavioral health care enrollees. United Health Group follows with an enrollment of 28.1 million people, and Aetna with 15.4 million.[36]

Many mental health care providers, including social workers, are concerned that in for-profit behavioral health MCOs, fiscal concerns may often influence clinical decision making, particularly in such areas as deciding how many treatment sessions a client should receive. They note that MCOs often decrease or eliminate reimbursement for important collateral work (e.g., interviewing the teacher of a depressed child or referring clients to community resources) on the grounds that it is not "medically necessary" and that they cut out field training for social work and other students by not reimbursing supervisors and not allowing students to do clinical work. And, finally, providers are not happy when fees for practitioners are decreased, as when Magellan cut reimbursement for social workers from $63 to $45 per hour.[37]

Social Analysis of Managed Care

In this section, we discuss the social values, assumptions, and manifest and latent goals underlying managed care, particularly care for those with mental illness. We also look at the state of research into this new approach to health care delivery.

Various values and assumptions support efforts to offer treatment to individuals with emotional problems. Humanistic motives compel us to want to help those in difficulty, especially when the problem does not seem to be their fault. Whereas mental illness was once seen as the result of immorality or possession by demons, we have come to view it either as a disease or as a set of reactions to "problems in living." The disease, or medical, model of mental illness is the more prevalent one in our society. It carries with it the assumption that psychological problems are a type of illness amenable to treatment by a psychiatrist or other highly trained mental health professional. Treatment can be on an outpatient basis or in a hospital. Medication is often part of the therapist's armament. Recently, those following a disease model have focused on genetic factors and the functioning of biological mechanisms in the brain.

The "problems in living" approach is part of what fuels a community mental health model of psychological problems. This model sees psychological difficulties in their broader social and economic context. It stresses interventions in people's environment in order to prevent or at least alleviate mental illness.

Mental health managed care has a stake in both approaches. Private sector MCOs tend to utilize the medical model, perhaps because the image of the highly trained therapist dealing out specialized treatments is a more credible and concrete one to "sell" to customers. MCOs working in the public sector with people who have more apparent economic and social stresses are gaining an appreciation of the importance of community-based and preventative services, even though this approach necessitates changes in the ways they have traditionally operated. MCOs in both areas have encouraged greater reliance on outpatient treatment than on hospitalization, in part for therapeutic reasons, in part because outpatient treatment is less expensive.

Managed care also builds on another set of values and assumptions in our society: the belief in the ability of market forces to solve both economic and social problems and the concomitant suspicion of government's ability to do so. Although Clinton's large-scale health reform proposals combined elements of government and private intervention, the plan was seen by many as relying too heavily on "big government." This created a highly favorable environment for entrepreneurial MCOs, which offered to prove the ability of private enterprise to grapple with the enormous problem of health costs in the United States.

The tension between the notion of a collective, societal response to health problems and the idea that market mechanisms should handle health needs is not new. In the United States, health care has always been a mixture of private and public responsibility. In the past few decades, however, there has been a pronounced swing toward private forms of organizing and delivering care. The rise of huge chains of private hospitals, including private psychiatric hospitals, is one manifestation of this swing. The development of MCOs is a further step in the "commodification" of health care. Much of the language of managed care is the language of business: customers, providers of products, customer service bureaus, market expansion, and so on. A good illustration is an advertisement for a mental health managed care conference for employers, MCO executives, and clinicians that promises to show participants how to "overcome downward price pressure . . . by enhancing behavioral healthcare value and implementing value-based pricing strategies." Participants will also learn how to "take advantage of 'focused factory' service production methods."[38]

The manifest goal of mental health managed care programs is to cut health costs while maintaining quality care. Latent goals include expanding into new markets, particularly at a time when the general health market is becoming saturated, and gaining control over providers. While this is particularly true of the for-profit MCOs that dominate the field, even nonprofits need to pay attention to maintaining a market share of enrollees. Although MCOs, as we have noted, do cut costs in many situations, critics describe latent effects of denying needed care, reducing client control, and avoiding accountability to the public at large.[39]

This discussion of assumptions and goals leads us to important research questions. For example, where managed care has cut costs, what is the source of these savings? Do they come from greater efficiency or from reduced access and/or quality? How effective are the treatment interventions used by providers in MCOs? How do access to care and treatment outcomes compare between managed care and fee-for-service arrangements? There are two sources of research on these issues: studies and surveys produced by outsiders such as academics and members of think tanks and the in-house quality and outcome assessments conducted by the MCOs. So far, the evaluative research has been sketchy, and a broad, comprehensive database has not yet emerged. The chief executive officer of a large MCO notes that after twelve years of development of mental health managed care, "managed mental health organizations and health services researchers are still strangers in a relationship [that has not been mutually productive]." Although the amount of research has been increasing, "there has been little effort to look at the extent to which changes that have taken place were influenced by how [MCOs] actually operate . . . what [MCOs] do well, and what they could be doing better." Health care analyst David Mechanic observes that although items such as cost reduction and access to care have been studied, data on quality of care and outcomes are more limited.[40]

There are a number of difficulties in doing research on mental health managed care. MCOs are set up as ongoing programs or businesses, not as experimental projects. The use of control groups, for example, does not fit well with the way they operate. Similarly, before-and-after studies, in which the same group of people is followed from an initial fee-for-service plan to enrollment in a managed care arrangement, are often not practical. Terms such as *treatment outcomes* are hard to define; should they be operationalized, for example, as reduction in symptoms, changes in diagnosis, or ability to stay out of the hospital? Should they be measured by therapist assessment, patients' report of improvement, or some scale of daily functioning? Even if *outcome* were well defined, the fact that most studies follow patients for a limited amount of time after treatment—often only six months—is problematic. For example, the effects of treatment for schizophrenia, "a chronic and fluctuating disorder with a widely variable clinical course," are hard to determine in the time allotted. Finally, the complexity and range in managed care organizations makes comparison and generalization of findings a challenging task.[41]

Despite these difficulties, research on various aspects of managed care is proceeding. One such aspect is the source of cost reduction. Some studies indicate that cost decreases are due to cuts in services, that is, reduced probability of inpatient admission and fewer inpatient days as well as fewer outpatient sessions per client. Lowering costs for services, including lowering payments to providers, has also contributed. However, it has also been found that some plans add coverage for residential facilities and partial hospitalization and stress emergency treatment while still containing costs. The notion that for-profit managed care plans tend to enroll healthier people than do nonprofit or fee-for-service operations has also been suggested as a reason for lower costs, yet several studies of specific health plans found little difference in the health status of enrollees in the different programs.[42]

Researchers have asked whether managed care plans increase or decrease people's access to mental health services. Access can be defined as the proportion of people in a health plan who have used a mental health service in a given year. A major study of the move to a Medicaid managed care system in Massachusetts showed increased access to outpatient treatment but decreased utilization of inpatient care. A large employer converting from a fee-for-service to a private-sector MCO plan reported similar results: greater use of outpatient services and a dramatic drop in inpatient care. In this case, however, although clients had greater initial access to outpatient sessions, the average number of approved sessions declined. Basically, the access findings appear to be mixed. Studies of outcomes and effectiveness of treatment are similarly varied. Here, the major finding is that although people who are moderately mentally ill tend to do as well under managed care as under traditional insurance, the picture is quite different for those with severe illness such as schizophrenia and serious depression. One large study found that primary care physicians in HMOs were less likely to recognize depressed patients; these patients tended to get less medication and to have poorer outcomes than those in fee-for-service plans. It also appears that people who are schizophrenic, and thus usually high users of services, get fewer services, such as hospitalization, under managed care. In addition, MCOs typically don't provide important nonmedical services such as housing and supervised daily activities.[43]

The internal research conducted by MCOs has tended to focus on measurement of cost, access, and utilization patterns. But more recently, perhaps because of criticisms of MCOs, companies have begun to stress quality of treatment, especially as measured by "report cards" on performance. Typical types of data for mental health MCOs include patient satisfaction with treatment, effective management of antidepressant medication, and follow-up after hospitalizations for mental illness. A private nonprofit accreditation group for MCOs, the National Committee for Quality Assurance (NCQA), collects and publishes data on quality. However, some of the largest MCOs refuse to let the NCQA release their data to the public, and so far much of the information is too general, not providing enough information on specific services such as availability of day treatment or data on quality of mental health staff. In response, a Presidential Commission on quality in the health care industry created a National Quality Forum to develop a public/private partnership that will devise and implement a national strategy for quality measurement and reporting. As we will see in the next section, growing dissatisfaction with the functioning of MCOs may produce the necessary pressure for a more effective system of quality control.[44]

The Political Context of Managed Care

By now you are no doubt well aware that the managed care revolution is a high-stakes phenomenon involving many different organizations and constituencies. It is a $2 billion industry, tackling a national problem, built on a specific ideology, and affecting Americans of all walks of life. The list of stakeholders is lengthy, including clients, employers, state health officials, providers, MCOs, federal and state legislators and other government leaders, advocacy groups, and the broader public. This section provides a brief overview of the major players and their points of view.

Clients and their families are at the receiving end of mental health managed care. They want effective and accessible help, and most would like some control over the type of assistance they get and the way it is delivered. Some are the people who provide the horror stories to newspapers and magazines— "After my allotted sessions were over, I could only see a psychiatrist fifteen minutes every three months to have my depression medication checked." Some may be concerned about confidentiality issues that arise when details of their problems are discussed between their therapist and an unknown gatekeeper. Others are largely satisfied with their care. However, surveys indicate a growing public concern about managed care in general. A 1997 study, for example, reports that 55 percent of people in managed care plans were concerned that if they were sick, their "health plan would be more concerned about saving money than about what is the best medical treatment." Only 34 percent of those with traditional insurance felt this way.[45]

Most mental health consumers are not organized with other clients or families to advocate for good treatment, although some have joined the ranks of client groups or organizations for family members, such as the National Association for the Mentally Ill, in order to influence MCO practices. Many clients have access to at least a rudimentary grievance procedure in their MCOs, and others have gone further and pursued lawsuits.

Employers and state health administrators who purchase managed care can be seen as driving the mental health managed care revolution. Their concern about controlling mental health costs underlies the move to MCOs. Yet they would also like to maintain some control over the premiums and practices of the MCOs with which they contract. The current rise in premiums is a problem for businesses, which will pass along a proportion of the increase to their employees. State Medicaid and mental health officials, who are more publicly accountable and whose health care planning decisions are more visible, are particularly likely to address concerns about quality of care, in addition to cost issues.

"Mental health providers" sounds like a unified group but actually encompasses a number of professions. Although the public often thinks of psychiatry as the major source of mental health practitioners, social workers actually dominate the field numerically: There are more clinically trained mental health social workers than all the other core mental health professionals combined. Other professionals include psychiatrists, psychologists, psychiatric nurses, and counselors. Thirty-seven percent of NASW members report mental health as their primary practice area.[46]

The use of different mental health providers has changed under managed care. Under traditional insurance, psychiatrists were used 85 percent of the time, at an average charge of $150 a visit; psychologists 10 percent of the time, at a $100 fee; and social workers and other licensed mental health professionals 5 percent of the time, at $85 a visit. Under managed care plans, social workers and other licensed providers are used 56 percent of the time, at an average charge of $65; psychologists 33 percent of the time, at $75; and psychiatrists only 11 percent of the time, at $90 a visit. These statistics indicate not only the replacement of higher-priced providers with "cheaper" ones under managed care, but also the decrease in fees received by all groups under the new system. Providers also face additional problems under managed care, including loss of autonomy and concerns about ethical issues, such as compromises to confidentiality. One mental health professional observes, "Seasoned clinicians with deep clinical knowledge now find themselves on the defensive, justifying a treatment plan to a managed care representative unfamiliar with clinical complexity."[47]

Physicians in general have been powerful stakeholders in health issues, with their major organization, the American Medical Association (AMA), often exerting enormous influence over health policy through lobbying activities. MCOs have emerged as a counterbalance to this power, subjecting managed care doctors' decisions to external review by gatekeepers and becoming a force in determining their incomes (often reducing them). In addition, physicians charge, managed care disrupts the relationship between doctor and patient and can create roadblocks to the delivery of appropriate treatments. Doctors have lately begun to contest managed care practices forcefully by refusing to accept new fee schedules, dropping out of MCOs, undertaking lawsuits, helping to pass legislation restricting MCOs' decision making, and even joining unions. In an extraordinary move, the AMA established a collective bargaining entity in 1999 to help salaried physicians in labor negotiations with hospitals and health systems.[48]

Even before they were largely squeezed out of mental health treatment financed through managed care, psychiatrists were highly critical of the movement to MCOs. The 1995 election of the president of the American Psychiatric Association became a referendum on the new system. A managed care opponent, who called MCOs "greed-driven sharks" that "manage health care for a profit," was chosen for the seat. For their part, managed care executives point to psychiatrists' high salaries and their tendency to engage patients in lengthy therapy when short-term treatments could be just as effective.[49]

Social workers have in some respects gained from the managed care revolution because they are more likely to be used as therapists by MCOs than by traditional insurers. Yet they have increasingly chafed at problems with the system. They are generally paid less than before, and MCOs have increasingly tightened their provider pools. Social workers in private practice who are not accepted into these pools must find clients with traditional insurance or people who can pay out-of-pocket. Social workers in agencies with managed care contracts face similar difficulties because the MCO policies dictate who will be paid for what services. And, like other providers, social workers are critical of limits on treatment sessions, excessive paperwork, and the vast amount of time spent getting approval for interventions from MCO gatekeepers.

Social workers have responded to these managed care problems in a variety of ways, with the National Association of Social Workers (NASW) playing a major role. NASW has joined other practitioner groups in class action lawsuits against MCOs. In one lawsuit, MCOs in New York State have been charged with antitrust violations such as fixing prices paid to mental health providers. Although the case was dismissed in two courts, it may proceed to the U.S. Supreme Court. NASW national and state offices have also helped introduce legislation modifying managed care practices. In Florida, the state chapter filed a complaint with the state Bureau of Managed Care alleging that an MCO acted unlawfully in dropping mental health providers from its provider pool. NASW has gained membership on an advisory council of the managed care industry's National Committee on Quality Insurance, where it has protested existing quality assurance standards that require social workers' referral decisions to be approved by psychologists. Finally, social workers, like physicians, are beginning to eye the benefits of unionization. The Rhode Island NASW chapter, for example, has voted to support the organization of health care unions that include social workers.[50]

Although many of these measures could be described as attempting to protect the profession, they often overlap with advocacy for clients and promotion of ethical practice in the mental health system. When a New Jersey HMO was going through bankruptcy, for example, and refused to allow clients to continue seeing the same providers, social workers successfully pursued legal remedies to ensure the continuity of those treatment relationships. This helped clients at the same time that it kept providers in the system. Similarly, social workers have pressured state legislators to make managed care Medicaid programs responsive to both practitioner and client issues. Pursuing its broad purpose of promoting social justice, NASW has advocated for "ethical, inclusive and comprehensive managed care policies and practices" and has lobbied for state and federal legislation to ensure patient rights in the managed care system.[51]

At the center of the managed care revolution, of course, are the MCOs themselves. Investors in for-profit managed care companies are also important players. We have already described the cost-cutting goals of MCOs and their objective of establishing remunerative markets. Investors count on these practices to bring them a good return for their money. As several Wall Street analysts comment, "What happens to managed care and financing for health care in the United States has both [short-] and long-term implications for the broader health care marketplace." Backlash against MCOs, they warn, can undercut investor earnings. Although MCOs generally don't intend to diminish the quality of health and mental health care, the practices they use to reduce costs have brought increasing protests. To counteract criticisms and the spector of greater government regulation, the industry has engaged in a $60 million congressional lobbying effort and an advertisement blitz predicting the negative effects of federal intrusion. New laws, one ad says, "could cause nearly two million hard-working Americans to lose their health coverage."[52]

Legislators, governors, presidents, and presidential candidates also have a large investment in the development of health care policies such as managed care. They must respond to the conflicting demands of powerful, well-organized stakeholders such as employers, MCOs, and physicians. They are sensitive to the voters' call to keep down taxes and to make health care affordable. They are also aware of public concerns related to the effects of managed care on accessibility and quality.

Legislators, public officials, and MCOs must also respond to the pressures of health care advocacy groups. Many such groups have taken an interest in mental health managed care. They include the National Association of Mental Health, a large and well-established organization that lobbies for increased funding for mental health programs and effective treatment for those with mental illness; the National Alliance for the Mentally Ill, a group composed of the families and friends of the mentally ill; the Bazelon Center for Mental Health Law, the leading national legal advocate for people with emotional problems; children's advocacy organizations such as the Federation of Families for Children's Mental Health; and client support and advocacy groups such as the National Mental Health Consumers' Self-Help Clearinghouse. Many national advocacy organizations have state branches that lobby for effective public managed mental health programs. In addition, professional associations, such as nurses' groups and the National Association of Social Workers, advocate regarding both client and provider issues.[53]

Mental health advocacy reflects the strong commitment that clients should receive adequate services from an accountable managed care entity. Advocates urge a number of improvements, changes, and protections in managed care, including effective grievance and appeal procedures; coverage of a full array of treatments and interventions, including community-based services such as housing programs and vocational training; greater use of outcome measures; parity or equality of insurance benefits for those with physical and for those with mental illness; and adequate attention to the needs of those with severe and chronic mental illness. As we will see in the last section in this chapter, the increasingly harsh climate for managed care created by consumers, providers, advocates, and others in the late 1990s is bearing fruit in a variety of new laws and legislative proposals.

Social Workers and Managed Care

Social workers play a variety of roles in managed care systems, including provider, gatekeeper, planner, and advocate. Although the movement first affected social workers in private practice, its impact has spread rapidly. Any social work setting that relies on third-party insurance reimbursement is likely to become involved in managed care. A number of social work agencies now contract with MCOs, as we saw earlier in the interview with Judith Kolb Morris. In addition, more and more Medicaid programs that utilize social work and other mental health practitioners have adopted a managed care approach. It is therefore vital for social workers to strive to make the system work well for their clients and themselves and to call for reforms when necessary.

Changing the system involves tackling a variety of concerns. A major issue, which involves one of the most sacrosanct of social work ethics, is the ability to ensure client confidentiality in a managed care environment. Managed care gatekeepers base their treatment approval decisions on information the social worker gives them about the client. Although clients sign "informed consent forms" to approve such disclosure, practitioners worry that people may sign these forms because they fear that otherwise the MCO won't cover the services they need. Social workers are also concerned about the number of managed care staff who might have access to client records. In one horror story, a clerk at a large MCO read confidential information in a client's file and revealed it to others at a party. The client sued the company, but the court ruled that "the clerk had not breached confidentiality as part of her job and that [the MCO] was not liable."[54]

The question of what constitutes adequate and effective treatment under managed care raises a whole constellation of issues, as illustrated in the following example from a social worker we know:

> I have a client who is a depressed and anxious high school student. She was recently suicidal. Her parents' MCO paid for my initial therapy work with her, which included getting some medication prescribed. She's still depressed and anxious, but she's no longer suicidal. The MCO refuses to pay for continued sessions with me. They argue that as long as she stays on medication, she's fine. Her parents are worried and they're paying out-of-pocket to continue counseling for her. I think managed care is fine for emergencies but not for follow-through. And it's the emergencies that cost the most.

Although many social workers acknowledge that MCOs have made a useful contribution in their promotion of short-term treatment, they stress that not all client problems fit this mold. Mental health practitioners use a variety of interventions for different types of problems; managed care may restrict their ability to choose what's appropriate for a given client, including a longer period of contact. People with severe and chronic mental illness often need ongoing community supports, yet these are rarely covered under managed care. In many situations, work with family members and others involved with the client (a particular skill of social workers) may be quite desirable, yet such interventions are not necessarily reimbursable.

The lack of discretion in determining the type or length of treatment contributes to providers' sense that they have lost autonomy under managed care. The system also produces a "high hassle factor"—extensive paperwork, constant phone calls to gatekeepers to approve treatment plans and allow additional sessions, and the application and review procedures to become a member of an MCO's provider pool. Social work agencies face similar difficulties; one director of a children and families agency noted that "managed care forces us to have a larger infrastructure that is an added weight around the agency's neck." Initially, these problems may have contributed to the decline in the number of those social workers engaged in private clinical practice. Twenty-one percent of social workers were private practitioners in 1996, but only 18 percent were in 1998. The proportion of those involved on a part-time basis fell from 44 to 35 percent.[55]

Although some social workers have chosen to leave the system, managed care will continue to have a major impact on the profession. What can you, as an individual social worker, do to affect managed care policies and practices? If you are a provider in an MCO pool, a frequent concern is what to do if the coverage runs out. Some therapists discuss the limitations of the MCO's coverage in the first interview with clients, suggesting that they think carefully about what their options will be if the reimbursement runs out before they choose to end their sessions. In one such situation, the client decided to pay for every other session herself, thus spacing out the amount she had to cover. In another case, a crisis involving a child who had been sexually abused, the MCO did not approve extra therapy sessions for the child even though the social worker had just begun to win his trust. The worker decided to present this to the MCO as an emergency case and also urged the child's mother to pursue a grievance with the MCO.

If you work in an agency, you can join in advocacy and change efforts at that level, such as the development of the in-house quality assurance system that gave more autonomy to Judith Kolb Morris's organization. You can band together with other staff members to influence the agency's policy and practices in order to protect your ability to carry out ethical practice.

You can also play a role in one of the many organized professional or health advocacy groups. As the broadest and most powerful voice of social work, NASW has undertaken a variety of lobbying and educational activities regarding managed care. The association grounds its work in an emphasis on accountable and ethical professional practice. It has produced numerous publications outlining practice guidelines and responsibilities for social workers in managed care. These responsibilities include the obligation to ensure that necessary services are made available to clients who still need help after their benefits have been used up. As we have seen, NASW also joins other groups in lobbying for legislation to make health and mental health care affordable, accessible, and effective. Local NASW chapters often have social action committees, which would welcome new members. Clinician groups, such as the Clinical Social Work Federation, have lobbied companies regarding such issues as client confidentiality and the denial of needed mental health services. State chapters of the National Mental Health Association offer similar opportunities for promoting policies to ensure that people's treatment needs are being met.[56]

States developing Medicaid managed care programs have aroused the interest of numerous advocacy associations and lobbying coalitions that are eager for involvement by citizens, clients and family members, and professionals. These groups have a real chance to affect change at the local and state level, both by exerting outside pressure on legislators and state health officials and by gaining representation on internal public managed care program planning groups. This last interview with a social worker gives an excellent picture of the sort of work that is there to be done.

Influencing the System

Interview with an Advocate

Shannon Robshaw graduated about twelve years ago from an M.S.W. program. Before she pursued her master's degree, she volunteered in a local chapter of the Mental Health Association of Louisiana in order to pursue her interest in improving mental health treatment for children with serious emotional disturbance. Her strong commitment to making the mental health system more responsive to children's needs helped propel her to the presidency of the association chapter. Along the way, she also discovered that she had a talent for lobbying. At her first visit to the Louisiana State Legislature, representing her chapter, she sat in on a legislative committee session to observe the hearings on a piece of mental health legislation. She had no plans to testify but did submit a written note stating her opposition to one provision of the bill. To her surprise, legislative aides sought her out at a recess because they wanted her to explain her objections. Because of their discussion, the bill was changed in line with Robshaw's suggestions.

At the School of Social Work, Robshaw did one of her internships with a children's services planning unit within the state Office of Mental Health. After graduation she continued her involvement with the Mental Health Association, this time with the state chapter in Baton Rouge. She went on to become the chapter's executive director. In this capacity, she engaged in lobbying and educational efforts to enhance public understanding of mental illness and to improve services for those with psychological problems. As Louisiana began to plan a managed care program for its Medicaid clients, Robshaw played a pivotal role in organizing the Mental Health Reform Coalition. This is a coalition of advocacy groups, including the state chapter of NASW, with the goal of influencing the goals and provisions of the proposed program.

Robshaw believes that states currently see managed care as a panacea or a magic wand that will "take care of" all problems of mental illness. The promise of cost savings reassures planners and legislators that there will be enough money to provide all needed services. But if there isn't enough money allocated now for mental health, she muses, there won't be enough under managed care either, particularly if private MCOs skim off the profits. Robshaw and others lobbied successfully at the legislature to restore some money that was being cut from a psychological rehabilitation services option within the Medicaid program.

When she visualizes a new public mental health managed care system in Louisiana, Robshaw argues persuasively that MCOs should provide a full range of services, including a hospitalization safety net, but maintain a strong emphasis on community-based care. Outpatient clinics will provide some of this care, but mentally ill adults will also need help in areas such as housing and employment.

Children could be assisted through school-based counseling, crisis residential centers, and other interventions. For children particularly, services will need to be coordinated across multiple providers and agencies, including child welfare and the juvenile justice system. Currently, more state money is allocated to the state hospital system than to community care; Robshaw feels this ratio needs to be reversed. A sound system should also include responsive grievance procedures and an independent ombudsman program for people to appeal denials of service.

What does Robshaw believe is the best tactic for achieving these goals? First, consumers and their advocates need to be included at the planning table. This is the first goal the Mental Health Reform Coalition pursued. The next step is to work to outline good contracts in which the state specifies what particular services it expects an MCO to deliver. Consumer, family, and advocate involvement can make sure these contracts stress community services and don't rely strictly on a medical model. As representatives on a planning board, they can also help develop appropriate outcome measures and quality assurance mechanisms.

As Robshaw notes, "Managed care is riddled with problems, but it's not as if we've had a really good system up to now." The dream of people such as Robshaw is that through strong advocacy efforts the managed care movement can be used to create an effective, coordinated, and innovative public mental health program.*

Current Proposals for Policy Reform

Headlines such as "The Revolt against Managed Care" and "HMOs Go under the Knife" symbolize the extensive backlash against the system that began to build in the late 1990s. As several Wall Street analysts note, despite the managed care industry's track record, it "has consistently received bad press and has become a societal, political, and legal target." Recognition of this hostile climate was reflected in the program for the April 2000 conference of the National Managed Health Care Congress, which focused on the needs of MCOs, purchasers, and large providers such as hospitals. Among the usual presentations on improving efficiency, measuring quality, and tracking market trends one finds sessions on "Media Training. . . : Win Back the Positive Image of Managed Care" and "A History of the Negative Perception of Managed Care and Effective Ways to Overcome It."[57]

Pressure from many stakeholders has led to proposals for regulatory and legislative reforms in managed care. Over a thousand bills have been introduced in state legislatures and in Congress "aimed at calming consumers' fears of losing

---

*Since our interview with Robshaw for the first edition of this text, she has played a major role in the passage of mental health parity legislation in Louisiana.

control of their health care while trying to retain some of the cost-saving, market-innovating features" of managed care. One important measure, the Mental Health Parity Act, has already been passed on the federal level. Yet the law is a limited one, leading to proposals for its expansion. Thirty-four states have passed parity laws, although some of these are limited to certain mental illnesses.[58]

Parity, the equal insurance coverage of mental and physical conditions, has been sought by mental health advocates since 1950. In 1996, Congress finally passed a parity law, sponsored by Republican Senator Pete Domenici (New Mexico) and Independent Senator Paul Wellstone (Minnesota). Increased receptivity for such legislation stemmed partly from revelations by Domenici, Senator Phil Gramm (Texas), and other public figures about the impact of mental illness on their own families. Opposition to the bill from insurers and employers led to its limited scope; the measure applies only to equality of lifetime and annual dollar limits for mental and physical health insurance coverage. It does not require parity in co-payments and deductibles and does not prohibit limits on the number of mental health treatment sessions or psychiatric hospital days. Smaller companies are exempted, and the provision does not apply if employers choose not to offer any mental health coverage at all.[59]

Advocates, consumers, and others were very concerned about the failure to end limits on mental health treatment. These limits are especially problematic for the severely mentally ill. The tragic death of Paul Wellstone, a champion of parity, in October 2002 added political and emotional energy to the drive to pass a bill explaining the 1996 law. In 2005, Representatives Jim Ramstad (Republican, Minnesota) and Patrick Kennedy (Democrat, Rhode Island) introduced the Senator Paul Wellstone Mental Health Equitable Treatment Act, which would require employers with more than 50 employees to provide comprehensive mental health and substance abuse parity. Although no such legislation was introduced in the Senate, Senators Pete Domenici and Edward Kennedy (Democrat, Massachusetts) have continued to work on the issue behind the scene.[60]

Laws protecting patients' rights in managed care have become the next important arena for reform. Such legislation might include the right to information about a health plan's procedures and policies, the right of access to a medical specialist without approval of a primary care doctor, the right to an independent appeals process, and the right to sue a health plan for damages when it improperly denies care. Most states have now passed at least limited patients' rights acts. Federal legislative proposals began to proliferate after a 1997 Presidential Commission on Protection and Quality in the Health Care Industry recommended laws to strengthen the patient's voice in managed care. Much political jockeying weeded these out until two major bills remained: a patients' rights measure promoted by the Senate Republican leadership and a bipartisan House bill coauthored by Democrat John Dingall and Republican Charles Norwood. A major difference between the Republican and bipartisan proposals related to the right to sue an MCO for damages, which the bipartisan bill granted and the Republican version, in line with the party's probusiness stance, did not. The House bill would have also covered far more people than the Senate measure. Six months after the passage of both bills, a conference committee of House and Senate members could not resolve their differences. Pressure has continued for strong patients' rights legislation.[61] Soon after his inauguration in 2001, President Bush announced a *New Freedom Initiative*. He established a New Freedom Commission on Mental Health, charged with studying the U.S. mental health system and proposing improvements. The commission's final report, released in July 2003, called for consumer and family-centered services, research-based treatment, and services tailored for culturally diverse populations.[62]

Conclusion

It is unclear how potential legislation on parity and patients' rights, or the responses to the President's New Freedom Initiative, will affect managed care in mental health and the lives of those with mental illness and their families. Social workers will have to walk their usual line between helping to make present policy and program arrangements as useful to clients as possible and working toward new and better systems.

Selected Web Sites on Mental Health and Managed Care

American Association of Health Plans

www.aahp.org

Web site of the organization representing HMOs, PPOs, and other managed care plans.

Bazelon Center for Mental Health Law

www.bazelon.org

Detailed information on mental health issues and on legislation related to managed care, community-based care, etc.

Center for Mental Health Services

www.mentalhealth.org/cmhs/index.htm

An agency of the Substance Abuse and Mental Health Services Administration, U.S. Department of Health and Human Services. Provides consumer/survivor information, mental health and managed care information, statistics, and information on advocacy.

Families USA

www.familiesusa.org

A national nonprofit organization that advocates high-quality, affordable health care for all. Information on managed care (including patients' rights proposals), Medicaid, and other topics is available.

National Alliance for the Mentally Ill

www.nami.org

Provides mental health information from a national organization of families of the mentally ill.

National Association of Social Workers

www.nasw.socialworkers.org

Covers various issues of interest to social workers, including managed care.

National Committee for Quality Assurance

www.ncqa.org

A nongovernmental organization that assesses and accredits MCOs.

National Mental Health Association

www.nmha.org

Provides reports, legislative alerts, and information on Medicaid managed care.

Notes

1. Robert Pear, "Rulings Chip Away at HMO Protection against Lawsuits," *New Orleans Times-Picayune* (15 September 1999), p. A27.

2. Robin Toner and Sheryl Gay Stolberg, "Decade After Health Care Crisis, Soaring Costs Bring New Strains," *New York Times* (11 August 2002), p. 1; Marguerite Ro and Lucy Shum, *Forgotten Policy: An Examination of Mental Health in the U.S.*, The Kellogg Foundation (May, 2001), p. 12 (online at www.communityvoices.org); Steven Findlay, "Managed Behavioral Health Care in 1999; An Industry at a Crossroads," *Health Affairs* 18 (September/October 1999), pp. 117–118.

3. David Prichard, "Managed Care: Who Manages Whom?" *Reflections* 10 (Fall 2004), p. 40; National Alliance for the Mentally Ill (NAMI), "NAMI'S Principles for Managed Care," (online at www.nami.org); National Mental Health Association, "Can't Make the Grade: NMHA State Mental Health Assessment Project," (online at www.nmha.org); "Aetna Settles Physicians' Suit," *Arizona Republic* (23

May 2003), p. D1; Milt Freudenheim, "Cigna's Cost in Settlement is Disputed by Plaintiffs," *New York Times* (26 November 2002), p. C1; Corinna Vallianatos, "Cigna Cut Reversed," *NASW News* 47 (February 2002), p. 1; "Firm to Modify Contracts," *NASW News* 46 (July 2001), pp. 1, 8.

4. Ellyn Spragins, "Does Your HMO Stack Up?" *Newsweek* (24 June 1996), p. 56.

5. Bruce Lubotsky Levin, "Managed Mental Health Care: A National Perspective," in *Health United States 1992*, National Center for Health Statistics (Hyattsville, MD: Public Health Service, 1993), p. 208; Daniel Goleman, "Battle of Insurers vs. Therapists," *New York Times* (24 October 1991), sec. D, p. 1; Susan M. Essock and Howard H. Goldman, "States' Embrace of Managed Mental Health Care," *Health Affairs* 14 (Fall 1995), p. 37; Philip J. Boyle and Daniel Callahan, "Managed Care in Mental Health: The Ethical Issues," *Health Affairs* 14 (Fall 1996), pp. 9–10.

6. Judith Graham, "Health Costs Rising Faster Than Expected," *Arizona Republic* (12 March 2002),

sec. 4, p. 1; Cynthia Smith, Cathy Cowan, Stephen Heffler, Aaron Catlin, and the National Health Accounts Team, "National Health Spending in 2004: Recent Slowdown Led by Prescription Drug Spending," *Health Affairs* 25 (January/February 2006), p. 1–2; Janelle Carter, "Rising Drug Costs Boost Health Spending by 8.7%," *Arizona Republic* (8 January 2003), p. 11.

7. Joe Sharkey, "Mental Health Hits the Money Trail," *New York Times* (6 June 1999), sec. 4, p. 5.

8. Sharkey, "Mental Health Hits the Money Trail"; Jolie Solomon, "Breaking the Silence," *Newsweek* (20 May 1996), p. 20; John O'Neill, "Mental Health System Said 'In Shambles,'" *NASW News* 48 (January 2003), p. 7.

9. Harriet Baum, "Mental Illnesses Deserve the Same Insurance Coverages as Other Illnesses," *Pittsburgh Post-Gazette* (4 June 2002) (online at www.post-gazette.com); Mary Jane England, "Capturing Mental Health Cost Offsets," *Health Affairs* 18 (March/April 1999), p. 82; Anthony Lehman, "Quality of Care in Mental Health: The Case of Schizophrenia," *Health Affairs* 18 (September/October 1999), p. 54.

10. Richard T. Frank and Thomas G. McGuire, "Health Care Reform and Financing of Mental Health Services: Distributional Consequences," in Ronald W. Manderscheid and Mary Anne Sonnenschein, Eds., *Mental Health, United States, 1994,* Center for Mental Health Services (Washington, DC: U.S. Government Printing Office, 1994), p. 13; Lehman, "Quality of Care in Mental Health," pp. 55–58; Solomon, "Breaking the Silence," p. 22.

11. Rita Vandivort-Warren, "How Social Workers Can Manage Managed Care," in Schamess and Lightburn, *Humane Managed Care?,* p. 255; Michael Malloy, *Mental Illness and Managed Care: A Primer for Families and Consumers* (Arlington, VA: National Alliance for the Mentally Ill, April 1995); National Association of Social Workers, *Social Work Speaks: NASW Policy Statements,* 3rd ed. (Washington, DC: NASW Press, 1994), p. 169.

12. Michael Malloy, *Mental Illness and Managed Care: Managing Managed Care for Publicly Financed Mental Health Services* (Washington, DC: Bazelon Center for Mental Health Law, November 1995), pp. 44–48.

13. Malloy, *Mental Illness and Managed Care,* p. 48.

14. David S. Hilzenrath, "Putting Their Money Where Their Health Is: Wall Street Is Betting on Firms That Are Revolutionizing the Medical Marketplace," *Washington Post Weekly Edition* (31 October–6 November, 1994), p. 19.

15. Transcript of Citizens' Health Care Group Public Meeting (17 August 2005) (online at www.citizenshealthcare.gov/resources).

16. Jodie Snyder and Susie Steckner, "Mental Health Agency $84 Million in Black," *Arizona Republic* (1 February 2004), pp. 1, 8.

17. Susan Steckner and Jodie Snyder, "Getting to Recovery," *Arizona Republic* (17 January 2001), p. 10; Kenneth Minkoff, "Community Mental Health in the Nineties: Public Sector Managed Care," *Community Mental Health Journal* 30 (August 1994), pp. 317–318; Findlay, "Managed Behavioral Health Care in 1999," pp. 117–118; Richard G. Frank, Howard H. Goldman, and Michael Hogan, "Medicaid and Mental Health: Be Careful What You Ask For," *Health Affairs* 22 (January–February 2003) p. 109.

18. Findlay, "Managed Behavioral Health Care in 1999," p. 121; Michael H. Bailit and Laurie L. Burgess, "Competing Interests: Public-Sector Managed Behavioral Health Care," *Health Affairs* 18 (September/October 1999), p. 112.

19. Findlay, "Managed Behavioral Health Care in 1999," pp. 119, 122; Frank, Goldman, and Hogan, "Medicaid and Mental Health," p. 109.

20. David Mechanic, *Mental Health and Social Policy: The Emergence of Managed Care,* 4th ed. (Boston: Allyn and Bacon, 1999), p. 139.

21. Paul Starr, *The Social Transformation of American Medicine* (New York: Basic Books, 1982), pp. 320–327.

22. Philip R. Popple and Leslie Leighninger, *Social Work, Social Welfare, and American Society,* 4th ed. (Boston: Allyn and Bacon, 1999), pp. 225–226; Starr, *The Social Transformation of American Medicine,* p. 386.

23. Levin, "Managed Mental Health Care: A National Perspective," pp. 208–209; *Third-Party Reimbursement for Clinical Social Work Services* (Washington, DC: National Association of Social Workers, 1995), p. 5.

24. Popple and Leighninger, *Social Work, Social Welfare, and American Society,* pp. 388–390.

25. Dan Morgan, "While Washington Talked: Health Care Reform Is Taking Shape in the Private Sector without Help from Congress," *Washington Post Weekly Edition* (12–18 September 1994), p. 31.

26. Bentson H. McFarland, "Health Maintenance Organizations and Persons with Severe Mental Illness," *Community Mental Health Journal* 30 (1994), p. 225; Levin, "Managed Mental Health Care: A National Perspective," p. 209.

27. Levin, "Managed Mental Health Care: A National Perspective," p. 210; Boyle and Callahan, "Managed Care in Mental Health: The Ethical Issues,"

pp. 7–8; Essock and Goldman, "States' Embrace of Managed Mental Health Care," p. 37.

28. "Parity: Plans May Lower Quality as Well as Cost," *NASW News* 43 (September 1998), p. 6; Mechanic, *Mental Health and Social Policy*, p. 156; David Mechanic and Donna D. McAlpine, "Mission Unfulfilled: Potholes on the Road to Mental Health Parity," *Health Affairs* 18 (September/October 1999), pp. 9–10.

29. Richard Wolf, "States Grabbing the Rope in Medicaid 'Tug of War,'" *USA Today* (3 November 1995), sec. A, p. 19; Colette Fraley, "The Blossoming of Medicaid," *Congressional Quarterly* (10 June 1995), p. 1638; Rita Vandivort-Warren, "Merging Managed Care and Medicaid: Private Regulation of Public Health Care," *NASW Social Work Practice Update* (Washington, DC: NASW, June 1995), p. 1; John Holahan et al., "Medicaid Managed Care in Thirteen States," *Health Affairs* 17 (May/June 1998), pp. 45–46.

30. Vandivort-Warren, "Merging Managed Care and Medicaid," pp. 3–4.

31. Essock and Goldman, "States' Embrace of Managed Mental Health Care," pp. 36–37; Robert J. Samuelson, "The Revolution's Started," *Washington Post Weekly Edition* (30 October–5 November 1995), p. 5; "Health Insurance," *Standard and Poor's Industry Surveys* 163 (2 March 1995), p. I-44; Robert Pear, "Medicine Panel Advises a Freeze on Hospital Pay," *New York Times* (19 January 1997), pp. 1, 11.

32. Katharine Levit et al., "National Health Expenditures in 1997: More Slow Growth," *Health Affairs* 17 (November/December 1998), p. 99; Katharine Levit et al., "Health Spending in 1998: Signals of Change," *Health Affairs* 19 (January/February 2000), pp. 124–126; Patricia Lamiell, "Health-Care Costs May Rise as Much as 10% by 1998," *Baton Rouge Advocate* (12 April 1997), p. 7C; Katharine Levit et al., "Trends in U.S. Health Care Spending, 2001," *Health Affairs* 22 (January/February 2003), p. 156.

33. Stephen Barr, "Health Insurance Costs Will Rise for Federal Employees," *Washington Post* (13 September 1998), p. A8; "Worrisome Changes Loom in the Private Health Insurance Market," *Health Action*, Families USA (November 2002), p. 1.

34. Amy Goldstein, "A Transfusion from Patients' Wallets May Be in Order," *Washington Post Weekly Edition* (21 November 1998), p. 31; "Getting Aggressive on Premium Price Increases," *Standard and Poor's Industry Surveys* 167 (5 August 1999), p. 1; "Growth in Global Pharmaceutical Market Accelerating," *Standard and Poor's Industry Surveys* 167 (29 July 1999), p. 10.

35. Srija Srinivasan, Larry Levitt, and Janet Lundy, "Wall Street's Love Affair with Health Care," *Health Affairs* 17 (July/August 1998), pp. 126–131; Steven Swartz, "Personal Business: Healthy Investments," *Wall Street Journal Sunday*, Supplement to *New Orleans Times-Picayune* (17 October 1999), p. F12; "Healthcare Spending Remains a Large Segment of U.S. Economy," *Standard and Poor's Industry Surveys*, pp. 8–9; "Even without Aetna Merger, Consumers Are Losing Choice," and Jamie Court, "Merger Hurts Patients," *USA Today* (28 June 1999), p. 15A; "Favorable Prognosis for Managed Care," *Standard and Poor's Industry Surveys* 2 (January 2003), pp. 1–10.

36. www.aishealth.com/managedcare/company intel/tenlargest.html

37. Jeffrey L. Geller, "Mental Health Services for the Future: Managed Care, Unmanaged Care, Mismanaged Care," in Schamess and Lightburn, *Humane Managed Care?*, p. 38; Findlay, "Managed Behavioral Health Care in 1999," pp. 116–118; Sue Matorin, "The Corporatization of Mental Health Services: The Impact of Service, Training, and Values," in Schamess and Lightburn, *Humane Managed Care?*, p. 159; John O'Neill, "Psychosocial Care Often Left with Crumbs," *NASW News* 44 (April 1999), p. 3.

38. Popple and Leighninger, *Social Work, Social Welfare, and American Society*, pp. 429–431; Lloyd M. Krieger, "How Managed Health Care Will Allow Market Forces to Solve the Problem," *New York Times* (13 August 1995), p. 12; The Institute for Behavioral Health Care, Final Program, Eighth Annual National Dialogue Conference on Mental Health Benefits and Practice in the Era of Managed Care: Behavioral Healthcare Tomorrow (September 1996).

39. Robert M. Johnson, "Ethics and Managed Care," *Health Decisions*, Publication of the Vermont Ethics Network (September 1995); Sharon R. King, "Mental Health Ventures May Gain from New Law," *New York Times* (20 October 1996), sec. 3, p. 3.

40. Saul Feldman, "Strangers in the Night: Research and Managed Mental Health Care," *Health Affairs* 18 (September/October 1999), pp. 48–49; Mechanic, *Mental Health and Social Policy*, pp. 160–162.

41. Feldman, "Strangers in the Night," pp. 50–51; H. Stephen Leff and Lawrence S. Woocher, "Trends in the Evaluation of Managed Mental Health Care," in Schamess and Lightburn, *Humane Managed Care?*, pp. 480–481; Steven S. Sharfstein, John J. Boronow, and Faith B. Dickerson, "Managed Care and Clinical Reality in Schizophrenia Treatment," *Health Affairs* 18 (September/October 1999), p. 69; Nancy W. Veeder and Wilma Peebles-Wilkins, "Research Needs in Managed Behavioral Health Care," in Schamess and Lightburn, *Humane Managed Care?*, p. 484.

42. William Goldman, Joyce McCulloch, and Roland Sturm, "Costs and Use of Mental Health

Services Before and After Managed Care," *Health Affairs* 17 (March/April 1998), pp. 40–50; Mechanic and McAlpine, "Mission Unfulfilled: Potholes on the Road to Mental Health Parity," pp. 11–12; Jan Blustein and Emma C. Hoy, "Who Is Enrolled in For-Profit vs. Nonprofit Medicare HMOs?" *Health Affairs* 19 (January/February 2000), pp. 210–219; Mechanic, *Mental Health and Social Policy*, p. 161.

43. James J. Callahan et al., "Mental Health and Substance Abuse Treatment in Managed Care: The Massachusetts Medicaid Experience," in Schamess and Lightburn, *Humane Managed Care?*, p. 139; Goldman, McCulloch, and Sturm, "Costs and Use of Mental Health Services Before and After Managed Care," pp. 46–47; Mechanic, *Mental Health and Social Policy*, pp. 161–162; Sharfstein, Boronow, and Dickerson, "Managed Care and Clinical Reality in Schizophrenia Treatment," p. 69.

44. Mechanic, *Mental Health and Social Policy*, p. 164; Allan Fine, "Although Illusive, Quality Continues to Be a Vital Measure for MCOs and Employees," *Executive Solutions for Healthcare Management* 2 (October 1999), pp. 2–3; Ellyn E. Spragins, "What Are They Hiding? HMOs Are Getting More Secretive about Quality," *Newsweek* (1 March 1999), p. 74; Tracy Miller and Sheila Leatherman, "The National Quality Forum: A 'Me-Too' or a Breakthrough in Quality Measurement and Reporting?" *Health Affairs* 18 (November/December 1999), pp. 233–237.

45. Vandivort-Warren, "How Social Workers Can Manage Managed Care," p. 260.

46. John V. O'Neill, "Profession Dominates in Mental Health," *NASW News* 44 (June 1999), p. 1; Brennan D. Peterson et al., "Mental Health Practitioners and Trainees," in Ronald W. Manderscheid and Marilyn J. Henderson, Eds., *Mental Health, United States, 1998*, U.S. Department of Health and Human Services (Washington, DC: U.S. Government Printing Office, 1998), p. 230; "Private Sector Employs Most Members," *NASW News* 48 (February 2003), p. 8.

47. O'Neill, "Psychosocial Care Often Left with Crumbs," p. 3; Matorin, "Corporatization of Mental Health Services," p. 161.

48. David S. Hilzenrath, "Finding Something Left to Squeeze," *Washington Post Weekly Edition* (14 July 1997), p. 20; Goldstein, "The Revolt against Managed Care: Florida Is the Beachhead for an Effort to Readjust the Balance of Medical Power," p. 6; Mark Hagland, "Physician Unionization: A Threat to Integration?" *Healthcare Leadership Review* (September 1999), p. 4; Jennifer Steinhauer, "Rebellion in White: Doctors Pulling Out of H.M.O. Systems," *New York Times* (10 January 1999), pp. 1, 20.

49. Jane Hiebert-White, "From the Editor: Managed Care and the New Economics of Mental Health," *Health Affairs* 14 (Fall 1995), pp. 5–6; James Sabin, "Organized Psychiatry and Managed Care: Quality Improvement or Holy War?" *Health Affairs* 14 (Fall 1995), pp. 32–33.

50. "Managed Care Suits Snagged," *NASW News* 44 (February 1999), p. 1; John V. O'Neill, "Managed Care Lawsuit Going Forward," *NASW News* 44 (September 1999), p. 1; John V. O'Neill, "Dropping of Providers Fought," *NASW News* 45 (January 2000), p. 8; "Managed Care Standards' Oversight Proviso Faulted," *NASW News* 44 (June 1999), p. 1; "Health Care Unionizing Gets Backing," *NASW News* 44 (February 1999), p. 4; Josephine Nieves (NASW Executive Director), "Social Work Collective Bargaining?" *NASW News* 45 (January 2000), p. 2. Note that independent practitioners are prohibited from collective bargaining by federal law, but they can affiliate with unions and receive lobbying help.

51. Kelley O. Beaucar, "HMO in Bankruptcy but Impact on Clients Deflected," *NASW News* 44 (September 1999), p. 14; "Program Goals: The Long and the Short of It," *NASW News* 44 (October 1999), p. 8; Colleen Galambos, "Resolving Ethical Conflicts in a Managed Health Care Environment," *Health and Social Work* 24 (August 1999), pp. 1–12.

52. Geoffrey E. Harris, Matthew J. Ropperger, and Howard G. S. Horn, "Managed Care at a Crossroads," *Health Affairs* 19 (January/February 2000), p. 156; Johnathan D. Salant, "Big Bucks Oppose, Promote Managed Health Care," *Baton Rouge Advocate* (28 November 1998), p. 7A; Terry M. Neal, "Bashing the HMO-Bashers," *Washington Post Weekly Edition* (6 July 1998), p. 11.

53. Jean Campbell, "Consumerism, Outcomes, and Satisfaction: A Review of the Literature," in R.W. Manderscheid and M.J. Henderson, Eds., *Mental Health United States, 1998*, U.S. Department of Health and Human Services (Washington DC: U.S. Government Printing Office, 1998), pp. 11, 16–17.

54. John V. O'Neill, "Trading Future Privacy for Services Today," *NASW News* 45 (January 2000), p. 3.

55. Holly A. Riffe, "Managed Mental Health Care and Job Satisfaction: The Impact of Third-Party Payers," *Journal of Applied Social Sciences* 23 (Spring/Summer 1999), p. 44; O'Neill, "Psychosocial Care Often Left with Crumbs," p. 3.

56. See, for example, *Third Party Reimbursement for Clinical Social Work Services* (Washington, DC: NASW, 1995) and *A Brief Look at Managed Health Care* (Washington, DC: NASW, 1994).

57. Goldstein, "The Revolt against Managed Care"; Watson, "HMOs Go under the Knife"; Harris,

Ripperger, and Horn, "Managed Care at a Crossroads," p. 157; *Final Program*, NMHC/2000, the 12th Annual National Managed Health Care Congress, April 16–19, 2000, Atlanta, GA.

58. Blendon et al., "Understanding the Managed Care Backlash," p. 81; National Mental Health Association, "It Is Time to Pass Comprehensive Health Insurance Parity!" August 2005 (online at www.nmha.org/state/parity).

59. Richard G. Frank, Chris Koyanagi, and Thomas G. McGuire, "The Politics and Economics of Mental Health 'Parity' Laws," *Health Affairs* 16 (July/August 1997), pp. 109, 112–114.

60. National Mental Health Association, "It Is Time to Pass Comprehensive Health Insurance Parity!"

61. Mary Graham, "What's Next on the State Policy Agenda? Consumer Protections!" *National Mental Health Association State Advocacy Update* (November/December 1998), p. 3; Peter Weaver,

"Patients' Rights Are Advancing in Legislatures," *AARP Bulletin* (January 2000), pp. 9, 12; G. J. Annas, "A National Bill of Patients' Rights: Clinton's State of the Union Address," *New England Journal of Medicine* 338 (5 March 1998), pp. 695–700; Helen Dewar and Amy Goldstein, "Senate Backs GOP's Modest Steps on Protecting Rights of Patients," *Washington Post* (15 July 1999), p. A8; Robert Pear, "House Bill Would Slightly Ease Lawsuits against H.M.O.'s," *New York Times* (10 September 1999), p. A18; "Thwarting Patients' Rights," *New York Times* (5 November 1999), p. A30; "Pressure Mounts against Law Cheating Patients of Power," *USA Today* (25 February 2000), p. 14A; Robert Pear, "Justice Souter Takes on a Health Care Taboo," *New York Times* (18 June 2000), sec. 4, p. 3.

62. President's New Freedom Commission on Mental Health, "Achieving the Promise: Transforming Mental Health Care in America, Executive Summary," July 2003 (online at www.mentalhealthcommission.gov/reports/Finalreports/FullReport.htm).

chapter **10**

Substance Abuse Policies

Frank Duchet, an M.S.W. student, is interning in a school social work setting. He's looking rather depressed in his supervision session today, and his supervisor asks sympathetically, "How's it going?"

"Well, I guess I wasn't really prepared for this kind of thing," Frank answers. "I was talking with Darren today, and he was telling me about how his oldest brother is in jail for dealing drugs and that last night he heard his mom yelling at his other brother because she overheard him talking about heroin with some friends. Darren was so matter-of-fact about it—and he's only seven years old! How am I going to help him with this?"

"It's the worst thing I've ever gotten myself into," says Lori, a sixteen-year-old whose life has been wrecked by an addiction to methamphetamine, commonly known as "meth." When she was eleven, she asked her father if she could get high with him. He gave her meth, and she liked it. Once she started using meth, she stopped going to school, stopped eating, and eventually ran away from home. She began having sex with older men who would continue her supply of the drug. She went on to burglarizing houses and stealing cars. She even traded her mother's jewelry for meth. Lori is now in a locked juvenile corrections facility. There she attends rehabilitation sessions to learn why she used meth and how to cope with it. Counselors say the entire healing process may take at least two years. Although she still suffers the side effects of her addiction (a poor memory, trouble paying attention, vision problems, and trouble breathing), she looks forward to going away to college someday. "Getting arrested," she says, "has turned out to be a blessing."

Josephina Sanchez is new in her job as a psychiatric nurse at the county mental health clinic. Passing through the lobby, she watches as an agitated-looking young woman is brought to the clinic's reception desk by an older woman, who tells the staff member at the desk, "Jenny's getting crazy again—she talks all the time, she doesn't sleep, and she keeps saying she wants to drive to California. She needs help!" The staff member asks Mrs. Marsh to wait with her daughter in the lobby while she contacts an intake worker.

Noticing Josephina watching these proceedings, the staff person waits until mother and daughter are settled and then turns to Josephina to comment quietly, "This is not going to be easy for Mrs. Marsh. They've been in before, and I bet it will be the same as usual—by the look of her, I'd guess Jenny's doing drugs again. That means the intake worker's going to tell them that she'll have to go to the substance abuse clinic first. She'll have to get treatment there and then later present her problems all over again to the people in the mental health clinic." Josephina looks puzzled, so the receptionist explains, "It's a strict policy. The mental health clinic never deals with someone with an acute alcohol or drug problem until after they've received treatment for their substance abuse—and the two staffs never get together to talk about these clients."

> Sue Chan is doing her policy analysis presentation in her Introduction to Social Policy class and is describing the new program of administering drug tests to all the state's welfare recipients. In her critique of the policy, she speaks with some passion about the fact that, as someone who works in the Department of Social Services, she feels this is unfair discrimination against people on welfare: "It's like we're assuming that all the folks on welfare are drug addicts or have something else wrong with them and we've got the right to do these tests to make sure they're entitled to help."
>
> Several classmates disagree. One notes, "I work in an insurance company, and they make us have drug tests, too. If I have to do it, why not welfare clients?"

As these vignettes suggest, the phenomenon of substance abuse affects many people in our society and has led to a variety of policy responses. In these few examples, individuals' use of alcohol or illegal drugs had ramifications for parents, siblings, friends, human service professionals, and their communities. Incarceration, drug testing, and agency treatment policies are just three of the myriad of policies relating to substance abuse, including laws prohibiting the possession, use, and distribution of drugs; state and local ordinances regulating the sale of alcoholic beverages; "no use" and even stricter "zero-tolerance" policies in elementary and high schools; and federal appropriations of funds to states with the requirement that these be spent on treatment and prevention of alcoholism and drug addiction.

According to the 2004 National Survey on Drug Abuse and Health, an estimated 19.1 million Americans age twelve and over, or 7.1 percent of the population, were current users of illicit drugs. This includes over 10 percent of the population aged twelve years or older. Another 121 million Americans aged twelve and over reported current use of alcohol, with close to a third reporting binge drinking and 6 percent qualifying as heavy drinkers.[1] The costs of substance abuse in terms of lost productivity, health care expenditures, and crime run into the billions of dollars each year. In addition, only a tiny percentage of those who abuse substances receive treatment (see Table 10.1). Clearly, substance abuse is an issue affecting many of the client groups, organizations, and communities that social workers work with.

In this chapter, we describe the historical, social, economic, and political contexts of substance abuse as well as the policies designed to deal with it. We will, however, take a different approach in this section from that taken in the other chapters, which analyze one particular policy in each field of practice. Instead, we briefly portray the vast array of policies dealing with substance abuse and then present, in more detail, two specific policies: drug testing of welfare clients and the practice of separating substance abuse treatment from the treatment of mental illness.

Table 10.1 Prevalence of Past Month Alcohol and Illicit Drug Use and Past Year Dependence and Treatment for Twenty-Five Metropolitan Statistical Areas

Metropolitan Statistical Area (MSA)	Past Month Substance Use		Past Year Dependence		Past Year Treatment	
	Any Alcohol Use	*Any Illicit Drug Use*	*Dependent on Illicit Drugs*	*Dependent on Alcohol but Not Illicit Drugs*	*Received Treatment for Illicit Drug Use*	*Received Treatment for Alcohol Use but Not Illicit Drug Use*
Anaheim–Santa Ana, CA	52.3	8.8	2.2	6.0	1.0	0.6
Atlanta, GA	51.0	5.9	1.2	4.5	0.7	0.4
Baltimore, MD	44.8	5.0	0.9	2.2	0.6	0.5
Boston, MA	61.5	6.7	1.7	4.4	1.0	2.2
Chicago, IL	53.8	5.5	0.9	3.5	0.5	0.7
Dallas, TX	50.2	5.7	1.6	3.3	0.7	0.5
Denver, CO	58.4	8.3	1.3	4.6	0.6	1.0
Detroit, MI	54.2	5.5	1.2	3.6	0.8	0.5
El Paso, TX	45.9	3.6	0.8	3.7	0.6	0.5
Houston, TX	50.9	4.1	2.1	2.0	0.8	0.7
Los Angeles, CA	49.3	6.7	1.5	7.1	0.8	0.5
Miami–Hialeah, FL	44.4	3.8	0.7	2.0	0.6	0.5
Minneapolis–St. Paul, MN	65.9	5.2	1.2	3.5	0.9	0.9
Nassau–Suffolk, NY	59.6	6.6	1.0	1.1	0.6	0.5
New York, NY	48.8	6.0	0.9	1.8	0.7	0.3
Newark, NJ	62.2	6.2	1.4	2.5	0.9	0.8
Oakland, CA	65.0	11.4	3.0	3.9	1.4	2.1
Philadelphia, PA–NJ	59.1	5.7	1.0	2.8	0.8	0.6
Phoenix, AZ	53.7	6.8	1.6	3.6	0.7	0.7
San Antonio, TX	54.4	4.4	1.4	2.5	0.5	0.4
San Bernardino, CA	49.1	7.4	2.1	3.9	1.2	1.2
San Diego, CA	49.1	7.1	1.4	3.0	0.7	0.5
St. Louis, MO–IL	55.0	5.2	1.0	2.5	0.7	0.6
Tampa–St. Petersburg, FL	41.2	5.3	1.0	2.1	0.7	0.4
Washington, DC	53.8	5.4	1.1	3.6	0.6	0.9

Note: All estimates represent prevalence rates (percentages) averaged over the three-year period from 1991 to 1993 for the household population age twelve or older.

Source: National Household Survey on Drug Abuse, 1991–1993, model-based estimates (SAMHSA, 1996).

The Problem of Substance Abuse

For starters, the designation of substance abuse as a "problem" has less consensus than does, say, a similar depiction of poverty or child abuse. The line between substance use and abuse can be unclear. Alcohol, for example, is a legal substance throughout most of the United States; many people use it in moderation in their everyday lives. Marijuana is classified as an illegal substance, yet there are arguments for its helpfulness in relieving the symptoms of illnesses such as AIDS, cancer, and glaucoma. As we will discuss later, some people urge a differentiation between the recreational use of drugs such as marijuana, and even cocaine and heroin, and the serious addiction to drugs that is harmful to the user and to others.[2]

Definitions of substance dependence and abuse do not always clarify the notion of harmful consequences. One definition of abuse speaks of "the nontherapeutic use of drugs to the point where it affects the health of the individual or impacts adversely on others." Yet how does one know just what constitutes adverse impacts? The American Psychiatric Association gives a more specific picture: Substance abuse is a "maladaptive pattern of use of alcohol and other drugs occurring within a twelve-month period leading to clinically significant impairment or distress," as manifested by such situations as a failure to fulfill major role obligations at home, work, or school; recurrent use of the substance in situations in which it may be hazardous, as in driving a car; or recurrent legal problems such as arrests for substance abuse related to disorderly conduct. These are clearer criteria for abuse, yet applying them may not always be easy. Failure to fulfill major role obligations, for example, may be due to a variety of factors, and the role of drug or alcohol use may be difficult to tease out.[3]

Although "abuse" is thus a somewhat slippery concept, we can at least define the "substances" involved in most substance abuse policies in the United States. These include illegal drugs, or those substances on a "controlled list" whose manufacture, sale, possession, or use is prohibited by law. These substances include marijuana, cocaine, inhalants, hallucinogens, methamphetamine, and heroin. Some substances on the controlled list, such as morphine, can also be used legally by prescription. In addition to illicit drugs, *substance abuse* also refers to legal drugs such as alcohol and tobacco. These are more loosely regulated. Although the dangers of tobacco use have been receiving more and more public attention, this chapter focuses largely on the use of drugs and alcohol.[4]

Substance abuse constitutes a problem on the national, state, community, organizational, family, and individual levels. For example, alcohol abuse incurs huge costs. A large portion of these result from the negative effects of alcohol consumption on health, but lost productivity is another important component. The picture is similar for drug abuse, although illegal use of drugs adds additional high crime costs. These include reduced earnings due to incarceration and national and state expenditures on the criminal justice system and drug interdiction. Both alcohol and drug abuse also lead to spending on various kinds of treatment.[5]

Individual businesses and other organizations suffer from reduced employee productivity and from job accidents caused by inebriated or incapacitated workers. All of us, for example, have read headlines about school bus crashes that were attributed to alcohol or drug abuse by the driver. Communities, too, feel the effects of substance abuse; again, a common newspaper story is that of the neighborhood group that has finally been able to close down the crack houses in its area or to take back the local park from drug dealers. Many of the local ordinances regarding retail liquor establishments stem from community concerns about public drunkenness or the use of alcohol on Sunday.

Social workers are well aware, of course, that individuals and their families can be adversely affected by substance abuse. One concern is the effects of drugs and alcohol on the development of the fetus. Research into the impact of maternal drug use is complicated and as yet not entirely conclusive. On the one hand, illicit drug use during pregnancy has been associated with very low infant birth weights. It also appears that a woman's use of cocaine, particularly during the last month of pregnancy, can have some effect on the fetus. Researchers have found, for example, that "at one month of age, cocaine-exposed infants were about three times as likely to be jittery, irritable, and difficult to console than nonexposed babies." On the other hand, the 1980s myth of the inconsolable and permanently damaged "crack baby" has now largely been debunked. As researchers have examined prenatal cocaine exposure more carefully, they have found that the effects on fetuses are subtle and that poverty, poor maternal health, and the use of multiple substances by pregnant women are also important factors.[6]

The effects of alcohol and other substances on the fetus have been more clearly demonstrated. Alcohol abuse by women who are pregnant can lead to fetal alcohol syndrome, which can cause mental retardation and physical defects. Women who smoke cigarettes also risk adverse effects on their infants.[7]

Social workers working with the families of those with substance abuse problems find that such abuse can seriously affect family functioning. For example, the children of alcoholic parents are often seen in social agencies for a variety of problems. One writer has even devised a title for their situation, calling them victims of the "Practicing Alcoholic/Addicted Parent Syndrome." Homelessness, domestic violence, and high-risk behavior by adolescents are among the many problems attributed in part to substance abuse within the family. Yet research does not substantiate all the claims of ill effects on families or theories about interaction between family members regarding substance abuse. For example, "codependency," or the idea that one family member may "enable" another to continue abusing alcohol or drugs, is not supported by empirical evidence.[8]

Finally, some population groups may encounter more problems related to substance abuse than others. Among people aged twelve to seventeen, rates of current illicit drug use varied greatly by major racial/ethnic groups in 2004. The rate was highest among American Indian and Alaska Native youths (26 percent). The rates were 11.1 percent for white youths, 10.2 percent for Hispanic youths, 9.3 for African American youths, and 6.0 percent for young Asians. In that same year, past-month alcohol use rates among individuals aged twelve to twenty were 16.4 percent among

Asians, 19.1 percent among African Americans, 24.3 percent among American Indians and Alaska Natives, 26.6 percent among Hispanics, and 32.6 percent among whites. Alcohol abuse is one of the five leading causes of death for American Indians, although this varies by tribe or community. Researchers have postulated that certain minority groups, including American Indians, may possess genetic traits that predispose them to alcoholism. However, few of these traits have yet been discovered. The highest prevalence of binge and heavy drinking in 2004 was for people aged eighteen to twenty-five (41.2 and 15.1 percent, respectively). Underage drinking is also a problem. Almost 11 million persons aged twelve to twenty reported drinking alcohol in the prior month. Of these, almost 20 percent were binge drinkers, and a little over 6 percent were heavy drinkers.[9]

Drug-related law enforcement has more serious effects for African Americans than for whites. Although African Americans constitute only 12 percent of the population, they account for about 40 percent of all arrests and over 30 percent of all convictions for possession of drugs. Nonwhites constitute almost 75 percent of drug offenders in prison. Analysts have noted the tendency in our country to exaggerate the use of drugs among minorities and to single them out for special attention. For example, when fears of a crack cocaine "epidemic" spread in the late 1980s, new laws established mandatory five-year sentences for possession of 5 grams of crack (used mostly by minorities). To receive the same penalty for powdered cocaine (used mainly by whites) required possession of 500 grams. As reporter Jonathan Alter notes, "Crack and coke are pharmacologically identical; only the delivery system (smoking versus sniffing) varies." Although African Americans are arrested and jailed for use of illegal substances more often than whites, the actual drug use patterns of the two groups are quite similar.[10]

The History of Substance Abuse Policies

Using the criminal justice system to deal with people who abuse drugs has a long-standing tradition in the United States, but it is just one of many responses to substance abuse in U.S. history. Interestingly, in the mid-1800s the notion of drug abuse was almost unheard of. Codeine, heroin, morphine, and similar substances appeared in such seemingly innocent concoctions as Gadway's Elixir for Infants, Dr. James's Soothing Syrup Cordial, and Victor Infant Relief. Opium was as common as aspirin is today. All were sold in nonprescription forms and advertised in family magazines. Morphine was used freely in the treatment of wounded soldiers during the Civil War. After the war, its use spread widely among civilians for pain relief and treatment of stomach ailments. Although physicians began to recognize the problem of morphine's addictive quality, there remained only minimal restrictions on its use. Warnings about the dangers of opium were similarly ignored.

As long as the use of these substances was seen as medically based and confined largely to the middle and upper classes, little public concern was aroused.[11]

Alcohol use was also initially a common and accepted part of normal life. Drinking was a ritual in social, political, and religious occasions during the colonial period. The colonists were serious drinkers, with the average male over fifteen years old drinking about six gallons of alcohol each year. Average consumption in the 1980s, in contrast, was less than three gallons. Attitudes began to change, however, during the early years of the republic. Leaders such as Thomas Jefferson and John Adams wanted new citizens to be people of "virtue," temperate in their habits. These ideas were supported by physicians such as Dr. Benjamin Rush, who had begun to see the alcohol addiction process as "a series of moral and physically degenerative stages."[12]

By 1855 the prohibition movement had become an important factor in U.S. life and thirteen states had passed temperance laws. About a decade or so later, drug addiction also became a public concern. One of the major reasons for these shifts in attitude in the later 1800s seems to be the changing context of alcohol and drug use. This use now appeared to many to be connected with race, class, and religion. White traders' introduction of whiskey to Native Americans, who were unaccustomed to this new substance, soon led to stereotypes of the "drunken Indian." Irish Catholics, Italians, other immigrants, and the urban poor in general were similarly criticized for heavy drinking. Middle-class Anglo-Saxon citizens used the slur of drunkenness to separate themselves from these "outside groups." Many charity workers of the times blamed "drink" as an important factor in a family's dependency on outside help.[13]

In the case of drugs, Chinese immigrants played a similar scapegoat role. Chinese laborers who came to the United States after the Civil War established the practice of smoking opium in the West Coast cities where they settled. First San Francisco, and then the California state legislature, passed laws against "opium dens" and imposed heavy fines or imprisonment for the smoking of opium. While medical use of opium and other drugs continued, the street use of such substances led to widespread concern similar to public reactions toward drug use today.[14]

The campaign against drugs, and particularly against alcohol, began to take on the form of a moral crusade. The temperance movement developed alliances with other reform groups, such as antislavery and populist organizations. Many in the first wave of feminists joined the ranks of the prohibitionists, forming the powerful Women's Christian Temperance Union. The business community also tended to support prohibition because it had an interest in maintaining the sobriety, and hence efficiency, of workers. By 1919 the movement had achieved its goal—the outlawing by the Volstead Act of the sale, manufacture, and transportation of all alcoholic beverages. With somewhat less fanfare, opponents of addictive drugs helped pass the Pure Food and Drug Act in 1906, which required the labeling of all medicines and other preparations containing habit-forming drugs. Eight years later a much stronger bill was passed. The Harrison Narcotics Act mandated the registration of, and imposition of a special tax on, "all persons who produce, import, manufacture, . . . sell, distribute, or give away opium or coca leaves" or their derivatives, which include heroin, morphine, and cocaine. Although the act was meant to regulate, not prohibit, the use of these drugs, eager U.S. Treasury agents turned it into a mandate for the prohibition of all such substances. Physicians were jailed for prescribing heroin and morphine to addicts and for using these drugs to alleviate the pain of the terminally ill. Both drug and alcohol control had come under the jurisdiction of the police rather than the physician or the moral reformer.[15]

Prohibition, of course, was a failed social experiment. Extremely difficult to enforce—and bringing with it the unintended consequences of increased criminal activity, gang warfare, and police corruption—the Volstead Act was repealed in 1933. Its repeal was helped by ideological arguments regarding individualism and free choice in the drinking of alcohol, posed particularly by a new coalition of urban dwellers, ethnic Americans, and a growing middle class. Making alcohol legal would also restore huge tax revenues to the government and provide jobs for the unemployed in the midst of the Depression. With the repeal of Prohibition, breweries and distillers began their transformation into today's powerful multi-million-dollar industry. By the end of the 1930s, one historian notes, "Prohibition was seen by most as a ridiculous and costly mistake, and an unacceptable intrusion by the government into personal behavior."[16]

However, support still remained for laws against drugs. The Harrison Act of 1914 had established a coercive national policy against habitforming drugs. In 1930 the Federal Bureau of Narcotics was formed to fight the perceived "drug menace." Drug addiction began increasingly to be seen as intrinsically criminal. It also continued to carry racist overtones, as shown in attacks on marijuana use by Hispanics and African Americans (despite the fact that marijuana was also being used by whites). Between the formation of the Narcotics Bureau and the early 1960s, thousands of drug users and dealers served lengthy prison sentences. The majority of those convicted were minorities of color, who were often unable to pay for lawyers who could raise constitutional rights issues such as entrapment by undercover agents and illegal search and seizure practices. Ironically, the bureau had to be replaced by a new agency in the early 1970s, as it was found to be full of agents who had taken bribes, sold confiscated drugs, and engaged in other acts of corruption.[17]

By the 1960s, the U.S. government had established two different policy approaches to the control of drugs: the reduction of the supply of drugs through law enforcement and the reduction of the demand for drugs through prevention and treatment. The "demand approach" was represented by the Narcotic Addict

Rehabilitation Act of 1966, which allowed for the nonpunitive incarceration of addicts for purposes of treatment. But the "supply approach" was clearly paramount and remains the government's dominant drug policy today. The foundation of this approach is a network of federal and state statutes and laws that define *controlled substances* and prohibit their possession, use, manufacture, and distribution. An important example of such legislation is the federal Comprehensive Drug Abuse Prevention and Control Act of 1970 (see Figure 10.1), which separates drugs into five classes according to their potential for abuse, their effects, and their medical usefulness. Among drugs included in the most serious and next most serious classes (based on greatest potential for abuse and so on) are heroin, marijuana, and cocaine.[18]

The act also created a commission to assess patterns of marijuana use and to study its impact on public health and safety. This was in part a reaction to the fact that marijuana use was growing among young people in the 1960s and was entering the mainstream. Users were now as likely to be white as African American and to come from both middle-income and poorer families. Encouraged by the drug use of avant-garde writers and artists, college students began experimenting with LSD and marijuana. During the Vietnam War, marijuana became for some a symbol of their protest against the war and "a statement against the hypocrisy, racism, and materialism of their parents." (Ironically, the horrors of that war helped lead to more serious drug addiction on the part of young soldiers, many of whom were African American.) Reacting against heavy sentences for college students charged with possession of marijuana, older adults helped create a more permissive attitude toward the use of the drug. The commission created by the 1970 act concluded that only sale, and not possession, of marijuana should be prohibited.[19]

The commission's recommendation met with strong resistance from President Nixon, who was elected in 1968 as a "law and order" president. During his term in office, Nixon launched a strong attack on drugs that included attempts to cut off supply by putting pressure on the major foreign producers of the U.S. supply, particularly Turkey and Mexico. The federal antidrug budget was doubled between 1970 and 1971 and doubled again the following year. A new agency was created, the Drug Enforcement Agency, to control supply. However, Nixon also promoted drug treatment as a way of diminishing the demand for drugs. As part of this effort, in 1973 he established the National Institute on Drug Abuse (NIDA) to help fund state and local antidrug treatment and prevention programs and to carry out research on drug use. During most of the years of Nixon's presidency, more stress was put on prevention and treatment than on controlling supply, with the former approach receiving two-thirds of the federal antidrug budget. The same treatment approach characterized Nixon's establishment, in 1970, of the National Institute on Alcohol Abuse and Alcoholism (NIAAA), which was the first major federal agency established to deal with alcoholism since the repeal of Prohibition.[20]

Figure 10.1 Schedule of Controlled Substances
Comprehensive Drug Abuse Prevention and Control Act of 1970

1. SCHEDULE I.
   A. The drug or other substance has a high potential for abuse.
   B. The drug or other substance has no currently accepted medical use in treatment in the United States.
   C. There is a lack of accepted safety for use of the drug or other substance under medical supervision.

   Examples: heroin, LSD, marijuana, mescaline, peyote

2. SCHEDULE II.
   A. The drug or other substance has a high potential for abuse.
   B. The drug or other substance has a currently accepted medical use in treatment in the United States or a currently accepted medical use with severe restrictions.
   C. Abuse of the drug or other substance may lead to severe psychological dependence.

   Examples: cocaine, opium

3. SCHEDULE III.
   A. The drug or other substance has a potential for abuse less than the drugs or other substances in schedules I and II.
   B. The drug or other substance has a currently accepted medical use in treatment in the United States.
   C. Abuse of the drug or other substance may lead to moderate or low physical dependence or high psychological dependence.

   Examples: amphetamines, barbiturate depressants, anabolic steroids

4. SCHEDULE IV.
   A. The drug or other substance has a low potential for abuse relative to the drugs or other substances in schedule III.
   B. The drug or other substance has a currently accepted medical use in treatment in the United States.
   C. Abuse of the drug or other substance may lead to limited physical dependence or psychological dependence relative to the drugs or other substances in schedule III.

   Examples: Valium, Phenobarbital

5. SCHEDULE V.
   A. The drug or other substance has a low potential for abuse relative to the drugs or other substances in schedule IV.
   B. The drug or other substance has a currently accepted medical use in treatment in the United States.
   C. Abuse of the drug or other substance may lead to limited physical dependence or psychological dependence relative to the drugs or other substances in schedule IV.

   Examples: compounds with low amounts of narcotics; stimulants, and depressants, such as codeine and opium

Source: P.L. 91-513, *United States Statutes at Large Containing Laws and Concurrent Resolutions Enacted during the Second Session of the 91st Congress of the United States of America, 1970–1971*, Vol. 84, Part I (Washington, DC: U.S. Government Printing Office, 1971).

It remained for Ronald Reagan to wage an all out War on Drugs in the 1980s, paradoxically at a time when drug use was actually declining in the United States. Marijuana use had fallen and cocaine use had leveled off. Despite these developments, Reagan, who came to office on a platform of getting tough on crime, immediately launched a decade-long war on drugs. This war was based chiefly on law enforcement, and the proportion of the federal antidrug budget spent on prevention and treatment plummeted. Looking back on the Reagan antidrug initiative, one federal official noted that the Reagan administration had presided over "the largest increases in drug law enforcement funding and manpower in the nation's history."[21]

In this war, drugs and crime were seen as intertwined enemies, with the 1984 Crime Control Act expanding the asset forfeiture laws that penalized drug traffickers, establishing mandatory sentencing guidelines for drug offenses, and increasing criminal penalties. The Defense Department and the FBI were given broad powers in the fight against drugs, and money and personnel were poured into border patrol efforts to stop drugs from crossing into the United States.[22]

The rise of the crack cocaine "epidemic" in the mid-1980s added further fuel to the Reagan administration's antidrug efforts. While the drop in drug use among the general population continued, crack, a cheap and highly addictive substance, recruited many new users from low-income and minority populations. This reinforced the notion that drug use was essentially a problem for lower-class, inner city African Americans. Although some citizens were genuinely concerned about the effects of crack on addicts and their families, others were quick to accept assumptions, often fanned by the media, that crack had turned inner city neighborhoods into violent wastelands. At any rate, drugs were seen more and more as a major national problem. A moralistic attitude—that is, a belief that drug use is the result of personal failing—is often easier to maintain when users, such as inner city residents, are perceived as people outside the U.S. mainstream. In the case of crack, this attitude led to the "Just Say No" campaign championed by Nancy Reagan. The traditional components of the war on drugs continued also, with two more antidrug laws being enacted that added more mandatory sentence categories, expanded international drug control efforts, and created a "drug czar" in the form of a cabinet-level official in charge of national efforts to control the supply of and demand for drugs.[23]

Responses to the abuse of alcohol were much less dramatic in the 1980s, but important legislation was passed. In part due to lobbying by an advocacy group, Mothers Against Drunk Driving (MADD), a 1984 act required states to raise the minimum legal drinking age to twenty-one in order to qualify for federal highway transportation funds. An alcoholic beverage labeling act mandated that all alcoholic beverage containers carry warning labels regarding issues such as using alcohol while operating motor vehicles; a 1988 law expanded the warning to the dangers of alcohol consumption by pregnant women. Most states added their own statutes about advertising of alcoholic beverages, public drunkenness, and drunk driving. One important change that affected treatment and prevention efforts aimed at both alcoholism and drug abuse was the Reagan administration's development of block grant programs that transferred much of the responsibility for drug and alcohol treatment and prevention programs to the states and decreased federal funding for these services.[24] The amount of private insurance coverage for the treatment of addiction dropped at the same time.

President George H. W. Bush continued much of the Reagan approach of using law enforcement to wage the battle against drugs and of pouring billions of dollars into this effort. Yet, by the end of the 1980s, many experts had concluded that attempts to cut off supply had failed as an antidrug policy. By the early 1990s, the number of inmates in U.S. prisons reached one million, with drug-related convictions playing a major role in this growth. Efforts had been made to help drug-producing countries apprehend suppliers. Bush ordered the invasion of Panama and had Manuel Noriega arrested on drug charges. Bush's drug czar, William Bennett, rallied against "whole cadres of social scientists, abetted by whole armies of social workers, who [feel] that the problem facing us isn't drugs at all, it's poverty, or racism." He reasserted the need for strict criminal penalties. But the problem of drug abuse remained. In part because of the spread of crack, more and more poor members of minority groups were ending up in prison on charges of possessing or selling drugs. The proportion of incarcerated drug offenders who were African American grew from 35 percent in 1983 to 48 percent in 1989.[25]

Approaches to combating drug abuse began to shift somewhat during the Clinton administration. Policy debate focused less on illegal drugs and more on the related problem of violent crime among juveniles. Federal drug control staff were reduced. Stress began to be put on police–citizen cooperation in the areas of drug enforcement and prevention. This latter, demand-focused approach was strengthened by federal grants for the creation of drug courts under the 1994 Violent Crime Control and Law Enforcement Act. Such courts combine intensive probation, mandatory drug testing, and treatment as alternative punishment for nonviolent and first-time drug offenders. There are now about 1,000 such courts nationwide. However, federal spending on drug abuse prevention and research remains less than that on antidrug law enforcement measures.[26]

One of the most intriguing developments in recent years, however, may have little to do with Clinton administration policies, state drug laws, police activity, or treatment programs. This is the rather sudden drop in the number of people using crack cocaine. One reporter describes this phenomenon in New York City in 1999:

> Today, in communities that used to have more open-crack markets than grocery stores, where children grew up dodging crack vials and gunfire, the change from

a decade ago is startling. On the surface, crack has all but disappeared from much of New York, taking with it the ragged and violent vignettes that were a routine part of street life.[27]

Although the New York City police commissioner attributed the change to the city's policy of "zero tolerance" for anyone openly using or selling drugs, almost every major U.S. city with drug problems, no matter what its policing policy, has witnessed the same decline in crack use. In a 1999 New York City study of drug use among people who were arrested, 35.7 percent of all arrested men over age thirty-six had used crack recently, but under 4 percent of those age fifteen to twenty had done so. Washington, D.C., has reported an even steeper decline. It appears that a generational revulsion against the drug may have occurred, with crack dealers being seen by the young as "the biggest losers on the street." One woman, whose mother had used crack, explained it this way: "If you were raised in a house where somebody was a crack addict, you wanted to get as far away from that drug as you could." But we must add a sobering note—the decline in use of one type of drug does not rule out the possibility that a different drug or drugs will rise in popularity. The use of marijuana in combination with alcohol, especially malt liquor, has now become popular in New York City. Heroin use also appears to be resurging, and young people are increasingly experimenting with new "club drugs" or "designer drugs" such as Ecstasy. In addition, college students are taking prescription stimulants like Adderall to help them study. There has also been an increase in the use of inhalants such as glue, shoe polish, and gasoline among eighth graders.[28]

Social and Economic Analysis of Substance Abuse Policies

How complete is our knowledge about substance abuse? As the story of the decline in crack indicates, there are important gaps in our understanding of the causes and patterns of drug and alcohol use. Some scientists link drug addiction to effects on brain processes. Some researchers who study alcoholism have systematically investigated whether there is a genetic component to the phenomenon. Yet both these approaches are still in fairly early stages, with hypotheses not fully confirmed. Similarly, research into the effects of treatment and prevention programs has had uneven success. Many evaluations of specific programs or interventions have not used good experimental designs or representative samples. Costs of these programs and possible unintended consequences have not always been examined and reported. Prevention programs are particularly difficult to assess, as it is hard to isolate the specific factors at work.[29]

However, progress is being made in some areas of treatment, prevention, and policy evaluation. One analyst observes, "Data now exist to support the conclusion that interdiction and crop eradication do not reduce the availability of drugs substantially for long time periods." On the other hand, random drug testing has reduced drug use in the armed forces. Drug prevention programs that utilize community involvement, a focus on the family, comprehensive services, and appealing activities as an alternate to drugs have been found to be more effective than prevention programs that focus on only one of these factors. Most studies examining the effects of state legislation raising the minimum legal driving age have concluded that these laws lead to declines in teenage night fatal crashes, which are those most likely to involve alcohol.[30]

As we noted earlier in this chapter, large numbers of people have difficulties with drugs and alcohol. Although the media and law enforcement activities often focus on minorities, substance abuse is found among people of all ethnic and racial backgrounds. One thing that the standard study of abuse—the U.S. government's National Household Survey on Drug Abuse—fails to show is the extent of substance abuse among homeless, institutionalized, and other populations who are not included in the Household Survey's sample. Insight into drug use among these populations can be found in an extensive survey of drug use among criminals, people who are in institutions, people who are currently in drug treatment programs, and homeless individuals and families that was carried out in Washington, D.C. The study indicates that all segments of the city's population show some degree of involvement in drug use, but there are marked differences in rates between household and nonhousehold populations. Twelve percent of households indicate the use of drugs, but the rate of drug use is 58 percent for the homeless and transient population, 50 percent for those who are institutionalized, 54 percent for adult offenders, and 50 percent for juvenile offenders.[31]

A particularly important factor in studying alcohol and drug abuse policy is an understanding of the conflicting values surrounding the use of these substances. One basic differentiation is between a view of the use (and particularly "misuse") of drugs and alcohol as criminal behavior and/or as a moral failing and a view of it as some type of illness or the outcome of certain environmental circumstances. Responses based on the first view include moral campaigns against substance abuse and the imprisonment of those who use or deal drugs. Responses consistent with the second view lead to therapeutic interventions, community development programs, and the like.

Another polarity in thinking about substance abuse is the contrast between the libertarian view that such behavior is a matter of individual right and the opposing view that it is the responsibility of the government to protect citizens from the threats to health and safety posed by drug and alcohol use. Libertarian policies might include free drug markets and the acceptance of recreational use of substances as long as such use does not harm others. Those who believe in government responsibility to prevent the misuse of drugs and alcohol would support controls ranging from incarceration of offenders to deterrence through law enforcement and rehabilitation.[32]

As we noted earlier, there is a definite economic aspect to substance abuse. In addition to calculating the financial costs of abuse to individuals, families, businesses, and the country as a whole, any analysis of economic issues related to abuse must also examine the economic role of large liquor producers and distributors, advertising companies, and, on the drug side, distributors and individual dealers. Although the profits of producers and dealers in the drug market may be hard to estimate, those of the alcohol industry are a matter of public record. The sale of alcoholic beverages is big business in the United States, bringing in 242 billion dollars in 2004. Moreover, this is a fairly concentrated industry, with three producers dominating the beer market (Anheuser-Busch, Miller Brewing, and Molson Coors) and five companies commanding most of the hard liquor market. A growing national movement toward moderation in the use of alcohol has led to slower growth in company profits; to counteract this, alcohol producers have sought new consumers through expansion into international markets and the development of new products. New and old products need advertising, itself a lucrative business. Critics have assailed the use, as well as the specific placement, of advertisements for beer, wine, and liquor. Their targets have included billboards promoting cheap liquor in low-income minority neighborhoods and television beer commercials aired when young children might be watching. One study found that children who were more aware of such advertisements "held more favorable beliefs about drinking and intended to drink more frequently as adults."[33]

Political Analysis

As in other policy areas, there is a long list of stakeholders involved in substance abuse issues. These include self-help groups such as Alcoholics Anonymous (AA), with its related groups for teens and for the families of those with drinking problems, and Narcotics Anonymous (NA). AA was founded in 1935 by two former alcoholics; currently the organization has approximately 2 million members in 150 countries. The only requirement for membership is a desire to stop drinking. Members meet regularly to share their experiences with alcoholism and to learn to follow AA's famous Twelve Step Program, which includes admitting their powerlessness over alcohol and the need to turn to a higher Power for help in overcoming alcoholism.[34] There are also citizens' organizations, such as Mothers Against Drunk Driving (MADD), which may constitute powerful lobbying bodies.

People who abuse alcohol and drugs, and the families of these individuals, are obvious stakeholders in substance abuse policies. Minority groups, as we have observed, are particularly vulnerable, as they often have specific alcohol and drug issues related to stigma and to interactions with the law enforcement and legal systems. Generally, however, neither those who abuse substances nor their families are organized into groups who could affect the development of legislative, legal, or treatment responses.

Professionals and direct care staff are another group of stakeholders. Although a relatively small percentage of social workers currently work directly in the substance abuse area, social workers do play important roles in the field. They function as case managers, counselors, administrators of substance abuse treatment programs, and policymakers. In addition, problems with drug and alcohol affect many clients and families with whom social workers work. A survey of members of the National Association of Social Workers found that 71 percent of those sampled had been involved with clients who had substances abuse problems in the previous year. These problems must often be addressed directly. In recognition of the growing importance of the field, and in response to membership interest, NASW decided to offer a specialist credential in substance abuse.[35]

The impetus for the new credential stemmed also from the profession's desire to enhance acceptance of social workers' competence in a multidisciplinary field that includes medical doctors, psychiatrists, psychologists (who have developed their own substance abuse certification), and drug or alcohol counselors, a number of whom are former substance abusers. These counselors have their own credentialing process, and there can be tension between them and psychiatrists, social workers, and others in the field. Those counselors with personal experience with abuse often argue that they alone can truly understand the situation of the addict or alcoholic, whereas the traditional professionals stress the importance of their advanced training and their greater ability to be objective about the client's problems. Because of the pervasive stigma against substance abuse in our society, some of these professionals may have difficulty working with counselors who have had substance abuse problems.[36]

Many groups within the legal and law-enforcement systems are also stakeholders. These include city and state police, county sheriffs, federal narcotics agents, lawyers, judges, and the U.S. Surgeon General. Both the U.S. Defense Department and the Bureau of Alcohol, Tobacco, and Firearms play a role in dealing with drug traffickers. These are just two of the over forty federal agencies, offices, and programs involved directly in substance abuse work.[37] Public officials and politicians on the city, state, and national levels also weigh in with their own approaches to substance abuse policy.

Groups with a strong financial interest in the consumption of drugs and alcohol don't necessarily come to mind immediately as major stakeholders, yet major stakeholders they are. Lobbyists for the multibillion-dollar alcoholic beverage industry seek to protect it from government regulation and higher taxes on its products. The industry actively promotes its products in stores, on billboards, and in the print and broadcast media. This use of advertising helps make the advertising industry another player in our field of interest groups. Public health advocates are a counterinterest group, pointing out the dangers of alcohol and criticizing the advertising business for its tendency to glamorize drinking, encourage the heavy consumption of alcohol, and target vulnerable groups.

Companies and farms that produce drugs, and the traffickers and dealers that deliver and sell them, are in a somewhat different position as stakeholders. Their activities are defined as illegal, and thus they cannot openly lobby politicians and officials. Yet they can sometimes exert a strong force under the table through bribery and extortion, and they can also fight back against those waging the war on drugs with physical force.

Finally, the average citizen and taxpayer often plays a major role in substance abuse policy. When public concern about abuse has been aroused, votes increase for "tough on crime and drugs" politicians, including presidential candidates. Public opinion polls regarding alcohol and drugs can influence policymakers at all levels.

It is important to recall the larger context in which all these stakeholder negotiations take place. When the use of alcohol and drugs can be seen as widespread across the various sectors of society, prohibition and government regulation become far less serious concerns. However, once drug and alcohol use is consistently identified with groups "outside the mainstream"—minority groups, "wild youth," or the homeless—the public becomes aroused to "do something about the problem" and to wage war on substance use and abuse through legal and other actions.

Analysis of Two Policies: Drug Tests for Welfare Clients and Separation of Treatment for Those Who Are Dually Diagnosed

Thus far we have briefly portrayed a number of policies related to substance abuse. In this final section, we look more closely at two policies of particular interest to social workers: state-level decisions to mandate drug testing of public welfare applicants and/or recipients and the practice of dealing with individuals experiencing both mental illness and substance abuse in separate treatment programs. The latter policy is clearly treatment related. Drug testing, however, can be used either to penalize people who use drugs or to refer them for help.

Drug Tests for Welfare Clients

Drug testing has been used most commonly in the workplace. It is estimated that about 2 to 3 percent of the U.S. workforce abuses legal and illegal drugs.[38] In an effort to maintain worker efficiency and productivity and to prevent safety hazards, public and private employers have set up a number of forms of drug testing for employees. These generally involve urine tests for traces of drugs in the body. They can be voluntary or required (usually the latter) and can be carried out at varying time intervals. In some cases, positive tests can lead to punitive measures, such as firing the employee. In other cases, employers may use the results of the test to refer employees for drug counseling and other treatment.

Of particular concern to us is the phenomenon of drug testing among groups that are essentially "captive audiences," such as people receiving welfare. St. John's County, Florida, was one of the first local governments to require such testing. In 1996, local officials ordered that anyone applying for county assistance for certain types of medical care must first submit to a urine test for illegal drug use. Those failing the test would be denied medical services. The new policy was in part an attempt to control costs, in part an effort to promote "personal responsibility" on the part of people receiving public aid.[39]

Maryland was the first state to propose mandatory drug tests for all AFDC applicants, a policy option approved in the Clinton administration's welfare reform act of 1996. In December of that year, a legislative committee of the Maryland General Assembly endorsed a drug testing policy in which an applicant who refused to take the test would be denied all cash benefits. Those for whom the test showed evidence of drug use would have to complete a state-paid treatment program; failure to enter or complete the program would lead to a reduction in the family's payments. Supporters of the proposal argued that it would strengthen families "by ensuring that cash benefits are spent on needy children, not on their parents' drug habits."[40]

Other states have initiated similar policies. South Carolina set up a program mandating treatment for welfare recipients suspected of abuse; the state randomly tests clients in treatment to make sure they remain drug-free during and after treatment. Those who do not can lose all of their welfare benefits. The Louisiana legislature, at the urging of Mike Foster, the state's governor, passed legislation in 1997 requiring drug screening, testing, education, and rehabilitation for all welfare recipients. Interestingly, this law was part of a larger package that required drug testing of state employees, elected officials, and college students on state scholarships. Governor Foster's initiative was described as part of "a drive to root out drug abuse by people who benefit from taxpayer money."[41]

Clearly, one assumption behind such policies is that a good number of welfare applicants and recipients abuse drugs. Yet, as our policy analysis framework asks, what do we actually know about this phenomenon? Maryland budget analysts estimated that 10 percent of welfare clients abused drugs and would need treatment, whereas the chair of the legislative committee proposing testing put the figure at 16 percent. South Carolina welfare officials weighed in with a 12 to 15 percent estimate for recipients in their state. Projections of the percentage of welfare recipients nationwide who are addicted to drugs range from 15 to 25 percent (compared to the National Household Survey on Drug Abuse estimate of 6 percent among the general public). In the first year of the mandated drug screening program for welfare clients in Louisiana, only 2 percent were identified as drug users. The range of all of these estimates, and the actual findings in one state, suggest that the focus on excessive substance abuse among welfare clients is not based on definitive research.[42]

In addition, policymakers should be looking for evidence of the effectiveness of drug testing. Studies of the effects of testing in the workplace show mixed results. One study by the federal Substance Abuse and Mental Health Services Administration (SAMHSA) found that workers who reported that their workplace used drug testing "also reported less current drug use than workers in places without testing." Yet an evaluation of drug testing in Silicon Valley companies revealed that tests reduced, rather than enhanced, worker productivity.[43] In the case of welfare clients, little is known as yet about the potential deterrence of drug testing or the lasting effects of the treatment programs that clients enter.

Certain values and assumptions underlie welfare-related drug testing programs; these are countered by other values and beliefs in our society. Policy supporters often stress the treatment aspect of the new approach, treatment that will enable welfare recipients to lead more productive and rewarding lives. This line of thought, however, can reflect an assumption that many people are on welfare because they are irresponsible and thus need guidance in changing their behavior. Client advocates question the assumption that substance abuse is widespread among welfare recipients. Legal experts argue that drug testing is an invasion of privacy. In 1999, the ACLU sued the U.S. District Court on behalf of all Michigan welfare recipients and won a restraining order to stop the testing. In April 2003, the 6th U.S. Circuit Court of Appeals ruled that Michigan's program, with its unreasonable searches, was unconstitutional. The NASW, along with a number of health and welfare organizations, had filed *amicus curiae* briefs opposing the Michigan policy. Denial of benefits due to a history of substance abuse may also go against provisions in the Americans with Disabilities Act. One commentator noted his concern "that there would be . . . drug testing for a whole universe of people without even some reasonable evidence that someone is using illegal substances." The stress on the individual rights of those on welfare has brought responses that reflect a concern for the larger community and sometimes the implied assumption that welfare clients are "sponging" on the rest of society. For example, a Florida state representative asserted: "There is no invasion of privacy. Is it their right to abuse their family and children by abusing drugs? Is it their right to abuse tax dollars?"[44]

There are, as usual, a variety of stakeholders in the drug testing debate. Although some welfare clients are organized and may work along with advocacy groups, in general clients are a vulnerable population with little input into welfare policy decisions or their implementation. Social workers, psychologists, and other professionals working in substance abuse are often critical of mandated drug testing but so far have had limited impact. Attorneys who focus on welfare rights, and particularly groups such as the ACLU, may have greater potential to alter or win the repeal of drug testing laws. What the critics are up against, however, is the ability of governors and other elected officials to tap into popular distrust of welfare programs and their clients. Louisiana's Governor Foster, a conservative Republican, received widespread support for his tough stand against a "lenient" welfare system. Political appeals to voters' wallets, such as a Florida official's statement that he didn't think the taxpayer "should be supporting the drug habits of anybody," constitute a further selling point for antidrug policies.[45]

Interestingly, the actual economics of drug testing may be the most potent factor in limiting its use. Simply put, drug testing on a large scale is expensive. The more accurate and complete the test, the more it costs. In the case of Maryland's policy, state budget analysts predicted it would cost 1.2 million dollars annually to test all welfare applicants. Outside experts calculated an even higher sum, adding that because the tests related to a public benefit, extra precautions would have to be taken to confirm their validity and protect against legal challenges. In addition, money would have to be put into increased treatment services, which one state senator estimated at $10 million a year. Less than two months after the proposal was made, the Maryland legislature dropped the testing plan, opting instead for in-depth interviews, conducted by professionals, to detect chronic drug addiction. Drug testing, the legislators concluded, would be too costly and might lead to lawsuits challenging test results. Advocacy groups, though still unhappy about sanctions against welfare recipients who didn't comply with the new drug screening, nevertheless applauded a system that "doesn't criminalize poor people nearly as much."[46]

Separation of Treatment for Those with Mental Health and Substance Abuse Problems

Our final example of substance abuse policy is an intervention policy: the decision to treat people with substance abuse and mental health problems in two different programs and at two different times or simply to treat one condition and ignore the other. The combination of substance abuse and mental illness is not at all unusual, and a number of clinicians argue that the most effective way to deal with the situation is to tackle both issues at once in a program specifically tailored for what is often called "dual diagnosis." Yet only recently have the barriers against coordinated treatment of the dually diagnosed begun to fall.

Concurrence of substance abuse and mental health problems (sometimes called *comorbidity*) is far more prevalent than most people, including many health and human services professionals, realize. Data produced by SAMHSA indicate that among persons with any alcohol, drug abuse, or mental disorder during their lifetimes, "56 percent will have two or more of these disorders." (Note that this and the following data refer to lifetime prevalence, or likelihood of coexisting conditions at some point in a person's life.) Various studies looking specifically at people with mental illness have found that as many as 50 percent of them will experience a concurrent substance abuse problem. Research focusing on those with substance abuse disorders estimates that about 35 percent of alcoholics will have coexisting mental disorders, whereas more than 50 percent of people addicted to drugs will have mental problems.[47] Within the phenomenon of dual diagnosis, certain combinations of disorders are particularly strong. The co-occurrence of bipolar (manic–depressive) disorders and addictive disorders is especially high, followed by the coexistence of schizophrenia and substance abuse problems. About 30 to 60 percent of those with alcoholism also suffer from clinical depression, and conduct disorders, such as aggressive behavior, frequently accompany alcoholism in men.[48]

As you read these figures, you may be wondering what coexistence actually means and how it comes about. For example, is depression a cause of alcoholism, which occurs when depressed people drink to make themselves feel better? (Researchers give this a fancy name: selfmedication.) Or, one might ask, can drug or alcohol abuse produce the kinds of delusions that characterize schizophrenia? Sorting out issues of "which came first" and whether one condition can mimic the symptoms of another has indeed been a problem in defining the phenomenon of dual diagnosis. Many of those who study this condition have come to the conclusion that while reactions to drugs or alcohol can produce symptoms similar to those of mental illness, the presence of two distinct disorders at the same time can also occur. This might simply take place simultaneously with no interdependence between the two conditions, or substance abuse and mental disorders might stem from common biological vulnerabilities, or one condition might be accentuated or aggravated by the other. Finally, some practitioners and program planners argue that regardless of the debates about the causes of the dual-diagnosis phenomenon, real-life clients are suffering from the condition and need to be helped.[49]

However, although treating dually diagnosed clients in programs specifically designed to deal with their problems sounds sensible, it has met with great resistance from professionals and policymakers in both the mental health and substance abuse arenas. One problem on the mental health side has been the negative attitudes of some clinicians toward people who abuse substances and their pessimistic assessments of the effectiveness of treatment for addiction. In the 1940s and 1950s, psychiatrists treated alcoholism with psychoanalysis; when this failed, they often concluded that alcoholism was not treatable with psychodynamic approaches. At the same time, AA members and others in the substance abuse field developed a critical attitude toward psychiatrists and psychotherapy.[50]

Negative feelings between these two sets of stakeholders have contributed to and been reinforced by organizational and economic arrangements in the fields of mental health, drug addiction, and alcohol abuse at the federal level. When the National Institute on Alcohol Abuse and Alcoholism was created, it was housed in the National Institute for Mental Health. However, in 1973 the two federal agencies were separated, and the National Institute on Drug Abuse was developed as a third distinct entity. Each had its own funding stream and particular set of missions. The federal divisions have generally been mirrored in state-level agencies. As noted in one analysis of the situation,

> [T]he federal, state, and local bureaucracies which deal with alcoholism, drug abuse, and mental health issues grew out of completely separate traditions. . . . The historical development of [these] three separate clinical and administrative worlds . . . has led to turf battles resulting in such problems as exclusionary criteria for acceptance of patients in each system and an inability to develop a holistic approach to clients with more than one diagnosis.[51]

The resulting failure to recognize and effectively treat dually diagnosed clients, especially younger ones, has led to "enduring patterns of maladaptive coping styles" among these clients, repeated and lengthy hospitalizations, and increased health care costs.[52]

Fortunately, the policy of using separate treatment facilities or of ignoring one condition entirely has begun to change. An apparent increase in the number of people with dual disorders has helped, along with research indicating both the high prevalence of dual diagnoses and the lack of expertise in managing these situations. In addition, the psychiatric profession has begun to accept the role that it can play in addictive disorders, as shown, for example, in the recent creation of a subspeciality of addiction psychiatry. On the federal level, substance abuse and mental health services have been combined under SAMHSA. Finally, treatment programs that focus on those with mental health and substance abuse disorders have begun to develop. The availability of appropriate services for dually diagnosed adolescents, for example, has increased significantly.[53]

The new treatment programs generally begin with detoxification in order for clinicians to get a clearer picture of what is occurring. Yet, unlike the situation of Jenny Marsh in the vignette at the beginning of the chapter, this is seen as part of a more comprehensive therapeutic approach, generally coordinated by a multidisciplinary team experienced in both mental health and substance abuse treatment. Although the methods of dealing with one disorder may conflict with those used in the other (for example, schizophrenic individuals often have great difficulty interacting with people in group settings such as AA meetings), the new treatment teams are developing appropriate adaptations for work with the dually diagnosed population.[54]

Conclusion

This chapter has described many types of policy responses to substance abuse, including specific treatment approaches. We included the latter in part to show that choice of treatment is indeed a type of policy, although not often recognized as such. The same policy analysis that you might apply to a piece of legislation or an agency regulation could be equally useful in understanding why a certain therapeutic approach has been adopted.

We hope that as you think about the array of policy responses to substance abuse presented here, you will increase your awareness of the importance to our society of (1) sorting out the many political, moral, and legal aspects of substance abuse policy; (2) reaching a consensus about the levels of seriousness of abuse; and (3) developing the most effective and humane ways of dealing with the phenomenon.

Selected Web Sites on Substance Abuse

Alcoholics Anonymous (AA)

www.alcoholics-anonymous.org

Provides information on Alcoholics Anonymous and its affiliated groups for professionals, recovering alcoholics, and others.

American Civil Liberties Union (ACLU)

www.aclu.org

This site includes information on legal and civil liberties issues related to drug policies.

Dual Diagnosis

http://users.erols.com/ksciacca

Provides information and resources for professionals, consumers, and family members about co-occurring mental illness, drug addiction, and/or alcoholism.

Mothers Against Drunk Driving (MADD)

www.madd.org

Provides information on this advocacy group, which includes fathers, young people, and others concerned about drunk driving and its victims. Press releases, research, information on MADD programs, and statistics are available.

Narcotics Anonymous (NA)

http://na.org

Provides information about Narcotics Anonymous for professionals, recovering drug addicts, and others.

National Institute of Mental Health

www.nimh.nih.gov

Discusses research on dual diagnosis and its treatment.

U.S. Substance Abuse and Mental Health Services Administration

www.samhsa.gov

Provides information on the federal agency within the Department of Health and Human Services charged with improving the quality and availability of prevention, treatment, and rehabilitation services in the United States. News releases, fact sheets, and statistics, including the National Household Survey on Drug Abuse, are available.

Notes

1. U.S. Department of Health and Human Services, Substance Abuse and Mental Health Services Administration, *2004 National Survey on Drug Abuse Health* (online at www.oas.SAMHSA.gov).

2. Barry Stimmel, *Drug Abuse and Social Policy in America: The War That Must Be Won* (New York: Haworth Medical Press, 1996), pp. xi–xii; Douglas N. Husak, *Drugs and Rights* (New York: Cambridge University Press, 1992), pp. 1–8.

3. Anna Celeste Burke, "Substance Abuse: Legal Issues," in Richard L. Edwards and June Gary Hopps, Eds., *Encyclopedia of Social Work*, 19th ed., Vol. III (Washington, DC: National Association of Social Workers Press, 1995), p. 2348; American Psychiatric Association, *Quick Reference to the Diagnostic Criteria*

from DSM-IV™ (Washington, DC: Author, 1994), pp. 108–109, 112.

4. David N. Saunders, "Substance Abuse: Federal, State, and Local Policies," *Encyclopedia of Social Work*, Vol. III, p. 2338; Robert M. Bray and Mary Ellen Marsden, Eds., *Drug Use in Metropolitan America* (Thousand Oaks, CA: Sage, 1999), pp. 38, 74.

5. U.S. Department of Health and Human Services, National Institute on Alcohol Abuse and Alcoholism, "Estimating the Economic Cost of Alcohol Abuse," *Alcohol Alert*, No. 11, PH 293 (January 1991), pp. 1–2 (online at http://silk.nih.gov/silk/niaaa1/publication/aa11.htm); U.S. Department of Health and Human Services, National Institute on Drug Abuse and National Institute on Alcohol Abuse and Alcoholism,

"Executive Summary," *The Economic Costs of Alcohol and Drug Abuse in the United States—1992*, pp. 1–5 (online at www.nida.nih.gov/EconomicCosts/Chapter1.html).

6. Bray and Marsden, *Drug Use in Metropolitan America*, pp. 252–257; Lawrence M. Berger and Jane Waldfogel, "Prenatal Cocaine Exposure: Long-Run Effects and Policy Implications," *Social Service Review* 74 (March 2000), pp. 28–37; David Lewis, The Center for Alcohol and Addictions Studies, Brown University, "Pregnant Substance Abusers Need Our Help" (30 June 1998) (online at www.jointogether.org); Patrick Zickler, "NIDA Studies Clarify Developmental Effects of Prenatal Cocaine Exposure," *NIDA Notes* 14, National Institute on Drug Abuse (September 1999), pp. 5–7; Beth Azar, "Researchers Debunk the Myth of the 'Crack Baby,'" *APA* (American Psychological Association) *Monitor* (December 1997) (online at www.apa.org/dec97).

7. Cynthia Crosson-Tower, *Exploring Child Welfare* (Boston: Allyn and Bacon, 1998), pp. 93–94.

8. Carl G. Leukefeld and Robert Walker, "Substance Abuse Disorders," in Janet B. Williams and Kathleen Ell, Eds., *Advances in Mental Health Research: Implications for Practice* (Washington, DC: National Association of Social Workers Press, 1998), pp. 191–192; Crosson-Tower, *Exploring Child Welfare*, p. 96.

9. U.S. Department of Health and Human Services, Substance Abuse and Mental Health Administration, *2004 National Survey on Drug Use and Health*, (online at www.oas.SAMHSA.gov).

10. Saunders, "Substance Abuse: Federal, State, and Local Policies," pp. 2338–2339; Bruce Bullington, "America's Drug War: Fact or Fiction?" in Ross Coomber, Ed., *The Control of Drugs and Drug Abusers: Reason or Reaction?* (Amsterdam, Netherlands: Harwood Academic Publishers, 1998), pp. 124–125; Michael Grossman, Frank J. Chaloupka, and Kyumin Shin, "Illegal Drug Use and Public Policy,"*Health Affairs* 21 (March/April 2002) p. 135; Jacqueline Cohen and Steven Jay Levy, *The Mentally Ill Chemical Abuser: Whose Client?* (New York: Lexington Books, 1992), p. 85; Adele Harrell, "Drug Abuse," in George Galster, Ed., *Reality and Research: Social Science and U.S. Urban Policy since 1960* (Washington, DC: Urban Institute Press, 1995), p. 172; Jonathan Alter, "The Buzz on Drugs," *Newsweek* (6 September 1999), p. 26.

11. Nanette J. Davis and Clarice Stasz, *Social Control of Deviance: A Critical Perspective* (New York: McGraw-Hill, 1990), pp. 122–123.

12. Davis and Stasz, *Social Control of Deviance*, pp. 92–93.

13. Davis and Stasz, *Social Control of Deviance*, pp. 93–94.

14. Davis and Stasz, *Social Control of Deviance*, p. 124; Cohen and Levy, *The Mentally Ill Chemical Abuser*, p. 85; Michael Woodiwiss, "Reform, Racism, and Rackets: Alcohol and Drug Prohibition in the United States," in Coomber, Ed., *The Control of Drugs and Drug Abusers*, pp. 13–14.

15. Davis and Stasz, *Social Control of Deviance*, p. 94; Woodiwiss, "Reform, Racism, and Rackets," p. 16.

16. Davis and Stasz, *Social Control of Deviance*, pp. 94–95; Woodiwiss, "Reform, Racism, and Rackets," pp. 18–21.

17. Cohen and Levy, *The Mentally Ill Chemical Abuser*, pp. 86, 88–89; Woodiwiss, "Reform, Racism, and Rackets," pp. 21–28.

18. Cohen and Levy, *The Mentally Ill Chemical Abuser*, pp. 86, 88–89; Husak, *Drugs and Rights*, pp. 27–30.

19. Harrell, "Drug Abuse," pp. 162–163.

20. Harrell, "Drug Abuse," pp. 163–164; Anna Celeste Burke, "Between Entitlement and Control: Dimensions of U.S. Drug Policy," *Social Service Review* 66 (December 1992), pp. 572–573.

21. Harrell, "Drug Abuse," pp. 167–168; Burke, "Between Entitlement and Control," p. 573.

22. Harrell, "Drug Abuse," pp. 168–169; Burke, "Substance Abuse: Legal Issues," p. 2350.

23. Harrell, "Drug Abuse," pp. 169–170; Burke, "Substance Abuse: Legal Issues," p. 2354.

24. Saunders, "Substance Abuse: Federal, State, and Local Policies," p. 2340; Burke, "Substance Abuse: Legal Issues," p. 2354.

25. David Stoesz, *Small Change: Domestic Policy under the Clinton Presidency* (New York: Longman, 1996), p. 97; Harrell, "Drug Abuse," pp. 171–172.

26. Harrell, "Drug Abuse," pp. 173–174; Saunders, "Substance Abuse: Federal, State, and Local Policies," p. 2341; James A. Inciardi, Duane C. McBride, and James E. Rivers, *Drug Control and the Courts* (Thousand Oaks, CA: Sage, 1996), pp. 86–88; Mike McCloy, "Eleven Counties Seek $9 Million for Drug Courts," *The Arizona Republic* (16 January 2001), p. B5.

27. Harrell, "Drug Abuse," pp. 173–174; Timothy Egan, "A Drug Ran Its Course, Then Hid with Its Users," *New York Times* (19 September 1999), p. 1.

28. Egan, "A Drug Ran Its Course, Then Hid with Its Users," pp. 1, 27; Bray and Marsden, *Drug Use in Metropolitan America*, p. 75; National Institute on Drug Abuse, *Community Drug Alert Bulletin* (Washington, DC: U.S. Department of Health and Human Services, December 1999); Kendra Nichols, "The Other

Performance-Enhancing Drugs," *The Chronicle of Higher Education* (17 December 2004), p. 42; Lyn Stoesen, "Drug Use among Teens Has Declined," *NASW News* 50, (March 2005), p. 9.

29. Alice M. Young, "Addictive Drugs and the Brain," *Phi Kappa Phi National Forum* 79 (Fall 1994), pp. 15–18, 23; National Institute on Alcohol Abuse and Alcoholism "The Genetics of Alcoholism," *Alcohol Alert*, No. 18, PH 357 (July 1995) (online at http://silk.nih.gov/silk/niaaa1/publication/aa18htm); Harrell, "Drug Abuse," p. 176; Brian E. Bride and Larry Nackerud, "The Disease Model of Alcoholism: A Kuhnian Paradigm," *Journal of Sociology and Social Welfare* (29 June 2002), pp. 125–141.

30. Harrell, "Drug Abuse," p. 176; National Institute on Alcohol Abuse and Alcoholism, "Alcohol Research and Public Health Policy," *Alcohol Alert*, No. 20, PH 330 (April 1993) (online at http://silk.nih.gov/silk/niaaa1/publication/aa20htm).

31. Bray and Marsden, *Drug Use in Metropolitan America*, pp. 304–305.

32. Harrell, "Drug Abuse," p. 160.

33. "Alcoholic Beverages and Tobacco," *Standard and Poor's Industry Surveys* 171 (23 January 2003), p. 9; Joel W. Grube and Lawrence Wallack, "Television Beer Advertising and Drinking Knowledge, Beliefs, and Intentions among Schoolchildren," *American Journal of Public Health* 84 (February 1994), pp. 254–258; Saunders, "Substance Abuse: Federal, State, and Local Policies," p. 2340.

34. Alcoholics Anonymous, *AA at a Glance* (online at www.alcoholics-anonymous.org), and *AA as a Resource for the Health Care Professional* (April 1999).

35. John V. O'Neill, "Expertise in Addictions Said Crucial," *NASW News* 46 (January 2001), p. 10; "Specialist Credentials Are Readied," *NASW News* 44 (September 1999), pp. 1, 10.

36. Cohen and Levy, *The Mentally Ill Chemical Abuser: Whose Client?*, pp. 18–21; Narcotics Anonymous, "Networking with Professionals" (26 March 2000) (online at www.na.org/networking.htm).

37. Harrell, "Drug Abuse," p. 157.

38. Saunders, "Substance Abuse: Federal, State, and Local Policies," p. 2344.

39. William Booth, "Florida County Sets Drug Tests for Welfare Clients," *Washington Post* (17 September 1996), sec. A, p. 3. J. Dennis Tyler, BCSAC, was a very helpful consultant on the material in this and other sections of the chapter.

40. John Jeter, "Maryland May Tie Drug Testing, Welfare Cash," *Washington Post* (4 December 1996), sec. A, pp. 1, 16.

41. Associated Press, April 10, 2003, Lelfarem listserv@hermes.gwu.edu; Booth, "Florida County Sets Drug Tests"; E. Anderson, "Drug Testing Begins for Welfare Recipients," *New Orleans Times-Picayune* (23 July 1998), sec. A, pp. 1, 12; D. Meyers and C. Redmond, "Stiffer Tests Urged," *Baton Rouge Advocate* (6 August 1998), sec. A, pp. 1, 4.

42. Jeter, "Maryland May Tie Drug Testing, Welfare Cash," sec. A, p. 16; Booth, "Florida County Sets Drug Tests," sec. A, p. 3; U.S. Department of Health and Human Services, *Highlights, 1998 National Household Survey on Drug Abuse*, Table 11; Guy Coates, "Welfare Drug Screening Off to Shaky Start," *New Orleans Times-Picayune* (1 August 1999), sec. A, p. 4.

43. Kelley O. Beaucar, "Federal Study Profiles Substance Abuse: Chamber of Commerce Notes Value of Employee Assistance Programs," *NASW News* 45 (January 2000), p. 10.

44. Joe Sexton, "Dependency's Double Edge," *New York Times* (9 November 1997), p. 38; Associated Press, April 10, 2003, Corinna Valliantos, "Association Backing Given in Two Cases," *NASW News* 46 (April 2001), p. 11; Jeter, "Maryland May Tie Drug Testing, Welfare Cash," p. A16; Karen Seccombe, *"So You Think I Drive a Cadillac?" Welfare Recipients' Perspectives on the System and Its Reform* (Boston: Allyn and Bacon, 1999), p. 107; Robyn Meredith, "Judge Halts Drug Tests of Welfare Applicants," *New York Times* (11 November 1999), p. A14.

45. Booth, "Florida County Sets Drug Tests for Welfare Clients."

46. Jon Jeter, "Drug Testing Plan Could Balloon Maryland Welfare Costs," *Washington Post* (5 December 1996), sec. E, pp. 1–5; Jon Jeter, "Welfare Panel in Maryland Alters Drug Strategy," *Washington Post* (30 January 1997), sec. C, pp. 1, 5.

47. John V. O'Neill, "Substance Abuse: The Common Thread," *NASW News* 44 (July 1999), p. 3; "Commentary: Drug Abuse and Addiction Treatment Research, the Next Generation," *Archives of General Psychiatry* 54 (August 1997), p. 692; Sheldon Zimberg, "Introduction and General Concepts of Dual Diagnosis," in Joel Solomon, Sheldon Zimberg, and Edward Shollar, Eds., *Dual Diagnosis: Evaluation, Treatment, Training, and Program Development* (New York: Plenum, 1993), pp. 5–6. We credit Todd Atkins with introducing us to the important topic of treatment policies for the dually diagnosed.

48. Zimberg, "Introduction and General Concepts of Dual Diagnosis," p. 7; Leukefeld and Walker, "Substance Abuse Disorders," p. 193.

49. Leukefeld and Walker, "Substance Abuse Disorders," pp. 192–193; Zimberg, "Introduction and General Concepts of Dual Diagnosis," pp. 4–5; Charles Ciolino, "Substance Abuse and Mood Disorders," in Mark S. Gold and Andrew E. Slaby, Eds., *Dual Diagnosis in Substance Abuse* (New York: Marcel Dekker, 1991), pp. 105–107, 111–112.

50. Zimberg, "Introduction and General Concepts of Dual Disorders," pp. 7–8.

51. Burke, "Between Entitlement and Control," p. 573; Cohen and Levy, *The Mentally Ill Chemical Abuser*, pp. 8, 21–22.

52. Gold and Slaby, *Dual Diagnosis in Substance Abuse*, p. iii.

53. Zimberg, "Introduction and General Concepts of Dual Diagnosis," pp. 3–4; Anne Marie Pagliaro and Louis A. Pagliaro, *Substance Use among Children and Adolescents: Its Nature, Extent, and Effects from Conception to Adulthood* (New York: John Wiley, 1996), p. 161.

54. See, for example, James A. Cocores, "Treatment of the Dually Diagnosed Adult Drug User," in Gold and Slaby, *Dual Diagnosis in Substance Abuse*, pp. 237–251.

chapter 11

Child Welfare: Family Preservation Policy

Life for many children in the United States is far more difficult than it should be. The Children's Defense Fund has gathered data indicating that on an average day in the United States 4 children are killed by abuse or neglect, 5 children or teens commit suicide, 8 children or teens are killed by firearms, 390 babies are born to mothers who received late or no prenatal care, 860 babies are born at low birth-weights, 1,186 babies are born to teen mothers, 2,076 babies are born without health insurance, 2,385 babies are born into poverty, 2,482 children are confirmed abused or neglected, and 3,742 babies are born to unmarried mothers, 4,262 children are arrested, and 16,964 public school students are suspended.[1] To these figures could be added the millions of children who each day suffer under conditions of extreme poverty or are afflicted by severe mental or behavioral disorders. Our society's concern for these problems is expressed in a formal service delivery system known as child welfare. This system is composed of government and private agencies that are given the responsibility to

- protect and promote the well-being of all children
- support families and seek to prevent problems that may result in neglect, abuse, and exploitation
- promote family stability by assessing and building on family strengths while addressing needs
- support the full array of out-of-home care services for children who require them
- take responsibility for addressing social conditions that negatively affect children and families, such as inadequate housing, poverty, chemical dependence, and lack of access to health care
- support the strengths of families whenever possible
- intervene when necessary to ensure the safety and well-being of children[2]

Although child welfare has a broad mandate, as a field of social work and of social welfare policy it has in recent decades focused more and more on the problems of child neglect and, even more so, abuse, providing what are known as child protective services. This narrowing of focus has been driven by two developments. The first is a rapidly increasing awareness among the general populace of the problem of child abuse, resulting in an ever-more efficient system for reporting abuse, and laws in every state mandating that professionals who deal with children report suspicions of abuse. The result of this is that maltreatment reports have increased from 9,563 in 1967 to about 3 million in 2003.[3] The other development contributing to the narrowing of focus is that funding for child welfare has not increased fast enough to allow agencies to deal with the massive increase in reports while still attending to broader child welfare concerns. Thus, broader concerns such as day care and child health have been pushed aside while agencies spend an ever-increasing proportion of their resources on child protection.

It is an old truism that every solution contains within it the seeds of a new problem. This has proven to be true in child protective services. One of the obvious ways to deal with a child in a substandard or dangerous home situation is to move the child from the home into substitute care. After the child is placed, the home can be assessed and, if there is hope for remediation, services can be delivered to strengthen the family and eventually return the child home. Predictably, as the number of reports of child abuse and neglect skyrocketed, the number of children in foster care kept pace. Unfortunately, as the number of children needing foster care has increased, the number of licensed foster homes has not kept pace. Between 1990 and 2003, the number of children in foster care increased by 27 percent while the number of foster homes increased by only 16 percent.[4]

At the same time the child welfare system is being subjected to increasing pressure to protect abused and neglected children, it is also being severely criticized for breaking up families and then not providing services to rebuild them. The child welfare system has been criticized for being overzealous, not following due process, and trampling on the rights of parents accused of abuse and neglect of their children. A political action group, VOCAL (Victims of Child Abuse Laws), has been formed to champion the cause of parents involved in the child welfare system.[5] Although many of these critics greatly overstate their case, it is true that the system deserves criticism for not putting enough effort into helping families resolve problems once a child has been removed. Child welfare researchers have found that once a child is removed from the biological parents, the amount of clinical services provided to the child and parents actually declines.[6] The National Center for Resource Family Support found that reunification was a goal for only 42 percent of foster children in 2000.[7]

The combination of these factors, as well as others that will be discussed later in this chapter, has led to great pressure on the child welfare system to reduce the number of children placed in foster care. One possible remedy, enthusiastically embraced by almost all stakeholders in the system, is an approach known as family preservation. This approach is based on the belief that in many cases in which placement appears to be imminent, it is possible to prevent placement by the provision of intense services delivered in the child's home over a brief, time-limited period. Elizabeth Tracy lists five primary goals of family preservation services:

- to allow children to remain safely in their own homes
- to maintain and strengthen family bonds
- to stabilize the crisis situation that precipitated the need for placement
- to increase the family's coping skills and competencies
- to facilitate the family's use of appropriate formal and informal helping resources[8]

Family preservation services begin, as do most child welfare interventions, with a child being referred to an agency as being in danger of serious harm. A social worker investigates the complaint and, if the complaint is confirmed, decides whether the family is a good candidate for family preservation services. For the family to be considered an appropriate case for family preservation services, the child must be at risk of placement, but the social worker must be convinced that the child can remain safely in his or her own home if intensive services are provided. Depending on the model of family preservation being applied, the family is given services for periods ranging from four to six weeks in the most intensive to three months or longer in the less intensive models. The social workers providing services have small caseloads and work with each family for many hours each week, sometimes twenty or more. After the provision of the brief, intensive services, the agency withdraws to a supervisory role and leaves the family to function—presumably with a greatly increased problem-solving capacity. Figure 11.1 summarizes the differences between traditional child welfare social services and family preservation services.

The several models of family preservation differ in length and intensity of service and also in psychosocial theory base. The original model, called Homebuilders,

Figure 11.1   Service Delivery Contrasts

Traditional Social Services	Family Preservation Services
Services in office	Services in client's home
Waiting list	Immediate response
50-minute hour	As long as session is needed
Weekly or less	Frequent—often daily
Business-only hours	7 days a week, 24 hours a day
Selective intake	Accept almost all cases
Worker defines solutions	Family selects solutions
Indefinite duration	Predetermined length
Long-term, often years	Short-term, four to six weeks
Large caseloads, 12 to 50	Small caseloads, 2 to 3
Focus on individual	Focus on family system
Concentrate on immediate symptom	Concentrate on underlying skills and interactions
Soft services only	Blend of hard and soft services
No special use of crisis	Use crisis as teachable moment
Solve problem for client	Help client solve own problem

Reprinted with permission, Edna McConnell Clark Foundation. From *For Children's Sake: The Promise of Family Preservation,* by Joan Barthel, 1992.

provides the shortest and most intense services. In this model, social workers carry only two cases at a time, spend as many as twenty hours a week with each case, are available twenty-four hours a day, and generally complete services within four to six weeks. This approach is based on cognitive–behavioral theory and relies heavily on devices such as behavioral checklists. The Homebuilders approach also focuses on concrete services. Another approach is based on structural family therapy, utilizes family systems theory, and emphasizes the relationship between the family and other systems. Special attention is given to improving the relations of the family with the community. In this model, social workers have somewhat larger caseloads and work with each family over a longer period of time, generally three to twelve months. Other variations of family preservation utilize psychodynamic and behavioral approaches and involve longer periods of contact with families.[9]

Since its inception in 1974 with the original Homebuilders program, family preservation has grown in popularity until it can now be said to be the policy of choice for dealing with child abuse and neglect. Some form of family preservation service is now in place in every state of the union. The services are provided by both public and private agencies, generally in some form of partnership. The approach is specified in laws at both the federal and state levels and in the policies of public and private agencies. The approach is probably undergoing the most thorough evaluation of any social welfare innovation in history; it has become so popular that a backlash has developed against it. We now turn to a detailed discussion of the development of child protective services and the growth and current dominance of family preservation as the service of choice.

Historical Analysis

If a time machine were to transport someone from the early nineteenth century into the present age, they would find child protective services almost as baffling as all of our technological marvels. Although few people during this earlier age would have approved of unnecessary cruelty or neglect toward children, the notion of children as a group with the right to protection, and of the government as having the right to provide such protection, was entirely foreign to the thinking of the era. By the end of the nineteenth century, thinking on this matter had undergone a remarkable transformation. Many people, particularly those in the middle and upper classes, had begun to believe firmly in the right of children to a certain level of care and the right of government to step in and enforce the provision of adequate care when parents were judged to be unable, or unwilling, to provide such care.

Two general developments during the nineteenth century account for the changing attitude toward the rights of children to protection and of government to provide it. The first is that during that century, the position of children in the economy changed radically, and along with this the method of valuing children. During the early years of the century, children had direct economic worth and their rights and value were judged accordingly. Viviana Zelizer, in her book *Pricing the Priceless Child*, documents how during the nineteenth century the concept of the "useful" child who made a valuable contribution to the family economy gradually evolved into the "useless" child of the twentieth century who is economically worthless, in fact very costly, to the family, but is considered to be emotionally priceless. The reasons for this transformation were many, including the decline in useful tasks that could be performed by children in a maturing industrial economy, the decline in birth and death rates, and the rise of the compassionate family. Because of this changed concept of the value of children, society began to view them as worthy of protection.[10]

The second general factor that accounts for the emergence of child protection at the end on the nineteenth century is, in fact, one result of the first. Stemming from the changed conception of the value of children, there evolved a change in the common law interpretation of children's and women's rights. Before the nineteenth century, the relationship between parents and children in this country generally followed English common law. Under the law at that time, children's rights were considered to be relatively unimportant. Likewise, mothers were entitled to "no power but only reverence and respect." The father, in contrast, was given practically absolute control over all matters pertaining to his wife and children. Although fathers were expected to protect and care for their children, the duty was "merely a moral obligation creating no civil liability." In other words, if a father was cruel or neglectful toward his children, society would not approve but was powerless to intervene. In the second half of the nineteenth century, the system of family law began to change. Two new legal principles emerged as dominant. One was the recognition of equal rights between mother and father, with the mother's rights, at least in regard to children, often being given preference. The second was the recognition by the legal system of children as being of paramount importance, vital to the future of society, and therefore as appropriate objects of the court's protection.[11]

The Child Rescue Movement

By the second half of the nineteenth century, the stage was set for outside intervention into family life for the purpose of protecting children. An incident in New York City in 1873 served to ignite what has come to be called the child rescue movement. Henry Bergh was a prominent philanthropist who had directed his efforts toward the protection of animals and, for this purpose, had in 1866 founded the New York Society for the Prevention of Cruelty to Animals (SPCA). It was to Bergh and his society that charity worker Etta Wheeler turned with her concern about the treatment of Mary Ellen Wilson, an eight-year-old girl who was being abused and neglected by her stepparents. Bergh directed his attorney, Elbridge T. Gerry, to seek custody of the child and prosecution of the stepparents. Gerry did this and, amidst much publicity, was successful. Media coverage of the Mary Ellen Wilson case caused a flood of public opinion resulting in the passage in New York in 1875 of "an Act of the incorporation of societies for the prevention of the cruelty to children."[12] The idea of organizing to protect children from cruel treatment caught on and in a very few years there was an anticruelty society in every major city in the country. In a manner similar to the SPCA, agents of the new child protection societies were quasi law-enforcement officers with power to "prefer a complaint before any court or magistrate having jurisdiction for the violation of any law relating to or affecting children." In 1877 the American Humane Association (AHA) was incorporated to provide coordination among the local societies and to disseminate information and provide assistance. By 1900 its membership was composed of 150 humane societies throughout the country, most dealing with both child and animal protection, but about twenty restricting their activities to protection of children.[13]

The Societies for the Prevention of Cruelty to Children (SPCC) did not view themselves as social welfare agencies. Rather, they viewed themselves as law-enforcement agencies specializing in the investigation of charges of child abuse and neglect. When they received a complaint, they would conduct an investigation and, if the charge was substantiated, remove the child and prosecute the parents. The child would be turned over to a child placement agency or children's home, and the SPCC would close the case and have no further responsibility for the child. Only in cases of lost or kidnapped children did the society ever consider returning the child to its parents. In describing the work of the Massachusetts Society for the Prevention of Cruelty to Children, its board chairman, Grafton Cushing, said in 1906, "There is no attempt to discover the cause of the conditions which make action by the [society] necessary, and therefore no endeavor to prevent a recurrence of these conditions. In other words, there is no 'social' work done. It is all legal or police work."[14]

Social Work Takes Over

From its onset, there were many problems with the child rescue approach. Among these were that it was not concerned with prevention of child maltreatment; it gave no recognition to the possibility that a child might love his or her family despite its problems and prefer to remain in the family of origin; and it had no appreciation for the difficulties of establishing a viable life for the child once the child was removed. At the same time the child rescue movement was emerging, social work as a profession and as a scientific approach to social problems was also emerging.

It was not long before people both inside and outside the child rescue agencies began to advocate for a social work approach to the problem of child maltreatment.

The foremost advocate for a social work approach to child welfare was C. Carl Carstens, a trained social worker appointed in 1906 as director of the Massachusetts Society for the Prevention of Cruelty to Children. Carstens advanced a new approach to child maltreatment that came to be known as child protection, as opposed to child rescue. The child protection approach involved providing personal services to families with the goal of preventing the recurrence of maltreatment; seeking out the causes of abuse, neglect, exploitation, and delinquency; and preventing maltreatment through environmental reforms. When the 1912 annual meeting of the American Humane Association rejected Carstens's proposal that the child rescue approach be replaced by a child protection approach, he withdrew the Massachusetts society from membership in the AHA and founded the Bureau for the Exchange of Information among Child-Helping Agencies, which in 1921 became the Child Welfare League of America (CWLA).[15]

Carstens became the first executive director of the CWLA and retained this position until his death in 1939. During his tenure, the CWLA and the AHA remained competitors around the issue of whether a child rescue or a child protection approach was the appropriate response to the problem of child maltreatment. However, gradually the AHA began to change and by the time of Carstens's death had adopted standards that referred to child protection and defined it as "a specialized service in the general field of child welfare" and recognized that the work involved "psychological factors" as well as "standards of physical care." The standards further called for member organizations to employ workers with college degrees and "special training in the social sciences and knowledge and experience in the social and legal phases of child protection work."[16]

During the same period that social work was taking over the field of child welfare, forces were also at work moving the responsibility from private to public auspices. The American Humane Association, the societies for the prevention of cruelty to children, the Child Welfare League of America, and all of the loosely affiliated agencies were all privately funded and operated. This arrangement befitted an era when government was small and took little responsibility for anything beyond "protecting our shores and delivering the mail," as the expression went. As the twentieth century progressed, government showed an increasing willingness to be active in the area of social welfare in general and child welfare in particular. The 1909 White House Conference on Children resulted in the establishment in 1912 of the U.S. Children's Bureau, located in the Department of Commerce and Labor. The Bureau was charged with investigation and reporting on "all matters pertaining to the welfare of children and child life among all classes of our people."[17] In 1918 the Infancy and Maternity Health

Bill (Sheppard–Towner Act) was passed, which set up infant and maternal health centers administered by state health departments. In 1935, child welfare services became a predominantly public function with the passage of the Social Security Act, which, under provisions of Title IV, Grants to States for Aid to Dependent Children, and of Title V, Grants to States for Maternal and Child Welfare, mandated that all states provide services for dependent children and provided funding for these services.

Child Abuse Becomes the Dominant Theme

During the earlier part of the twentieth century, when child welfare was becoming a social work function and a responsibility of the public sector, it was a relatively small and broad-based area of social welfare. In 1955, for example, there were only slightly more than 5,000 professional employees of public child welfare agencies nationally.[18] The eleven-page entry on child welfare in the 1949 *Social Work Yearbook* devotes only two paragraphs, less than one-third of a page, to "Protection from Neglect and Cruelty." The remainder of the entry deals with a wide range of child welfare concerns including poverty, health care, disabilities, and juvenile delinquency.[19] A series of related events that began in the 1950s has resulted in the child welfare system experiencing tremendous growth while at the same time narrowing to an almost exclusive focus on child abuse and neglect.

The event that triggered these changes in the child welfare system was the discovery of child abuse by the medical profession. Due to advances in radiological techniques, physicians began to identify traumatic injuries in children that did not fit any known explanation. Physicians were hesitant to blame these unexplained injuries on parents until 1955, when P. V. Woolley and W. A. Evans investigated the home situations of a sample of children displaying such injuries and found that the infants "came invariably from unstable households with a high incidence of neurotic or frankly psychotic behavior on the part of at least one adult."[20] The wide public attention given the findings of Woolley and Evans virtually exploded into an anti–child abuse crusade six years later when pediatrician Henry Kempe published the results of his research on child abuse under the catchy name the "battered child syndrome." Social policy expert Alvin Shore considers this to be a

> blow to child welfare . . . with the identification of child abuse as a specific family and social problem. The model of child abuse that was offered and was bought by legislatures and the public was the so-called medical model: a distinguishable pathological agent attacking the individual or family that could be treated in a prescribed manner and would disappear. This model does not characterize child abuse accurately, but belief in it leads to public frustration, if not fury, that abuse persists. So identifying child abuse as a problem led to public dissatisfaction with child welfare agencies and an enormous number of children to care for.[21]

Table 11.1   Increase in Reports of Child Abuse

Year	Abuse Reports	Rate per 1,000 Children
1967	9,563	0.1
1975	294,796	4.5
1980	1,154,000	18.0
1985	1,919,000	30.0
1990	2,559,000	40.0
1994	3,110,000	46.0
1997	3,195,000	47.0
1999	3,244,000	46.0
2004	3,000,000	42.6

Source: Duncan Lindsey, *The Welfare of Children* (New York: Oxford University Press, 1994), p. 93; Karen McCurdy and Deborah Daro, *Current Trends in Child Abuse Reporting and Fatalities: The Results of the 1994 Annual Fifty State Survey* (Chicago: National Committee to Prevent Child Abuse, 1995), p. 5; Ching-Tung Wang and Deborah Daro, *Current Trends in Child Abuse Reporting and Fatalities: The Results of the 1997 Annual Fifty State Survey* (Chicago: National Committee to Prevent Child Abuse, 1998), Table 1; Nancy Peddle and Ching-Tung Wang, *Current Trends in Child Abuse Prevention, Reporting and Fatalities* (Chicago: National Center on Child Abuse Research, 2001), p. iv; and U.S. Department of Health and Human Services, Administration on Children, Youth and Families, *Child Maltreatment 2004* (Washington, DC: U.S. Government Printing Office, 2006).

A major result of the "discovery" of child abuse by the medical profession and the corresponding widespread public knowledge and interest in the problem was the development of child abuse reporting laws. In the early 1960s, the Children's Bureau developed a model law that was adopted by thirteen states by 1963. By 1966, every state had passed a mandatory child abuse reporting law. The original laws required only physicians to report, but objections by the medical profession led to the laws being quickly broadened to also require other professions with frequent contact with children to report.[22] As a quick inspection of Table 11.1 illustrates, the combination of these reporting laws with the heightened public awareness caused by radio, television, and press coverage resulted in a huge increase in the number of child abuse reports to public agencies.

The massive increase in child abuse referrals created a major problem for child welfare agencies. The heightened public awareness of the problem led to large increases in staff, but these have not nearly kept pace with the increased demand for services. As Table 11.2 illustrates, the size of the child welfare staff increased by 128 percent between 1967 and 1977; however, during this same time period, the number of child abuse complaints requiring investigation increased by 8,663 percent. This trend has continued and has resulted in child welfare agencies assigning an ever-increasing proportion of staff to the function of protective services until this one service has virtually taken over public child welfare agencies. In their 1990 analysis of child welfare, Sheila Kamerman and Alfred Kahn confirmed this phenomenon, concluding,

Table 11.2   Increase in Child Welfare Staff as Related
               to Child Abuse Referrals

Year	Child Welfare Professional Staff	Child Abuse Referrals
1967	14,000	9,563
1977	32,000	838,000
Percent increase	128%	8,663%

Source: Duncan Lindsey, *The Welfare of Children,* 2nd ed. (New York: Oxford University Press, 2004), p. 20; Karen McCurdy and Deborah Daro, *Current Trends in Child Abuse Reporting and Fatalities: The Results of the 1994 Annual Fifty State Survey* (Chicago: National Committee to Prevent Child Abuse, 1995), p. 5.

Child Protective Services (CPS) (covering physical abuse, sexual abuse, and neglect reports, investigations, assessments, and resultant actions) have emerged as the dominant public child and family service, in effect "driving" the public agency and often taking over child welfare entirely. . . . Child protective services today constitute the core public child and family service, the fulcrum and some-times, in some places, the totality of the system. Depending on the terms used, public social service agency administrators state either that "Child protection is child welfare," or that "The increased demand for child protection has driven out all other child welfare services."[23]

Foster Care—From Solution to Problem

The beginnings of foster care in the United States were characterized by the same child rescue approach that characterized the societies for the prevention of cruelty to children. The originator of the idea of foster care was the Reverend Charles Loring Brace, who founded the New York Children's Aid Society in 1853. Brace's idea was to take homeless children from the streets of New York, where they were begin-ning to be perceived as a serious threat to social order, and transport them to rural regions of the country to be placed with farm families. Brace perceived this to be a win–win proposition, as the result would be homes for homeless children and ad-ditional hands to help the farm families with their labor-intensive lifestyle.

The technique of the Children's Aid Society was to gather homeless children in shelters in New York City and, when a large enough group was gathered, to send them by train to towns in the Midwest. Agents of the Children's Aid Society would precede the train into each town, organize a local placement committee of prominent citizens, and advertise the location and the date the children would be available for placement. When the day arrived, local families would inspect the children, and families who were deemed suitable by both the society's agent and the local committee could select one or more children. No money was exchanged between the parents and the society. As Verlene McOllough reports, "Willing families would sign placing-out agreements guaranteeing the child the same food, lodging, and education children born to them would receive. In return the child would become part of the family, which in the nineteenth century generally meant taking on a sizable share of the work."[24] The work of the Children's Aid Society grew quickly and eventually became extensive. By 1873 the society was placing more than 3,000 children a year. Its peak year was 1875, when 4,026 children were placed.

The policies and techniques of the Children's Aid Society were the target of some well-deserved criticism. A major concern was that, in true child rescue fashion, if a child had living parents the society made no attempt to work with them so the child could return home. Quite the opposite; "as the Children's Aid Society ferreted out neglected children from the poorer districts, they convinced many impoverished parents that a child's best chance lay in permitting the society to find the child a new home far beyond the urban slums and its miseries."[25] Another criticism was raised by Catholics, who felt that the Children's Aid Society, founded and run by Protestants, was snatching Catholic children off the streets and sending them to the West to be reared as Protestants. Many of the states receiving children soon lost their enthusiasm for the society's work. Many of the children—one study estimated nearly 60 percent—became sources of trouble and public expenditure when their placements failed to work.[26] Finally, the most serious criticism was the lack of study, the generally casual nature of the placement process, and the almost total absence of follow-up supervision after a placement was made.

Although the Children's Aid Society's program had many flaws, the basic idea of placing dependent children in a family setting caught on and had a tremendous impact on child welfare practice. Toward the end of the nineteenth century, advocates for a social work child protection approach to child welfare, notably John Finley of the New York State Charities Aid Association, Charles Birtwell of the Boston Children's Aid Society, and Homer Folks of the Children's Aid Society of Pennsylvania, began to develop sound administrative procedures for child placement. These procedures included placement of the child in his or her home community, if possible; thorough study of the child and the prospective foster home; some financial support for the child; and careful supervision of the placement. By the turn of the twentieth century, foster care had replaced institutional placement in a number of cities. In 1909 the report of the first White House Conference on Children gave support to the foster care movement with the recommendation that "it is desirable that [children] should be cared for in families whenever practicable. The carefully selected foster home is for the normal child the best substitute for the natural home."[27] The spread of foster care continued until, by midcentury, it was the placement of choice for normal children who, for one reason or another, were not able to remain with their natural families.

Foster care became a standard item in the child welfare worker's tool kit and existed with little question or examination until the late 1950s. At this time, two things happened that began to profoundly shake social workers' and public policymakers' confidence in the foster care system. The first development was the publication of several studies of foster care that found serious deficiencies in the system. The second was the explosion of child abuse referrals, which led to a consequent explosion in the number of children placed in foster care and hence a huge increase in cost.

The study that opened the floodgates for criticism of the foster care system, conducted by Henry Maas and Richard Engler, was entitled *Children in Need of Parents*, published in 1959. Maas and Engler chose nine counties that were thought to be representative of the United States in general. They sent a research team into each community. The team

> studied these nine counties and, simultaneously, the children in care in each of them. Information about the children and their families was gathered from all sixty agencies serving the communities at the time of our study. Key persons were interviewed in each of the communities which produced these dependent children and/or offered placement resources. The legal systems through which many of these children came into care, or which influenced their destinies in care, were studied. And the networks of agencies serving these children and families were also examined.[28]

As there was no central data-reporting mechanism for foster care, the Maas and Engler study provided the first valid look into the overall picture of foster care in the United States. What they discovered was not comforting. They found that the assumption that foster care was a temporary respite for children and families experiencing difficulty was not true—the average length of a foster placement was three years; many children were destined to grow up in foster care, and in fewer than 25 percent of the cases was it probable that the child would ever be returned home. Equally disturbing was the finding that the parents of foster children indicated, in most cases, that they either had no relationship or a negative relationship with the child placement agencies, and in only one-third of the cases did a parent ever visit the child in care. In an afterword to the study, Child Welfare League of America Executive Director Joseph Reid referred to foster children as "orphans of the living."[29]

Following the study by Maas and Engler was a series of research studies revealing deficiencies in the foster care system and in the whole concept of foster care as the plan of choice for dependent and neglected children. A 1962 Children's Bureau national survey of child welfare agencies conducted by Helen Jeter corroborated the findings of Maas and Engler, estimating that 31 percent of children in placement were "in danger of growing up in foster care." Jeter found that for 64 percent of the children in public foster care, the only plan the agency had was to continue them in placement. Little evidence was found of work being done to address the problems that led to children being placed in foster care.[30] In 1966, David Fanshel and Eugene Shinn examined data from 659 children entering the New York foster care system and followed these children for the next five years. They found that the system was not guided by any systematic scientific knowledge or principles. Although they concluded that foster care had little harmful effect on the children, they also found that those children who eventually went home were returned to home situations that were little, if any, better than when they left. As in the Maas and Engler and the Jeter studies, Fanshel and Shinn found that many children were in foster care for long periods of time with little probability of ever returning home and with virtually no contact with their natural parents.[31]

These studies, along with a number of journalistic and legalistic treatises on foster care, such as Goldstein, Freud, and Solnit's influential *Beyond the Best Interests of the Child*, identified three major concerns regarding foster care. The first is that foster care was in many, if not most, cases not a temporary but rather a long-term situation. The second concern is with what came to be called "foster care drift." This referred to the finding that many children in foster care were not in one stable foster home but placed in a series of homes. The final problem was that agencies placing children in foster care rarely had any kind of long-term plan for the children other than for them to remain in care until such time as they could be returned home (often never). As a result of these concerns, a new approach to foster care was developed in the late 1970s and 1980s known as the permanency planning movement.

Permanency planning is based on several interrelated ideas:

1. The child's own home is the best place for him or her, and removal should occur only under extreme circumstances.
2. In instances in which a child is removed, a specific plan should be developed immediately, closely monitored, and revised as needed. The focus of the plan should be obtaining a permanent living arrangement for the child in as little time as possible.
3. The primary goal of the plan should be to return the child to his or her own home. If this is not possible, steps should be taken to legally free the child for a permanent placement at the earliest possible time.
4. The preferred plan for a child who cannot return to his or her biological home is adoption. No child is considered unadoptable.
5. If adoption is not an option, then a long-term foster care plan should be developed with the child, the agency, and the foster family all making a commitment to a permanent placement.

Permanency planning became a part of national social welfare policy with the passage of P.L. 96-272, the Adoption Assistance and Child Welfare Act of 1980. This act directs federal fiscal incentives toward permanency planning objectives—namely, the development of preventive and reunification services and adoption subsidies. For states to be eligible for increased federal funds, they must implement a service program designed either to reunite children with their families or to provide a permanent substitute home. They are required to take steps, such as the establishment of foster placement review committees and procedures for regular case review, that ensure that children enter foster care only when necessary, that they are placed appropriately, and that they are returned home or else moved on to permanent families in a timely fashion. The act also creates fiscal incentives for states to seek adoptive homes for hard-to-place children, including children who are disabled, older, or minority group members.[32]

When the permanency planning approach was implemented in the 1970s and 1980s, it appeared, for a while, that the problem of foster care was under control. The number of children in foster care declined from 520,000 in 1977 to 275,000 in 1984. However, after 1984 a number of factors in the social environment kicked in and caused this trend to reverse. Among these factors were the crack cocaine epidemic, economic problems leading to increased poverty and unemployment, AIDS, and a sharp rise in births to single mothers, particularly teenagers. By 1991 the number of children in foster care had risen to 429,000, and it is estimated that the number is currently at an all-time high of 581,000. Compounding the problems caused by the rapid increase in the number of children needing foster placement has been the corresponding decrease in the number of foster families. Between 1984 and 1989, the number of foster homes declined from 137,000 to 100,000.[33] Among the factors generally thought to explain the decline of foster homes are the increased employment of women outside the home, the low payments made to foster parents, inadequate support services for foster parents, and a lack of training opportunities for foster parents.[34]

The Emergence of Family Preservation

Selecting a beginning point for the history of a social policy is always somewhat arbitrary, but the date and event generally cited as the beginning of the family preservation movement is 1974, when the Homebuilders Program was piloted in Washington State. To hear the originators describe the program, it appears to have begun almost by accident. Three psychologists, Jill Kinney, David Haapala, and Charlotte Booth, submitted a grant application proposing to develop "super foster homes," which they conceptualized as foster placements backed up with lots of training and professional consultation.

Our funding agent, however, insisted that before placement, we try "sticking a staff member in to live with a family." This idea sounded outlandish, but it also seemed interesting. We knew we would learn about families, and since we wanted the super foster home funding, we decided to try the in-home services, assuming they would fail, our funding agent would be convinced, and we could then continue with our super foster home approach. . . . We were wrong: The approach was surprisingly effective.[35]

Two factors caused the idea of family preservation to be widely and rapidly embraced by the child welfare community. The first is the "reasonable efforts" provision of P.L. 96-272, the Adoption Assistance and Child Welfare Act of 1980. This provision requires that child welfare agencies provide services to prevent the necessity for placement and that courts determine whether the agency has made "reasonable efforts" to accomplish this end. The act does not specify what these reasonable efforts might be, but states have seized on family preservation services as a way to demonstrate that they are in compliance with the law. The second factor is the explosive increase in the number of children in foster care. Faced with a trend with no end in sight, and the accompanying increase in costs, states began to perceive foster care as a situation that was out of control. Family preservation offered a way to rein in the situation. In 1982 there were 20 family preservation programs nationwide; by 1988 this number had increased to 333 and by 1991 to more than 400.[36] Most of these programs were initially funded by federal demonstration grants and by grants from private foundations, notably the Annie E. Casey Foundation and the Edna McConnell Clark Foundation.

In 1993, family preservation became an explicit part of federal policy with the passage of P.L. 103-66, the Family Preservation and Support Program, which was part of the Omnibus Budget Reconciliation Act. The provisions of this act had a federal cost of one billion dollars over five years to provide states with funds for services to avoid foster care placement for children and to preserve and strengthen families. As this act included a 25 percent matching requirement from the states, the actual amount to be spent on family preservation services over five years was actually 1.25 billion dollars. As reported by the Congressional Research Service,

The legislation was developed in response to a widespread perception of crisis in the child welfare system, as indicated by dramatic growth in the numbers of child abuse and neglect reports and children entering foster care, beginning in the mid-1980s. As the caseload has grown, the child welfare system also has faced high staff turnover and low morale, a shrinking supply of foster parents and foster homes, and a shortage of related support services such as drug and alcohol treatment and mental health care.[37]

In 2003 the Child Abuse Prevention Act (CAPTA) was again reauthorized (P.L. 108-36, the Keeping Children and Families Safe Act) through fiscal year 2008. In addition to reauthorizing CAPTA, the new law, among other things, strengthens research goals and greatly expands child welfare worker training. The bill authorizes appropriations beginning at $315 million in 2004 and increasing to $498 million in 2008, plus adjustments for inflation should any be made. The Congressional Budget Office estimates that authorizations will total about $2.2 billion over the 2004–2008 period. The CBO further estimates additional authorizations totaling an additional $1.4 billion over the course of the act.[38]

The combination of P.L. 96-272, with its requirement that agencies demonstrate "reasonable efforts" to prevent foster home placement of children, and P.L. 103-66 and 108-36, each providing massive federal financial incentives to provide family preservation services, made family preservation the policy of choice in the twenty-first century for dealing with child maltreatment. Although a backlash developed to family preservation programs, embodied in the passage in 1997 of the Adoption and Safe Families Act, this continues to be the policy of choice for dealing with the problem of child dependency. Virtually every state in the Union developed some form of family preservation program by the end of the twentieth century.

Social Analysis

Problem Description

Family preservation is one aspect of society's response to the problem of child dependency. Child dependency as a problem has at least three levels. The primary level is the problem of child poverty. The secondary level, derived from the primary, is the problem of child maltreatment. Derived from the first two levels is the tertiary problem of the explosive growth of the foster care population.

Descriptive Data

A number of statistics regarding child welfare and family preservation were previously cited; a brief recap is provided here. Note that, despite years of concern, there is no good centralized source of data regarding child maltreatment and foster care. From 1974 to 1986, a good source of data was the annual *National Study of Child Neglect and Abuse Reporting*, conducted by the American Humane Association and funded by the federal Children's Bureau. This was funded for a reduced study for 1987 and has not been funded since. The national study consisted of a nationwide compilation of data derived from official reports of child maltreatment documented by state child protective service agencies. This task has now been assumed by the Administration on Children and Families of the U.S. Department of Health and Human Services, under the name National Child Abuse and Neglect Data System. This system is providing ever better data, but is still plagued by the problem of missing data from states, making precise reports of national incidence difficult. Data regarding children in foster care were in the past even more limited than data pertaining to reports of maltreatment. A system has now been developed by the U.S. Department of Health and Human Services called the Adoption and Foster Care Analysis System. This system is designed to collect uniform, reliable information on children in all forms of out-of-home care.

Four levels of data are important for understanding family preservation as a social welfare policy. The first level is data that estimate the actual incidence of child maltreatment—("estimate" because it is not possible actually to know the incidence of abuse and neglect due to the secret nature of the acts involved). The U.S. Department of Health and Human Services contracts for periodic National Incidence Studies of Child Abuse and Neglect (NIS). The most recent was NIS 3, published in 1996 and reporting on data collected for 1993. NIS 4 is currently under way, but data from it has not yet been released. These studies employ a scientific sampling procedure to attempt to uncover incidences of child maltreatment that have escaped the formal reporting machinery. NIS 3 estimated that in 1993 1,553,800 children in the United States were abused or neglected. The report found that only about 28 percent of these cases were investigated by child protective services. These data indicate that the actual incidence of abuse and neglect is far greater than indicated by official reporting statistics.

The second type of data that is important for understanding family preservation summarizes actual reports of child maltreatment. This information is presented in Table 11.1, which indicates that the number of reports has increased from 9,563 in 1967 to currently over three million. Most of this increase is undoubtedly a result of increased public awareness of the problem and more efficient reporting systems. However, there also is little doubt that a portion of the increase reflects an actual increase in incidence resulting from trends such as increased poverty, homelessness, drug use, and births to young single mothers.

The third type of data for understanding the family preservation policy is the number of confirmed reports. As the number of reports has increased, the proportion that are substantiated by protective services investigation has decreased. In 1975 about 60 percent of reports were substantiated; by 1987 this had fallen to 40 percent, and currently about one in three reports is substantiated.[39]

The final figure—the one most directly relevant to family preservation policy—is the number of confirmed reports that lead to child placement. This was previously referred to when discussing the development and early success of permanency planning. To review, the number of children in out-of-home placements went from a high of 520,000 in 1977 to a low of 275,000 in 1984, at which time the number began to increase rapidly until it is estimated that as of September 30 2004 the population was about 518,000.

Relevant Research

There is a huge body of research relevant to child protective services. However, here we will address only the research most relevant to family preservation as a policy response to child placement. This research regards parent–child bonding, the effect of foster placement on child development, and the relation of poverty to child maltreatment. Research on program effectiveness will be described in the evaluation section.

Although Harry Harlow and his colleagues at the University of Wisconsin Primate Center had no specific interest in child welfare, their findings on infant–parent attachment were extremely interesting to social workers in the field. Duncan Lindsey describes the studies as follows:

> An experimental psychologist, Harlow wanted to understand the importance of a mother's nurturing on the growth and development of a child. He examined what happened to an infant monkey that was raised in a wire cage that provided necessary physical nourishment but did not permit any emotional interaction or attachment with other monkeys. The monkey's cage allowed it to see and hear other monkeys but did not allow any physical contact. Harlow observed that the infant raised in an isolated cage suffered from intense neurotic behavior when compared to an infant monkey raised with a cloth surrogate mother. . . . Further, the effects of social isolation continued for the experimental monkey into adulthood. . . . Harlow's experiments provided dramatic evidence of the importance of parental affection and care to the developing child. The research emphasized the importance of providing children with parental nurturing. Children growing up in institutions or in a series of foster homes were deprived of the essential bonding and attachment that comes from a parent.[40]

Research by John Bowlby on children who were separated from their parents at age two or three confirmed Harlow's primate studies. Bowlby found that these children tended to suffer from severe psychological distress and concluded that separation from parents has severe consequences for a child's development.[41] A recent and thorough analysis of attachment theory research in relation to child welfare written by Mennen and O'Keefe concludes, "Research on maltreated children has supported many of the theoretical propositions of attachment theory."[42]

Given the importance of the question, it is surprising that there are not more studies of the actual effects of foster placement on the development of children. The one major, but now somewhat dated, study of this question is the longitudinal study of children in foster care conducted by Fanshel and Shinn. This study resulted in data contradictory to what would be expected based on the findings of Harlow and of Bowlby. Fanshel and Shinn employed a wide array of behavioral indicators and checklists to assess the adjustment of children returned home and of those still in foster care at the end of the five-year period covered by their study. They conclude, "From our involvement in these data and other investigations, we feel that children who enter foster care as infants and live stable lives in the same setting emerge as teenagers who are relatively free of problems." Children who entered care when they were older and those who did not have stable, long-term placements were found to have significant problems.[43] However, this can be at least partially explained by the findings of several studies that children entering foster care at an older age are more likely already to have severe behavioral and adjustment problems.[44]

Two recent studies—one sponsored by the Pew Commission and one by the Chapin Hall Center for Children—have demonstrated how harmful foster care is to the successful development of children. These studies confirmed the earlier findings of Maas that foster care is often not temporary care and that many children languish in foster care for five or more years. Each year 20,000 children "age out" of foster care—that is, reach their eighteenth birthdays and legally become adults without first returning to their own homes. The Pew Commission and Chapin Hall studies looked at the outcomes for those children who aged out of foster care and the findings can only be described as grim: They experience mental health problems at three times the rate of a comparable national sample; one-quarter have been tested or treated for sexually transmitted diseases, more than four times the rate of the national sample; two-thirds of the males and one-half of the females have been arrested, convicted of a crime, or sent to a correctional facility; nearly 40 percent fail to graduate from high school and over one-half read at or below the seventh-grade level; and nearly 40 percent end up on welfare.[45] These studies make clear that attempting to divert children from foster care by working with their own families is a really good idea.

Unlike the question of the effects of foster placement on children, the effects of poverty are well researched and consequently well understood. One study concluded that the incidence of abuse and neglect is ten times higher among families with incomes below the poverty line than among those with middle-class incomes. In a 1969 survey of abusive families, Gil found that nearly 60 percent had been on public assistance at some time and that slightly more than 34 percent were receiving welfare at the time of the report. A journalist looking into abuse and neglect found that more than half the children removed from their homes as a result of abuse or neglect came from families receiving welfare. Leroy Pelton surveyed child protective service records in New Jersey and found that 79 percent of the families had incomes below the poverty line. Gelles conducted two nationwide surveys on family violence and found that "violence toward children, especially severe violence, is more likely to occur in households with annual incomes below the poverty line."[46] After two separate, thorough reviews of the research, Lindsey and Pelton conclude that poverty is at the root of nearly all child welfare problems. Making the situation worse are data indicating that the rate of child poverty has been steadily increasing.[47]

Is Family Preservation Policy in Accord with Research Findings?

One of the cornerstones of family preservation policy is the belief that foster care is bad for children. As reviewed in the preceding section, the research on this question is incomplete and results to date have been contradictory. However, when looked at more carefully, the results do not appear so contradictory. The study by Fanshel and Shinn concluded that children in foster care did not appear to suffer any serious consequences, with the caveat that the children they were talking about were those who entered foster care at a young age and who had stable placements. In *Beyond the Best Interests of the Child*, Goldstein, Freud, and Solnit argue that what is important to a child is a psychological parent, not necessarily a biological parent. A psychological parent is any caring adult who meets the child's day-to-day needs and does so over an extended period of time.[48] It seems clear that the children studied by Fanshel and Shinn were fortunate enough to find psychological parents in their placements. Thus it appears that the attachment and outcome research of foster care would lend support to either permanency planning (strive to provide a psychological parent to a child if the biological parent is unavailable) or to family preservation (support biological parents in their efforts to also be psychological parents). The Chapin Hall and Pew Commission studies, on the other hand, demonstrate that the outcomes of long-term foster care are highly detrimental to human development and in so doing lend strong support to a family preservation approach to child welfare.

Although family preservation policy may be consistent with the research and theory regarding attachment, it is hard to discount the arguments of scholars such as Lindsey, Pelton, and Gil that the real problem behind child maltreatment is poverty. It is ironic that just as our society is pouring money into family preservation programs in an attempt to hold families together, we are slashing financial assistance programs that provide many of these families their only hope for stability. Lindsey refers to child abuse as "the red herring of child welfare," arguing that it is a highly charged issue that draws attention away from the real and more difficult problem of child poverty.[49]

Major Social Values Related to Family Preservation

Family preservation policy occurs at the intersection of some of the most deeply held, and deeply dividing, of our society's values. These are children's rights, family rights, and the government's right to act in *parens patriae*, the ultimate parental authority. As you saw in the historical analysis section, up until the nineteenth century children were considered to have few rights, and those they did have were clearly subservient to the rights of their parents, particularly the father. As time has passed, children have been given considerably more rights, and it now is quite clear that they have a right to a certain—albeit vague—level of care. Lagging only slightly behind the recognition of children as beings with certain rights was the recognition of the right of government to intervene in family life to safeguard the rights of children. Susan Downs, Ernestine Moore, Emily McFadden, and Susan Michaud observe that support for government intervention has increased in recent years due to a fear that U.S. society is experiencing breakdown in the family as a social institution and to "the realization that virtually all governmental actions directly or indirectly affect families."[50] Nevertheless, Americans still have great ambivalence about this, being ever-fearful of government and believing that the government should be allowed in family life only in cases of the utmost urgency.

Family preservation policy represents a clever attempt to reconcile these seemingly contradictory rights. It recognizes the right of children to be protected but does it in such a way as to maximize the rights of parents to rear their own children. By its generally time-limited nature, family preservation seeks to make government intervention as short as possible and to get out of family life in the least possible time. This balancing of rights makes family preservation a very marketable policy to legislators and to the general public and, in part, explains its rapid spread.

Family Preservation Goals

Because family preservation policy includes an explicit and well-funded evaluation requirement, the manifest goals of the policy are clearer and more explicitly spelled out than is the case in most social welfare policies. This is because a basic requirement of program/policy evaluations is that goals be specified; if they are not, you have nothing to evaluate. The basic, stated goals of family preservation are

1. To prevent placement of children in families in crisis. This is the cornerstone of family preservation. The idea is to intervene in family situations that would normally be assessed as requiring placement of the children with intensive, time-limited services, which quickly improve family functioning to a degree that the children can remain in the home.
2. Protect children and prevent subsequent child maltreatment. Family preservation policy does not consider it enough simply to prevent placement. This must be done in a way that ensures that the children are protected from subsequent harm both in the short and in the long term.

3. Improve family functioning. Family preservation services seek to leave families with better daily-living and problem-solving skills than were present before intervention.
4. Prevent child abuse and neglect. This goal is sometimes categorized as family support, as opposed to family preservation, but in any case is generally a component of family preservation policy. This goal is to improve the general social environment of families and to enable more families to care for their children adequately without the necessity of intervention of any kind. This may be viewed as an institutional approach to the problem of child maltreatment, as contrasted to the other services, which represent a clear residual approach.

Somewhere between a manifest and a latent goal of family preservation is the goal to decrease the cost of child protective services. One of the major motivating factors in the rapid spread of family preservation has been that it is perceived as a cost-efficient way to deal with child maltreatment. This goal lies between manifest and latent because, although few people would deny it, it is generally not listed among the stated goals. We suspect that if within a few years the costs of child protective services do not decline or at least the growth shows signs of slowing, policymakers will lose considerable enthusiasm for family preservation, regardless of how well it achieves its stated goals.

We are not able to identify any purely latent goals of family preservation policy. A few scholars, for example, Ann Hartman and L. Diane Bernard, have argued that a latent goal of all family policy is to preserve the existing patriarchal family structure and, along with it, existing power relationships in society. Bernard states,

> The oppression and exploitation of women in society is reflected and initiated in the family, which reinforces continued gender discrimination. The primary function of the family is to maintain the status quo. Preservation of the family and family stability are the primary goals of patriarchy, ensuring obedience and continuity. . . . The major purpose appears to be to restore stability and reestablish control by returning to traditional values.[51]

We see little evidence that this is the case in family preservation policy. Nowhere in the policy is there a definition of the type of family that is to be preserved. In fact, many of the cases described in the literature appear to be female-headed, single-parent households, and changing these to traditional nuclear families is never mentioned.

Hypotheses
There appear to be two major hypotheses derived from family preservation goals. The first can be stated as, "If intensive, time-limited social work services are

provided to families with children at risk of placement, and these services are provided in a timely fashion, then placement of the children can be permanently avoided." As we discuss in the evaluation section, we have serious doubts that this hypothesis will be upheld given the severity of the problems most of the target population is experiencing, the decline of supporting resources and services, and the relatively primitive state of social work intervention technology.

The second hypothesis appears to be, "If child placement is avoided via provision of intensive family preservation services, then reduction in foster home placement will save more money than the family preservation services cost." Once again, given the seriousness of the problems in the target population, we doubt that it will be possible, in most cases, to limit services to a brief period, and therefore services will cost more than anticipated. Also, as is discussed in the evaluation section, there is some evidence of a "net-widening" phenomenon in family preservation. This is a phenomenon first identified in probation and diversion services in criminal justice. What appears to happen in some instances is that, with the option of family preservation being available, social workers are referring cases to family preservation that would not even have been opened were these services not available.

Political Analysis

Family preservation is one of those rare social policies that contains significant elements that appeal to stakeholders across the political spectrum. Liberals (a group that includes most social workers) favor family preservation because it operationalizes many of their most sacred values. Among the aspects of family preservation that appeal to this group are:

- It does not blame the victim.
- It proceeds from a strengths perspective.
- It emphasizes cultural sensitivity.
- It emphasizes a belief in people's capacity to change and desire to do so.
- It defines family in a flexible fashion and approaches each family as a unique system.
- It respects the dignity and privacy of family members.

Conservatives also find much to like about family preservation as a response to the problem of child maltreatment. Among the aspects of family preservation this group likes are:

- It shortens the time government is involved in people's lives.
- It emphasizes that people are ultimately responsible for solving their own problems.

- It emphasizes independence and seeks to wean people from the social service system.
- It resonates with the conservative emphasis on "family values."
- It is viewed as a potentially more cost-efficient way of protecting children.

Because family preservation policy exists at this intersection of liberal and conservative values, it has—up to this point—experienced little meaningful political opposition. At the Committee on Ways and Means hearing on the legislation that eventually led to P.L. 103-66, Family Preservation and Support Services, forty-three groups either testified or submitted testimony for the record. Not a single submission expressed any opposition to or even reservations about the act.[52]

There are, however, a few groups that oppose family preservation policy. One group consists of those very conservative ideologues who see in family preservation a continuation of trends that they believe are eroding the very foundations of our society. They believe that family preservation is another policy that removes accountability for responsible behavior from the individual and places it on society. Patrick Murphy, the Cook County (Chicago) public guardian, for example, states, "The family preservation system is a continuation of sloppy thinking of the 1960s and 1970s that holds, as an unquestionable truth, that society should never blame a victim. But in most cases, giving services and money to parents who have abused their children does nothing but reward irresponsible and even criminal behavior."[53] Murphy introduced a bill in the 1993 Illinois legislature that would require court approval for family preservation in cases of physical or sexual abuse. The bill passed, but in response to strong opposition by the Department of Children and Family Services and the American Civil Liberties Union, among others, Governor Jim Edgar vetoed it. Murphy and his allies persisted, however, and later in 1993, in response to the murder of a young girl whose family was receiving family preservation services, Illinois ended its Family First program. However, as Heather MacDonald, another critic of family preservation, reported, "This decision does not mean, however, that Illinois is rejecting family preservation. It is now introducing the original Homebuilders model, which, though it has a vastly better safety record than the Family First program, embodies the identical philosophy."[54]

Opposition to family preservation policy also comes from competing human service providers who see it as cutting into their "market." The National Council for Adoption, a group favoring policies that free more children for adoption, argues that family preservation programs often harm children who could be removed from hopeless parents and placed in good adoptive homes. The group's vice president, Mary Beth Seader, complains, "I know people who have been trying for two years to adopt these crack babies that have been abandoned in hospitals, but . . . the state is not terminating parental rights even if there is no contact with the biological mother."[55] Residential treatment center personnel are another group who question family preservation. They argue that family preservation is being embraced so enthusiastically by policymakers because it offers an alternative much cheaper than residential treatment for children experiencing severe problems in their family setting. However, the argument goes, in many instances there is no substitute for the more expensive alternative. For example, David Coughlin of Boys Town says, "Family preservation? Who can be opposed to that? But some of these kids are going to be in trouble all their lives. These kids are always going to need help. You can't just blow across the top of a family for three months and expect their woes to go away."[56]

Perhaps the most important opposition to family preservation policy is currently coming from an increasingly influential segment of the social work profession that asserts that our emphasis on family preservation has been misguided and has put children at risk. The leader of this effort is Richard Gelles, now dean at the prestigious University of Pennsylvania School of Social Policy and Practice, who condemned family preservation in no uncertain terms in *The Book of David: How Preserving Families Can Cost Children's Lives*. In this book, Gelles uses the case of one child who was murdered by his parents while supposedly under the protection of the state child welfare division. Gelles argues that the agency's policies were so skewed toward the goal of preserving families that the social workers ignored all sorts of evidence that the home was unsafe, and the result was a child death that should have been prevented. Gelles states,

> The most compelling argument for abandoning the uniform policy of family reunification and family preservation comes from the data on children killed by their parents. Research clearly reveals the damage done by rigidly following the family preservation model. . . . 30 to 50 percent of the children killed by parents or caretakers are killed after they were identified by child welfare agencies, were involved in interventions, and were either left in their homes or returned home after a short-term placement.[57]

Gelles is currently establishing a center at the University of Pennsylvania School of Social Work dedicated to shifting policy away from family preservation and toward being child centered.

In 1997, Congress reauthorized the Child Abuse Prevention Act (CAPTA) with a bill titled the Adoption and Safe Families Act that makes the safety of children a priority in all child welfare decision making. This act was viewed by some as representing a shift in federal policy away from family preservation and toward child-centered policy. The main aspect of the act that leads to this belief is its clarification of the requirement that agencies must demonstrate that they have made "reasonable efforts" to preserve a family before parental rights are terminated. Under this new law, reasonable efforts are not required when the court has found that

- the parent has subjected the child to "aggravated circumstances" as defined in state law (including but not limited to abandonment, torture, chronic abuse, and sexual abuse);
- the parent has committed murder or voluntary manslaughter or aided or abetted, attempted, conspired, or solicited to commit such a murder or manslaughter of another child of the parent;
- the parent has committed a felony assault that results in serious bodily injury to the child or another one of the parent's children; or
- the parental rights of the parent to a sibling have been involuntarily terminated.

In these specified cases, states are not required to make reasonable efforts to preserve or to reunify the family. They are required to hold a permanency hearing within thirty days and to make reasonable efforts to place the child for adoption, with a legal guardian, or in another permanent placement. In addition, the act mandates a permanency hearing by the end of every twelve-month period a child is in care.

The 1997 act was not as anti–family preservation as family preservation advocates initially feared. Although agencies are relieved of the requirement of making family preservation efforts in the preceding specified instances, they continue to be required to make reasonable efforts to preserve and reunify families in all other cases. More important, the new law specifically continues and expands the Family Preservation and Support Services Program, renaming it the Promoting Safe and Stable Families Program. Funding levels for the program were increased. In 2003 CAPTA was again reauthorized with the passage of the Keeping Children and Families Safe Act. This act once again contains provisions designed to rein in family preservation efforts, notably procedures requiring referrals and services to infants born with substance abuse symptoms, as well as case monitoring, management, and tracking procedures. However, this act also increases funding for family based, as well as other, child welfare services.

Economic Analysis

Although many good arguments have been made for the policy of family preservation, we think it is clear that economic considerations are the driving force behind its rapid growth. In the opening statement to the Committee on Ways and Means, Representative Fred Grandy said, "Principally, federal spending on foster care and adoption through Title IV-E of the Social Security Act has increased from $474 million to $2.5 billion, or roughly a 418 percent increase since 1981. And in the last five years, IV-E has increased by an average of $360 million a year."[58]

Policymakers and administrators are desperate to get control of what is perceived as a runaway increase in costs, and family preservation advocates have successfully used this as a way to sell the policy.

If family preservation can produce the results it promises—prevention of foster home or institutional placement through the provision of time-limited, intensive services—the potential cost savings are significant indeed. The Edna McConnell Clark Foundation has produced media kits stating that family preservation programs cost an estimated average of $3,000 per family per year, as compared to foster care at $10,000 per year per child, or institutional care, which costs $40,000 annually per child. Carolyn Brown and Susan Little, writing about the Full Circle Program, a California family preservation program, assert, "Besides helping children and their families, this work has saved hundreds of thousands of tax dollars: Reunification services for a family cost an average of $2,600[,] . . . less than one month of residential care in California."[59] Kinney, Haapala, and Booth, founders of the original Homebuilders Program in Washington State, report their costs as $2,700 per family. They report the costs of alternatives as $5,113 for foster care, $19,673 for group care, $25,978 for residential treatment, $42,300 for placement in an acute psychiatric hospital, and $100,200 for long-term psychiatric care. Marianne Berry evaluated a family preservation program in California and kept detailed per-hour cost records. She found that families in the program received an average of 67.35 hours of service at a cost of $41.22 per hour, for a per-case average cost of $2,776.17. Comparing this with foster care costs, she concluded that this "translates into a savings of $4,648 for every foster care placement this program prevented. . . . When placement is prevented for more than one child in a family, this savings is multiplied, resulting in an even greater economic benefit from this program."[60]

The critical question on which the future of family preservation rests is whether the projected cost savings will actually materialize. To do so, the number of foster placements will have to begin to decrease or, at the very least, the rate of increase will have to slow and evaluation results will have to establish that family preservation is the reason. If this does not happen, policymakers will undoubtedly lose their initial enthusiasm for family preservation, critics such as Patrick Murphy will gain more credibility, and child welfare policy will turn to some other proposed solution. The results of evaluations of family preservation programs are continuing to come in and are being widely disseminated. It is to these results we now turn.

Policy/Program Evaluation

It is probably not stretching the truth to say that family preservation is one of the most carefully studied social welfare innovations in history. There are a number of reasons for this, principally that the program involves leaving children in potentially harmful situations, which calls for extremely vigilant monitoring. The increasing skepticism with which policymakers are now receiving claims of social policy advocates also has resulted in calls for close monitoring of innovations. The prototype family preservation program, the Homebuilders Program, was originally funded under a National Institute of Mental Health research grant, which, of course, had knowledge development as a primary goal. When the Family Preservation and Support Program was passed in 1993, Congress included $2 million in fiscal 1994 and $6 million per year from 1995 through 1998 to fund research and evaluation as well as training and technical assistance. The act also requires states to develop new foster care and adoption information systems. The 2002 extension of the Promoting Safe and Stable Families Program includes $6 million per year for research, training, and evaluation out of the mandatory funding and dedicates 3.3 percent of discretionary funding for these purposes.

When family preservation models were first implemented during the 1970s, they reported wildly positive outcomes. The Homebuilders Program reported placement prevention rates varying from a low of 73 percent to a high of 91 percent of families served. Some of the more recent studies have reported success rates almost as high. An evaluation of a Connecticut program claimed that 82 percent of children at risk of placement were still in their own homes after one year of service. Berry's study of a family preservation program in California concludes, "A full 88 percent of the families receiving services in this program avoided otherwise imminent child removal for a year after being served."[61]

These studies, sometimes referred to as "first generation studies," have come under serious criticism for methodological problems. The major problem identified is that they lack any kind of control or comparison group. Thus, if a study finds that 90 percent of the children in the program were not placed, it cannot, without a control group, conclude that the services prevented placement, because there is no way of knowing whether the children really were at risk in the first place. It is possible to argue that, without the services, fewer than 10 percent of the children would have been placed and therefore the program actually *increased* that rate of placement. This effect was in fact indicated in an analysis of data from the Illinois Family First program conducted by Littell in which she concludes, "Intensive FPS may have 'case finding' effects, resulting in increases in out-of-home placements and substantiated reports of maltreatment and decreases in case closings."[62]* In response to these criticisms, a number of more rigorous studies

---

*This effect has also been seen in the finding of evaluations of intensive social services to people released from prison on parole. The more services a parolee is given, the more likely he is to be caught for some violation of parole and sent back to prison. It is quite possible that intensive supervision of families with children defined as being at risk of placement could have similar results.

have been implemented. The results of these studies have been mixed. Some have found no significant differences in placement rates between experimental and control groups.[63] An Oregon study found that significantly fewer children in less difficult cases were placed, but there was no significant difference in placement rates for children in families with more difficult problems.[64] In one study, the experimental group—or the one receiving intensive family preservation services— actually experienced a *higher* rate of placement than the control group.[65]

Dagenais, Begin, Bouchard, and Fortin have conducted a useful meta-analysis of the net effect of intensive social service intervention on placement rates and the impact of these interventions on children and their families. They collected 156 reports of family preservation program evaluations and selected those that met criteria of good scientific methodology. The result was thirty-eight reports related to twenty-seven programs deemed scientifically worthy. The results of these evaluations were disappointing. The authors found that children who received the services evaluated in the studies were placed in substitute care almost as often as the children in the comparison groups. They did find, however, that the services had a positive impact on children and their families, but that it was slight: "only one variable—neglect, with reference to health care—from just one study indicated statistically lower rates of maltreatment subsequent to intervention."[66]

The most significant study of family preservation to date was conducted in Illinois by the University of Chicago's Chapin Hall Center for Children, under contract with that state's Department of Children and Family Services. The study began in 1989 after Illinois had implemented a version of the Family First program. The study ran for four years and involved three levels of data collection. The first level involved collecting descriptive data from all 6,522 cases involved in Families First in 1989. The second level was a randomized experiment, with a sample of 1,564 cases, to test program effects of subsequent placement and harm to children. The third level, involving a sample of 278 cases, was a series of interviews with parents in both the experimental and control groups to gather data on the effects of the program on child and family well-being over time and to assess clients' experiences and views on the services they received. The results of this study were that the Family First program in Illinois had no effect on either the frequency or the duration of placements.[67] A subsequent reanalysis of the data from this study, applying more powerful statistical techniques, confirmed the original conclusions finding that "it appears that the duration, intensity, and breadth of family preservation services have little impact on subsequent child maltreatment, out-of-home placement, or the closing of cases in child welfare."[68] After a general review of family preservation programs, Pecora, Whittaker, Maluccio, and Barth conclude:

To date the field lacks conclusive evidence that FBS [family-based services] prevent child placement, and about which types of FBS programs are most effective with different client subpopulations including those involved in physical abuse, neglect, parent–child conflict, or other areas. We also need a better understanding of effectiveness with different age groups of children and of program components that contribute to success with different families (e.g., in-home services, active listening, client goal setting, concrete services). . . . Because the programs that have been evaluated varied significantly in target group, model consistency, program maturity, and services provided, it is premature to draw any conclusions about the effectiveness of any particular type of service for any particular clientele.[69]

A number of scholars in child welfare have recently begun to criticize what they believe is the overemphasis on placement prevention as the major criterion for effectiveness of family preservation services. They argue that there are a number of other, equally or more important, possible outcomes from services. Pecora and colleagues, for example, suggest the following additional types of outcomes:[70]

- Improvements in child functioning (e.g., behavior, school attendance, school performance, self-esteem)
- Positive changes in parental functioning (e.g., depression, employment, substance abuse, anger management, self-esteem) or parenting skills such as the use of appropriate discipline techniques and child care
- Improvements in family functioning (e.g., family conflict, communication, cohesion, adaptability, or social support)
- Reunification of families after child placement

Berry has argued that our focus on placement prevention has deflected attention from important questions regarding just which elements of intensive services contribute to family preservation and which do not.[71] This knowledge would lead to an improvement in services rather than a simple judgment of whether the services were cost efficient.

We agree that there are a number of dimensions of family preservation services that could profitably be examined for the purpose of increasing social worker effectiveness in designing programs and in responding to family needs. However, keep in mind that the family preservation policy has been touted and implemented based on the belief that it will eventually help manage the child welfare crisis by reducing the population in placement and (consequently) the huge and rapidly increasing cost of services. If family preservation does not live up to the cost-efficiency promise, regardless of how effective it is demonstrated to be as a social work practice approach, it will be abandoned by policymakers, who will then continue the search for cost containment in child protection.

Current Proposals for Policy Reform

Family preservation has probably reached its zenith as a policy supporting specific program initiatives. In spite of the data coming in indicating a number of areas of effectiveness, it seems clear that it is not leading to a reduction in foster care rates. As these data continue to be collected and disseminated, it is likely that policymakers will begin to look for other answers.

There is a strong reform movement afoot in the area of foster care and family preservation. This is a steady movement toward kinship care, described by the Child Welfare League of America as "one of the most stunning changes in the child welfare system." Kinship care is simply the practice of looking to a child's extended family for a placement resource before looking to foster care with an unrelated family. Data reported by the U.S. Department of Health and Human Services and the Child Welfare League of America indicate that the percentage of children placed with relatives increased from 18 to 33 percent of the foster care caseload from 1986 through 1997. Most children placed with relatives are members of racial and ethnic groups, mostly African American. In other ways, the population placed in kinship care appears to be identical with the general foster care population.[72]

The movement in foster care policy toward kinship care has been an interesting mix of macro- and micropolicy initiatives. On the macrolevel, there have been two significant events. The first is the Child Welfare League of America's National Commission on Family Foster Care, which convened in 1991 and developed *A Blueprint for Fostering Infants, Children, and Youth in the 1990s*. One of the major thrusts of this document was to support the significance of kinship care. The other significant macrolevel event was the 1979 Supreme Court ruling in *Miller v. Youakim*, in which the court ruled that relatives not be excluded from the definition of foster parents eligible for federal foster care benefits.

Mark Courtney makes an interesting observation that the movement toward more kinship care may well be the result of microlevel as much as macrolevel policy change:

> Various states, localities, and individual social workers and judges have no doubt contributed to this trend in ways that cannot be easily observed, let alone described, given the decentralized nature of child welfare services. . . . Current permanency planning philosophy in child welfare places emphasis on keeping children "with family," even when they are removed from the home of their birth parents. . . . Common sense suggests that staying with relatives is likely to be less

traumatic for a child removed from parental care than placement with unfamiliar foster parents or group care providers. . . . Paying kin to care for a child, as opposed to having to find an appropriate foster home, makes the difficult decision to remove a child from home easier for social workers and judges.[73]

Early data indicate that kinship care is an effective tool for the goal of permanency but works to the detriment of family preservation/reunification if the family to be preserved is that of the biological parents. In a rigorous study of reunification of families with children placed in foster care in Chicago, Robert Goerge found that placement in the home of a relative was one of the strongest variables in reducing the probability of reunification.[74] Courtney found that children in kinship care are more likely than children placed in family foster homes or group care to remain in the foster care system for long periods of time.[75]

Kinship care is appealing to policymakers on two fronts. First, because it leaves children in the care of relatives, although not the parents, it appeals to profamily sentiments. Second, kinship care is cheaper than family foster care. Families are now eligible for licensure and payment as foster parents for related children, but under current policy in thirty-four states, they can receive only the amount of the child's public assistance payment. This amount is much lower than the prevailing foster care rate in most states, and it is even lower if more than one related child is placed in the same home. It appears that the inequity in this situation is becoming apparent, and pressure is mounting for states to provide the same level of support for children in kinship care as for those in family foster care. Thus this foster care system reform, too, may eventually prove to be no cost saver.

Conclusion

By way of conclusion, we wish to make several observations regarding family preservation as a policy response to child maltreatment. The first is the recognition of the difference between family preservation as a philosophy behind child welfare policy and family preservation as a specific programmatic response to the problem of child maltreatment. As a programmatic response implemented in programs such as Homebuilders and Family First, family preservation produces evaluation results that are, at the very least, casting doubt on the claims of the programs' designers that they will save money through placement prevention. Although it may well prove to be true that the programs are effective on a number of other dimensions, such as elevating a family's general level of problem-solving ability and child care, this is pretty much beside the point. The programs have been advertised and implemented on the basis of cost effectiveness, and if they do not demonstrate effectiveness according to this criterion, they will lose support.

Family preservation, however, should not be interpreted to mean only one specific type of program or method. Family preservation is first and foremost a philosophy of practice with families in crisis. Robin Warsh, Barbara Pine, and Anthony Maluccio offer the following broader definition of family preservation:

> Family preservation is a philosophy that supports policies, programs and practices which recognize the central importance of the biological family to human beings. It underscores the value of individualized assessment and service delivery, with adequate system supports, in order to maximize each family's potential to stay, or again become, safely connected.[76]

This general philosophy of family preservation can be expressed through any number of specific programs and techniques, including kinship care, shared foster care (in which the foster family and the biological family are in direct contact and share childrearing responsibilities), open adoption, family reunification programs, and a number of other profamily approaches, some of which undoubtedly have not even been thought of yet. Warsh, Pine, and Maluccio argue that defining family preservation in terms of one model, such as Homebuilders, confuses the concept. Thus we conclude that although the specific family preservation models that have recently spread so quickly seem to be falling short of their goals, family preservation as a philosophy of child welfare policy is alive and well and has yet to demonstrate its full potential.

The second observation we wish to make is that true family preservation will, of necessity, involve a much wider range of interventions and benefits than just a direct response to incidents of child maltreatment. We have reviewed arguments concluding that poverty is actually the central child welfare problem. Lindsey, for example, analyzed national survey data and demonstrated that family income is the best predictor of a child's removal from home.[77] Courtney has analyzed cost data and concluded that it costs the federal government over eleven times as much per child to provide foster care as to provide welfare assistance to the child's family.[78] Putting these findings together, we could argue that if poverty is the leading variable related to placement, and *if* placement is much more expensive than increased welfare payments, *then* we could save money and improve the lives of children and families by increasing welfare benefits to a level that enables people to live and care for their children decently. However, as with specific family preservation services, increased welfare supports are only a small part of the total response needed to deal adequately with the problem of child maltreatment. As Edith Fein and Anthony Maluccio have stated,

> No solutions to child welfare issues will be viable without supports to families. These include adequately compensated employment, availability of housing,

accessible medical care, and decriminalization of substance abuse to remove the economic incentive for drug dealing. Other supports are also important, such as good day care, parenting education, and readily available mental health services. As we noted over a decade ago, "permanency planning [or family preservation programs] cannot substitute for preventive services and for increased investment in our children."[79]

Thus we conclude that it is unrealistic to expect any one specific approach to have a great impact on placement rates. Perhaps if family preservation programs were evaluated as one of a whole set of interventions to reduce placements, they would fare better.

Our final observation is derived from the first two: Although it is understandable to look for a "silver bullet"—a simple one-step remedy to a problem such as child maltreatment—it is highly unrealistic. Child maltreatment results from a huge number of variables, some relating to individual psychology and some to macrosocial and macroeconomic conditions, all interrelated along an almost infinite number of dimensions. As a society, we have a modest understanding of a few of the relevant variables and no knowledge of a number of others; as to how they are interrelated, our understanding is at an even more primitive level. To think that one program approach, such as family preservation, will be *the* solution is simplistic. The conclusion of Fein and Maluccio regarding permanency planning is also an appropriate conclusion for this policy analysis of family preservation:

> The complexity of human interactions precludes simple solutions, and the certainty of having solved a problem is destined to elude our grasp. These considerations, however, are not negative. They help define the dimensions of the problem and provide a challenge to those who choose to work seriously with children, society's most precious resource.[80]

Selected Web Sites on Family Preservation

Annie E. Casey Foundation

www.casey.org

Provides information on one of the biggest advocates for and supporters of the family preservation approach to child protective services. Includes information on grants, reports, press releases, and activities of the foundation. Includes data from the National Center for Resource Family Support.

Children's Bureau Express

www.calib.com/cbexpress

Displays an online newsletter supported by the Children's Bureau, the National Clearinghouse on Child Abuse and Neglect Information, and the National Adoption Information Clearinghouse.

Children's Defense Fund

www.childrensdefense.org

Provides information on one of the largest and most prominent child advocacy organizations in the country. This site includes information about the organization, discussions of current issues, news and reports, and other features related to a broad definition of child welfare.

Child Welfare League of America

www.cwla.org

Contains information on one of the oldest and largest child welfare organizations in the country. This site includes a description of the organization, news and events, policy advocacy tips, current activities of the CWLA, a calendar of upcoming events, membership information, links to other sites, and other useful features.

Family Preservation and Child Welfare Network

www.familypreservation.com

Supported by the Public Health Administration Department of the University of South Carolina, includes data, program descriptions, and links to other sites.

National Clearinghouse on Child Abuse and Neglect Information

www.calib.com/nccanch

This site is a vast repository of child welfare information sponsored by the U.S. Department of Health and Human Services. Includes information on new programs and initiatives, publications and fact sheets, a clearinghouse catalog, specialized services (information on statistics, child welfare, child abuse and neglect prevention, and state statutes), conference information, online databases and directories, and links to related sites.

Notes

1. Children's Defense Fund Action Council, *Stand Up for Children Now! State of America's Children Action Guide* (Washington, DC: Children's Defense Fund, 2006).

2. David S. Liederman, "Child Welfare Overview," in Richard L. Edwards and June Gary Hopps, Eds., *Encyclopedia of Social Work*, 19th ed. (Washington, DC: NASW Press, 1995), p. 424.

3. Karen McCurdy and Deborah Daro, *Current Trends in Child Abuse Prevention, Reporting, and Fatalities: The 1999 Fifty State Survey*, Working Paper Number 808 (Chicago: National Center on Child Abuse Prevention Research, 2000), p. iv; Child Welfare League of America, National Data Analysis System, "Child Abuse and Neglect—Reports Alleging Maltreatment" (online at http://ndas.cwla.org).

4. E. Kaye and R. Cook, *National Survey of Current and Former Foster Parents* (Washington, DC: U.S. Department of Health and Human Services, Administration on Children, Youth and Families, 1993); Child Welfare League of America, National Data Analysis System, "Out-of-Home Care Homes and Facilities, 2003" (online at http://ndas.cwla.org).

5. Richard Wexler, *Wounded Innocents: The Real Victims of the War against Child Abuse*, rev. ed. (Buffalo, NY: Prometheus Books, 1995).

6. David Fanshel and Eugene B. Shinn, *Children in Foster Care: A Longitudinal Investigation* (New York: Columbia University Press, 1978); Ellen Gambrill, *Critical Thinking in Clinical Practice: Improving the Accuracy of Judgements and Decisions about Clients* (San Francisco: Jossey-Bass, 1990); Duncan Lindsey, *The Welfare of Children* (New York: Oxford University Press, 1994).

7. Casey Family Programs, National Center for Resource Family Support, "General Foster Care Statistics" (online at www.casey.org) (18 February 2003) .

8. Elizabeth M. Tracy, "Family Preservation and Home Based Services," in Edwards and Hopps, *Encyclopedia of Social Work*, p. 973.

9. John R. Schuerman, Tina L. Rzepnicki, and Julia H. Littell, *Putting Families First: An Experiment in Family Preservation* (New York: Aldine De Gruyter, 1994), pp. 20–21.

10. Viviana A. Zelizer, *Pricing the Priceless Child: The Changing Social Value of Children* (New York: Basic Books, 1985).

11. Susan Tiffin, *In Whose Best Interest? Child Welfare Reform in the Progressive Era* (Westport, CT: Greenwood Press, 1982), pp. 142–143.

12. Gertrude Williams, "Protection of Children against Abuse and Neglect: Historical Background," in Gertrude J. Williams and John Money, Eds., *Traumatic Abuse and Neglect of Children at Home* (Baltimore, MD: The Johns Hopkins University Press, 1980), p. 77.

13. Robert H. Bremner, Ed., *Children and Youth in America—A Documentary History*, Vol. II: 1886–1932 (Cambridge, MA: Harvard University Press, 1971), p. 201.

14. *Annual Report of the MSPCC* 26 (December 31, 1906) p. 4, quoted in Paul Gerard Anderson, "The Origin, Emergence, and Professional Recognition of Child Protection," *Social Service Review* (June 1989), p. 224.

15. Anderson, "The Origin, Emergence, and Professional Recognition of Child Protection," pp. 224–227.

16. Anderson, "The Origin, Emergence, and Professional Recognition of Child Protection," p. 223.

17. Walter I. Trattner, *From Poor Law to Welfare State—A History of Social Welfare in America*, 3rd ed. (New York: Free Press, 1984), p. 115.

18. Lindsey, *The Welfare of Children*, p. 20.

19. Emma O. Lundberg, "Child Welfare," in Margaret B. Hodges, Ed., *Social Work Yearbook, 1949* (New York: Russell Sage Foundation), pp. 98–109.

20. P. V. Woolley and W. A. Evans, "Significance of Skeletal Lesions in Infants Resembling Those of Traumatic Origin," *Journal of the American Medical Association* 181 (September, 1955), pp. 17–24, cited in Lindsey, *The Welfare of Children*, p. 91.

21. Alvin L. Shore, "The Bleak Prospect for Public Child Welfare," *Social Service Review* (March 2000), p. 126.

22. Lindsey, *The Welfare of Children*, pp. 91–92.

23. Sheila B. Kamerman and Alfred J. Kahn, "Social Services for Children, Youth and Families in the United States," special issue of *Children and Youth Services Review* 12 (Dec. 1990), pp. 7–8, quoted in Lindsey, *The Welfare of Children*, p. 96.

24. Verlene McOllough, "The Orphan Train Comes to Clarion," *The Palimpsest* (Fall 1988), p. 146.

25. McOllough, "The Orphan Train Comes to Clarion," p. 146.

26. Trattner, *From Poor Law to Welfare State*, p. 118.

27. Trattner, *From Poor Law to Welfare State*, pp. 118, 202.

28. Henry S. Maas and Richard E. Engler Jr., *Children in Need of Parents* (New York: Columbia University Press, 1959), p. 3.

29. Joseph H. Reid, "Action Called For—Recommendations," in Maas and Engler, *Children in Need of Parents*, p. 380.

30. Helen Jeter, *Children, Problems and Services in Child Welfare Programs* (Washington, DC: U.S. Children's Bureau, 1963).

31. Fanshel and Shinn, *Children in Foster Care*.

32. Mary Lee Allen and Jane Knitzer, "Child Welfare: Examining the Policy Framework," in Brenda G. McGowan and William Meezan, Eds., *Child Welfare: Current Dilemmas—Future Directions* (Itasca, IL: Peacock, 1983), pp. 120–123.

33. Susan Whitelaw Downs, Ernestine Moore, Emily Jean McFadden, and Susan Michaud, *Child Welfare and Family Services: Policies and Practice*, 7th ed. (Boston: Allyn and Bacon, 2004), p. 274.

34. Joyce E. Everett, "Child Foster Care," in Edwards and Hopps, *Encyclopedia of Social Work*, p. 385.

35. Jill Kinney, David Haapala, and Charlotte Booth, *Keeping Families Together: The Homebuilders Model* (New York: Aldine De Gruyter, 1991), pp. 3–4.

36. Peter Pecora, James K. Whittaker, and Anthony Maluccio, with Richard P. Barth and Robert D. Plotnick, *The Child Welfare Challenge: Policy, Practice, and Research*, 2nd ed. (New York: Aldine De Gruyter, 2000), p. 278; Elizabeth M. Tracy, "Family Preservation and Home-Based Services," in Edwards and Hopps, *Encyclopedia of Social Work*, p. 974.

37. Karen Spar, "The Family Preservation and Support Program: Background and Description," *CRS Report for Congress* (Washington, DC: Congressional Research Service—Library of Congress, 1994), p. i.

38. Congressional Budget Office, Cost Estimate, S. 342, Keeping Families and Children Safe Act of 2003, Report to the Senate Committee on Health, Education, Labor, and Pensions (February 12, 2003).

39. Nancy Peddle and Ching-Tung Wang, *Current Trends in Child Abuse Prevention, Reporting, and Fatalities: The 1999 Fifty State Survey* (Chicago: National Center on Child Abuse Prevention Research, 2001), p. 6.

40. Lindsey, *The Welfare of Children*, p. 32.

41. J. Bowlby, "The Nature of the Child's Ties to His Mother," *International Journal of Psychoanalysis* 39 (March 1958), pp. 350–373, cited in Lindsey, *The Welfare of Children*, p. 32.

42. Ferol E. Mennen and Maura O'Keefe, "Informed Decisions in Child Welfare: The Use of Attachment Theory," *Children and Youth Services Review*, 27 (2005), pp. 557–593.

43. Fanshel and Shinn, *Children in Foster Care*, p. 449.

44. N. J. Hochstady, P. K. Jaudes, D. A. Zimo, and J. Schachter, "The Medical and Psychosocial Needs of Children Entering Foster Care," *Child Abuse and Neglect* 11 (Jan. 1987), pp. 53–62; A. McIntyre and T. Y. Kesler, "Psychological Disorders among Foster Children," *Journal of Clinical Child Psychiatry* 15 (Winter 1986), pp. 297–303; M. E. K. Moffatt, M. Peddie, J. L. Stulginskas, I. B. Pless, and N. Steinmetz, "Health Care Delivery to Foster Children: A Study," *Health and Social Work* 10 (May 1985), pp. 129–137.

45. Pew Commission on Children in Foster Care, *Fostering the Future: Safety, Permanence and Well-Being for Children in Foster Care*, (Washington, DC: Author, 2004); Mark Courtney, S. Terao, N. Bost, *Midwest Evaluation of the Adult Functioning of Former Foster Youth: Conditions of Youth Preparing to Leave Care* (Chicago: Chapin Hall Center for Children, 2004).

46. National Center on Abuse and Neglect, *Study Findings: National Study of Incidence and Severity of Child Abuse and Neglect* (Washington, DC: Department of Health, Education, and Welfare, 1982); David Gil, *Violence against Children: Physical Abuse in the United States* (Cambridge, MA: Harvard University Press, 1970), p. 112; Barbara Vobejda, "Are There No Orphanages?" *Washington Post Weekly Edition* (October 26–November 1, 1995), p. 32; Leroy Pelton, "Child Abuse and Neglect: The Myth of Classlessness," in Leroy Pelton, Ed., *The Social Context of Child Abuse and Neglect* (New York: Human Sciences Press, 1981), pp. 37–42; Richard J. Gelles, "Poverty and Violence toward

Children," *American Behavioral Scientist* 35 (1992), pp. 258–274.

47. Lindsey, *The Welfare of Children*; Leroy Pelton, *For Reasons of Poverty: A Critical Analysis of the Public Child Welfare System in the United States* (New York: Praeger, 1989).

48. Joseph Goldstein, Anna Freud, and Albert J. Solnit, *Beyond the Best Interests of the Child* (New York: Free Press, 1973), pp. 16–20.

49. Lindsey, *The Welfare of Children*, p. 157; Pelton, *For Reasons of Poverty*.

50. Downs, Moore, McFadden, and Michaud *Child Welfare and Family Services: Policy and Practice*, p. 15.

51. Ann Hartman, "Ideological Themes in Family Policy," *Families in Society: The Journal of Contemporary Human Services* (March 1995), pp. 182–192; L. Diane Bernard, "The Dark Side of Family Preservation," *Affilia: Journal of Women and Social Work* 7, No. 2 (Summer 1992), pp. 156–159.

52. Subcommittee on Human Resources of the Committee on Ways and Means, House of Representatives, 103rd Congress, First Session, "Hearings on President Clinton's Budget Proposal for New Funding for Child Welfare Services Targeted for Family Support and Preservation Services" (21 April 1993).

53. Patrick Murphy, "Family Preservation and Its Victims," *New York Times* (19 June 1993), p. 21.

54. Heather MacDonald, "The Ideology of 'Family Preservation,'" *The Public Interest* (Spring 1994), p. 52.

55. Quoted in MacDonald, "The Ideology of 'Family Preservation,'" p. 51.

56. Quoted in Mary-Lou Weisman, "When Parents Are Not in the Best Interests of the Child," *Atlantic Monthly* (July 1994), p. 62.

57. Richard J. Gelles, *The Book of David: How Preserving Families Can Cost Children's Lives* (New York: Basic Books, 1996), pp. 148–149.

58. Fred Grandy, "Opening Statement," Subcommittee on Human Resources of the Committee on Ways and Means, House of Representatives, 103rd Congress, First Session, "Hearings on President Clinton's Budget Proposal for New Funding for Child Welfare Services Targeted for Family Support and Preservation Services" (21 April 1993), p. 3.

59. Carolyn L. Brown and Susan Little, "Family Reunification," *Children Today* (November–December 1990), p. 23.

60. Marianne Berry, "An Evaluation of Family Preservation Services: Fitting Agency Services to Family Needs," *Social Work* 37 (July 1992), p. 320; Jill Kinney, David Haapala, and Charlotte Booth, *Keeping Families Together: The Homebuilders Model* (New York: Aldine De Gruyter, 1991), pp. 186–187.

61. Kinney, Haapala, and Booth, *Keeping Families Together: The Homebuilders Model*, p. 185; Charles E. Wheeler, Grietje Reuter, David Struckman-Johnson, and Ying-Ying T. Yuan, "Evaluation of State of Connecticut Intensive Family Preservation Services: Phase V Annual Report" (Sacramento, CA: Walter R. McDonald & Associates), cited in Schuerman et al., *Putting Families First*, p. 34; Berry, "An Evaluation of Family Preservation Services," p. 316.

62. Julia H. Littell, "Effects of the Duration, Intensity, and Breadth of Family Preservation Services: A New Analysis of Data from the Illinois Family First Experiment," *Children and Youth Services Review* 19 (1997), p. 34.

63. D. N. Willems and R. DeRubeis, "The Effectiveness of Intensive Preventive Services for Families with Abused, Neglected, or Disturbed Children: Hudson County Project Final Report," (Trenton: Bureau of Research, New Jersey Division of Youth and Family Services, 1990); Stephen J. Leeds, "Evaluation of Nebraska's Intensive Services Project" (Iowa City, IA: National Resource Center on Family Based Services, 1984), reviewed in Schuerman et al., *Putting Families First*, pp. 34–35.

64. Steven A. Szykula and Matthew J. Fleishman, "Reducing Out-of-Home Placements of Abused Children: Two Controlled Field Studies," *Child Abuse and Neglect* 9 (March 1985), pp. 277–283.

65. Hennepin County Community Services Department, "Family Study Project: Demonstration and Research in Intensive Services to Families," 1980, reviewed in Theodore J. Stein, "Projects to Prevent Out-of-Home Placement," *Children and Youth Services Review* 7 (Fall 1988), pp. 109–121.

66. Christian Dagenais, Jean Begin, Camil Bouchard, and Daniel Fortin, "Impact of Intensive Family Support Programs: A Synthesis of Evaluation Studies," *Children and Youth Services Review* 26 (2004), pp. 249–263.

67. Schuerman et al., *Putting Families First*, pp. 53–79, 143–191.

68. Littell, "Effects of the Duration, Intensity, and Breadth of Family Preservation Services," p. 34.

69. Peter Pecora, James K. Whittaker, Anthony N. Maluccio, and Richard Barth, with Robert D. Plot-nick, *The Child Welfare Challenge*, 2nd ed. (New York: Aldine De Gruyter, 2000), p. 294.

70. Peter J. Pecora, James K. Whittaker, and Anthony Maluccio, with Richard P. Barth and Robert D. Plotnick, *The Child Welfare Challenge: Policy, Practice, and Research* (New York: Aldine De Gruyter, 1992), p. 295.

71. Berry, "An Evaluation of Family Preservation Services."

72. Everett, "Child Foster Care," p. 383; Child Welfare League of America, *Kinship Care: A Natural Bridge* (Washington, DC: Child Welfare League of America, 1994); Rebecca L. Hager and Maria Scannapieco, *Kinship Foster Care: Policy, Practice, and Research* (New York: Oxford University Press, 1999); Child Welfare League of America, "Kinship Care Fact Sheet" (October 2005).

73. Mark E. Courtney, "The Foster Care Crisis and Welfare Reform: How Might Reform Efforts Affect the Foster Care System?" *Public Welfare* (Summer 1995), p. 31.

74. Robert M. Goerge, "The Reunification Process in Substitute Care," *Social Service Review* (September 1990), p. 436.

75. Mark E. Courtney, "Factors Associated with the Reunification of Foster Children with Their Families," *Social Service Review* 68 (March 1994), pp. 81–108.

76. Robin Warsh, Barbara A. Pine, and Anthony Maluccio, "The Meaning of Family Preservation: Shared Mission, Diverse Methods," *Families in Society: The Journal of Contemporary Human Services* 76 (December 1995), p. 625.

77. Duncan Lindsey, "Factors Affecting the Foster Care Placement Decision: An Analysis of National Survey Data," *American Journal of Orthopsychiatry* 6 (Spring 1991), pp. 272–281.

78. Mark Courtney, "Managed Care and Child Welfare Services: What Are the Issues?" *Children and Youth Services Review* 22 (February 2000), pp. 87–91.

79. Edith Fein and Anthony N. Maluccio, "Permanency Planning: Another Remedy in Jeopardy," *Social Service Review* 37 (September 1992), pp. 344–345.

80. Fein and Maluccio, "Permanency Planning," p. 345.

Conclusion

At the end of a sentence, you expect a punctuation mark; at the end of a road, you expect a destination; at the end of a book, you expect a conclusion. After writing three hundred and some odd pages about social welfare policy, we think there are two logical types of conclusion. The first regards what lessons we believe we have learned from the process of developing our policy analysis framework and applying it to the five areas in the previous chapters. The second is a discussion of how we can take the lessons we have learned and develop an action strategy to address the problems uncovered.

Lessons from Policy Analysis

When in graduate school, one of the authors had a favorite economics professor who was fond of saying that the key to understanding economics is the realization that everything is related to everything else—in at least two ways. This is also a useful observation for social welfare policy. All parts of policy are infinitely complex and interrelated in a seemingly endless variety of ways. This same professor also used to say that if you took all the economists in the world and laid them end to end, they would never reach a conclusion. Although a cynic might also say this about social welfare policy analysts, we do not want to end this book on such a note. We think several broad, general conclusions can be drawn from the analyses we have presented, and we will identify these in the following sections.

The Bottom Line Is the Bottom Line

The primary issue in practically every area of social welfare policy is *cost*. Put another way, social welfare policy is always subservient to economic policy. Every policy reform we have discussed has as its driving goal the reduction of expenditures, or else a fear that costs will get out of control. The 1996 welfare reform legislation has as its centerpiece requirements that recipients become employed, with time limits for this to happen. The argument is that we are spending too much and that work requirements will reduce costs. The main argument for family preservation is that by intervening in a family quickly and intensively, we can avoid foster care and thus reduce total long-range cost. Most proposals for reform of Social Security are based on assumptions that the system will go broke at some future date unless costs are reined in. Managed care is a system designed to deliver medical and mental health services at a cheaper rate. Issues of humanitarianism, quality of life, promoting a good society, and mutual responsibility are all secondary to doing it cheaper.

As social workers, we have often been pulled into the cost game and we have sold policies we wished to pursue based on promised cost reductions. Lindblom's notion of partisan policy analysis is why we do this. (If you will remember from Chapter 3, Lindblom is the political scientist who argues that people perform policy analyses directed toward the goals of those they wish to influence.) Realizing that policymakers are greatly concerned with cost, social workers try to sell policies based on cost reduction. Social workers did this in 1962 when we convinced Congress that providing social services to welfare recipients would help them solve the problems leading to their dependency, get them off welfare, and thus save costs. We did this again in 1993 with arguments advocating for the Family Preservation and Support Program. Legislators quickly soured on the 1962 Social Service Amendments when they did not produce the expected cost savings. Now that family preservation is firmly in place and foster care placement rates—hence costs—are continuing to rise, it is highly likely that Congress will also sour on this, even if it can be demonstrated that by other criteria the concept is a success.

Compassion and Protection: Dual Motivations for Social Welfare Policy

Our review of current social welfare policies has confirmed Ralph Pumphrey's historical review of social welfare in the United States. He argued that all social welfare is driven by two more or less compatible motives. On the one side is the desire of people to make the lives of others better. "This aspect of philanthropy may be designated as *compassion:* the effort to alleviate present suffering, deprivation, or other undesirable conditions to which a segment of the population, but not the benefactor, is exposed." On the other side are aspects of policies that are designed for the benefit of their promoters and of the community at large. Pumphrey called this motivation *protection* and stated, "It may result either from fear of change or from fear of what may happen if existing conditions are not changed." Pumphrey concludes by offering the hypothesis that social welfare policies that have proved effective have been characterized by a balance between compassion and protection.[1]

Aspects of compassion and protection have been evident in all the policies we have analyzed. Public welfare policy is concerned with helping poor people (actually the children of poor people) but is also concerned with protecting society against the threat of dependent adults; family preservation policy seeks to help keep families together but also seeks to protect society from the excessive costs of an escalating foster care population; Social Security is designed to assure that the elderly are afforded a reasonably comfortable retirement, but it also protects families from having to assume responsibility for the care and support of aging relatives.

Ideology Drives Out Data in Social Welfare Policy Making

Social welfare policies are influenced much more by social values than they are by data from empirical research. It causes policy analysts no end of frustration to see situations such as the welfare reform debate. Even though masses of data have been presented to Congress demonstrating that many poor people can't work and that there are not jobs for a majority of those who can, Congress continues to pass reform packages that feature time limits on assistance.[2] These time limits are based on the work ethic, with its assertion that work can be found by anyone who tries hard enough. As empiricists and social scientists, we express outrage, sometimes amusement, at what we view as antiscientific, anti-intellectual behavior.

Is this tendency to promote values over data really so difficult to understand? We don't think that it is. Even social workers and allied social scientists find it hard to accept data that contradict deeply held values. For example, we are finding the research that casts doubt on the effectiveness of family preservation programs difficult to deal with because these programs are embodiments of some of our most cherished values. When Richard Herrnstein and Charles Murray published *The Bell Curve: Intelligence and Class Structure in American Life*, social workers immediately rejected the book's main theses, in most cases never having bothered to read the book. We have read the book and found ample grounds on which to reject Herrnstein and Murray's assertions empirically. However, and this is our point, many of our colleagues rejected it without objectively assessing the arguments because these were so out of line with social work values.

Although we understand the tendency for ideology to drive out data in policy making, we do not excuse it. One of the ongoing challenges to policymakers will always be to make the process more rational and data based. This is the only way we will ever bring about meaningful social change and a more just society.

Policymakers Are Generally More Sophisticated Than They Appear

Political scientists Theodore Marmor, Jerry Mashaw, and Philip Harvey argue that the central feature of social welfare policy is misinformation. They say,

> A quite remarkable proportion of what is written and spoken about social welfare policy in the United States is, to put it charitably, mistaken. These mistakes are repeated by popular media addicted to the current and the quotable. Misconceptions thus insinuate themselves into the national consciousness; they can easily become the conventional wisdom.[3]

However, policymakers themselves generally know better. With the legion of consultants, expert staff members, and social scientists providing testimony before committees and all of the data and expertise available from government bureaus and private think tanks, all at the beck and call of legislators, they usually have a pretty good grasp on the reality of social welfare problems. Also, some policymakers, for example Daniel Patrick Moynihan, were experts in social welfare–related areas before they were elected to office. Others specialize in one or two areas of policy after election and quickly become quite expert.

With popular misconceptions about social welfare so strongly entrenched, how can legislators make policy in this area and hope to remain in office? Marmor, Mashaw, and Harvey present three options. They can try to correct the conventional wisdom, they can act as if the conventional wisdom is true, "or they can speak in terms that reflect popular understanding but attempt to govern on the basis of their quite different conception of the facts." The first option is a sure road to political death; the second is generally too cynical even for career politicians. So most see "dissembling as the only path available to policy reform combined with political success."[4]

These observations explain why reforms of social welfare policy have such a high failure rate. If reforms are marketed in terms of dominant misconceptions, they are destined to fail. As we saw in the chapter on welfare reform, nearly every politician is currently on the bandwagon supporting the two-year time limit on welfare benefits. However, all except for perhaps the most dense have seen the data that, having now passed two years, there are large numbers of welfare recipients for whom there simply is no work. They further realize that taking the steps necessary to guarantee work will result in a more costly, rather than less costly, welfare program. Thus, because social welfare policies are designed and marketed in a way that virtually assures eventual failure, reform will always be a key feature, perhaps even focus, of the system.

Our Expectations for Social Welfare Policy Are Unrealistic

The common denominator of all the policies we have analyzed, with perhaps the exception of Social Security, is that, for some of the reasons already mentioned, they have had disappointing outcomes. In an interesting analytical twist, the prominent sociologist Amitai Etzioni argues that the problem may well be not that the policies are failures, but rather that people expect too much from them. He argues that human behavior is extremely difficult to change and that the very act of attempting to do so is a tremendous challenge. He says, "We all know how difficult changing human behavior is, but this knowledge has not changed our basic optimistic predisposition. Once we truly accept that human behavior is surprisingly resistant to improvement, however, some rather positive, constructive lessons follow."[5] These lessons are summarized below.

Lower Your Expectations—Expect Change to Cost Much More Than Predicted

Because behavior change is so difficult to accomplish, we should be happy with any positive results at all. Viewed from this perspective, we should celebrate the fact that family preservation programs are successful in reaching and helping a few families, that a welfare-to-work program places 10 or 15 percent of participants in jobs, that boot camps for young offenders have a 50 percent graduation rate. Regarding this last example, Etzioni observes, "We must acknowledge that hoping to assimilate people raised for twenty years in one subculture (say, the inner city, as a gang member) into a different subculture (of work and social responsibility) in only a few months is laughably ambitious."[6]

Creaming Is Okay

Social programs are often criticized for concentrating on the part of the target population with the fewest problems. For example, welfare-to-work programs often admit recipients with a comparatively high level of education, few problems, and recent work experience because they are easy to place in jobs and make the program look effective. As we saw in the review of family preservation, that policy is currently under criticism because the clients selected for services are not the most serious cases. Researchers have concluded that most of family preservation's clients were never in danger of having the children removed in the first place. Critics say that the practice of creaming is undesirable because it directs services to people who may not even need them and it avoids dealing with the really tough problems. Etzioni disagrees, arguing that we never have enough money to help everyone and so it only makes sense to concentrate our efforts on those most likely to benefit. "The resources saved this way can then be applied to some of the more difficult cases. Policymakers should, though, recognize the fact that the going will get tougher and tougher."[7]

Don't Expect to Scrape the Bottom of the Barrel

We must recognize that even with concentrated and persistent effort, no social welfare policy will ever be able to reach everyone and every social problem. In a situation analogous to a medical patient with an illness too severe to cure, there are some people who will never be adequate parents, some welfare recipients who will never be able to get a job, some criminals who see no percentage in being "rehabilitated," and some social problems, such as poverty, that may never be completely eradicated.

Don't Allow the Best to Defeat the Good

We generally tend to evaluate social welfare policies relative to the original promises of their sponsors rather than to some reasonable level of achievement. Because of the nature of the political process, policies are almost always oversold initially in order to get enough support to be enacted. Because, as we have noted again and again, social welfare policies rarely exhibit spectacular success, they should be measured against other policies rather than against some ideal standard. For example, a welfare-to-work program that increases the level of paid employment by nine hours a month will be considered a failure if measured against the standard that all participants should find full-time jobs. However, if compared with other programs that increased work by only five hours per month, this program could look very good. "As long as the social goal at hand must be served, we must settle for the comparative best (which is often not so hot), rather than chase elusive perfection."[8]

Be Multifaceted But Not Holistic

In social work school, we teach students to utilize a systems approach. This approach illustrates how the various aspects of a person's life and problems are related and that anything affecting one aspect of a system will reverberate throughout the system. This approach also illustrates that policies must address a number of facets of a person's life to be truly effective. Probably the best example in this book is child welfare policy. It is now quite fashionable to point out that it is impossible to address child abuse and neglect effectively without at the same time addressing poverty. Etzioni accepts this but argues that a holistic approach would cost so much and be so complex that it would never be practical for the large number of people who need help. We must search for policies that recognize the systems aspect of problems but are less exacting than a holistic approach. Thus, while we recognize that poverty is the major factor leading to child neglect, we can still provide therapeutic day care programs that address only a few targeted aspects of the neglect and by doing so make children's lives better. As Etzioni concludes,

> It's no use pretending that poverty or welfare will be abolished, AIDS or cancer cured in this century, drug abuse or teen pregnancy sharply reduced. Let's instead dedicate our efforts to effective but clearly delineated projects in each of these areas. This humbler approach is likely to have a very attractive side effect: it may enhance public willingness to pay for such projects and may also restore public trust in our leaders and institutions.[9]

There are slight indications that Etzioni's advice about lowering expectations is beginning to sink in for program evaluators, at least. In their meta-analysis of scientifically adequate evaluations of family support programs, Dagenais,

Begin, Bouchard, and Fortin found evidence of only very slight effects by the twenty-seven programs evaluated. After discussing the disappointing data they surprisingly conclude, "Investigators would, therefore be wise to give up on obtaining spectacular results and content themselves with more modest program gains. Not even a small change in a family should be taken lightly, however."[10]

Taking Action—Policy Practice for Social Workers

The focus of this book, quite intentionally, has been on the development of a set of largely passive skills, those of the policy analyst. Social work, however, is an action-oriented profession, and social workers are action-oriented people. We therefore end this book with a brief discussion of the skills that social workers can develop to take the results of policy analysis, results that almost always reveal that policies are deficient in a number of ways, and translate them into action strategies to improve policies to better fit our vision of a just and equitable society. We wish to note, however, that although policy analysis is a passive activity, it is a necessary prerequisite to any type of action strategy. For an action strategy to be effective, it is imperative that the people taking the action have a firm grasp on the problem they are dealing with and on achievable goals. Doing your homework is necessary before action is taken, and that homework is policy analysis. The following strategies are all built on solid policy analysis.

Program Evaluation

You've been working at the Greenville Family Services Center for about a year. This agency, funded by the United Way as well as several small state contracts and client fees, provides counseling, parent education, and a variety of other services to children and their families. The agency's clientele ranges from middle-class to lower-income families. Six months ago the center began to implement a pilot community outreach project, in which it delivers its services directly in schools and several neighborhood community centers.

Today the center's director stopped you in the hall. "I've been thinking," she said, "about a new project for you. You're pretty fresh out of school, and so your knowledge about research and policy issues is probably more up-to-date than that of a lot of the other staff. And you've been here long enough to have a feel for our philosophy and how we operate. I'd really like you to take on an interim program evaluation of how this new community project is going."

"Wow," you answer, both flattered and inwardly terrified. "I know we've talked about these things in class, but I've never actually done an evaluation. But I guess I can try."

"Good!" she exclaims, "Then that's settled. Come into my office on Monday and we'll talk about how you'll proceed."

Saturday rolls around and you are sitting in your favorite coffeehouse wondering what you've gotten yourself into. But then again, how hard can it be? You've saved texts and notes from your classes. There are probably some straightforward steps in the books on how to go about an evaluation.

Actually, a text will only get you so far in this process. It can describe some techniques to use. More important, it can orient you toward the sorts of questions you need to ask as you plan your evaluation. Even policy analysis texts like this one—although they don't aim to teach you specific macropractice or research skills—can still offer a frame of reference for approaching your new task. (And note that Chapter 3 in this book describes several types of policy and program evaluation.) The following are the basic components in the program evaluation process and the questions that can guide them. (See Figure 12.1 for a sample program evaluation.)

1. Most important, you need to find out the *goals* of the program because achievement of these goals is what you'll be evaluating. Was the agency trying to reach out to new clients? To make services convenient for existing clients? Or perhaps to make services more successful by locating them in the actual environment where clients may be experiencing their difficulties so that the worker can observe some of their daily problems firsthand, watch their interactions with the environment, and help them to practice new behaviors? Are some goals manifest, or direct, and others latent, or not openly communicated? Perhaps the director wants staff to see and more fully understand the actual challenges—such as low incomes, crowded schools, and inadequate recreation facilities—that some clients face.

This could be pretty easy, you think. And it may not be hard to find out all the formal and some informal goals by talking with the director, board members, and key staff persons, and by reading the official description of the project. You may find different goal expectations on the part of supervisors and direct service staff and should take this into consideration as you think about how to structure your evaluation. Another factor may further complicate your life: Human "experiments," especially program experiments, are "messy" ones. You can't put a glass dome over the project to shield it from outside occurrences and from staff and administrative reactions. As two social scientists noted in their description of an evaluation of antipoverty programs in the 1960s, goals for these programs often changed in midstream and new approaches were added. "As soon as staff discovered a better way of serving [program participants] they adapted their procedures, methods, and techniques accordingly. It was impossible to be inventive, flexible, and expedient . . . and at the same time do careful, scientific, controlled research."[11]

Figure 12.1 An Outcome Evaluation Instrument for Residential Programs

The person who developed the following outcome evaluation instrument is a staff member in a state Office of Children's Services. At the time that she devised this set of outcome measures, she was also a social work student enrolled in a required course in Program and Practice Evaluation. She decided to meet the class assignment of presenting a sample program evaluation by creating an instrument that could actually be used by her agency.

Problem: To develop an outcome instrument that would allow the state office to monitor and evaluate the work of a large variety of residential programs for troubled youth that contract with the state to provide services.

Solution: The following outcome data will be provided annually to the Office of Children's Services by the residential program:

> How many youths are served in the facility, by age and sex?
> What is the average length of stay per child by each level of care (i.e., mild, moderate, or controlled)?
> What is the number of children in this placement at least six months whose level of care at the end of the review period was (1) less severe than at placement, (2) more severe than at placement, (3) the same as at placement?
> What is the number of behavioral incidents reported, documented, or investigated internally by the program? (Behaviors to count include running away, abusing substances, becoming pregnant, committing a crime, contracting an STD, and initiating sexual perpetration.)
> How many children have exhibited (1) good or markedly improved school attendance, (2) good or markedly improved grades, (3) good or markedly improved school behavior?
> How many children have learned an art, sport, or other skill not normally obtained from daily living experiences?
> How many children have been discharged (1) because they successfully completed their treatment plan; (2) because of difficulty with their behaviors or emotional states and the provider did not feel they were appropriate for the facility; (3) because they were admitted to a psychiatric hospital, ran away, or were incarcerated; (4) because of other reasons beyond the control of the provider (e.g., court decision to return child to family)?
> How many children have been discharged (1) to a less restrictive environment, such as a family setting; (2) to a more restrictive environment, such as a boot camp, psychiatric hospital, or other institution?

This response to the class assignment became the first draft of an outcome evaluation instrument that was adopted by the state office. It has been in operation for one year, and the student is helping to evaluate and refine it for further use.

Source: Adapted from an evaluation instrument developed by Sybil Willis. Used with her permission.

So some compromises in your evaluation design will become inevitable as you try to accommodate changes in goals and services.

2. You will want to describe the *characteristics of the organization* in order to set the context for the new approach and to help you determine what changes have occurred. This includes a description of the *types of clients* involved in the new program. The backgrounds and practice techniques and interventions of *staff* are also important pieces of information related to the services that are being carried out to meet project goals. The *organizational structure* of the agency and of the new project will also be helpful in understanding how the new services are delivered and what constraints might hinder full execution of the goals.

3. You will probably find it helpful to do some process evaluation, which involves examining the way services are being carried out in the new program. For example, one program goal may be to treat clients with respect. You will need to devise ways to find out if direct workers, the receptionist, and other members of the staff are "doing this right"—for example, by observing whether they address clients by their last names and respond to them in a timely way when they come in for appointments or meetings.

In both the process evaluation and the outcome evaluation we describe later, it is crucial that you understand the demands that a program evaluation generally makes on the direct service workers, secretaries, financial officers, and similar staff members. These are the people who will be supplying you with various kinds of information, such as client statistics, financial reports, and responses to questionnaires about counseling outcomes. This means additional work for them; each interview with the evaluator, for example, cuts into time that a direct service worker might be spending with a client. It will be important, therefore, to bring staff members on board and to help them see that the evaluation not only will be useful to the agency but also could help them carry out their jobs. One good way of doing this is to find out what the direct service and other staff members would like to learn from this evaluation. What additional information would they like you to seek that would assist them in their work? This gives you new questions to add to the study.

4. Next, you will want to define *outcomes* that can be measured to determine whether the projects' goals are being met. Defining outcomes is a basic step in finding out whether a program achieved what it wanted to. In other words, you need a fairly concrete way to think about the program's goals, which will give you something to observe and measure. Usually, you will involve the agency director, key program staff, and anyone else who played a major role in setting the project's goals in this endeavor. Together, you can decide how the goals could be operationalized into outcomes, such as an increase in clients served by the agency, a change in types of clients being seen (maybe more lower-income families or youth, or more people from a particular neighborhood), and differences in the "presenting problems" or perhaps psychiatric diagnoses of the people being worked with. You may be thinking, "But this isn't finding out about changes in clients' satisfaction with the agency's services or about whether people's problems are alleviated more quickly or effectively since the program began to be offered outside the agency." And you would be right. In order to find out about the success of many of the agency's efforts, you would really need a *baseline*, or knowledge of what clients were experiencing before the change was enacted. For example, what was the level of client satisfaction with services, and how quickly and effectively were problems handled in the past? This kind of information is necessary for before-and-after comparisons. The outcome goals we've described are the sorts of things your agency has probably kept records on, such as number of clients and families served in a given month. You will therefore be able to measure changes in these particular outcomes. It may well turn out that your interim evaluation will include a design for a fuller evaluation and specify what baseline data—such as client satisfaction information—the agency should now begin to gather.

5. You will need to *measure* the outcomes of the program. Here's where things get complex; there are many different kinds of measurement to use, some simple and some sophisticated (consultation with a research methodologist, for example a social work faculty member who teaches program evaluation, might be helpful here). There are two major types of measurement—qualitative and quantitative. Studies can use one or combine both. One example of a qualitative approach would be to interview clients about their level of satisfaction with the new way of receiving services: What do they like or not like about it and why? You could also ask about the usefulness of the community-based intervention and, if a client was served by the agency before the project was implemented, you could explore which of the two approaches seemed most helpful and why. You could also observe client–worker interactions in both settings and look for differences in such measures as levels of relaxation and rapport. Finally, you could develop a set of interview questions to use with the agency workers.

The quantitative approach means producing data that can be statistically manipulated. We have already discussed some simple versions of this approach, such as noting the number of clients using agency services under the new program in comparison to the number using services under the old one. You might also use a written survey of client satisfaction and analyze the responses in a variety of ways, such as looking at the different ways in which particular variables (age, ethnicity, income level) seem to affect specific responses.

6. At the end of all of this, you will need to write a *report* or otherwise *disseminate* your findings. This might include suggestions for change. The report or other presentation of the study should be as clear and concise as possible. In the practical world of program evaluation, one hopes that one's findings, both positive and negative, will help organizations further refine their programs. This could involve expanding them, adding new elements, and abandoning approaches that don't seem to be meeting program goals. The report stage can be a delicate one. Your interpersonal skills and your awareness of the political elements in policy making will be called on, especially when you need to explain what parts of the program aren't working without arousing defensiveness among administrators and staff. Most important, you need to work to make sure that your evaluation doesn't end up on the shelf but instead continues to help the agency as it moves forward.

Building Coalitions

Most social work students know something about the value of coalitions. The notion of joining with others to make a change is probably a familiar one. You may have heard more about this in courses covering community organizing or social action, however, than in policy courses. Although coalitions can serve a variety of purposes, including large-scale political reform, we will talk here only about those that focus specifically on formulating, promoting, changing, or opposing a policy.[12] Such coalitions could focus on agency policies, court cases and legal decisions, city and county ordinances, legislative rules and regulations, rulings by government administrators, and state or federal legislation.

The typical coalition draws together representatives of a variety of groups that have some interest or concern regarding the policy in question (the notion of stakeholder, which we discussed in Chapter 6, is useful here). Members agree to work together on a particular policy issue, and the coalition gains its power from the combined efforts of its member organizations. These organizations represent different constituencies with a variety of sources of influence and power; when the coalition speaks, it is not the number of coalition members that matters, but the number and influence of people and interests it represents. As Bruce Jansson notes, this is particularly important in dealing with issues related to those with less power in our society, such as low-income families, homeless people, and those who are institutionalized.[13]

Coalitions take shape in various ways. The Mental Health Reform Coalition in Louisiana had its informal beginnings in the cooperation between lobbyists and directors of several advocacy groups that occupied the same office building. Because organizations advocating with and for those with mental illness and their families are relatively few in number in Louisiana, it was not difficult to identify and bring in other groups. Because these organizations had somewhat different agendas, however, a certain amount of negotiating and reaching consensus on common goals had to take place before all agreed to join. In other situations, it might take more effort to find potential coalition members. Sometimes, in doing preliminary research on a policy issue for your organization, you will come up with the names of other local, state, or national organizations that are working on the same issues. These can be contacted with the idea of making a common cause. It's important to remember, also, that fairly different groups may share an interest in one particular issue, as we will see in the example at the end of this section.[14]

Once the representatives of different organizations have come together, they typically engage in negotiating goals and an agenda and devising strategies for their work. In the case of the Mental Health Reform Coalition, all the organizations represented were interested in having a greater impact on the funding and service delivery decisions of the state Office of Mental Health and in promoting a mental health parity law in Louisiana. However, the groups had to agree on goals and priorities in these two areas. Negotiations regarding an agenda to promote with the state office called for some compromise between those groups valuing community-based mental health services and those lamenting the closing down of such institutional programs as a children's mental health facility in New Orleans. Similarly, in planning a lobbying campaign for a mental health parity law, an agreement had to be reached that both children's mental health services and adult services would be covered in the legislation.

The following scenario further illustrates the process of developing a coalition. Suppose a large development corporation has proposed a major development project at the edge of a university campus. The current area is home to several student bars, a bookstore, a branch of the Gap, a comfortable coffeehouse, several fast-food restaurants, a great Vietnamese restaurant, an old-time diner, a popular sandwich shop, and a middle-sized grocery store convenient for those families living in university housing. The area targeted by the developers also includes several blocks of a low-income, mostly African American neighborhood. The development proposal includes plans for a major conference center hotel, individual office buildings, and a large mall with spaces for upscale stores and restaurants. The design is intended to convey a sophisticated city atmosphere, but it will include old-fashioned touches such as gas street lights and balconies on many of the buildings. Some of the existing restaurants and stores may relocate into the new mall, but not all will be able to afford the rent. In addition, the several blocks of the low-income neighborhood on the project site would be razed, with compensation paid to homeowners and landlords. The woman who heads the development corporation has been quoted as saying that tearing down this area would be "no great loss."

The proposed project is attractive to some groups, including the city government and the Chamber of Commerce, which visualize business expansion and additional tax revenues. But an unusual collection of opposing bodies is beginning to emerge. The first, interestingly, is a faction within the student government, which worries that such a "glitzy" project will change the funky, comfortable atmosphere of the existing commercial area and that the new stores and restaurants will be too expensive for most students. Married students in university housing, many of whom are international students with no cars, are concerned that their closest grocery store will disappear. Most faculty are not yet sure what to make of the development proposal, although some echo student concerns about the loss of at least part of the existing campus restaurant and shopping area, and others worry about increased parking problems. Those business owners who suspect they won't be able to relocate into the new project are clearer in their opposition to it.

A community economic development group in the African American neighborhood, made up largely of local businesspeople and clergy, has also raised concerns about the effects of the development on their neighborhood, especially the loss of three or four blocks of housing. Interestingly, several departments in the university have created a university–community partnership program through which university faculty and students and the economic development group work together on community improvement projects in the neighborhood. The program is carried out with the blessing of university administrators.

The university–community partnership program hired a recent social work graduate several years ago to staff the program. This person has become the catalyst in bringing the various interest groups together in opposition to the new project, at least in its present form. She has spoken individually with the community development group members, business owners, leaders of the informal faction in student government, members of the international student association, and members of the Faculty Senate. As she proceeds, she is identifying common goals and possible actions, including questioning the zoning regulations that allow construction of such a large development close to campus as well as the destruction of several blocks of homes. There is also some question whether the city should be issuing building permits for structures that might strain existing roads and utilities.

As you can see, this is a promising scenario for the creation of a unique and potentially strong coalition of a variety of groups opposed to the development project. Its success will depend in part on the groups' ability to work together on a common agenda, to gain support from presently uncommitted bodies such as the university administration, and to fashion successful strategies aimed at influencing policies on commercial development.

Information Dissemination

As Haynes and Mickelson point out, data on social problems or needs are absolutely essential to any type of policy change strategy:

> No matter what form of intervention a social worker may undertake—community organization, casework, administration, or political activity—the resource most needed and used is information. Before any diagnosis can be reached or community organization strategy developed, information about the client's background and presenting problem or the community's problem and demographics must first

be obtained. Intervention in the political arena has the same basic requirement because the same processes are used by the social worker in the political arena as in case or community work.[15]

The first step in information dissemination is documentation. As social workers, we keep copious records and notes on all our cases, so we are already in possession of a great deal of documentation. Policymakers have a great deal of macrolevel data available to them to help in their decision-making process, and social workers are perfectly capable of adding to this data. Our professional organizations, such as the National Association of Social Workers and the Child Welfare League of America, keep massive databases, which are available to policymakers. However, this information is available from a number of sources and is not the most valuable contribution social workers can make. What social workers are in a unique position to provide is a human face to go with the statistics.

One of the authors once served on the budget committee of a large social service funding organization. One of the agencies that received much of its funding from this group provided rehabilitation services to people who were alcohol or drug dependent. The executive director of the agency was a brilliant, Ivy League–trained public administrator who came to the budget committee year after year with beautifully detailed and presented materials on needs, services, trends, outcomes, and the historic decline in funding to the agency. When he began his presentation, the budget committee would listen attentively, albeit with a somewhat glazed-over look, and would, in the end, cut the agency's appropriation. One year, however, he did something different. He began his presentation by handing out copies of all the charts, graphs, and tables on which he usually based his presentation. He then said that he was going to do something different that year, and he introduced a woman who was the agency's senior clinical social worker. She took over the presentation and spent twenty minutes describing a case she had worked with for many years. She described the client, a woman who came to the agency alone, crack addicted, and asked the agency to find a home for her two grade school–age children because she could not take care of them and, in any case, felt she would not live much longer. The social worker described how she convinced the mother to try getting off drugs one more time; she placed the woman and the children in the agency's shelter and got the mother into drug treatment, job training, and intensive counseling. The children were enrolled in a tutoring program, support groups for children of addicted persons, and recreation groups. A team was formed between the agency, the state department of social services, the county mental health agency, and the children's schools. Eventually, housing was found in a safe neighborhood, the mother got her drug habit under control, and she found a job. At the conclusion of the presentation, the social worker passed around pictures (with permission, of course) of the two children who were now young adults. One was working as a certified auto mechanic and the other was a college student preparing to be a grade school teacher. Following the presentation, the budget committee voted to give the agency the largest budget increase in its history. The reason was clearly that the social worker had provided a type of documentation that made the executive director's charts, graphs, and statistics come alive and have real meaning and import for the decision-making committee.

There are a number of ways in which social workers can provide documentation to influence the policy-making process. One is giving testimony. Whenever legislative bodies consider a policy change, they hold a public hearing in which anyone can address the body. Social workers can provide documentation based on their practice experience, which can lead to particularly persuasive testimony. The National Association of Social Workers and several other professional social work and social work education organizations work through Action Network for Social Work Education and Research (ANSWER) to promote legislation that supports the profession and the people and communities with which it works. In the last several years, social workers have lobbied extensively to maintain funding for child welfare services in the face of proposed cuts by the Bush administration and a Republican Congress. Advocacy work by ANSWER and individual social workers in Spring 2006 helped defeat the Health Insurance Marketplace Modernization and Affordability Act, which would have rolled back state provider mandate laws and repealed state mental health parity laws as well as other mental health coverage mandates. Social workers have also fought for a fair, equitable, and comprehensive plan regarding the latest wave of immigration across the country's border with Mexico. NASW's position is that "immigration is the foundation and essence of American society. . . . Any proposal that diminishes the well being of immigrant citizens and denies immigrant workers basic protections is detrimental to the ideals of this great nation." NASW has lobbied against bills that discriminate against immigrants and which criminalize those who would assist undocumented immigrants in need.[16]

Social workers can also act as expert witnesses when legislative committees or administrative bodies request testimony about an issue. For example, a school board considering establishing a program of after-school activities may request that a social worker from one of the communities targeted provide testimony on the activities of gangs in the area and proved strategies for deflecting children from gang membership. Unlike providing testimony, which anyone can do simply by signing up, serving as an expert witness requires an invitation. In order to be invited to serve in this role, one must be able to demonstrate that by some combination of education and experience one is indeed an "expert."

The most accessible and practical means of providing documentation is written communication. Social workers should regularly communicate with their elected representatives regarding pending legislation relevant to social welfare.

Contrary to popular opinion, legislators do pay attention to their mail, and a communication from someone who can establish professional expertise regarding an issue can have a real effect. A letter to the editor of a newspaper or news-magazine or, even better, an op-ed piece can help sway public and decision-maker opinion. Letters should be neat and professional appearing. You should start by stating the subject and your credentials for discussing it, clearly state and back up your opinion, recommend specific action, and sign your name, address, and phone number.

Lobbying

Supplying documentation, testifying, acting as an expert witness, and engaging in written communication can be identified as individual components of the larger process of lobbying. Lobbying is simply the purposive, goal-directed, planned process of attempting to influence the position of a decision maker, usually an elected one. In the past, many social workers have tended to shy away from formal lobbying, believing that it is a self-serving activity that has no place in an altruistic profession, that it requires a lot of money, and that it requires formal training in politics and the political process.

Although it is true that much of lobbying is self-serving, not all is. Many decisions regarding the welfare of oppressed and disadvantaged groups are made in the policy arena of Washington, D.C., state capitals, and city and county court-houses. If, as social workers, we are serious about improving the lives of these groups, we need to actively attempt to influence decisions that affect their lives. We should also realize that being self-serving is not always a bad thing. Many of the lobbying activities of professional social work are in regard to issues such as licensing and Medicare reimbursement rates for social workers. These issues could be seen as self-serving, but they have wider implications.

It is also true that money plays a part in lobbying. However, great deals of money are not essential. The activities we have described cost very little and can be very effective.

Finally, social workers are already trained in most of the skills essential for effective lobbying. Lobbying is mostly a process of developing relationships and effective communication, both skills central to social work training. The specific knowledge needed for lobbying, such as familiarity with the legislative process, correct forms of address for various officials, and understanding the various roles of officials, are easily obtainable from literature available from groups such as the League of Women Voters.

The specifics of lobbying are beyond the scope of this book, but we do want to make one essential point. A social worker considering lobbying should realize that lobbyists, rather than being perceived as a nuisance, are an essential source of information, and even a personnel resource, for legislators. Elected officials are required to deal with an incredible range of complex, technical issues, most of them in areas in which they have no expertise. These officials rely on lobbyists who have—either as individuals or as representatives of groups—the needed technical knowledge. A legislator who is trained as an engineer and is on a committee dealing with a piece of child abuse legislation will welcome input from a group of social workers trained and experienced in child welfare. Moreover, much of the legislation lawmakers introduce is written for them by lobbyists or by professionals acting as lobbyists. The vignette on childhood sexual abuse legislation at the beginning of Chapter 6 is a good example of a professional's involvement in this process.

Social workers have been involved in lobbying in many ways for many years. In the early years of the twentieth century, social worker C. C. Carstens, General Secretary of the Massachusetts Society for the Prevention of Cruelty to Children, had the Speaker of the Massachusetts House of Representatives on his board of directors. Each year, Carstens would prepare an agenda of children's issues, which the speaker would proceed to introduce to the House. During the New Deal, President Roosevelt's chief of staff was social worker Harry Hopkins, and social workers had substantial influence on the development of the Social Security Act. In the 1950s, the profession became formally involved in the legislative process through the establishment of a legislative office in Washington by the National Association of Social Workers. Most NASW state chapters now have a government relations director (a title that means, essentially, "lobbyist").

Political Action for Candidate Election

Another important social policy action strategy for social workers is working to put people in elected office who reflect values and goals consistent with those of social work. Social workers can, of course, individually work for political candidates. Campaigns for political office rely heavily on volunteers to do everything from answering the phone, to stuffing envelopes, to going door to door to promote the candidate, to helping raise money, to developing issue papers and campaign strategy. The political process is, for better or worse, one of quid pro quo (you scratch my back and I'll scratch yours), so one of the best ways of gaining influence with an elected official is to have a record of campaign participation. Those involved in the early stages of a campaign, particularly one waging an uphill battle, will earn particular gratitude from the candidate.

Another strategy is to work through a political action committee (PAC). PACs are organizations set up to collect and disburse voluntary contributions from members of special-interest groups for the purpose of furthering the political goals of the groups. In 1976 the National Association of Social Workers established a PAC called Political Action for Candidate Election. This was initially established to support candidates for national-level offices. Since 1976, all but four NASW chapters have set up state-level PACs. Haynes and Mickelson observe, "Poor people, sick people, the elderly, and children do not make political campaign contributions, and indeed often don't or can't vote. Thus, a social workers' PAC is a necessary advocacy group, not for professional self-interest and protection, but for the disadvantaged and disenfranchised as well."[17]

Running for Office

Calls for social workers to become involved in electoral politics are as old as the profession itself. In 1896, James B. Reynolds, speaking at the most prestigious professional conference of the era, urged social workers to go into politics.[18] Jeffrey Brackett, founding director of the Boston School for Social Workers, was elected to the Baltimore city council in 1900; Zebulon Brockway, a progressive prison administrator and reformer, was elected mayor of Elmira, New York, in 1905; Thomas Osborn, another penologist, was elected to the Auburn, New York, Board of Education in 1885, was nominated for lieutenant governor in 1888, and was elected mayor in 1903. The first woman elected to the U.S. House of Representatives was Jeanette Rankin, a social worker and Republican from Montana, in 1916. More recently, Ronald Dellums, a psychiatric social worker, was elected to Congress in 1970; Barbara Mikulski, another social worker, was elected to the House and subsequently the Senate; and Ed Towns was elected to the House from New York City.[19]

With the vast number of elected offices on the national, state, and local level, it is hard to fix the exact number of social workers currently holding office. However, it is clear that it is rapidly increasing. In 2005, six social workers served in Congress and sixty-eight were members of state legislatures. In addition, 101 social workers held local positions, such as service on a city council or membership on a School Board.[20] When one of the authors was director of a medium-size midwestern school of social work, he had on his faculty and staff the city mayor, a member of the city commission, and the chairperson of the county Democratic party. Apparently, the interest that NASW focused on electoral politics is sifting down to the membership, who are becoming involved on an individual level.

The famous social caseworker Mary Richmond once spoke of social work as retail and wholesale. *Retail* meant one-on-one social work with individual clients to solve individual problems. *Wholesale* meant social action social work attempting to find collective solutions to problems affecting thousands of people. We hope that the policy analysis skills and the policy analysis examples that we have presented in this book have, at the very least, sensitized you to the absolute necessity for wholesale approaches to the problems we as social workers address. All social workers learn conventional macropractice skills for intervention in large systems.

Less commonly taught is what we consider to be the ultimate macropractice approach: that of becoming involved in the electoral process and, ideally, becoming an elected official.

Notes

1. Ralph Pumphrey, "Compassion and Protection: Dual Motivations in Social Welfare," *Social Service Review* 23 (1959), pp. 21–29.

2. For example, see "Testimony of Sheldon Danziger, Professor, School of Social Work and School of Public Policy, University of Michigan, Before the Senate Finance Committee, February 29, 1996."

3. Theodore R. Marmor, Jerry L. Mashaw, and Philip L. Harvey, *America's Misunderstood Welfare State* (New York: Basic Books, 1990), p. 213.

4. Marmor, Mashaw, and Harvey, *America's Misunderstood Welfare State*, pp. 213–214.

5. Amitai Etzioni, "Incorrigible," *Atlantic Monthly* 274 (July 1994), pp. 14–16.

6. Etzioni, "Incorrigible," p. 16.

7. Etzioni, "Incorrigible," p. 16.

8. Etzioni, "Incorrigible," p. 16.

9. Etzioni, "Incorrigible," p. 16.

10. Christian Dagenais, Jean Begin, Camil Bouchard, and Daniel Fortin, "Impact of Intensive Family Support Programs: A Synthesis of Evaluation Studies," *Children and Youth Services Review*, 26 (2004), p. 259.

11. Peter Marris and Martin Rein, *Dilemmas of Social Reform* (New York: Atherton Press, 1967), pp. 197–198.

12. Norman L. Wyers, "Policy-Practice in Social Work: Models and Issues," *Journal of Social Work Education* 27 (Fall 1991), p. 242.

13. Bruce Jansson, *Becoming an Effective Policy Advocate* (Pacific Grove, CA: Brooks/Cole, 1999), pp. 302–303.

14. Willard C. Richan, *Lobbying for Social Change*, 2nd ed. (New York: Haworth Press, 1996), pp. 188–189.

15. Karen Haynes and James S. Mickelson, *Affecting Change: Social Workers in the Political Arena*, 5th ed. (Boston: Allyn and Bacon, 2003), p. 84.

16. NASW, Government Relations Updates (online at www.socialworkers.org/advocacy).

17. Haynes and Mickelson, *Affecting Change: Social Workers in the Political Arena*, p. 153.

18. J. B. Reynolds, "The Settlement and Municipal Reform," in *Proceedings of the National Conference of Charities and Correction* (Boston: George H. Ellis, 1896), pp. 138–142.

19. Toby Weismiller and Sunny Harris Rome, "Social Workers in Politics," in Richard L. Edwards, Ed., *Encyclopedia of Social Work*, 19th ed. (Washington, DC: NASW Press, 1996), pp. 2305–2313.

20. www.naswdc.org/pace/state.asp

appendix A

Library Research for Practitioner Policy Analysis

Lynn Tobola, M.L.S.
Social Work Librarian
University of Alabama

Information Self-Reliance

Since the first edition of this book was published in 1998, our world has changed. We have become more unified and torn apart than ever before. The ability to locate accurate, reliable information has gained unprecedented global interest and concern. Unquestionably, the ease and process of locating information has changed dramatically in the last few years. In the past, librarians could provide patrons with virtually all of the information available at their fingertips. Now, with the growing numbers of electronic resources available and the growth of the Internet, that is not easy, perhaps even impossible. Therefore, it is essential for social workers to move in the direction of becoming "information self-reliant," which can be defined as the ability to independently identify, locate, evaluate, and use information effectively. Locating information is a process-oriented task. As you become fluent with the process of identifying and locating print and online resources, you will be empowering yourself with information self-reliance skills.

Get to Know Your Librarians

There is nothing terribly complex about collecting information for policy analysis. Although the information itself is not unduly complicated, it is vast and becoming available at a dizzying pace. Many people still have the curious idea that the main function of librarians is to check out books and then return them to the shelves. They think that asking a librarian a question is an imposition on the librarian's time and often feel embarrassed to do so. Many times library users approach the reference desk only after failed attempts to locate specific information. Considering the abundant avenues for searching and the enormous numbers of resources to wade through, waiting to confer with a librarian can cost you valuable time.

Librarians are professionals trained to help people make efficient and effective use of the library. They assist individual patrons with particular research problems on a daily basis. Modern libraries contain a fascinating yet bewildering assortment of online, CD, machine-readable, and laser disc information retrieval systems, as well as the older print resources. A few sessions with your librarian, ideally focused on a research topic, will save you an immense amount of time and trouble. Librarians are keenly interested in teaching you the skills you need to learn as much as helping you find good relevant resources. Perhaps you feel comfortable or skilled searching the Internet, but learning to use other library resources with the assistance of a librarian can still be quite productive.

After you have become familiar with the major information-retrieval sources available in your library, your dependence on the reference librarians will begin to decrease. However, there will always be valid reasons to consult your librarian. For example, there may be a new resource available of which you are not aware. Stop by the reference desk occasionally and ask if there are any new additions to the collection that might be of value to your current research.

The quickest and easiest way to become information self-reliant is to go to the library and begin exploring the building by simply walking around. Get a visual sense of what is where. Where are the current journals shelved? Where is the reference department? What is the location of the interlibrary loan office? Bring a planned research strategy, ask for assistance, follow through on the instructions and suggestions of the librarian, and give it your best shot. You'll probably surprise yourself. You are on the way to becoming an information self-reliant social worker.

Explanation and Organization of Information Self-Reliance Topics

This appendix contains three items. The first two are worksheets designed to assist you in planning research strategies and to practice communication skills with librarians. The third is a set of checklists that you can use to determine whether a library has a particular title in print or electronic form, the locations of those titles, and the usefulness of those resources for specific information needs.

The checklists can be used, depending on your strategy, for more than one library to help make the most productive use of your time. Space has been provided next to each title in the lists for you to write call numbers, government document classification numbers, and the physical or online locations of materials, as well as any notes you care to include in order to get back to a particular resource easily.

Space is also included to allow you to review these resources with a critical eye and make notes. Try to include the value of the resource as well as some limitations. For example, a resource could have extensive, up-to-date statistics on mental health services but be limited to adult populations, whereas you might need statistics on mental health services for children. Making one or two comments on the usefulness of a resource the first time you use it can save time on future projects.

It is important to consider the kinds of information included in each resource (e.g., names and addresses, statistics, or historical information), the subject areas covered (e.g., health, mental health, or child welfare), and the scope (e.g., geographic limitations, specific populations, time frame, or intended audience). Although this might seem to be a lot of work, it is not. Take a moment to determine whether a particular resource is appropriate for your current information needs.

Searching for a known title can often be the simplest strategy for beginning researchers. Most major academic and many large public libraries now have on-line catalogs. Therefore, the entries on the checklists are arranged by title.

Much of the information appropriate to a given topic should be as current as possible; however, it is important to know the history of a policy when doing policy research. Some of these titles have been published for a number of years and are still updated or published on an annual, biannual, monthly, weekly, and even daily basis, often online. Some titles are updated on an irregular basis. Dates of publication for titles that have been updated either regularly or irregularly will appear as *latest ed.* in the date field. Publication dates of several titles are rather old. They have been included because they have historical value. Speak with a librarian if you have a question regarding the current edition of a title.

To further assist you in building information self-reliance skills, annotations (i.e., brief summaries) of the resources are not included. Many of these resources are unique and can provide an abundance of useful information, including names of people to contact, association and research society publications, and information on free publications. The only way you can understand the value of some of these resources is to find a good table and a comfortable chair and look at them yourself.

The resources listed vary according to level of intensity. Some tend to be more popular than academic, but all are certainly helpful for policy analysis. Both levels are included in order to make the checklist useful for a variety of libraries. After reviewing the content of each worksheet, you can either systematically complete all the checklists or use them selectively to explore resources useful for specific kinds of information.

This appendix is intended to encourage social work students to begin learning information self-reliance skills and to encourage practitioners to rediscover known resources and explore the changing nature of information retrieval. It is offered in the conviction that careful and skilled research will improve social policy, social programs, social work education, and social work practice. The best way to learn how to do library-oriented research is go out and do it.

Worksheet for a Planned Research Strategy

1. Create a list of possible areas for a policy analysis.
   a. _____
   b. _____
   c. _____

2. What is the purpose of the analysis?
   a. course requirement
   b. legislative testimony
   c. grant proposal
   d. job related
   e. other

3. Check all of the relevant types of information needed for your policy analysis.
   ____ background
   ____ charts, graphs, tables
   ____ definitions
   ____ history
   ____ expert interviews
   ____ laws/legal information
   ____ legislative histories
   ____ primary sources
   ____ public opinion
   ____ statistics

4. Determine the time frame for completion of the first round of research _____
   Determine the time frame to begin writing the first draft _____
   Determine the time frame for the second round of research _____
   Determine the time frame to begin writing the second draft _____

5. Go to the library to become familiar with the organization (where things are) and with the services (e.g., reference assistance, interlibrary loan, photocopying).

6. Stop at the reference desk and determine whether there is a social sciences and/or government documents librarian to speak with regarding your information needs. Ask for a brief introduction to the online or card catalog if you are not familiar with the system.

continued

7. Spend some time becoming familiar with the library's catalog and electronic resources. Find out what databases are available that are relevant to your topic. Most libraries have databases arranged by subject area. A librarian can also make good suggestions regarding an appropriate database depending on your policy topic. Set aside a time to simply explore what your library has online. Many electronic resources can now be searched remotely. Find out how to determine what they are and know how to correctly access these resources from off-campus locations.

8. Use the list of indexes, abstracts, journals, and other resources in the appendixes as a checklist for the holdings in the library. What does your library have?

9. Begin an initial search for information related to your topic. Locate one or two books, three or four journal articles, and one or two government documents.

10. Begin reading. Concentrate on the information you have located and whether it is what you will need for the analysis. Make some notes on each one of the books, articles, government documents, and web sites. Include bibliographical information in your notes, bearing in mind the information you will need for your reference list should you decide to use a particular source.

11. Determine what resources are available for locating federal, state, and local experts knowledgeable in your policy area. Make a list of names and numbers. Plan ahead. Write down three to five carefully worded questions to ask the experts when you contact them. Make the calls.

12. Refine your research question based on the initial review of the literature and your conversations with the experts.

13. Communicate with the librarian to get suggestions regarding additional resources you might need to consult.

14. Communicate with your instructor regarding the results of your initial findings and ask for suggestions.

15. Don't get frustrated. Plan your library time, your reading time, your thinking time, and your writing time. And especially, your rewriting time.

16. As you begin to become comfortable using the library resources, you are likely to find additional information that can be added to your analysis. Incorporate new information in your rewrites.

17. Know when to stop. There is an enormous amount of information available on topics related to policy analysis. Don't get caught up in the amount of information you collect. Concentrate on relevance to the analysis.

18. A well-written paper is as important as the resources you choose to use. Ask a friend or colleague to read your analysis for clarity and style.

19. Once you begin following planned research strategies, you should notice a difference in the quality of the finished product.

Worksheet for an Interview with a Librarian

This form was developed to assist students with communicating in an effective and efficient manner when talking to a reference librarian. It can be used in conjunction with the Planned Research Strategy Worksheet. The desired outcome of this worksheet is to instill confidence in students when communicating with a librarian or other information specialists.

Most people feel completely at ease ordering food in a restaurant. We know what we want and how we want it prepared. This is not always true in communicating what we want when it comes to information. Put yourself in control. Make statements as opposed to asking questions. "I would like to find information . . ." on is a stronger positive introduction than "Can you help me find . . . ?" and they convey the same need for assistance.

Pay attention. Be inquisitive. Librarians are no different from other professionals when it comes to jargon. When something is said that you don't understand, ask for an explanation. "What are 'the stacks'?" "What is a SUDOC number you just mentioned?" "What does keyword mean?" "What is PDF full text as opposed to HTML full text?" Present yourself in a prepared manner and the results will be a productive exchange between you and the librarian. A planned strategy for talking with a librarian is one of the skills needed to become information self-reliant. Complete the following form.

1. Decide on a topic using the Planned Research Strategy Worksheet as a guide.

2. Form an introductory statement in one sentence. For example, "I would like to find some current articles and a couple of books on [your topic]."

3. Write down the next two statements to include more detailed information. The more information librarians have, the easier it will be for them to determine their strategy for assisting you. For example, "I am working on a ten-page paper for my social work policy analysis class. I know I'll need some statistics and the historical background of [your topic]."

4. Listen to the librarian. Are you being asked to clarify your subject? Are you being directed to resources? Do you understand what the librarian is saying? If not, admit it and ask to have the instructions repeated. For example, "Gee! That's great—but I have no idea what you just said. Could you run that by me again?" You are still in control. Practice a couple of positive responses if you are not sure what you have been told.

5. Depending on when you go to the library, there could be a different librarian at the reference desk than the one you spoke with initially. Make use of the variety of expertise available to you. For example, one librarian might specialize in searching

continued

electronic resources, whereas another might have more experience in locating state or regional resources. Also, you may find that you feel more comfortable with one than another. Practice the communication exercises suggested earlier with more than one librarian.

6. Remember that librarians are there to help you. Help them to help you by coming prepared.

The Internet

It is essential to mention here the vast amount of information available on the Internet that can be used for policy analysis. Many college, university, and public libraries now have computers available for people to connect to the Internet. One of the best ways to learn some of the search strategies is to find someone who has experience and ask for a demonstration. If you don't really know what the Internet is or haven't actually done any searching, find out and devote some time to learning how to locate information on the Net. Searching for information on the Internet is quite different from strategies used for searching finite databases. Please refer to the section on Electronic Resources and Indexes for additional comments on strategies. There are numerous books on navigating the Net, some specific to social work, as well as resources that list various sites containing a broad array of information. Four fairly recent publications unique to social work are listed in the Beginning Resources section that follows. Check with your librarian or local bookstore to see what is available. Because Internet sites change and grow every day, specific addresses are not included here.

Newspaper Indexes

Newspapers are an excellent source for locating analyses of current or historical events and issues. Policy developments can be followed on a day-to-day basis, whereas magazines and academic journals can be weeks or months behind. Most major libraries subscribe to a variety of national newspaper indexes, such as the *New York Times* and the *Washington Post*, that regularly print in-depth analyses of social welfare policy issues. Check your library holdings for national, regional, state, and local newspaper indexes and newspaper holdings either in print or electronically. Often, online versions of major state papers have searchable archives. Many public libraries also maintain clip files for local and state newspapers.

Beginning Resources

The titles listed below are general resources that can be helpful when beginning a research project. Names, addresses, and telephone numbers in some of the publications can help get you in touch with experts in a given field. Other titles provide guidelines for writing or recommend additional resources to consider.

Allyn and Bacon Quick Guide to the Internet for Social Work, by Joanne Yaffe and Doug Gotthoffer (Allyn and Bacon, 1999).
Call Number _____   Location _____
Notes _____

Find It Fast: How to Uncover Expert Information on Any Subject, 5th ed., by Robert I. Berkiman (HarperResource, 2000).
Call Number _____   Location _____
Notes _____

Guide to Information Sources for Social Work and the Human Services, by Henry Mendelsohn (Oryx Press, 1987).
Call Number _____   Location _____
Notes _____

Internet and Social Welfare Policy: A Supplement to American Welfare Policy: A Pluralist Approach, by Howard J. Karger and David Stoesz (Allyn and Bacon, 2002).
Call Number _____   Location _____
Notes _____

Professional Writing for the Human Services, edited by Linda Beebe (NASW Press, 1993).
Call Number _____   Location _____
Notes _____

Reference Sources in Social Work, by James H. Conrad (Scarecrow, 1982).
Call Number _____   Location _____
Notes _____

Social Worker's Guide to the Internet, by Rey C. Martinez and Carol Lea Clark (Allyn and Bacon, 2001).
Call Number _____   Location _____
Notes _____

Social Worker's Internet Handbook, by Gary B. Grant and Linda May Grobman (White Hat Communications, 1998).
Call Number _____   Location _____
Notes _____

continued

Sources of Information for Historical Research, by Thomas Slavens (Neal-Schuman, 1994).
Call Number _____ Location _____
Notes _____

Encyclopedias/Dictionaries/Directories/Biographies

The titles listed below provide a variety of different kinds of information. For example, the encyclopedias are great resources for a quick review of a given topic. The dictionaries can be useful for providing a specific definition for a word or phrase that plays a key role in your policy analysis. Information on people who played significant roles in developing or changing existing policy can be located in the biographical material. Profiles of interest groups and information on numerous associations, organizations, and societies that can be contacted for information are included in some of the resources.

American Reform and Reformers: A Biographical Dictionary, edited by Randall M. Miller and Paul A. Cimbola (Greenwood, 1996).
Call Number _____ Location _____
Notes _____

American Reformers: An H. W. Wilson Biographical Dictionary, edited by Alden Whitman (H. W. Wilson, 1985).
Call Number _____ Location _____
Notes _____

Biographical Dictionary of Social Welfare in America, edited by Walter I. Trattner (Greenwood Press, 1986).
Call Number _____ Location _____
Notes _____

Biographical Directory of the Governors of the United States, 1988–1994, by Marie Marmo Mullaney (Greenwood Press, 1994).
Call Number _____ Location _____
Notes _____

Biographical Directory of the United States Congress, 1774–present (available online through the WorldCat database).
Call Number _____ Location _____
Notes _____

Dictionary of Public Policy And Administration, by Jay M. Shafritz (Westview Press, 2004).
Call Number _____ Location _____
Notes _____

continued

Directories in Print (Gale Research Co., latest ed.).
Call Number _____   Location _____
Notes _____

Encyclopedia of Associations (Gale Research Co., latest ed., also available online as Associations Unlimited).
Call Number _____   Location _____
Notes _____

Encyclopedia of Social Work, 19th ed. (NASW Press, and the 1995, 1997, and 2003 supplements).
Call Number _____   Location _____
Notes _____

International Encyclopedia of the Social Sciences (Macmillan, 1968–1979).
Call Number _____   Location _____
Notes _____

Public Human Services Directory (American Public Human Services Association, latest ed.).
Call Number _____   Location _____
Notes _____

Social Work Almanac, 2nd ed., by Leon Ginsberg (NASW Press, 1995).
Call Number _____   Location _____
Notes _____

Social Work Dictionary, 5th ed., by Robert L. Barker (NASW Press, 2003).
Call Number _____   Location _____
Notes _____

Social Work Speaks: NASW Policy Statements, 2003–2006, 6th ed. (NASW Press, 2003).
Call Number _____   Location _____
Notes _____

State Legislative Sourcebook 2005: A Resource Guide to Legislative Information in the Fifty States, by Lynn Hellebust (Government Research Service, 2005).
Call Number _____   Location _____
Notes _____

Think Tank Directory: A Guide to Independent Nonprofit Public Policy Research Organizations, 2nd ed., edited by Lynn Hellebust (Government Research Service, 2001).
Call Number _____   Location _____
Notes _____

continued

United States Executive Branch: A Biographical Directory of State and Cabinet Officials, rev. ed., by Robert Sobel and David B. Sicitta, (Greenwood Press, 2003).
Call Number _____   Location _____
Notes _____

U.S. Aging Policy Interest Groups: Institutional Profiles, by David D. Van Tassel and Jimmy Elaine Wilkinson Meyer (Greenwood Press, 1992).
Call Number _____   Location _____
Notes _____

U.S. Criminal Justice Interest Groups: Institutional Profiles, by Michael A. Hallett and Dennis J. Palumbo (Greenwood Press, 1993).
Call Number _____   Location _____
Notes _____

Electronic/Print Indexes and Abstracts

____ ABI/INFORM Complete (a ProQuest database) (administration/management/business)
____ Academic Search Premier (an EBSCOHOST Research Database) (interdisciplinary)
____ Academic Universe (LEXIS/NEXIS)
____ Abstracts in Social Gerontology (Sage)
____ AGELINE (American Association of Retired Persons)
____ America, History and Life (ABC-Clio)
____ American National Biography Online (Oxford University Press)
____ American Memory
____ ArticleFirst (OCLC)
____ Associations Unlimited (Gale)
____ Books in Print (Bowker)
____ Child Abuse, Child Welfare, and Adoption (National Information Services Corporation)
____ CINAHL (a ProQuest database) (health/nursing)
____ Criminal Justice Abstracts (National Council on Crime and Delinquency, Information Center)
____ Education Full Text (Wilson)
____ ERIC (Educational Resource Information Center)
____ Ethnic NewsWatch (a ProQuest database)
____ Expanded Academic ASAP (Gale)
____ Family Index Database (Family Scholarly Publications)
____ Gender Watch (a ProQuest database)
____ GLBT Life (an EBSCOHOST database)

continued

____ Health Source (an EBSCOHOST database)
____ Human Resources Abstracts (Sage)
____ International Bibliography of the Social Sciences (London School of Economic and Political Science)
____ Newspaper Source (an EBSCHOHOST database)
____ Opposing Viewpoints Resource Center (Thomson/Gale)
____ PAIS International (OCLC Public Affairs Information Service)
____ ProQuest Historical Newspapers (a ProQuest database)
____ ProQuest Newspapers (a ProQuest database)
____ PsychArticles (an EBSCOHOST database)
____ PsycINFO (American Psychological Association)
____ PubMed (National Library of Medicine)
____ Research Library Complete (a ProQuest database)
____ Sage Family Studies Abstracts (Sage)
____ Social Sciences Citation Index (Institute for Scientific Information)
____ Social Sciences Index (H. W. Wilson)
____ Social Services Abstracts (Cambridge Scientific Abstracts)
____ Social Work Abstracts (National Association of Social Workers)
____ Sociological Abstracts (Sociological Abstracts, Inc.)
____ Women's Studies Abstracts (Transaction Periodicals Consortium)

U.S. Government Documents

Approximately 1,400 research and public libraries have been designated as selective or regional depository libraries. These libraries, based on their classification, regularly receive either unclassified selected publications from the Government Printing Office (GPO) or all unclassified publications available in the depository program. The U.S. government is one of the most prolific publishers in the world. Government documents are an unparalleled source of information. Locating the closest selective or regional depository library can provide you with extensive information on most topics for doing a policy analysis. However, many government agencies and departments now have their own web sites and are easily accessible through the Internet. These sites will end with the 'gov' domain. A few of these resources are repeated under differing titles reflecting the variety of ways in which your library may subscribe to them. Government documents librarians are specially trained to assist you with locating these unique and various kinds of publications. Use their expertise, as they can be tremendously helpful.

What follows is a list of basic relevant resources published by either the GPO or research presses that will aid in policy analysis. Several of the resources belong in more than one of the categories listed below. They have only been listed once in the most appropriate category. Use the spaces provided to check your library's holdings.

continued

Getting Started

Complete Guide to Citing Government Information Resources: A Manual for Social Science and Business Research, by Debora Cheney, Diane L. Garner, and Diane H. Smith (Lexis/Nexis Matthew Bender, 2002).
Call Number _____ Location _____
Notes _____

Directory of Federal Libraries, 3rd ed., edited by William R. Evinger (Oryx Press, 1997).
Call Number _____ Location _____
Notes _____

Directory of Government Document Collections and Librarians, 8th ed., (American Library Association, 2003).
Call Number _____ Location _____
Notes _____

Encyclopedia of Governmental Advisory Organizations (Gale Research Co., latest ed.).
Call Number _____ Location _____
Notes _____

Federal Database Finder, 4th ed., compiled by Matthew Lesko (Information USA, Inc., 1995).
Call Number _____ Location _____
Notes _____

Government Online: One-Click Access to 3,400 Federal and State Web Sites, by John Maxymuk (Neal-Schuman, 2001).
Call Number _____ Location _____
Notes _____

Guide to U.S. Government Publications, edited by John L. Andriot (Gale Research Co., latest ed.).
Call Number _____ Location _____
Notes _____

How Congress Works and Why You Should Care, by Lee H. Hamilton, (Bloomington Indiana University Press, 2004).
Call Number _____ Location _____
Notes _____

Introduction to United States Government Information Sources, 6th ed., by Joe Morehead (Libraries Unlimited, Inc., 1999).
Call Number _____ Location _____
Notes _____

continued

Tapping the Government Grapevine: The User Friendly Guide to U.S. Government Information Sources, 3rd ed., by Judith Schiek Robinson (Oryx Press, 1998).
Call Number _____   Location _____
Notes _____

United States Government Manual (online at www.gpoaccess.gov/gmanual).
Call Number _____   Location _____
Notes _____

Using Government Information Sources: Electronic and Print, 3rd ed., by Marilyn K. Moody and Jean L. Sears (Oryx Press, 2001).
Call Number _____   Location _____
Notes _____

Keeping Up with New Government Publications

The best and most current electronic resource for keeping up with new U.S. government publications can be located at www.gpoaccess.gov/index.html.

Names and Numbers

The following resources contain the names, addresses, and phone numbers of people working with or for the U.S. government. They can be used for contacting individuals or offices for information on the current status of specific legislation or to express concerns, opinions, or ideas.

American Lobbyists Directory (Gale Research Co., latest ed.).
Call Number _____   Location _____
Notes _____

Congress and the Nation (Congressional Quarterly Service, latest ed.).
Call Number _____   Location _____
Notes _____

Congress A to Z, 4th ed., edited by Ann O'Connor and David R. Tarr (Congressional Quarterly, Inc., 2003).
Call Number _____   Location _____
Notes _____

Congressional Yellow Book (Washington Monitor, latest ed.).
Call Number _____   Location _____
Notes _____

continued

Federal Yellow Book (Washington Monitor, Inc., latest ed.).
Call Number _____   Location _____
Notes _____

NASW Register of Clinical Social Workers Database (NASW).
Call Number _____   Location _____
Notes _____

Washington Information Directory (Congressional Quarterly Service, latest ed.).
Call Number _____   Location _____
Notes _____

Government Indexes

There are a wide variety of indexes for locating government documents. The appropriate resource to use depends on what kind of information you are looking for. Depository libraries now have many of their indexes available electronically. Find out what your library has in electronic format that relates to government publications.

The indexes listed below will direct you to hearings, reports, debates, articles in government publications, and other relevant information related to your policy area. Other indexes and search aids are listed in more specific sections of this appendix. Please also refer to the section on Legal Resources.

Catalog of United States Government Documents, 1994–present (U.S. Government Printing Office, available online at www.gpoaccess.gov/cgp/index.html). *Note:* The online database MARCHIVEWEB DOCS, July 1976–present can be searched for older publications.
Call Number _____   Location _____
Notes _____

Catalog of U.S. Government Documents [MOCAT], 1895–present [print version of the previous entry], (U.S. Government Printing Office).
Call Number _____   Location _____
Notes _____

CIS/Index to Publications of the United States Congress, 1970–present, (Congressional Information Service, latest ed., and also available online through the LEXIS/NEXIS Congressional Universe database).
Call Number _____   Location _____
Notes _____

continued

Congressional Research Service Index database (division of the Library of Congress)
Call Number _____   Location _____
Notes _____

FEDSTATS: The Gateway to Statistics From Over 100 U.S. Federal Agencies (available online at www.fedstats.gov).
Call Number _____   Location _____
Notes _____

Library of Congress THOMAS, dates vary depending on what you are looking for (available online at www.thomas.loc.gov).
Call Number _____   Location _____
Notes _____

U.S. Government Periodicals Index (Congressional Information Service, latest ed.).
Call Number _____   Location _____
Notes _____

Statistical Sources

American Statistics Index: A Comprehensive Guide and Index to the Statistical Publications of the U.S. Government (Congressional Information Service, latest ed.).
Call Number _____   Location _____
Notes _____

CENSTATS, current (United States Bureau of the Census, available online at www.census.gov).
Call Number _____   Location _____
Notes _____

Guide to U.S. Government Statistics (Documents Index, latest ed.).
Call Number _____   Location _____
Notes _____

Historical Statistics of the States of the United States: Two Centuries of the Census, 1790–1990, by Don Dodd (Greenwood Press, 1993).
Call Number _____   Location _____
Notes _____

Historical Statistics of the United States, Colonial Times to 1970 (U.S. Government Printing Office, 1975 and supplements; Bicentennial Edition also available online at www.census.gov/prod/www/abs/statabs.html)
Call Number _____   Location _____
Notes _____

continued

LEXISNEXIS Statistical, 1973–present, (LEXIS/NEXIS) [also available in print as American Statistics Index].
Call Number _____   Location _____
Notes _____

STATISTICAL MASTERFILE (and the accompanying Retrospective database in the series).
Call Number _____   Location _____
Notes _____

Statistical Abstract of the United States (U.S. Government Printing Office, latest ed.; also available online at www.census.gov/statab/www).
Call Number _____   Location _____
Notes _____

United States Bureau of the Census (U.S. Bureau of the Census, latest ed., also available online at www.census.gov).
Call Number _____   Location _____
Notes _____

Legislative Histories

A thorough policy analysis requires a detailed review of the information provided to the policymakers that leads to the passing of a law. The resources listed below all have a unique role in tracking past and present policy histories at the federal level. Many of these are now available electronically. Remember, making good notes the first time you use a resource is important. Working with a number of resources that provide similar kinds of information in a variety of ways can be confusing. Two or three comments about a resource can save time when you go back to use them again. Several of the resources listed in the Getting Started section of this appendix provide descriptions of the content of the following titles and why and when to use them. Please also refer to the section on Legal Resources.

Historical Government Bibliographies

Bibliography of United States Government Bibliographies, 1968–1973, by Roberta A. Scull (Pierian Press, 1975).
Call Number _____   Location _____
Notes _____

continued

Bibliography of United States Government Bibliographies, 1974–1976, by Roberta A. Scull (Pierian Press, 1976).
Call Number _____   Location _____
Notes _____

Cumulative Subject Guide to U.S. Government Bibliographies, 1924–1973 (Carrollton Press, 1976).
Call Number _____   Location _____
Notes _____

Code of Federal Regulations and Index (U.S. Government Printing Office, latest ed.).
Call Number _____   Location _____
Notes _____

Congressional Record Daily Digest (U.S. Government Printing Office, latest ed.).
Call Number _____   Location _____
Notes _____

Federal Legislative Histories: An Annotated Bibliography and Index to Officially Published Sources, compiled by Bernard D. Reams (Greenwood Press, 1994).
Call Number _____   Location _____
Notes _____

Federal Register (U.S. Government Printing Office, latest ed., also available online from 1994–present at www.gpoaccess.gov/fr).
Call Number _____   Location _____
Notes _____

Legislative Histories (Congressional Information Service, latest ed.) [Volume 3 of the printed CIS/Index listed under Government Indexes; also available through the LEXIS/NEXIS Congressional Universe database].
Call Number _____   Location _____
Notes _____

Major Acts of Congress, 3 vols., Editor-in Chief, Brian K Landsberg (Thompson/Gale, 2004 or latest ed.).
Call Number _____   Location _____
Notes _____

U.S. Congressional Serial Set, 1789–1969 (LEXIS/NEXIS).
Call Number _____   Location _____
Notes _____

continued

United States Code (U.S. Government Printing Office, latest ed., also available online at www.gpoaccess.gov/uscode).
Call Number _____   Location _____
Notes _____

United States Code Congressional and Administrative News (West, latest ed.).
Call Number _____   Location _____
Notes _____

United States Statutes at Large (U.S. Government Printing Office, latest ed.; an online version of Statutes dating from 1789–1875 is available online at www.memory.loc.gov/ammem/amlaw/lwslink.htm).
Call Number _____   Location _____
Notes _____

Selected U.S. Government Department and Agency Periodical Publications

Following is a short selected list of government department and agency publications. There are many more. These sources often provide useful and easy-to-follow summary material on policy issues. Some articles in these publications can be located using the *Government Periodicals Index* and the *Catalog of United States Government Documents*. Most of them are available through the agency or department web site.

Aging News (U.S. Administration on Aging, quarterly, available online [2002–present] at www.aoa.gov (click on PRESS ROOM, then "Aging News," and then "Aging News Archives" for older material)
Child Support Report (U.S. Office of Child Support Enforcement, monthly).
Health Care Financing Review (Centers for Medicare and Medicaid Services, quarterly and supplements).
Juvenile Justice Journal, (U.S. Office of Juvenile Justice and Delinquency, irregular).
Mental Health, United States (U.S. Department of Health and Human Services, annual).
Psychopharmacology Bulletin (MedWorks Media, quarterly).
Public Health Reports (U.S. Public Health Service, bimonthly).
Social Security Bulletin (U.S. Social Security Administration, quarterly).
Sourcebook of Criminal Justice Statistics (U.S. Bureau of Justice Statistics, annual).

State and Local Information Resources

There are a variety of places to locate information at the state and local levels. A growing number of state and local resources are available on the Internet that are citizen-oriented and user friendly. Much information can be obtained on the United States Bureau of the Census web site. State departments of public health often publish vital statistics on an annual basis. Departments of human resources can provide statistics on social services, program and project status reports, and information related to the elderly, children, youth, families, health, mental health, and crime in the state. Many state universities publish economic almanacs and statistical atlases. Contact your state department of human resources and state universities to obtain information on regularly published newsletters, reports, and fact sheets. Many of these can be subscribed to on a minimal or no cost basis. Chambers of commerce and county courthouses can also provide valuable information at the local level.

Almanac of the 50 States: Basic Data Profiles with Comparative Tables, edited by Manthi Nguyen, (Information Publications, 2005 or latest ed.).
Call Number _____ Location _____
Notes _____

Associations Unlimited (available electronically and in print as *Encyclopedia of Associations*, Gale Research, latest ed.).

Book of the States (Council of State Governments, latest ed.; an Internet search on the Council of State Governments and the National Conference of State Legislators home pages can also provide up-to-date information).
Call Number _____ Location _____
Notes _____

County and City Data Book (U.S. Government Printing Office, latest ed.; county and city data can also be obtained on the United States Bureau of the Census web site).
Call Number _____ Location _____
Notes _____

State Reference Publications: A Guide to State Blue Books, Legislative Manuals and Other General Reference Sources (Government Research Service, latest ed.).
Call Number _____ Location _____
Notes _____

Legal Resources

A large number of public documents related to social welfare policy are in the form of laws or regulations. Many of these can be located in the federal and state documents collections of most large libraries. However, a thorough analysis will generally require the resources available in a law library and the services of a trained law librarian. Listed below are some of the most widely available resources in academic, public, and law libraries that are useful for policy analysis. Also included below is a brief summary of the different types of law and resources specific to those laws to assist in clarifying what kinds of resources to use related to your particular policy.

Brief Description of Laws and Basic Resources
Statutory Law

Statutory law: consists of session laws—a collection of federal laws in chronological order of their enactment—and statutory codes that arrange statutes according to subject matter. The publisher of the first two following titles is the U.S. Government Printing Office and mentioned in the Government Documents section for location.

Statutes at Large—Used to locate federal session laws in their chronological order of enactment.

United States Code—Used to locate federal statutory laws by subject.

United States Code Annotated (West, latest ed.) and the *United States Code Service* (Lawyers Co-operative Pub. Co., latest ed.). Provide more than just the text of the laws. Each includes (1) notes of court decisions interpreting, construing, and applying code sections; (2) editorial notes and analytical discussions on particular statutes or provisions; and (3) references to attorney general opinions, administrative regulations, various secondary sources, and legislative history.

Legal Research in a Nutshell, Morris L. Cohen and Kent C. Olson (St. Paul, MN: West Publishing, 1992).

Administrative Law

Much authority has been delegated to administrative agencies by Congress and the president. Administrative law is "The law governing the organization and operation of the executive branch of government (including independent agencies) and the relations of the executive with the legislature, the judiciary, and the public" (*Blacks' Law Dictionary*, St. Paul, MN: West Group, 1999, p. 46). The administrative rules of these agencies can be located using both government and commercial indexes.

The Federal Register—Chronologically arranges all new rules adopted by federal agencies and gives a brief synopsis of the content of the regulation, a preamble to clarify the contents, and then the complete text of the regulation.

continued

The Code of Federal Regulations and the Index to the Code of Federal Regulations—Provide subject access to regulations listed in the Federal Register. Each volume contains an alphabetical list of federal agencies indicating the title and chapter of each agency's regulation.

Shepard's Federal Citations—Citations to cases at the federal courts of appeals as well as district court levels.

Shepard's United States Citations—Citations to U.S. Supreme Court decisions and congressional statutes, trademarks, copyright, and patents.

Common Law

Common law is "The body of law derived from judicial decisions , rather than from statutes or constitutions" (*Blacks' Law Dictionary*, St. Paul, MN: West Group, 1999, p. 270). Decisions of these courts are collected chronologically in volumes called "case reporters," and summarized by subject matter in references works called "case digests."

Federal Reporter—Contains U.S. Court of Appeals decisions.

Supreme Court Reports—Official government report of Supreme Court decisions.

United States Supreme Court Reports: Lawyers Edition—Similar to the *Supreme Court Reports*, but also includes editorial comments on decisions.

Getting Started

Almanac of the Federal Judiciary: Profiles of all Active United States District Court Judges (Lawletters, annual as well as semi-annual supplements).
Call Number _____   Location _____
Notes _____

Black's Law Dictionary (West, latest ed.).
Call Number _____   Location _____
Notes _____

Law and Legal Information Directory, edited by P. Wasserman (Gale Research Co. latest ed.).
Call Number _____   Location _____
Notes _____

Legal Newsletters in Print (Infosources Publishing, latest ed.).
Call Number _____   Location _____
Notes _____

Legal Research in a Nutshell, by Morris L. Cohen and Kent C. Olson (Thompson/West, 2003).
Call Number _____   Location _____
Notes _____

continued

U.S. Code and Administrative News (West, latest ed.). This publication contains the full text of all recently passed public laws as well sections of documents, such as hearings and committee reports that can provide brief legislative history information.
Call Number _____   Location _____
Notes _____

West's Encyclopedia of American Law, 2nd ed., edited by Jeffry Lehman & Shirelle (West, 2005).
Call Number _____   Location _____
Notes _____

Legal Indexes: Electronic and Print

Current Law Index (Information Access Corp., 1980–). (*Note:* LegalTrac listed below under Electronic Legal Indexes is the counterpart to this print title).
Call Number _____   Location _____
Notes _____

Index to Legal Periodicals (H. W. Wilson Co., 1908–). (*Note:* This is also available electronically 1994–).
Call Number _____   Location _____
Notes _____

Legal Indexes: Electronic

As mentioned in the earlier section on electronic and print resources, some dates are not included. The coverage will depend on the kind of subscription your library has.

Legal Resources Index (Information Access Corp.).
Location _____
Notes _____

LEXIS/NEXIS (LEXIS/NEXIS).
Location _____
Notes _____

WESTLAW (West Publishing Co.).
Location _____
Notes _____

Journals

The following list of journals is provided for two purposes. First, it can be used as a checklist to determine what titles are in a library. Second, it is an attempt to demonstrate the variety of publications that contain information related to policy analysis.

There are a couple of things to keep in mind when searching for articles in journals. The most current issues of a journal, usually located in a current periodicals section of the library, are not yet indexed in printed resources. However, more and more journals are being included in online indexes available through your library's computer, and many articles can be printed out full text. If this is the case and you have the option to print the PDF version as opposed to the HTML version, do so. The reason is that the PDF version is a scanned version of the original text and has actual page numbers for direct quotes and the tables, graphs, and charts are in the original location of the article. In some cases, the HTML versions have them at the end of the article and can be difficult to read. These indexes are generally updated often enough to include current articles. For each research project in progress, make a list of a few journals most relevant to those topics. Train yourself to browse regularly through the current issues for articles not yet indexed.

A second reason to browse the current as well as the previous issues of a journal is that not all of the articles in any given journal are indexed. Some indexing is done selectively, depending on the policies of the publishers. This means that a relevant article might not be located if you rely strictly on print or online indexes. This is not as time consuming, tedious, or boring as it might sound. After a couple of browsing sessions, you'll be surprised at how quickly you can go through an enormous amount of published information and determine whether it is relevant to your research needs.

Descriptions of content for several of the titles listed below are given in the two following publications.

An Author's Guide to Social Work Journals, 4th ed., by Henry Mendelsohn (NASW Press, 1997).
Call Number _____
Location _____

Understanding Social Problems, Policies, and Programs, 2nd ed., by Leon Ginsberg (University of South Carolina Press, 1996). (See appendix.)
Call Number _____
Location _____

Place a checkmark next to the titles held by your library.

continued

A

____ *ABS, American Behavioral Scientist*
____ *Administration and Policy in Mental Health*
____ *Administration in Social Work*
____ *Affilia: The Journal of Women and Social Work*
____ *American Journal of Public Health*

B

____ *Behavioral Sciences and the Law*
____ *British Journal of Social Work*

C

____ *Child Abuse and Neglect*
____ *Children and Schools: A Journal of Social Work Practice* (formerly *Social Work in Education*)
____ *Child and Youth Services*
____ *Children and Youth Services Review*
____ *Children's Health Care*
____ *Child Welfare*
____ *Community Mental Health Journal*
____ *Congressional Quarterly Researcher*
____ *CQ Weekly Report*
____ *Crime and Delinquency*

E

____ *Evaluation and Program Planning*
____ *Evaluation and the Health Professions*

F

____ *Families in Society*
____ *Family Process*
____ *Family Relations: An Interdisciplinary Journal of Applied Family Studies*

G

____ *Gallup Poll Tuesday Briefing*
____ *Gerontologist*

H

____ *Health and Social Work*
____ *Home Health Care Services Quarterly*

continued

J

____ *Journal of Aging and Social Policy*
____ *Journal of American History*
____ *Journal of Applied Gerontology*
____ *Journal of Behavioral Health Services and Research* (formerly *Journal of Mental Health Administration*)
____ *Journal of Criminal Justice*
____ *Journal of Drug Issues*
____ *Journal of Family Issues*
____ *Journal of Family Social Work*
____ *Journal of Gay and Lesbian Social Services: Issues in Practice, Policy and Research*
____ *Journal of Gerontological Social Work*
____ *Journals of Gerontology*
____ *Journal of Health and Social Behavior*
____ *Journal of Health and Social Policy*
____ *Journal of Mental Health Administration* (now titled *Journal of Behavioral Health Services and Research*)
____ *Journal of Progressive Human Services*
____ *Journal of Research in Crime and Delinquency*
____ *Journal of Social History*
____ *Journal of Social Issues*
____ *Journal of Social Policy*
____ *Journal of Social Service Research*
____ *Journal of Social Work Education*
____ *Journal of Social Work in End-of-Life and Palliative Care*
____ *Journal of Social Work in Long-Term Care*
____ *Journal of Social Work in Mental Health*
____ *Journal of Social Work Practice*
____ *Journal of Sociology and Social Welfare*

L

____ *Legislative Studies Quarterly*

N

____ *NASW News*

continued

P

____ *Policy and Practice* (formerly *Public Welfare*)
____ *Policy Review Policy Studies*
____ *Policy Studies Journal*
____ *Policy Studies Review* (now titled *Review of Policy Research*)
____ *Political Science Quarterly*
____ *Public Administration*
____ *Public Administration Quarterly*
____ *Public Administration Review*
____ *Public Health Reports*
____ *Public Interest*
____ *Public Policy*
____ *Public Welfare* (now titled *Policy and Practice*)

R

____ *Research in Social Problems and Public Policy*
____ *Research on Social Work Practice*
____ *Review of Policy Research* (formerly *Policy Studies Review*)

S

____ *Social Forces*
____ *Social Philosophy and Policy*
____ *Social Policy*
____ *Social Policy and Administration*
____ *Social Problems*
____ *Social Science Research*
____ *Social Security Bulletin*
____ *Social Service Review*
____ *Social Work*
____ *Social Work in Education* (now titled *Children and Schools: A Journal of Social Work Practice*)
____ *Social Work in Health Care*
____ *Social Work Research*

Y

____ *Youth and Society*
____ *Youth Policy*

Associations/Organizations/Societies Publications

In addition to journal articles, books, government documents, and newspapers, the publications of national, regional, state, and local associations and organizations are excellent resources for information. Included in newsletters, fact sheets, bulletins, and reports are calendars of upcoming events, such as political rallies related to pending legislation, status reports on programs funded by state and federal laws, as well as the names and addresses of experts who can be contacted for specific information. Both the national and state and local editions of the *Encyclopedia of Associations* (now available electronically as the Associations Unlimited database) provides names, phone numbers, addresses, member information, conference announcements, and titles of publications of thousands of large and small associations including the ones listed here. Many of the publications are free. Check with your librarian if you have questions related to locating association and organization information.

The following list is intended as a small example of the variety of associations, organizations, and societies that can be contacted for information related to policy that affects whole populations at the federal, state, and local levels, as well as for specific populations, such as Alzheimer's patients and their families or the homeless. Internet addresses are included as there are a variety of links to resources from the homepages.

Alzheimer's Association
www.alz.org
Alzheimer's Association Newsletter
Brochures/Fact sheets/Video kits

American Association of Retired Persons
www.aarp.org
The AGELINE database is available from this web site

American Public Human Services Association
www.aphsa.org

American Society on Aging
www.asaging.org
Aging Today: The Bimonthly Newspaper of the American Society on Aging
Generations: The Journal of the American Society on Aging

Bazelon Center for Mental Health Law
www.bazelon.org

continued

Center on Hunger, Poverty and Nutrition Policy
www.centeronhunger.org

Children's Defense Fund
www.childrensdefense.org

Child Welfare League of America
www.cwla.org

Council on Social Work Education
www.cswe.org

Institute for Research on Poverty/University of Wisconsin–Madison
www.irp.wisc.edu
Discussion papers and special reports

National Alliance for the Mentally Ill
www.nami.org

National Association of Social Workers
www.naswdc.org
Social Work Speaks: NASW Policy Statements, 2002–2006 (in print only)

National Coalition for the Homeless Safety Network
www.nationalhomeless.org

Social Welfare History Group (An Affiliate of the American Historical Association)
www.historians.org/affiliates/social_welfare_his_group.htm
Newsletter

Information Self-Reliance
School of Social Work
The University of Alabama

The following is a statement approved by the faculty at The University of Alabama School of Social Work regarding information self-reliance competencies for students in the social work program. It is included as an example and as encouragement for other schools to adopt similar statements to demonstrate a common goal of working toward information self-reliant social work students.

> The School of Social Work is dedicated to preparing social work students with the ability to retrieve, identify, and assess information relevant to professional social work practice during their course of study at the school. Our goal is that students be competent to identify, locate, and effectively use information in print, machine-readable, and electronically-transmitted formats. These skills are essential to the competent practice of professional social work.

The faculty believes that these competencies not only contribute to the quality of professional practice and scholarship, but can also enhance an individual's lifelong information needs and quality of life.

Historical Policy Analysis Research

Research for a historical policy analysis may draw on some of the library sources described in Appendix A, but it will generally rely on more specialized historical resources. Several of these are described in Appendix A, such as *Historical Statistics of the United States, Colonial Times to 1970* and Thomas Slavens's *Sources of Information for Historical Research*. This appendix* will give you more extensive information on the types of sources necessary for understanding the history of a social welfare policy.

As we described in the chapter on historical policy analysis, historians distinguish between primary and secondary sources of data. Primary material consists of records made at the time an event occurred by participants or direct observers of the event. Secondary sources are reconstructions of an event by persons without firsthand knowledge of the event. Secondary sources often do an important job of orienting you to the area you want to study. They can provide an overview and a context for your policy history. However, they generally present conclusions drawn by the author, based on his or her interpretation of the evidence existing at the time the material was written. These conclusions may not always be accurate. If you want to draw your own conclusions based on the evidence, and particularly to use new data that has come to light or new theories about the development and nature of social welfare policies, you will need to examine the original sources yourself.

This is not to say that primary sources are bias-free. They too represent the values, judgments, and preconceptions of the observer or participant recording an event. However, historians attempt to control for bias by using a variety of primary sources—and, indeed, of secondary sources. If you were investigating the history

*Some information in this appendix was taken from Leighninger, "Historiography," *Encyclopedia of Social Work*. Copyright © 1995 National Association of Social Workers, Inc. Reprinted with permission.

of an agency decision regarding which sorts of client problems to deal with and which to refer, for example, you would want to interview staff at various levels and not just the agency director.

In using secondary sources for social policy history, the library is a basic place to start; bibliographic and catalog subject headings such as Child Welfare often include History as a subheading. Abstracts of historical articles can be found electronically, as well as in hard copy, in sources such as *American History and Life* and *Historical Abstracts*. Other tools for finding books and articles on social welfare history include a new heading (Social Welfare and Public Health) in the Recent Scholarship Section of the *Journal of American History;* a category on Social Work Profession—History in *Social Work Abstracts;* Trattner and Achenbaum's *Social Welfare in America: An Annotated Bibliography;* and the annual annotated bibliography, including books, articles, and dissertations, produced by the Social Welfare History Group.[1]

Among social work journals, *The Social Service Review* and *The Journal of Sociology and Social Welfare* are particularly likely to publish historical articles. Review articles in *Reviews in American History* offer excellent orientations to current trends and debates in social welfare history.

The Encyclopedia of Social Work covers historical topics and biographies of social welfare leaders; Walter Trattner's *Biographical Dictionary of Social Welfare in America* is also a good source of information about important figures in social welfare.[2] *The Dictionary of American Biography, Dictionary of American Negro Biography*, and *Notable Women: The Modern Period* are other helpful sources of biographical data.

Once you have an overview of a policy history area, you will want to turn to the original sources. Using original sources may seem daunting at first. The range of evidence is vast: memoirs, correspondence, minutes of committees, agency manuals containing rules and policies, client case histories, court testimony, government reports, and census reports. You may be further intimidated to learn that the historical evidence is not always written and can include interviews with key policymakers and staff of social work agencies, oral histories, photographs, films, and even songs. Our policy history of the Benton Park Crisis Center, for example, drew in part from a large scrapbook that included news clippings, photographs, and other material documenting major events in the life of the agency. Yet, as you pursue a historical analysis, you may find yourself caught up in the fun of this "sleuthing" game, in which you use your imagination to determine what has gone on in the past. Occasionally, one stumbles across an exciting "find," such as a mouldering box of case records dating back to the early 1900s in an agency basement. More usually, a painstaking search is involved, in state and local libraries, archival collections, organization headquarters, individual agencies, and collections of oral histories, in order to locate pertinent sources. Fortunately, there are guides to a number of these holdings and collections.

Archives are places where unpublished records are collected, cataloged, and made available to researchers. They may be housed in libraries, organizations, universities, and museums. Tracking where the records of particular individuals or organizations are stored can be a tricky task. One help is the *National Union Catalogue of Manuscripts*, available in libraries. There are several important archival collections in social work and social welfare; these include the Social Welfare Archives at the University of Minnesota, the Social Work Archives at the Smith College School for Social Work, and the records collection at the Center on Philanthropy, Indiana University, Indianapolis. Individual archives have their own directories, for example, the directory of the University of Minnesota's Social Welfare History Archives Center (1970) and supplements to it.[3]

The articles "Archives of Social Welfare" by Clarke Chambers in the eighteenth edition of the *Encyclopedia of Social Work* and "Social Welfare History Archives" by David Klaassen in the nineteenth edition are excellent starting points for locating primary sources. The nineteenth edition also contains Leslie Leighninger's entry "Historiography," which gives an overview of the use of historical sources.[4] In addition, authors of books on social work and social welfare history generally describe the archival sources they have used in their notes and bibliographies.

Libraries can also be sources of primary material on social welfare history topics. The social work collection will often include issues of social work journals dating back to the early 1900s, as well as the complete *Proceedings* of the National Conference of Social Work (formerly National Conference of Charities and Correction), dating from the 1980s back to 1874. You will also find the annual published reports of various social welfare organizations, such as your state's public welfare or mental health departments and selected private agencies and institutions. A search in the Louisiana State University library, for example, produced a fascinating set of reports regarding the patient census, types of treatment, and size and condition of the physical plant in large state hospitals in the 1930s and 1940s.

Newspapers and newsmagazines provide firsthand reports of social welfare developments and interviews with both policymakers and the recipients of social services. Many of these, such as the *New York Times* and the *Washington Post*, have their own indexes. As we noted earlier, the *Times* index goes back to 1851. Finally, the government documents departments of libraries offer a wealth of information regarding the history of public social welfare policies.

A special kind of individual record is the oral history, which is a tape-recorded interview with a person about his or her past and often about that person's participation in particular historical events. These interviews are transcribed and then made available through special oral history collections, often housed in university libraries. Historians may use oral histories conducted by others or carry out their own.[5] The Smith College Social Work Archives and the Social Security Project at the Oral History Collection of Columbia University are important repositories of oral histories related to social work and social welfare.

Related to oral history is a research technique known as interviews with key informants. This technique, more familiar to journalists than to social scientists, consists of interviewing people who by virtue of job and/or training are recognized as experts. People commonly used as key informants are academic researchers, agency executives, legislators and their aides, and social activists. Often forgotten, but possessing an important perspective, are clients of programs created by social welfare policies. Gaining the firsthand perspective of people actually involved in the policy you are analyzing can be extremely useful, whether their perspective is from the top down or the bottom up.

Social welfare organizations, agencies, and schools of social work also create their own unpublished records. These include annual reports, minutes of committee meetings, agency manuals and regulation books, memos, client surveys, and case records (such as those used by Eve Smith in her study of orphanages). Sometimes these are still locked in some dusty file cabinet in a school or agency office. Sometimes they have been donated to local or state libraries, archives such as the Social Welfare History Archives, or state history collections. In figuring out whether these records still exist and where they are located, one place to start is the organization itself. The records of many national social welfare organizations can be found at the Social Welfare History Archives, as can the committee minutes, yearly conference proceedings, and other memorabilia of professional associations such as the National Association of Social Workers.

The case records of social agencies are particularly helpful to social welfare historians as they try to understand the lives of ordinary citizens.[6] If you are planning to use an agency's client records, you must be sure to receive permission from the agency administration and to follow your university's Human Subjects Review Board policies for protecting subject rights.

The addition of a client perspective helps make policy histories more complete. So does attention to the issues of women and minorities, who constitute a large proportion of the clientele of social welfare programs and who have also played significant roles in the development of the social work profession. In addition, women and minorities have been a driving force behind informal self-help organizations. There is a growing body of historical literature on the roles and position of women and minorities in the social welfare system. These include studies of women and public welfare by Abramovitz and Gordon; biographies of African American social welfare leaders by Carlton-LaNey, Peebles-Wilkins, and Rouse; and histories of the women's clubs and self-help movement by Lerner and Scott.[7] The works of these authors include a number of references to archival and other sources related to race and gender in social welfare. There are, for example, specialized oral history collections, such as the Black Women Oral

History Project at the Schlesinger Library, Radcliffe College; archival collections at Howard University and other institutions; and programs such as the Center for Research on Women, Memphis State University, which provides computerized searches of databases in its particular topic area.

The list of sources in this appendix is extensive, but necessarily so, because the best history relies on a variety of kinds of data. Taking the time to learn the history behind a policy, whether it's the federal Equal Opportunity Act or your field agency's rules on eligibility for services, will greatly enrich your understanding of the policy's goals, scope, weaknesses, and strengths.

Notes

1. Walter I. Trattner and W. Andrew Achenbaum, Eds., *Social Welfare in America: An Annotated Bibliography* (Westport, CT: Greenwood Press, 1983). The annual Social Welfare History Bibliography is available through membership in the Social Welfare History Group, School of Social Work, East Carolina University, Greenville, NC 27858-4353.

2. Walter I. Trattner, *Biographical Dictionary of Social Welfare in America* (Westport, CT: Greenwood Press, 1986).

3. The directory of the University of Minnesota's Social Welfare History Archives can be found in many university libraries. Other useful archives include the U.S. National Archives, the Archives of Labor and Urban Affairs at Wayne State University, Temple University's Urban Archives Center, and the Rockefeller Archive Center in North Tarrytown, New York. The social work and other libraries at Columbia University in New York have an extensive collection of materials on social welfare history, including a large collection of annual reports, publications, and conference proceedings from leading social agencies and organizations. Many states maintain archives that include material on public social welfare programs and policies, and some agencies also store their administrative and client records.

4. In fact, portions of this appendix were adapted from Leslie Leighninger, "Historiography," in Richard L. Edwards and June Gary Hopps, Eds., *Encyclopedia of Social Work*, 19th ed., Vol II (Washington, DC: NASW Press, 1995), p. 1254. Copyright 1995, National Association of Social Workers, Inc., *Encyclopedia of Social Work*.

5. B. Allen and W. L. Montrell, *From Memory to History: Using Oral Sources in Local Historical Research* (Nashville, TN: American Association for State and Local History, 1981).

6. See, for example, Linda Gordon, *Heroes of Their Own Lives: The Politics and History of Family Violence* (New York: Penguin Books, 1988); Beverly Stadum, *Poor Women and Their Families: Hardworking Charity Cases* (Albany: State University of New York Press, 1992).

7. Mimi Abramovitz, *Regulating the Lives of Women: Social Welfare Policy from Colonial Times to the Present* (Boston: South End Press, 1988); Linda Gordon, *Pitied but Not Entitled: Single Mothers and the History of Welfare* (New York: Free Press, 1994); Iris Carlton-LaNey, "The Career of Birdye Henrietta Haynes, A Pioneer Settlement House Worker," *Social Service Review* 68 (June 1994), pp. 254–271; Wilma Peebles-Wilkins, "Black Women and American Social Welfare: The Life of Fredericka Douglass Sprague Perry," *Affilia* 4 (Spring 1989), pp. 33–44; Jacquelyn Anne Rouse, *Lugenia Burns Hope: Black Southern Reformer* (Athens: University of Georgia Press, 1989); Gerda Lerner, "Community Work of Black Club Women," *Journal of Negro History* 59 (1974), pp. 158–167; Ann Firor Scott, *Natural Allies: Women's Associations in American History* (Urbana: University of Illinois Press, 1992). See also Steven J. Diner, "Chicago Social Workers and Blacks in the Progressive Era," *Social Service Review* 44 (December 1970), pp. 393–410; Linda Gordon, "Black and White Visions of Welfare: Women's Welfare Activism, 1890–1945," *The Journal of American History* 78 (September 1991), pp. 559–590; Robyn Muncy, *Creating a Female Dominion in American Reform, 1890–1930* (New York: Oxford University Press, 1991); Susan Kerr Chandler, "Almost a Partnership: African Americans, Segregation, and the Young Mens' Christian Association," *Journal of Sociology and Social Welfare* 21 (March 1994), pp. 97–111; and N. Yolanda Burwell, "North Carolina Public Welfare Institutes for Negroes, 1926–1940," *Journal of Sociology and Social Welfare* 21 (March 1994), pp. 67–82.

Index

Credits